# MIRACULOUS MERCY THE BEST BLESSING OF MUSLIM MONOTHEISM

### GREGORY HEARY

While monotheistic worship is the reason humans were created it is not enough to worship the Creator alone, without proper knowledge of the Creator obtained through authentic prophetic information. All genuine prophets sent by God taught and practiced Tawheed (Unique singular monotheism) while rejecting and fighting against all that opposes Tawheed. Yet merely knowing and practicing upon correct Tawheed is not enough to enter paradise without Tawbah (Repentance) for both our sins and our lack of doing good deeds. The main purpose of Tawheed is so we can make Tawbah. Without Tawbah (Repentance) Tawheed doesn't benefit as much and Tawbah without Tawheed won't work and would actually be a crime/sin punishable by God. So, I have composed this book to give an Islamic incitement to attain Salvation through sincere repentance and as a reference guide to remind myself when I fall into mistakes. Godwilling this composition will give us all better understanding of our merciful forgiving Creator and the duties we owe to the Maker of the Universe and assist us in fulfilling our purpose in life. There are many crimes associated with repentance due to ignorance, insincerity, or both. As mentioned, a non-monotheistic repentance is a further crime in addition to sins, worse than the sins themselves; despite the placebo effect the adherents of false religions will feel causing them to think they have attained the sweetness of salvation due to their delusion.  For Satan's ultimate goal is maximum misguidance.  Whereas since Satan knows many people will regret their evil crimes instinctively, both emotionally and mentally, then false methods of repentance have been devised to mislead people into blasphemies and heresies that they subsequently fail to repent from.

      As an example, pertaining to comparative religion, my Christian parents taught me as a child that the first two humans were the original sinners of our species.  Allegedly I inherited their sin and would've gone to hell because of what they did unless I was baptized.  Baptism is a Christian ritual involving "holy water" being sprinkled on the baptized person while a special phrase is said during the sprinkling or full-body immersion in water, depending on which Christian denomination it is.  Since I was baptized as a baby without even knowing it or what baptism was for, I was allegedly forgiven and the original sin of the first humans was no longer held against me.  Although when you recall all the people who lived and died before the ritual of baptism started, this would mean that all the great prophets I used to read about daily in the bible went to hell because they weren't baptized.  This incorrect doctrine of original sin led me to grow up thinking everyone was born inherently evil and sin was human nature and that religion was fundamentally to correct the natural instinctive evilness of humans and that less sinful humans were somehow superhumans.

    This is also why Christians are typically adamantly opposed to abortion, because since the baby is scientifically alive at the embryo stage then they believe that baby has the stain of original sin on its soul. Therefore, if it dies in the womb without being baptized, Christianity teaches that such a baby will burn in hell forever because of the original sin that was never removed via their Christian baptism ritual. The only difference of opinion among the traditional Christian religions is which part of hell the baby will be in forever. Some believe there is a specific place in hell specially reserved for such babies called limbo. To overcome the guilt this baptism requirement complex causes medical professionals to have many Christian nurses or doctors perform what is called a secret unauthorized baptism on every newborn they deliver to ensure babies get baptized; just in case their parents never choose to baptize or raise their children as Christians. Even though this baptism without the parents' knowledge or consent is illicit, illegal and unprofessional many Christian denominations teach it is still valid and virtuous. Secret unauthorized baptisms are also performed on adults. This is another tidbit of information I think non-Christians would want to know. A non-

Christian adult could enter a hospital and explicitly declare he or she did not want to be baptized and while unconscious he or she could get baptized without knowing against their will. Despite Christians having good intentions, I consider the practice of non-consensual or secret baptisms to be a violation of a human being's right to choose their religion. From a technical human rights perspective every baby who is baptized is forced to become a Christian whether they want to or not, which may be the reason why they oftentimes cry during the baptism. Many Christians want to force their primary ritual of forgiveness for the sins of our ancestors upon others due to sincere convictions of concern. Of course, Anabaptists and those Christian denominations that evolved from them or copied parts of their doctrines don't allow infant baptisms for several reasons, but the majority of Christian denominations support and practice infant baptism. Which is actually a semi-contradictory type of doctrine, because if humans must be required to be mature and willing in order to get baptized then they should also have to be mature and willing in order to get sins as well. So, if there is original sin then infant baptism should be valid, since there are infant sins. Yet if infant baptism is invalid then infants cannot justifiably be born with original sin either. Basically, what I'm saying is that if the babies aren't dirty with sin they don't need a baptismal bath, but if they do have sin on their soul then they do need a baptismal bath, or at least based on Christian doctrines regarding baptism. In order to avoid a double standard, there either has to be baptism for all infants globally because they have original sin or else baptism must have nothing to do with alleged original sins that get inherited by our ancestors at all and there can't be original sin. So that's where while one might initially think babies should grow up and choose to be baptized, however based on the doctrine of original sin they shouldn't get a choice. While if one says it's ok to baptize a baby to save their soul, then one would also have to say it's ok to baptize an unconscious adult to save their soul and maybe even a baby in the womb because one has to determine that if original sin is inherited then at what stage does the original sin get inherited? Once inherited then baptism should be performed no matter what according to Christian doctrine, so the day the sin is on the soul must be declared by Christians. Yet thus far none have declared the specific second or day which this original sin stains the soul. Many will say we are just born with it but they don't define what that means. Does the baby have it only after the umbilical cord is cut? Do they have it when the head pops out but the rest of the body is still in? Do they have it when the water breaks? If they get it at all then when do they get it? At the very moment of conception? If so, then theologically people should be baptized immediately after a woman's egg is fertilized. Which to be truly accurate means Christians would have to perform a baptism every time they have intercourse, just in case an egg was fertilized and original sin got passed on. Whereas then the question also arises about a pregnant woman getting baptized at any stage during pregnancy. If a woman gets baptized for the first time while pregnant, does it count for her baby too? Regarding twins that come from one fertilized egg which has split, do both of them get original sin, or does only one of them get it, or does it get split 50/50? What about triplets or multiple numbers of babies all born from the same egg? Furthermore, if we baptize at conception and only one baptism is performed and it is later discovered that more than one baby is developing does the baptism count for both or just one? What if they are of different eggs? If it doesn't count for all then there could be a possibility of the non-baptized infecting the already baptized. Yet how would we be able to tell? Also let's say a person was baptized before they got pregnant, if the baby has original sin on its soul while in the womb then what's to stop that original sin from spreading to the mother? If babies catch it from their parents, then a mother could catch it from her baby in the womb. It must also be declared whether original sin is in the sperm or the egg. If in the sperm then since only one egg is usually fertilized, all those other sperms would be carrying original sin and since they remain in the woman's body, they could contaminate her. Likewise, if sperm contains original sin, then the man could get infected by his sinful sperm while it's inside his body, and since sperm is produced for life, he would be constantly at risk of his sperm staining his soul with original sin transmission.  While if original sin is in the eggs only then every woman has capsules of original sin that are likely to infect her at any time in her life, spiritually she could never be safe until every egg is gone and she completely goes through menopause.  I don't mean to offend any Christian who may read this but if people are getting this original sin on their soul we have to determine exactly when they get it and how so that they can be purified as soon as the spiritual infection occurs.  Most Christians agree that this sin is transmittable, so I want to know exactly when it is transmitted and how?  It's a question that deserves to be answered.  If it's unknown when it's transmitted or how, then only symptoms would alert us to its presence.  Which leads me to ask what are the symptoms of someone contaminated with original sin?  If we don't know when it's transmitted and we don't know how and we don't know of any symptoms then how can we even know whether this impurity exists?  How would we know when it's gone?  If absolutely nothing is known about this stain of original sin and it's all just guesswork then how can it possibly be cured? Any cure for such a mysterious contamination could only come through guesswork.  Why didn't a single prophet teach us about original sin?  If a prophet told us how to cure it, they would've told us when/how we got it and how to prevent it from being transmitted. If there is any problem whatsoever with any type of baptism, then the problem would have to come from the doctrine of original sin before there could be a problem with any ritual of baptism. On the other hand, Mormons don't believe in original sin being passed on to others, nor do they believe in baptizing infants, but they do believe in baptizing dead people and they do it via proxy. They actually baptize dead people, and do it without their consent nor that of their families. The ritual of baptism is more disputed amongst the various Christian denominations than one would guess. To date, there is no consensus yet, so I don't expect any answers to my previous questions anytime soon. Despite all the talk one hears about "freedom of religion" in reality if Christians don't baptize you in the womb, or as a baby, or as an adult whether conscious or unconscious, then Mormons may baptize you in the tomb after death. Baptism is almost unavoidable. However, there are many different types of baptisms done different ways for different reasons and many Christians will reject those baptisms done by other Christians. So, it's not really about if you'll get it, it's more about which type will you get and what does baptism count for; if anything.

Honestly reflect, does it make any sense at all that everyone would have to get a spiritual vaccine ritual for eternity due to a sexually transmitted ancestral sin or else they are damned to eternal hellfire? It'd make more sense for God to miraculously cut the chain of transmission off. Especially with historical records of God eliminating the entire world of disbelievers and starting afresh with Noah's nation, if at any time baptism would be taught it would've been at the time of Noah or earlier. Noah's nation could've easily ended the transmission of original sin for everyone so why didn't God teach them a method? Yet Christians purport that all the Jewish prophets from Adam onwards were clueless about original sin and how to repent from it until John the Baptist came, despite John himself never making baptism obligatory as a necessity of faith. Then Christians fraudulently claim God/Jesus/God's son died in a deal to forgive all sins, only if you believe it happened. Yet even then such a belief that cures all sins before you are even born or commit them, still doesn't cure humanity from the original sin from being transmitted according to them. The fact is this original sin dogma is merely a pathetic excuse for explaining why people can be evil, concocted by people influenced by racist jinni called Satan who wants us to hate the original humans whose creation was the catalyst for Satan turning into a devil and being exited from paradise himself due to his racism and jealousy of humans. Which leads us to another topic which is the existence of the jinni Satan and the wisdom and power of God in creating Satan despite the mischief caused and the misguidance Satan creates through false heretical blasphemous religious doctrines like original sin.

    Naturally it's crystal clear that everyone is entirely responsible for themselves and nobody can blame their parents or their kids for anything; much less their original ancestors. The various different bibles usually say God said the day Adam eats of the tree of knowledge he will die. On the very same day he ate, not hundreds of years later. This means the death caused by sin is a spiritual death not literal. Or else God is a liar. Or else those bibles are lying about God. The soul or person "dying" is like a dead battery, it doesn't work or fulfill the purpose for which it is created but it can be recharged through repentance and fixed so that it can once more fulfill the purpose for which it was created which is to worship and obey its Creator. The way to recharge the soul is to follow the instruction manual(s) God has sent through the Messengers he has sent. For example, being brain dead, doesn't mean the brain ceases to exist but just that it's malfunctioning and has a problem, which might or might not get fixed. For many verses in religious scriptures sins causing death refers to spiritual death, although sometimes it can refer to the expiation for a sin. The scriptures say some sins cause one to be put to death such as adultery or murder and some sins don't such as theft. Such verses mean that if you don't follow the laws of God then by default you are sinning, not automatically because of any sinful action but due to being guilty of inaction which is sinful. Just as by not following the laws of your government would make you a criminal even though you may not have committed a felony or misdemeanor. This is because failing to do what is obligatory is to be guilty of what is prohibited. The scriptures also equate sin with being dead because sins can kill your relationship with God. While if you don't have the correct relationship with God then you are basically dead spiritually and are comparable to a spiritual zombie. You might walk, talk, breathe, eat etc. but that's just in a physical sense. Likewise, not all sins cause spiritual death. For example, worshipping an idol causes spiritual death and makes one a disbeliever yet minor sins generally do not by themselves cause a spiritual death, they are merely spiritual wounds. Although a single wound is very capable of causing death, and death is also a possibility when repeatedly getting wounded. Yet physically God is the one who causes death when he sends the angel of death to extract a person's soul. Every mortal being must die or else they would be immortal and none is immortal except God. (Which is also why Jesus cannot be God since the human prophet Jesus will eventually die after returning to earth to kill the antichrist and proving he has yet to die by any method due to a miraculous safe escape to paradise from his enemies; despite what Christians allege due to multiple contradictory biblical tales written by pseudonymous authors in Greek, a language never known or spoken by Jesus transmitted by copyists unknown. For definitive proof prophet Jesus was not crucified nor killed refer to my book *"Contradicting Biblical Conjecture about the Crucifiction"*.) Everything created by God will eventually die including animals, plants, cellular life, etc. However, many of these things will have died sinless such as trees, birds, fish, flowers, rocks, time, angels, etc. The death in which God takes no pleasure refers to the "spiritual death" aka disbelief or sin. When evil people like Goliath die then God is pleased by their physical death despite being displeased by their spiritual death. The angel of death will be the last thing to physically die and then later the Day of Resurrection will come when we shall be resurrected, judged, etc. Yet those spiritually dead, also known as disbelievers, since they lived and died as disbelievers in this worldly life then they will be raised as disbelievers and will remain spiritually dead without a relationship with God and will be eternally punished for it; aside from the punishment of having no relationship with God. While spiritually dead the eternal physical torment will indeed be real, and really painful at that, just as their worldly existence was real despite their being spiritually dead. Physical death is like a court date with God.

**Abu Huraira reported Allah's Messenger (ﷺ) as saying:**

*There was an argument between Adam and Moses in the presence of their Lord. Adam got the better of Moses.*

*Moses said: Are you that Adam whom Allah created with His Hand and breathed into him His sprit, and commanded angels to fall in prostration before him and He made you live in Paradise with comfort and ease. Then you caused the people to get down to the earth because of your lapse.*

*Adam said: Are you that Moses whom Allah selected for His Messengership and for His conversation with him and conferred upon you the tablets, in which everything was clearly explained and granted you the audience in order to have confidential talk with you. What is your opinion, how long would the Torah have been written before I was created?*

*Moses said: Forty years before.*

*Adam said: Did you not see these words: Adam committed an error and he was enticed to (do so).*

*He (Moses) said: Yes. Whereupon, he (Adam) said: Do you then blame me for an act which Allah had ordained for me forty years before He created me?*

*Allah's Messenger said: This is how Adam got the better of Moses.*

Source: Sahih Muslim 2652c

**It was narrated from Ash'ath, from his father that a man from among Banu Tha'labah son of Yarbu' said:**

*"We came to the Messenger of Allah when he was speaking to the people, and some people stood up and said: 'O Messenger of Allah, these are Banu Tha'labah who killed so and so.' The Messenger of Allah said: 'No soul is affected by the sin of another.'"*

Source: Sunan an-Nasa'i 4838 Grade: Sahih

**It was narrated that Abu Rimthah said:**

*"I came to the Prophet with my father and he said: 'Who is this with you?' He said: My son, I bear witness (that he is my son). He (the Prophet) said: 'You cannot be affected by his sin or he by yours.*

Source: Sunan an-Nasa'i 4832 Grade: Sahih

The original sin doctrine doesn't even exist in Judaism, it's purely a Christian heresy of tribalistic guilt which God has never pronounced upon us. According to Islam both Adam and Eve ate the forbidden fruit and whoever was first isn't even ostracized. Rather than be known as the first sinners, Islamically they are known as the first humans to have successfully repented from sin. There is a great wisdom in this, because people will often blame either the first man or the first women for all their hardships, thereby falling for the same trap. The important thing is not who broke the rules first, but why? Satan, our most dangerous enemy, is the one who persuaded the first humans to disobey God. He made what was wrong seem right to the first human couple.  Satan has had much practice since then in tricking people to do wrong and has even made us forget that he was the instigator who led our ancestors out of paradise.  Satan even got us to forget how he did it.  Satan tricked them through a lie, that's why he thinks it's so funny when we tell each other "Funny lies" especially if people laugh at them, he laughs at them laughing not realizing that we learned how to lie from him and got here because he lied to our ancestors in paradise.  Satan got our parents evicted from paradise and made homeless as a result of 1 lie and then we tell lies "to have fun" via jokes or by bearing false witness via the acting entertainment industry.  People often claim they don't lie or support liars but acting in any capacity is lying, thereby all fictional stories are sinful.  So those who truly don't witness falsehood don't watch fictional television tales or movies.  <u>The first sin humans ever did wasn't in eating the forbidden fruit, it was in taking Satan to be a friend, trusting and obeying his desires and false promises when God had warned us about him being an enemy</u>.  Satan swore to our ancestors in God's name that he was a truthful sincere advisor and they believed him and suffered because of it.  Thus, our species lost our privileges and got sent to earth, to be taught a lesson to treat Satan as our enemy on earth as God had told us to do originally in paradise.  If we don't take Satan and his friends as enemies here, or enjoy entertaining him and imitating him by telling each other "Funny lies", or lies we don't yet recognize as lies as in the case of religious innovations or heresies, then we'll be sent to hell with Satan after we die. Yet when the next move comes, we could go our separate ways and let Satan go to hell alone while we go back to paradise. Rather than be angry at our ancestors (after all they were humans prone to make mistakes) we should be aware of our enemy who has the same plan to deceive us and puts it into action every single day. Let us not be among those who forget the enemy and become divided prior to being conquered. Adam and Eve were taught how to ask for forgiveness with four primary conditions for repentance, and a fifth condition that is sometimes applicable:

1. **To admit you sinned.** (many people don't even think they did anything wrong)
2. **To regret it.** (some know it's a sin but don't care)
3. **Ask the Creator _alone_ to forgive you.** (it's his law you broke, so only he can forgive)
4. **Sincerely promise not to do it again.** (if you plan on doing it again you didn't do step 2 properly, step 4 is to prove step 2 through action)
5. **Right the wrong you did to the harmed parties if possible if your sin involved the rights of another creature.**

The Creator subsequently forgave them. For those who disagree why stop at Adam and Eve?

Why not say we inherit all the sins of all our ancestors, including the ones done by our parents before we were born? Why just the first sin (which is technically the second sin) of the first humans who erred? Because contemplating the sheer injustice of an entire species being held accountable for other people's sins generations and generations afterwards would be realized and the false notion disposed of. If a person commits a crime and gets a criminal record, that doesn't get inherited or passed on to their descendants. Neither is sin inherited, and the bibles even say this right in the book of Ezekiel: "*The child will not share the guilt of the parent, nor will the parent share the guilt of the child.*" Is that not fair and completely just? Furthermore, forgiveness was dependent upon the guilty party repenting. No parent could get their kid out of trouble with God and likewise no kid could get their parent out of trouble with God. As the legal saying goes: "*If you do the crime you got to do the time.*" Well, we are innocent of the crime committed by Adam and Eve, we got enough of our own share of personal crimes/sin which God could condemn us for. God would never punish someone for something they didn't do or even intend to do, and universally everyone would recognize it to be unjust oppression if he did. Even in worldly terms if you commit a crime do you think any judge would sentence you and again all your descendants to jail forever, then thousands of years later the judge decides to forgive your descendants for your crime by killing his own innocent son so that your distant descendants could be forgiven and not punished for a crime they never committed? Some may say that with God it's different because Adam and Eve were evicted from paradise and sent to earth as a result, therefore we suffer on earth because of it. So, they postulate the original sin must also pass on to us since we are on earth. This idea is unfounded. For instance, let's say a landlord tells their tenants of an apartment complex not to eat from the apple tree "or else". Later the landlord catches the tenants eating from the tree and tells the tenants they are no longer welcome on the premises and have to go live elsewhere. The tenants leave and have kids in the new location who have kids for generations afterwards. Now would the landlord have any problem with the kids of those tenants who ate the "forbidden fruit", or the next generations of descendants? Not at all. Despite the kids living in a different geographical location than their ancestors lived in while tenants, their location or DNA has nothing to do with their relationship with the landlord. God is the landlord and we are those kids whose ancestors broke the rules and had to move, their sin is between God and them. It has nothing to do with us and God. Our God made it clear, that with him all of our crimes/sins that we are guilty of can be forgiven, if we fulfill the criteria for repentance before we get escorted to meet the Judge (God) by the angel of death. The goal is not to be forgiven for sins we didn't commit or have somebody else pay our penalty but to be forgiven for our own sins and lessen our evil while increasing our goodness.

Factually God does not want every human to be sinless and worship him. Do you know why? Because God already has creatures who do 100% what God wants them to do. They are called angels. Every angel believes in the right thing, does the right thing and never sins. So those who insist God could make everyone believe and stop us from doing evil if he wanted to are right, God could, but he doesn't want to because he already has angels to be like that so why create a repeat species of angels? Is there some rule that says God can only create sinless angels and no other type of creature? Why do some humans think God can only create angels or it's unfair? God is creative and doesn't want to only create angels, God wants plants, animals, humans, devils, etcetera because it displays his immense power and to truly understand why you would need the knowledge of God anyways. Yet let's consider some attributes of God such as being forgiving and merciful. Now if nobody ever disobeyed God then how could God be forgiving if he never forgave anybody for doing wrong? God could not be forgiving if nobody ever sinned so God could forgive them. God is also the most severe in punishment, but if God never punished anybody how could he be the most severe in punishment? Basically, for God to be God as God has defined himself then God has to act accordingly. Since God is merciful there must be opportunities to display that mercy, so by us humans existing and repenting it allows God to be merciful and forgive, likewise humans existing and not repenting from disbelief or sins shows God as forbearing and then as just and powerful when God finally does punish the guilty ones. So, the existence of human freewill shows the depth and complexity of God, because if only angels existed that would be a very bland boring one-dimensional under-developed God. Such a "god" would have an ungodly personality and character that would be emotionally inferior to us. For such a "god" to exist would be impossible because by definition the Creator must be more complex than its creation, so God could never give us such a wide range of attributes or characteristics if God was such an undeveloped entity that was less complex than its creatures. Emotionally God must be more complex than us, but God couldn't be if everyone believed and obeyed. If God created only angels or 100% obedient beings and nothing else then that would be an uncreative and nearly insecure God rather than the full God we have which can create such a diverse universe and have such a wide range of various treatments for the things within it.

Insecurity about your relationship with God is necessary to have the correct healthy relationship with God as befits him as God and you as his creation. If you don't feel your relationship with God is vulnerable and there is a chance of rejection due to your beliefs or actions then you can never truly feel love from God. Since to feel true love there must be the possibility of there being no love. This is the problem with Christianity and Judaism, they have no sense of vulnerability with their relationship with God. Jews think God loves them due to their race and Christians think God loves them so much automatically that he died for them or sent a son of his to die for them, thus Christians feel God loves them more than he does Christ himself since he allegedly harms innocent Jesus for their sake. Thus, both the Jews and Christians are spiritually immature and have a "Baby Love" selfish attitude with God where they expect God to love them and only wonder about how much God loves them rather than if. Truly Judaism and Christianity fundamentally teach that God loves you and/or everyone by default and it's only a question of how much do you want God to love you, thus they do good and avoid evil only to get more love never to avoid/decrease God's hatred. It is because of this doctrine of special unconditional divine love as taught by Judaism and Christianity combining with the philosophical poisonous doctrines of freedom of belief and human equality along with arrogance and Satanic influences that cause people to think that God doesn't love only the people of 1 religion while hating all the rest and that if God did then everyone would agree religiously. This baseline equality of love belief is also similar to what ancient pagans believed about religion. Today people took this notion and mixed it with freedom, so they think God has to distribute his love for people equally and that exercising freedom cannot cause God to stop loving or start hating them.

The foolish think God shouldn't let them be evil if he doesn't want them to be evil, but that's like a child telling a parent that they shouldn't ever allow any possibility for them to break any rules if they really don't want them to break the rules. Such an argument is crazy because only an irresponsible person would make such a claim. Such a policy they purport to want would not allow growth. Likewise, no accredited school would ever be allowed to function if it was impossible to fail the courses or exams.  Responsibility is a fact of life, just because people don't like the consequences of their beliefs/actions doesn't mean there is anything wrong with responsibility.  Without responsibility one cannot succeed or get rewarded.  If there is no possibility of failure no success or reward can ever exist.  Hence for Heaven to exist as a possibility then Hell must exist or else that would not be just.  It's not like God doesn't help us at all, that would be unfair.  God actively tries to guide everybody as much as he can without making the test of life invalid.  For you to get the reward for passing the test of life, God can't take it for you or make it impossible for you to fail because then it wouldn't be a true test and there would be no justifiable reason/excuse to give you any rewards at all.  God chooses to guide or allows people to go astray based on them and whether they truly want guidance to submit or not.  God gives extra help only to those who truly want it and appreciate it.  Equal opportunity is a fictional fantasy since our opportunities are not all equal, as some have an easier religious environment than others and no human is equal nor has equal opportunity as another in all of history.  So, we do not have equal opportunity but we in reality are all unique individuals in special circumstances with those blessed to be guided blessed, and those allowed by God to be cursed with misguidance cursed. God won't go out of the way to guide people who don't sincerely want God's help on the test of life thus God allows some to be accursed because of knowledge about their spiritual reality. On a personal and general level God wants every individual to believe correctly but regarding destiny God doesn't want a world with 100% believers. Since if everyone passed the test of life then that would be an unfair test that in effect means it's impossible to fail since nobody failed it. Another reason for the existence of false religions is because if 100% of people believed then lots of the benefits of disbelief and disbelievers would not exist. Yes, false religions and disbelievers actually do have a positive effect on the world and God desires this positive effect of disbelief and disbelievers even though God hates disbelief and disbelievers. An example is Satan. God hates Satan but he allows him to exist despite that hatred because he is more pleased with the long-term effects that Satan's actions bring about than God would be if Satan didn't exist at all. The benefit of Satan existing is greater than his harm despite the hatred God has for Satan and his ultimate plan to harm him eternally, the same applies to people upon false religions. Yet just because danger exists in a religious context or environment doesn't mean safety is automatic, nor impossible to attain. A dual balance between hope in God's mercy and fear from God's punishment must be simultaneously within an individual. The fearfulness prevents future crime while the hopefulness prevents despair over the past. The trouble is living in the present many people become hopeful over future sins being forgiven and fearless about our past sins by assuming they are already forgiven. Such an attitude leads many people to transgress and abusively treat God's opportunity of forgiveness as a guarantee through their actions though they may say or believe otherwise. Then when the delusion of Satan disappears the same people who believed their past and future sins were forgiven in the midst of their decision to sin go to the exact opposite extreme pushed by Satan to think that God will never forgive their past nor future under any circumstances and therefore despair. Such despair is what leads to increased evil through accepting and embracing sin thinking the game is over while it is ongoing, or even worse the adoption of false religious means of repentance through slanderous savior religions or supplications and prayers to intermediaries seen to be less sinful and somehow on a higher than human level.

As it pertains to Christianity the proliferation of sin leads wicked sinners to see the cross/Christ as their only life-raft and chance to get to paradise. This is because if society wasn't so sinful and so immoral and people weren't instinctively evil then Christians would have no target audience desperate for a savior because they'd realize God can just forgive them directly. Sinful societies promote Christianity. Moral societies are anathema to Christian proselytization. If people weren't "hopeless sinners" they wouldn't think they need to be "saved" with a fatal sacrifice paid with the blood of God and/or his son. Whereas the most intense suffering possible on earth cannot compare with the eternal suffering of hell which man is liable to receive, and if one said Jesus Christ was infinite then his ability to endure suffering would be infinite but even if a being with an infinite pain threshold were to suffer, which is impossible, that cannot atone for eternal suffering. Because the level of suffering could only atone for that level, it cannot account for an eternal time. So, if Jesus allegedly endured maximum pain equivalent enough for all to be saved from hell for X hours, then they'd only get saved for X hours from hell, and only those who sinned before the event could be saved since he couldn't atone for sins not yet committed. Whereas if one argued Jesus could atone for future sins not yet committed then that means there is no repentance or even such a thing as God's forgiveness because baptism would be a stamped ticket to paradise which no sin could revoke.  All sins would be atoned for before they were committed and before God could forgive them.  Thus, if Trinitarianism and the doctrine of Atonement were true, a Christian could do anything they wanted and didn't need any rules at all.  But this would apply to everyone, because if Jesus had atoned for sins and could offer infinite payment then people wouldn't even need baptism either because if Jesus could save anyone and everyone then he would.  In reality Jesus wasn't even crucified nor was he divine, nor a son of God as Christians mistakenly claim based off of blindly following preachers who mistakenly believe the heretical corruptor Paul and those students of Paul who wrote Greek manuscripts about Jesus, which Emperor Constantine instigated others to unscholastically compose and eventually declare as the authoritative Christian biblical text several hundreds of years after Jesus; thereby replacing the actual Injeel which was the text of Divine Revelation revealed to the 100% human prophet Jesus.

That the Creator of everything could be biologically related to a mortal human with all the flaws and disgusting aspects that humans are known for is akin to atheism and insults God. Some Christians will maintain that their anthropomorphic man-god-ghost dogma is true and not offensive to anyone. Since that is the case they make we will take it and prove why it is offensive to Jesus and Mary, whom Christians claim to love, to say such a thing. Most people will agree that Mary was a virgin when she gave birth to Jesus. If Christians then say that God is the Father it would imply that Jesus is a bastard. The dictionaries define "*bastard*" as "*a person born of parents not married to each other*". Since no modern Christian claims that the Creator married the human mother of Jesus then by claiming God is the father, or that God begot Jesus, and Mary is the Mother it means that Jesus must be a bastard according to Christianity. Of course, this is extremely offensive to anyone who has any iota of respect for Jesus, but Christians don't think about what it fully entails to believe and say that Jesus is the "son of God". What do you think Mary would think about someone who calls her miraculously born son a bastard, but just in different words? What do you think Jesus would do to those people who proudly proclaimed this slander against him? To believe Jesus is the son of God means to believe that Jesus is a bastard. Now do you think that Jesus went around preaching that he was a bastard of divine lineage and that if people believe he is a bastard of God, then they would go to heaven forever? Obviously not. Yet this is what Christians profess and promote, thinking they are showing respect to Jesus or God in some way by slandering such a righteous Messenger of God who was miraculously born to the best woman of all time. If such Christians also believe that Jesus is God then to believe that means to believe that God is a bastard. Is that what the prophets taught? Officially according to the English language Christianity teaches that Jesus was a bastard. And for those Christians who say Mary was married to Joseph at the time she was impregnated with Jesus then they are saying God unjustly impregnated a married woman while hypocritically making adultery punishable by death. Other Christian sects, like Mormons, even go the full distance alleging God performed physical adultery to give birth to himself/son. Most Christians won't admit that Christianity teaches Jesus was a bastard yet they still maintain him to be a son of God, born of a virgin who wasn't married to God, who was crucified for mankind's salvation. If that is the case where God punished his offspring for our sins it would mean God is an abusive parent. To send one's innocent son to death in the most painful and humiliating manner in order to forgive someone you're not related to is criminal, unjust, abusive and insane. If someone wrongs me and subsequently apologizes, I'd never say: "*I can't forgive you until I crucify my only beloved son.*" Muslims believe that God is the Most Merciful. Humans can forgive one another without having to kill their children as a prerequisite. By Christians saying that God had to send his son to death for our salvation means that humans are more merciful to humans than God is. Christianity fundamentally teaches incorrectly that humans are more merciful than God and that God is an abusive parent.

Most Christians are taught and believe that salvation is practically guaranteed, thinking Jesus died for their sins despite that alleged sacrifice not covering the original sin somehow nor the sins of those who don't believe the blasphemous non-monotheistic Christian creed. Many Christians consider salvation a foregone conclusion not worth much attention or effort. Then there is a Holy Ghost that nobody really knows much about except it is 1/3rd of God and inside every Christian protecting them from evil despite their constant sins, even though there are no tests that can be done to determine when the ghost is in you or how much of it is in such people. Realistically if you study and compare every religion in the world, Christianity is fundamentally the easiest religion in the world that requires the least from its adherents and is the most offensive to common sense. Typically, the easiest way to do something is not the right way, but Christians tend to ignore this reality of life when it comes to their religion. Throughout history people have shifted the blame and refused to accept responsibility and accountability for their actions, Jews have a scape-goat, Egyptians had a scape-ox, Hindus had a scape-horse, Chaldeans a scape-ram, Brahmans a scape-bull, Aztecs a scape-lamb, Tamalese a scape-hen and Christians have a scape-God/son of God. This is why the average Christian is typically the least moral or religious person if they're grouped together with average adherents of other religions. The vast majority of Christians think that all they have to do is go to church once in a while, believe what they're told about Jesus (which is blasphemously anthropomorphic polytheism), give money to church and it makes them a "good person" who is certain to enter paradise. It is only if everyone is really wicked can Christianity make a case for the bloody atonement via Christ. Christians essentially say that humans are so sinful it's impossible for God, merciful as he is, to forgive so many sins unless he physically transforms into a human and gets killed as a sacrifice for us; as if that makes any sense even though the Holy Ghost never dies or gets hurt thereby technically making it a partial divine sacrifice in theory.  On the other hand, if people could successfully stop sinning then this nonsensical oxymoronic theology would be rejected immediately.  Super sinful environments are a breeding ground for Christian blasphemy because it makes people think God cannot forgive all the sins they've seen, much less all the rest ever committed.  Therefore, a government that stops sin is actually preventing an environment conducive to Christian propaganda from spreading.  If as a whole people "aren't that bad" we don't need God to bleed and die for us, so this is why Christians inherently promote sin even if it's unintentional because their theology requires obnoxiously evil societies or nobody would ever accept Christianity as plausible in any way.  Politicians and Clergy know this and that's why clergy rarely/barely complain when politicians create sinful societies because the clergy knows sinful societies help them preach and get people involved with Christianity.  A sinless society doesn't need a savior sacrifice, in reality neither does a sinful society either because God can forgive sins as God wills whether it makes sense to us or not.  The clergy also likes war because then they can pray for peace.  During war lots of people go to church to pray, and while in church they tend to make monetary donations as well.  If the world is not a sinful evil immoral place filled with evildoers, then Christians have no sales pitch they can make. This is why sinful governments historically have been very friendly with Christian clergy. It's a symbiotic relationship. Hence this is why the Roman Empire actually became more degenerate AFTER Christianity spread throughout it, because even the pagans had a moral code of conduct but Pauline Christianity gave states a blank check to cultivate sin as unofficial policy. Do the research, the Roman Empire and morality declined as the citizenry converted from Paganism to Christianity. Thus, Christians were and are generally more immoral than polytheistic Pagan Idolaters. Christianity was and is a religion where governments of Christian peoples never actually have to morally reform themselves and improve their citizens because Christian clerics need and subconsciously desire the opposite. Except for the rare minority who actually believe and try practicing the minute level of morality their nonscholastic corrupted texts tell them they are supposed to preach. Governments + Christianity = the economics of sin + a theological necessity for an economy/nation based upon sinfulness. But worst of all Christians claim adherence to genuine prophets while preaching creeds contradicting the core message of God's prophetic faith. In my opinion, as a former Christian leader, someone claiming a prophet is God or a son of God or God in human form and that such a being died as a sin transferring sacrifice and that you have a God-ghost inside you is worse than someone disbelieving in a prophet and practicing polytheism; though all false faiths lead the practitioner to eternal hellfire despite containing false recipes for repentance that lead to a placebo effect where the person "feels forgiven" for their sins despite getting more and more sinful since their very religion is sinful to start with. Whereas if you are upon a false religion like Christianity or anything other than Islam then it doesn't do much good to stop the obvious major sins if you still adhere to the ultimate sins of disbelief and polytheism. For the remorseful major sinner of the monotheists has a better chance of forgiveness than the pious polytheist or innovator despite whatever prejudices humans have. Foolishly some people imagine they need another person to improve their connection with their Creator in some type of manner and they commit themselves to this goal of obtaining an intercessor with God in sinful ways thinking they need such because of their own sinfulness, despite many going farther astray in such a pursuit. It is Satan who wants people to hope in a savior intermediary because once an intermediary is between you and God the relationship is ruined and you have lost your connection with the Creator.  So, a sinful person with Tawheed is better off despite their sins than a sinless person who puts an intermediary between them and God.  Yet sins themselves corrupt our mind and make people desperate and foolish so they forget that sins are strains on the relationship and not capable of severing it.  There is only one sin that severs the relationship and that is Kufr (Disbelief) and Shirk (polytheism, including savior faiths or so-called saintly intermediaries) but even Shirk or Kufr if committed can be recovered from if one ceases, desists and repents correctly and completely.  So, putting someone or something else into the mix with your worship of God is the worst thing one can do religiously.  True monotheistic worship is between you and God only.  Nobody else, not even an angel, has any business being involved or invoked in your rituals of worship after you learn them from a genuine prophet of God.  Prophets are our teachers of monotheism not saviors or semi-deities.  So, supplications, as with all other types of worship are only to be done to/for the Creator of everything exclusively.

    Inevitably and blasphemously people occasionally ask me to pray for them not realizing that asking a Muslim to do that "for you" is similar to asking someone to pay for your ticket to paradise.  Everybody has to do their own daily prayers, I can make a supplication to Allah asking for something for someone else as long as I am alive and able, but I can't do someone else's prayers for them.  Even then, generally it is somewhat blameworthy to ask others to supplicate for you for personal benefit, because if Allah won't answer your supplications himself then someone else supplicating for you won't be of much benefit.  That's like one person who's drowning asking another person who's drowning to help them stop drowning.  It can also make the one asked to supplicate for someone else arrogant themselves by Satan causing them to think they are more righteous than others and have some special relationship with Allah.  Furthermore, asking others to make supplications for you makes one rely on others, similar to how polytheists rely on others to a heretical intercessory extent and ask dead righteous people to pray for them, when Allah has given us a direct connection to ask him directly.  If the beggar begging for supplications from a human were to beg the King of the Universe one-on-one they would receive the answer directly without delay.  But if the person is too arrogant to ask the King or too afraid or too shy or whatever excuse Satan will give them to place an intermediary between them and performing an act of worship, then what answer do they expect their fellow test-taking servant to get for them when God is aware of the moment they asked someone else to ask God for goodness for them.  Such a question in itself betrays belief in God because if you knew God was all-hearing you would be ashamed to ask another to ask God for goodness for you while God is listening to you ask.  So, if someone ever asks you to ask God through prayers or supplications or something then tell them, do you believe God heard you ask me to do that for you?  Then proceed with that line of questioning until they see the idiocy of them asking you to ask God within earshot of God.  It is disrespectful to ask an assistant to a President or King while in the presence of the ruler to have that assistant ask the ruler for something.  So why then do people ask a petty human to ask Allah on their behalf when God is actively paying attention to every word they utter themselves?  Kindly explain that them asking you is either polytheism or sin or at the least an act of not worshipping God which is futile and wasteful.  Personally, I refuse to worship my Creator on behalf of others.  I'm not going to pray or supplicate to God because somebody else requested me to do so because then it's not sincere.  I am in so much need myself of God's bounty that I don't have time or care about others to bother to worship for them.  It is pure laziness and lack of trust in God that leads people to ask for others to pray to God for them for any reason whatsoever.

Besides, others might ask the Creator to give you something that you don't want. I do deliberately do that sometimes, people will come up to you and say *"Can you ask God to help me with my visa or help me with X or pass a test or bla bla bla or to recover from an illness?"* I then deliberately do the opposite and make dua for what I think is best saying things like *"O God make them be happy to get deported away from this sinful place. Forgive their sins through their sickness and help them enjoy it for as long as you decree it to afflict them, if being sick helps them avoid sins then help them avoid sins. Or help them to enjoy being poor."* Really it pisses me off when people tell me what to pray for X on their behalf. How arrogant can they be to dictate your dua? You're the one they want to pray yet they don't even want you to pray for them the way you want to. They basically want you to be their slave and worship God on their behalf giving them the blessing of God despite you putting in the effort. Who are they to tell you how, what, when and for who to pray for? Are they a prophet of God? If not then you can say no, you probably shouldn't refuse rudely but you should say no in order to teach them; whether you actually refuse to comply entirely is not advisable but it's not sinful to tell them no and then do it in secret. Sometimes it can be fun to do, just to get a reaction and to teach them.  Other times it's obligatory to say no because people can ask you to pray God helps them to do something sinful like steal, gamble, murder, get intoxicated or have illicit sexual relations or any number of sinful things.  In reality they just want X from God and they want you to pray and get it for them.  They may say they don't really think you can get what they want from God, but if that's the case then why do they ask?  If they really didn't think you invoking God would improve the odds of them getting what they want then they wouldn't have asked you to make dua for them or for anything.  So, they really do think you can get them what they want in a very real sense.  In truth God doesn't grant blessings due to a democratic numbers game.  Please stop trying to play a numbers game with God thinking the more people who you recruit to worship him on your behalf the more likely of getting what you want when you are too lazy and insincere to worship God yourself.  If it isn't a democratic numbers ploy to get others praying for your benefit then what would you call it?  It truly betrays the faith of an individual to ever ask another to pray or supplicate on their behalf.  It is better for them to go years without voluntary supplications and then supplicate to God by themselves alone than to have armies of others supplicating for them due to their request. If you truly trust in God then you trust that God will respond when you supplicate. To ask others on your behalf displays a lack of tawakkul or trust of reliance upon God. Trust in God's reply and do what you need to do in order to get God's blessings when you request them from God yourself.

**Abu Sa'id al-Khudri reported:**

*The Prophet, said, "There is no Muslim who calls upon Allah, within which is no sin or cutting family ties, but that Allah will give him one of three answers: He will quickly fulfill his supplication, He will store it for him in the Hereafter, or He will divert an evil from him similar to it."*

*They said, "In that case, we will ask for more."*

*The Prophet said, "Allah has even more."*

Source: Musnad Aḥmad 11133

Grade: *Jayyid* (very good) according to Al-Arna'ut

**Abu Huraira reported:**

*The Messenger of Allah, said, "Every one of you will have his supplications answered, as long as he is not impatient and he says: I have supplicated but I was not answered."*

Source: Ṣaḥīḥ al-Bukhārī 6340, Ṣaḥīḥ Muslim 2735

Because people have imagined they have a weak relationship with God, they ask you to be a middleman, but of course they'll deny you are their middleman because they also say their own prayers and know such a concept can be sinful disbelief and polytheism, yet at the very least they are making you their sidekick, cheerleader or wingman. While the energy used to ask another to supplicate for you could've been more wisely used in supplicating to the Creator yourself. If someone asks me to make supplication or prayers for them I respond by saying, "*I know someone even better than me who has every dua they make answered immediately. He's nearby, do you want me to introduce you right now so you can ask them to ask Allah to make dua on your behalf?*" Then I say "*The one who you should ask to make dua to Allah for you is ... Allah.*" When they get frustrated or confused then say, "*Well if you think it's silly for you to ask God to ask God for something then it's even sillier for you to ask me to ask God. Whereas if you asked God to ask God for you then surely the outcome is not going to be any worse than if I ask for you, because God has a much better relationship with God than I do. If you want to get God's attention then God is the only one to ask, not me or any other creature.*" Yet sometimes they still persist and ask me to make a dua. In such a case right then on the spot make dua in front of them so they can hear you saying something like, "*O Allah please help this person to trust entirely in you with certainty. O Allah make them such that they never ever ask another person to make dua or pray for them again in their life and that they encourage others to ask you directly for everything and anything they want and need. Make them satisfied with what you decree so they never ever ask anyone to make dua for them again. And if they never ask anyone except for you then grant them the easy entry into paradise and forgive all their sins without account."* Then you can tell them that is your dua which you just made for them, and it'd be dumb to make any others because if God doesn't accept that one then you got your own big problems with God to deal with. Tell them it is a conditional dua that is linked to them never asking anyone else to make dua for them again, if they ask for dua then your dua can't come true, so to ever ask for another dua is to reject the dua you made for them and that even applies to if they ask you ever again. Some Muslims think it's good to ask dua from others but this is due to weak hadith and customs. The companions of Muhammad only asked specific individuals to make dua for them because Muhammad told them ask X person from X city to make dua for you because God will answer it. It was not a promotion of asking others, it was a specific case only applicable to them and it falls under obeying Allah's Messenger's direct orders regarding specific individuals. Other hadith mention how duas of certain people are accepted but it doesn't mean to ask them to ask for you, and most hadith of such incidents are people responding to others asking them to make dua by saying rather you should make it for me rather than asking me to do it for you. In reality they weren't asking for others to make dua for them but discouraging people asking them by saying they should make a dua rather than asking a dua be made. And the few weak hadith that promote asking dua from others are considered inappropriate by the very people who ask others to supplicate for them. For example there is a Daif weak hadith in Sunan Ibn Majah 1441:

**It was narrated that 'Umar bin Al-Khattab said:**

*"The Prophet said to me: 'When you enter upon one who is sick, tell him to pray for you, for his supplication is like the supplication of the angels.'"*

But do people who ask others for supplications go to hospitals and ask the sick to supplicate for them or do they consider that bad manners? So those who ask healthy people rather than sick people are contradicting the very evidence they could possibly use in their favor. They will oppose the weak hadith and invent their own method for getting others supplications under duress and anything done insincerely is not accepted anyways. Therefore, they would be more sincere supplicating for themselves than you would be on their behalf after being requested.  So, it is purely for the imagined comfort of the placebo effect that they ask people to supplicate for them instead of worshipping their God themselves.  Others take this to a further extent and arrogantly brag about praying for others thus invalidating any sincerity they might've had by boasting about their worship thereby rendering their "prayers for you" null because of sharing what was a secret between them and God.  Others will even go so far as to claim supplicating for others when they are not even capable of remembering all the people they promised to supplicate on behalf of, so they end up lying about their alleged supplications or promises of supplicating.  Thereby the devil gets people to go from thinking they are performing good deeds of worship to sinfully lying and it is a widespread communal disaster that people ask others to ask God for stuff for them.  The peoples communally blessed by God were blessed because all of them individually had better more sincere and less sinful relationships with God than entire buildings of worshippers of our modern societies do.  Your community, even if they tried to, cannot fix your relationship with God.  It is your responsibility alone, so grow up and supplicate your own supplications as your prophet taught you.  You can't have others worship your way to paradise for you.  Trust in God exclusively and don't bother others asking for spiritual favors they are incapable of providing even if they tried.  Prophets themselves couldn't sway God's opinion of people whom they tried to bless and people they tried to curse, so if even prophets couldn't control God through supplication on behalf of others why bother asking anyone of lesser status for such favors?  Don't disgrace yourself with such beggary.  Plus, supplicating for people you know due to them asking for it is biased prejudice and not sincere in my opinion because there is undoubtedly pressure there to conform to the request.  A great all-encompassing supplication for somebody to make would be something like: *"Bless all the Muslims and guide humans and jinn to the straight path of Islam."*  That covers everybody believer and disbeliever of multiple species.  So, if you made that dua on a daily basis and you come across someone begging for supplications without time to correct their creed then you can inform them they already were covered in your generic daily dua of blessings for Muslims and guidance for all humans and jinn.  And what could be more sincere than supplicating for two entire species allowing God to choose best who to bless most amongst them, whether they are living or dead, human or jinn?  Why waste words on one person exclusively, other than yourself, when you can supplicate for goodness for all free-willed creatures?

Rather than ask someone to ask God for you, just ask God yourself. Seriously if you are not in paradise and are not safe from the hellfire then what business do you have asking God to do something for someone else? Worry about yourself! After the Day of Worldwide Judgement and Global Resurrection, when you are in paradise safe from the hellfire then you can start asking God to help out others, but truly it's a better use of your time to ask God directly yourself for your own stuff. You are taking the test of life, you don't have time to be asking God to help others out on their test of life, you need God to help you yourself. If people ask you to pray for them then tell them you are too busy asking God for your own stuff to have time to ask on behalf of others and they should likewise be talking to Allah instead of you. Seriously ask them if they think you can help them better than God can. Don't you know there will be people burning in hell forever and while alive they used to pray to God on behalf of others? Imagine how much regret they'll feel hating themselves wishing they had asked God to forgive them 1 extra time rather than "*praying for others*" or "*keeping others in their duas*". It's best to never ask somebody to ask God for something on your behalf. God is not some friend of a friend; God is your personal Creator and personal provider. Do you ask others for oxygen? No, God gives it to you. Do you ask others to give you sunshine or rain? No, God provides everything. So why ask other people for stuff when God is already giving you what you want and need without even asking? If you ask the only way he'd not grant your request is if you were a disbeliever, or if you didn't fulfill the conditions to get your dua accepted, or if what you asked for wasn't in the best interest of the world. Never be shy to use the abilities God gave you to ask God directly for things, that's precisely why God gives you the abilities. The prophets were sent with the specific mission to tell people to only ask God alone directly for everything. God sent prophets and books to us simply to let us know that God wants us all to ask him only and him alone for all we want and need. So today we shouldn't ask others to ask God on our behalf. We have a direct connection with the divine, there are no middlemen, middlewomen, middlechildren or ghosts or any created intermediate intermediaries between us and the Creator of the entire Universe, the All-Hearing, All-Seeing. Just consider that God actually hears and sees people when they go and ask others "Can you pray for me or ask God for me?" How stupid is that? Don't they know God can hear them and see them when they are asking others instead of God directly? Really how do you think that makes God feel? If they truly believe God is as God described his divine attributes, they wouldn't ever ask anything to pray to God on their behalf. Ask God yourself directly! In all of history God hasn't bitten any hand that was raised in prayer to him so you got no reason to be shy. Satan made it his lifelong job merely to break up your relationship with God by inserting incapable intermediaries so you and God don't talk. God created you specifically to ask him for stuff. A single dua you make to Allah is better than asking everyone in the world to supplicate for you. Instead of asking people to supplicate for you, if you still feel comfort in the democratic numbers game thinking God is persuaded by quantity instead of quality then you could always do specific good deeds as specified in the prophetic hadith that make the angels or animals supplicate for you. Or better yet just ask God to be satisfied with whatever he wills for you. If you become a friend of Allah then you won't ask others to supplicate for you because you will supplicate to God directly. Whereas if you are an enemy of Allah then it doesn't matter if all the prophets and angels and every creature of all time supplicates in your favor, you will be destroyed. Fix yourself and your faith instead of falling for the trap of the false security of having others supplicate on your behalf. Truly your Creator destined for you to read this so that you would supplicate to him directly for all you need/want. It'd be insulting to God to ask anyone to supplicate for you after you read this about asking only God for everything. In a Sahih hadith in Al-Tirmidhi's collection of hadith Al-Jami 2418, prophet Muhammad said what means: "*Verily the person who does not ask Allah, Allah gets angry at him.*" From this I understand it to be almost sinful to ask people to ask Allah on your behalf, because in the moment you are asking people to make dua then you are not asking Allah and Allah gets angry at sins. God commands you to ask him directly, there is no proof at all to say God wants you to ask so-and-so to ask God for you. (In the past there were some people God wanted some people to ask to supplicate for them, but nobody on earth today is known to be on such a list and there is no order to ask others to ask. Likewise, even when people asked prophet Muhammad to supplicate for them the prophet would often say that if they remained patient enduring their difficulties then they would be rewarded more than if he supplicated for them. After they heard their reward for not asking the prophet to supplicate they refrained and did not ask the prophet to supplicate for them.) It is both obligatory to ask God directly and obligatory to avoid God's anger and block the spread of Bida (religious innovations).  Even if you think it might not be sinful to ask others in certain situations it's considered to be best to ask only Allah going to the divine source directly.  The odds of you getting what you want are better if you only ask God because God answers and aids those who rely only upon him more often and more readily than those who ask others to ask for God for them.  That is what all the prophets taught.  Satan told people to ask others to ask, then ask dead people to ask, then ask statues of dead people to ask, then ask idols to ask God.  That's what idolatry is and how it originally started, most idol worshippers didn't/don't think idols were/are gods but just intercessors with God who convey their requests to God on their behalf.  Asking others to pray for you is similar to idolatry except your idol is a living creature instead of lifeless.  Just ask your Creator, and leave the other creatures alone.  There is nothing that will make one happier than doing that which pleases the Creator and avoiding that which displeases the Creator.

  There is a famous saying that one can never live morally and appreciate it unless they have lived immorally before.  Although I do not recommend one tries living immorally because this is what

Satan wants, yet sometimes Satan leads humans astray and the detour ends up taking them to the straight path which Satan was trying to make them avoid thereby making his plan backfire. So regardless of how many times Satan has fooled you and led you into error, you can turn the tables on him, choose the right path and be forgiven by Allah to Satan's consternation. For instance, I was once deceived into following a false Satanic religion called Christianity, but by the blessing of Allah I was guided and able to use my experience and knowledge from my time of misguidance to write books hopefully exposing the false religion(s) and immorality Satan has spread, God-willing. Every time Satan misleads us, we should use it as an opportunity to come closer to Allah. If Satan leads us to do a sin, then we repent and start doing extra good deeds hoping to be forgiven for the sin. Even though we messed up and did wrong, we end up doing better because our mistakes put pressure on us to reform and improve. Every time you do a sin you should try to start an extra habitual good deed so that you will make improvements to your lifestyle. This is one reason why Allah has created Satan, because when he tricks believers into falling they get back up and climb to greater levels of goodness. However, we should never regard any sin as being small because all it took was one sin for

Adam to be ejected from paradise and one sin for Iblis to become Satan, thus by us doing one sin it could also prevent us from entering paradise and cause an alliance with the devil.  Rather than think of how small or trivial a sin we do is, we should contemplate on the power and greatness of Allah whom we offend when we sin.  The small sins which are consistently committed eventually add up into a mountain of sin.  Persistence in sinning causes minor sins to become major sins.  Many of the deeds we view as harmless our Creator considers to be felonious.  Yet Allah is so great that we could be potentially forgiven for all our major and minor sins as long as we don't commit the ultimate sin.  The ultimate sin would be to worship other than Allah, or associate partners with Allah in his attributes/names or worship or obedience, or to lie about Allah by claiming he has children, parents or relatives, or to reject any of the Prophets whom Allah has sent.

So, whoever you are, wherever you are, Allah will help you to worship him and follow the true religion, you are capable don't let Satan discourage you.  You may have a feeling that "*I'm so sinful and have done so many bad things I don't think Allah will ever forgive me and let me into paradise.  I just know I'm going to hell no matter how hard I try.*"  That feeling is directly from Satan.  I have heard this statement so many times from so many different people who didn't know the other people said it with each thinking the feeling was something new and that they were the first to ever speak such a phrase that I've lost count.  Most of the times I hear this idea the people utter this with exactly the same words as others do.  I have heard people say this very statement word for word only to me and they all think it's an original unique statement.  None of them heard the others say it, they all think it's coming from themselves.  This is an example of one of Satan's whispers, it is a satanic statement of despair; it's a catchphrase of his.  Really think about it, take that italicized text and imagine having a serious conversation with Satan asking him how he feels and this is exactly what Satan would say and it is exactly what he wants us to feel and say.  We make mistakes, the biggest mistake one can make is to think Allah cannot easily forgive all their mistakes.  This is because only disbelievers' despair of the mercy of Allah.  If you are alive reading this sentence right now, then you can potentially enter paradise.  It isn't over until it's over and it is not over yet.  One of the worst sins one can commit is to think that Allah cannot forgive your sins because it constitutes disbelief in the mercy of Allah.  Don't be tricked by the popular Satanic slogan of "Sorry doesn't cut it" that leads you to hopelessness, despair, depression, more sins and false pagan polytheistic idolatrous religions in which a "savior" gets punished in your place and you pray to them hoping for them to intercede with your Creator to obtain paradise and safety from the hellfire.

When mankind was created to be established on the earth the angels asked Allah why he was making us when we would cause mischief and bloodshed on earth while they (the angels) were devout worshippers who never disobeyed him or sinned. Allah said because he knows what they do not know. Elsewhere Allah said that had you, I or humans been sinless he would have destroyed us all and replaced us with people who would sin. Do you know why? Because Allah is the Most Merciful and loves to forgive. Allah enjoys when a person repents. That is all you and I need to do, no matter what we've done with our lives. If we acknowledge we did wrong, sincerely regret it, tearfully apologize to Allah only, desperately asking for forgiveness and promise and try our very best to never do it again, then Allah has promised to forgive such a person. If we then mess up again and do the same sin or even worse sins and then repent again then again Allah will forgive us, every single time. Allah will continue to forgive us again and again and again and again more times than is possible to calculate, as long as we are sincere and alive. Even when we die Allah may still forgive us because he is that merciful and loves to forgive. However, there is one sin so great so abhorrent so ugly filthy rotten disgusting and evil that if you die upon it then Allah will never ever ever forgive you for all eternity. That sin is to associate something with Allah or to elevate something above Allah in your heart or disbelieve/reject the way of life God has ordained for us. This is what all the false religions other than Islam do. They associate with Allah other beings that have no power to Create the universe, to give life or death, who have no authority on the Day of Judgement and don't even know what or when it is and are themselves created who are either creatures themselves or figments of a satanic imagination. One may do this by saying there is more than 1 God, or that God has children, or by denying some of the attributes of God. Maybe instead they take their desires to be their God. Whereas if God says to do or not to do something they do what they want in opposition to God's command thereby elevating their own cravings above Allah obeying themselves instead of their Creator. Maybe they make other people their god by obeying a priest, rabbi, politician, employer, friend, spouse, child, parent, or imam, instead of Allah when they conflict. Maybe they reject God's prophets because other people told them to or they don't like what the prophets say or where they're from or think they know better than a prophet even though God has said the prophets know better and should be followed.  Maybe they even worship the prophet unintentionally thinking they are doing what the prophet wanted or honoring the prophet out of respect despite the prophets setting clear limits to the love they deserve and warning not to exceed those limits.  This sin of worshipping people or other than Allah is the one which will cause eternal damnation for those who die without repenting from it.  Anything else may be forgiven.  Still, we must remember that Allah is the most severe in punishment as well as the most forgiving.  Thus, if any sins we haven't repented from aren't forgiven on the Day of Judgement we may have to temporarily suffer for them a severe punishment much more than we would like and much more painful than we would like.  But a person who submits to the will of Allah (Muslim) and worships him alone dying in a state of such submission (Islam) will eventually go to paradise and be taken out of hell.  Yet we are so blessed to be alive we could be forgiven for everything before we die if we repent and go into paradise without any suffering at all if Allah wills.  All we have to do is repent, believe and do good deeds.  If you are alive to read this then that means you still got a chance.  Even if you make such a foolish mistake as to knowingly commit a major sin, utter a statement of disbelief or temporarily start worshipping your desires, even after all that you could still be forgiven if you repent like you've never repented before and have a life-changing moment becoming a better person then Allah may forgive you; but not only may Allah forgive you he may actually LOVE you.  That is what we need.  Allah doesn't need us to love him, rather you and I absolutely must obtain the love of our Creator.  What are we waiting for?  Soon we will die, be resurrected and meet him.  If he loves us then we will experience unimaginable _____.  There is no way to finish the previous sentence of how glorious and amazing being loved by the Creator for all eternity will feel.  Words and emotions cannot simulate it for us.  Yet remember if Allah hates us when we return to him then likewise we will experience unimaginable_____ the terror and sorrow of which words and emotions cannot simulate for us, it would be a depression worse than the kind that makes people kill themselves and those they love.  Today may be our last.  I may not even be alive when you are reading this.  We want Allah to love us for eternity, then the least we could do is demonstrate to Allah in public and private that we love him with all our heart, mind, soul and body by following the true religion he has ordained for us and created us to follow.

What about addictions? Drug, Alcohol, Cigarette, Music, Luxury, Videogame, Sexual, Food, Fiction, Fortune and there are many more things and behaviors which one can have "addictions" with such as the internet or the phone and every addict has their own.  However, in reality there is no such thing as an addict or an addiction, this is a satanic deception.  No prophet ever told someone they were an addict or addicted to something to which they couldn't control themselves.  When we were born nobody was an addict, this means one voluntarily chooses to oppress oneself and become an addict.  Therefore, everyone can voluntarily choose to stop being "addicted" regardless of how long it's been or how much damage has been done. Neuroplasticity in particular proves this.  The brain is designed to heal and recover from any programming it has been conditioned to, it just takes time and habits to start new brain neuron circuits.  The 12 step recovery programs that involve people admitting they are addicted and will just have to try to manage their addiction for life are setting themselves up for excuses, despair and failure despite possibly achieving abstinence from whatever vice they have.  The inventor of Alcoholics Anonymous, Bill Wilson, actually founded A.A. after being pumped full of hallucinogens at a detox facility which made him "feel a white light". He came up with 12 steps in a rush one night while sitting in bed based on the idea that Jesus had 12 apostles, which is another false notion Christianity spews underestimating in lieu of them adopting the pagan zodiac which deems the number 12 sacred. Alcoholics Anonymous wasn't based on science or addiction therapy at all, Bill Wilson just made his social habit of drinking alcohol into a social habit of confessions about drinking alcohol. In 2014 CE, A.A. came under the microscope and it was discovered only 5-10% of their members actually stop drinking alcohol. So, the most famous 12-step alcohol addiction recovery program has a 90-95% rate of failure. Why then is it so popular and well-respected? Could it be due to government funding and sponsorship? Maybe. Such 12-step programs tend to offer resignation, shame and excuses neglecting to tell their members that some things can only be cured by the Creator and as a policy most are agnostic in order to increase membership. Those who think they are addicts incapable of change just haven't learned of the cure or haven't successfully implemented it yet. Such people with problems would be better off using a torture device when tempted to sin rather than exposing their sins at a social pity party for similar sinners.  Or safely lighting something on fire whenever tempted to sin can greatly help one get through difficult tempting seconds.  Even if one had to singe themself a little to avoid indulgence sometimes that's better and can help addicts avoid relapses.  The burning of a fire is more potent than the burning from withdrawal symptoms.  Every addict prefers withdrawal.  Ideally one shouldn't hurt oneself but fire can be a great reminder and motivator when Satan tempts us to do something that leads to the hellfire.  It's rare for Satan's false promises about sin to make a stronger argument than fire.  Yet Satan frequently makes addicts forget how great a friend fire can be.  Fire can give someone a better incentive to not sin than almost any "sponsor".  That's why these addict support groups didn't come into existence until after fire became rare amongst the masses and it's also why communities who still frequently use fire on a daily basis typically don't have any of these addict support groups.  Most addiction groups turn "your problem" into a club membership pairing you with a "sponsor" making you rely on them instead of God.  Many religiously believe/teach that people "need people" to recover from addiction.  Whereas while people and therapy can be very helpful, if an addict were the only person on an island or on earth they could still fully recover if God helped them.

Most of the addict clubs/programs always stress that one must rely on God and "surrender" but then rely on healthy social networking more than God or alongside God it seems. Not to nock healthy relationships with people but there is a way to recover from addiction without people, and while that may not be the way for every sinner/addict God really will help people be his friend and recover from addictions, with or without using people to do so. People can help quite a bit but God helps more when relied upon alone, it may take a long time but the help of God is always near, God may help people with people but God should be the one relied upon 100%. Many addiction recovery groups unknowingly teach a religion and a method of repentance not proscribed by prophets, and that's why they tend to perpetually fail to rehabilitate their members. Since the addict club is like a social cult in many ways, subconsciously to stay in the club part of the addicts ensure that "their problem" persists. Which is why addict cults say you're in for life with such clubs aiming for sobriety and not recovery. A recovered addict quits going to addict groups just like a recovered patient leaves the hospital and surrounds themselves with healthy people now that they are no longer sick. Addiction clubs say that sick people have to stick with sick people or they'll never get healthy. They become addicted to confessing their flaws and troubles because it is a way to dump their guilt. They become addicted to addiction recovery and addiction therapy. Most of the addict recovery programs are cults. Useful cults, beneficial to many in many ways but still cultlike in their methodology and unprophetic in doctrine. Imagine a hospital that said everyone who enters it is in for life; we would know that such a hospital must not be helping anybody. Rather these "addictions" are diseases. All diseases can be cured completely as there is no disease which Allah has sent down except that Allah has also sent down the cure. We may not know the cure for everything, but Allah does and will provide the cure. Reading the Quran is a cure for many things, especially ignorance and arrogance which are the two fundamental causes of sin. The cure may even be just sincerely asking Allah to cure oneself. So many times we ask God to help us stop sinning but we should also ask God to protect us from having sinful desires to begin with. If you have a consistent problem with X desires that lead you to do X sin then sincerely and consistently ask God to protect you from having X desires as well. Even if you keep sinning always keep asking, God wants you to ask and Satan wants you to stop asking. In fact, asking God alone for a cure itself is a type of medicine for spiritual diseases. Yet asking

God is not enough it is upon us to take the medicine that Allah proscribes to heal from the diseases completely as well as to prevent future infections from satanic diseases. Allah can and will cure us of any "addiction" or disease if we ask, but we have to take the steps to develop a spiritual immune system by getting proper spiritual nutrition and exercising the correct spiritual hygiene, which can only be done by following the examples of the prophets. Could God cure us upon request? Yes, but God knows how best to heal us and it may sometimes take many attempts at healing/repenting to be fully cured because God is the best doctor and wants us to appreciate spiritual health and develop healthy habits. Many doctors know that for some people getting sick and not getting better is/was better in the long run for their health than if they never got sick or got cured quickly because of the person seeking the cure for a prolonged difficult journey led them to become. For some cases the medicine could be as simple as staying away from other diseased people so you can develop an immune system without exposure to the virus. Some diseases we may never get and some we may contract repeatedly. While things like addictions are special diseases which are symptoms of diseases as well. Addiction is a side effect of another disease. Fixing an addiction can only be done by fixing the lifestyle that led one to pick up that addiction, addiction is just a symptom and side-effect of an unislamic mentality, personality and lifestyle. The cure can only be found with the true prophetic guidance for life. A disbeliever can never be free from addiction, they might attain sobriety from certain substances or behaviors but they will always have the mentality, personality and lifestyle which causes destructive addictions. I repeat every non-Muslim disbeliever is an addict of something and most have the personality of an addict; or at the very least the personality of a disbeliever which is very similar and only slightly different than that of an addict. Sadly, not every Muslim has a 100% Islamic personality and this leads them to have unislamic behavior. Hence prophets were sent by Allah to humanity to guide us all; if the guidance they brought to humanity can't cure an addiction nothing can. Addictions have always existed and so has the cure for them, the cure is the prophetic faith. A sophisticated "modern approach" is not the solution, God understands humans better than modern scientists so his solutions work, we don't need to know and may never know the precise science behind it because science can't explain it all. Science doesn't account for Satan and Satan plays a role in addiction. Yes, science can add useful insight but Islam is the cure. The problem is with the way people today and historically failed to correctly accept and use the prophetic medicine of Islam for all the spiritual diseases they ever contract. Muslims still have the faith but many fail to use it correctly, the prophetic medicine is available most just don't know how to use it or fail to use it appropriately with consistency. When many try, they fail and then fail to try again improving with sincerity, knowledge and patience until they die in the process. Every patient always dies in the process of seeking good health, so too does the believer die in the process of seeking good spiritual health. To stop sinning one needs patience because it usually takes many attempts to be successful and true success is in the struggle for the success in the afterlife. God doesn't tell mankind "Struggle to stop sinning." God tells us to struggle to enter paradise so truly success does not exist in this life. The only "successful person" is the one in paradise. If you are still alive on earth and never died then you are not "successful" because you are still taking the test of life. So, accept that "success" does not exist on earth; "striving" is the best you can experience. Be patient, be patient. Death and success or failure comes sooner than you think, don't rush it. Typically, we are enslaved to our own impatience, of which impatience is a root cause of all types of sins. We tend to think that "One day I'll wakeup and never feel like sinning." Such a day will never exist because Satan exists, other sins may replace your current ones but everyday Satan will try something. While one can recover from addiction, Satan will always be around to mislead us. It's not that "once an addict, always an addict" it's just that Satan works 24/7. But Satan's work in a sense is worthless as he is simply a slaver trying to enslave us, whom we strive to defeat. Slavery is unenforceable, all slaves choose slavery. "Addiction" is another form of slavery; every addict is a slave to a certain vice. In Islam the Muslim is the slave of Allah, nothing else. Yet never does a Muslim or non-Muslim ever get forced into slavery of any type. Satan likes us to think we are powerless slaves to sin but our freewill is stronger than all Satan can use. No Satanic slavery is too much for us to get out of and keep away from. Only Allah has authority, Satan has none unless we delusionally choose to obey him when he pesters. Our patience must be greater than Satan's to be successful. Satan might lay a billion traps for us but it's never too many, even if we fall into every trap he sets we can still travel the road to paradise and achieve forgiveness and success. If we fail it's because we choose to fail and let Satan lead us to disaster. Just as Satan had no power over Adam, Satan has no power over us. Satan is a creature and is thus powerless since all might and power belongs to Allah alone and Allah has refused to allow Satan to have any power over his true slaves. God wants us to sincerely with knowledge and patience seek refuge with him from Satan, not just once but every time. How do we seek refuge with God from Satan? Not through mere words only but with our beliefs, intentions and deeds too.

Allah says in his Quran 14:22

وَقَالَ ٱلشَّيْطَٰنُ لَمَّا قُضِىَ ٱلْأَمْرُ إِنَّ ٱللَّهَ وَعَدَكُمْ وَعْدَ ٱلْحَقِّ وَوَعَدتُّكُمْ فَأَخْلَفْتُكُمْ ۖ وَمَا كَانَ لِىَ عَلَيْكُم مِّن سُلْطَٰنٍ إِلَّآ أَن دَعَوْتُكُمْ فَٱسْتَجَبْتُمْ لِى ۖ فَلَا تَلُومُونِى وَلُومُوٓا۟ أَنفُسَكُم ۖ مَّآ أَنَا۠ بِمُصْرِخِكُمْ وَمَآ أَنتُم بِمُصْرِخِىَّ ۖ إِنِّى كَفَرْتُ بِمَآ أَشْرَكْتُمُونِ مِن قَبْلُ ۗ إِنَّ ٱلظَّٰلِمِينَ لَهُمْ عَذَابٌ أَلِيمٌ (٢٢)

*"And <u>Shaitan (Satan) will say when the matter has been decided</u>: "Verily, Allah promised you a promise of truth. And I too promised you, but I betrayed you. <u>I had no authority over you except that I called you, so you responded to me. So, blame me not, but blame yourselves.</u> I cannot help you, nor can you help me. I deny your former act in associating me (Satan) as a partner with Allah (by obeying me in the life of the world). Verily, there is a painful torment for the Zalimun (polytheists and wrong-doers, etc.)"*

This means that in the end when Satan and those he misled are thrown into hell, Satan will then admit he had no power or control over us and that all he had done was call upon us and we listened and obeyed him.  But we don't have to.  God would never punish a person for doing something they couldn't stop themselves from doing.  This means at all times a person is in total control of their actions and will be held accountable for them all.  Satan wants us to think that we've sinned so much that now we can't stop ourselves from sinning no matter how hard we try, but this is false and Allah tells us the truth of it.  Allah is not lying to us when he reveals that Satan has no control over us.  It is Satan who lies and tricks us into thinking we are hopeless sinners that can never reform and be cured.  Whatever your disease is it can be cured this instant 100% so that you never fall into that sin or vice again, just ask Allah to cure it and to protect you; by being his slave as a Muslim it protects you from all other forms of slavery.  Humans don't need recovery programs, we need Islam.  Satan has the same power over us as a fisherman has over fish.  Satan just presents some sinful opportunities baiting us with a plan to hook us after we take the bait, so that we end up getting damaged, taken out of our natural state (or fitra) and then suffer for the rest of our life in sin until we are grilled over the hellfire for eternity.  Those are Satan's main moves; he casts bait and calls us just as a fisherman says "Here fishy fishy fishy".  We don't have to obey Satan or take the bait no matter how tempting it may be or how pleasurable it may be to take a nibble or a bite.  Even if we do make a mistake or many and get hooked many times we must fight back and not get taken off the path.  How do you fight Satan?  You seek refuge in God and follow the prophets' teachings.  Obviously, it's best not to get hooked at all, but Satan uses as many lines and nets as possible to catch us, so if we get hooked that doesn't mean it's game over, it just means we have to work harder when we're hooked.  Satan is just a skilled fisherman who will be trying to catch us all our life.  He has no authority over us, we can take his hooks out or sever his lines, nets or any other trap we fall into.  Even if we swallow a sinful satanic hook and it hooks into our heart that doesn't mean we're done for, because the line can always be cut by God and the hook surgically/spiritually removed, but it does mean we might suffer some damage and hardship for a while as a result of swallowing Satan's hook or having bitten into it.  Yet clever as he is Satan tries to make us think when caught that in order to get out of his net we should nibble then bite then swallow a baited hook or bigger hooks.  Of course, Satan never comes out and says to swallow he just tells us to look at the bait or listen to it or touch it or think about it, then a while later he persuades us to nibble and nibble and nibble until before we know it we swallowed the whole hook and it's inside us allowing Satan to pull our heart with great force.  At that point some of us can feel something is wrong and we sincerely want to change lest we get barbequed in hell.  Then Satan will pretend to tell us how to get his hook(s) out but in reality, he simply offers painkillers which have bigger hooks in them as well to weaken our resistance and make his job easier, or he tells us to go into an electrified net which will numb us so we feel better, or that we're already hooked so we might as well keep eating the bait and have fun before we're grilled in hell.  Therefore, to repent we need both sincerity to change and knowledge from God as to how to correctly fix ourselves which we can learn only through God's divine revelation and prophets, with only the prophet of our time Muhammad giving us the specific solutions we need in our lives.  If we commit a sin, instead of repeating, or despairing, Godwilling we can turn that sin into sincere repentance and gain forgiveness so we aren't seared in the hellfire for that sinfulness.  So, we are going to have the sin and the cere or the searing one way or the other.  It's just a matter of whether we will have the pious repentful sincerity, or the sinful searing in the hellfire suffering severely for eternity.  Thus, we must repent as soon as possible, because for anyone to delay repentance is a sin itself.

Adam, the first man, was made by Allah from clay.  He became the worst man alive and then became the best man alive.  Adam was the worst man alive because he committed the first sin and was the most sinful man for a period of time.  Yet then Adam repented, was forgiven and subsequently was the best man alive since he was the only man to have repented for a period of time.  Throughout both his worst moment and his best he was still of clay.  This shows you, me and everyone else that humans can indeed be reformed and reformed and reformed just as clay changes forms.  Some can be good forms and some can be bad forms.  Some forms can look good but be bad and some forms can look bad but be good.  Outside foreign forces may influence and shape us, but we can change and be molded into what Allah desires.  Sure, we may be in a bad state or even in the worse state we have ever been before in our lives but because we are human we can reform ourselves and our ways and our Creator will help us to be who he wants us to be and to do what he created us to do.  As humans are made from clay it means worshipping prophets, governments, family, culture, any human system or even worshipping ourselves by being slaves to our desires is tantamount to worshipping an idol of clay.  As clay we want what is good for us this is why Allah promises righteous believers Gardens in Paradise, because Gardens are great for clay to be in. While Allah threatens the disobedient and disbelievers with Hellfire because fire is terrible for clay. As clay our hearts can grow hard and hard clay is bad without much worth. The solution to hard clay is water, meaning sincere tears for the sake of Allah and the sweat of doing good deeds for the sake of our Maker alone. Also using water to perform Islamic ablution prior to prayer removes one's sins and protects one from shaitan. Islam is the perfect mold for us, all we have to do is enter it wholeheartedly, knowledgeably stick to it and let Allah guide us while we are patient and grateful. Yet it goes both ways, as long as we are alive we can be misinformed, disfigured and transformed by Satan and our own flaws and lose our good form Allah has guided us to and suffer the tragedy of dying in a bad form. The bottom line is that as long as we are alive, we can change for better or worse just as clay can. God-willing we will die in a better condition than we are currently in today. It's not about the past, what's done is done; what's important is what you do next. The test of life isn't over yet. The only catch is the test of life isn't over for everybody so we can't say what the final judgement of most of those living today will be (aside from the antichrist or yajuj and majooj). Yet we do know the categories that are available and we know that everyone is currently in one category or the other or many. We can see where people currently are in order to judge them as God has judged and how the prophets judged and taught us to judge. But people change remarkably quickly. The prophets came to pass judgement on mankind before God judges mankind, so that way there are no surprises. Saying that "Only God can Judge" is like a criminal saying "Only the Judge can determine whether I committed a crime or not." which is a foolish statement to make because the law determines who the criminals are. The Judge doesn't judge if you are a criminal, the judge just passes the sentence so you can be justly punished for crimes committed. So, a more accurate saying is "*Only God can Sentence*".

When we die the most important thing that matters is what our Creator/ Judge will think of us and do to us. The opinions of our family, friends and everyone else will not outweigh the importance of the opinion of Allah. It would be better for people to curse you a million years after you die and to have Allah love you, than to have the entire world mourn your death a billion years afterwards with Allah cursing you. When you are in that grave the people will leave, abandoning you to your fate, to go on with their lives laughing, playing and partying without a second thought to your rotting foul-smelling decomposing corpse. These "loved ones" will throw dirt on your dead body, at the least, some may do even worse things, like embalming, stuffing or burning. Maybe they will even dance on your grave, urinate or defecate on it. Surely, they will spend all the wealth you left behind, as if you worked your entire life just for them. You will become an excuse. The only time they will mention you will be to lighten the mood and they will say things like, *"we better have fun now before we end up like ____ (your name)"*. You know this is true because you know people who have died before you that have been treated in this manner; the people probably liked them more than they like you. So *"What will they say when you die?"* shouldn't even be a thought in your mind, let alone something you care about. Hypothetically let's say people loved you, praised you and after death you became the most famous well-liked person of all time. If you were to go to hell on the Day of Judgment then what will they think of you then? What would all that fame and praise be worth when your flesh is constantly burning and being remade to burn again and out of sheer thirst you drink boiling water which destroys your intestines and melts your mouth, face, lips and teeth? How much sleep do you think you will get using blankets of hellfire? How will it feel never being able to sleep ever again and having no tears left to cry so that you cry blood out of pain and sorrow? If you have to endure that for eternity, whatever nice things people may have said or thought about you will be of no consolation; it will only add to your misery. Death is a fact of life. Instead of caring about the opinions of people, always ask yourself: *"What will Allah think of me when I'm judged?"* This does not mean that you go to extremes with the *"Only God can judge me, who do you think you are?"* attitude and start being bad without a care in the world for what anybody else thinks. If one where to make a case that *"Only God can judge me"* then that includes compliments too, so if someone was told they were smart or beautiful, such a person should reply *"Only God can judge me, who do you think you are?"* This double standard reveals that such people actually mean *"Only God can judge me negatively, everyone can judge me positively."* Everyone is a judge to some extent, but few judge with justice or rule in matters according to the way God instructs us to. The type of Judgement reserved to the Creator alone, refers to Allah being the only one who can judge concerning whether you go to heaven and hell. Although divine laws have been sent to us in order for judgments to be passed in this life as well. Those who break the divine laws are to be punished in this life and the next, if they are unrepentant. We have been given the criteria to know what laws we'll be judged by in this life so there are no surprises in the afterlife. Ignorance of the law would be an excuse if there was no way to know it, but the prophets came with it and the law of God has been preserved. It explains if you do certain sins you will get certain punishments and so on and so forth unless you repent. The prophets David and Solomon were just judges and kings, if the slogan "*Only God can judge*" were true, then why were these prophets judging people? Prophets came to judge people on earth. No one told Moses: "*Hey Moses, only God can judge, who do you think you are?*" People might say: "*but he was a prophet, you're not*", well the laws God gave to the prophets to judge by are still around. You wouldn't say that because the ruler who signed the law into existence isn't alive today then that means we don't have to follow the law. God, who made the law, always exists and we are expected to keep the law and communally on the governmental level punish the lawbreakers whether the original enforcer (prophet) is here or not. The code of conduct is still in effect. You don't stop following the laws just because a new cop is on the beat, or because no cops are around. The law of God doesn't have an expiration date. It can only change if a prophet says so on the authority of God.

No more prophets means no more changes. It doesn't have to be written in stone, all that matters is that it was decreed by God. The law of God was not put up for a vote. The reason Satan uses this clever seemingly religious slogan "*Only God can judge*" is to make people feel they have a license to do whatever sin they want and no one has the right to tell them they are wrong. The point is when people die and the world mourns saying that they are going to heaven, because they were famous and loved by people, don't put too much value on what they say. After all, the dead person is punished in the grave if people wail and tear their clothes out of grief for them. It actually hurts the dead person when people get too emotional and commit sins over their death. Having the world wail for the death of someone can be a bad indication of what is happening to them in the grave. Extreme displays of affection only serve to torture the deceased object of affection. Such people are judging the final destination of the dead based on their own opinions of them. Only Allah knows what you were really like when nobody was looking and what was in your heart and mind. The eulogy at your funeral is of no value to you. Realistically it's possible to deceive the people of the world into thinking you are a saint while doing all sorts of evil behind closed doors. The world's estimation of you will not determine your eternal destination when you are placed in the grave. The opinions of people will be the last thing on your mind when the angels Munkar and Nakir forcefully awaken you to begin the interrogation in the grave. Conveniently people wailing at funerals forget their slogan of "*Only God can judge*". They are deluded into thinking they really knew the person. Then they equate their sense of good and bad with what God thinks is good and bad. This slogan is usually an indication the person saying it practices microtheism. Microtheism is when a person acknowledges God with reduced reverence. In which a person "worships" God, but they do it on their own terms. Such a person might go to houses of worship once in a while, but they don't think God has any right to control their private lives or personal behavior. Basically, they believe in God but they don't care how God wants them to live. This belief is similar to the religion of Satan. Sadly, most humans are not even aware of the word microtheism and don't realize they are practicing a different religion than what they think. Such people will be surprised when they die and discover how far astray they were. May Allah help us to discern the true religion from the false religions in all their forms and to practice the true religion with sincerity and consistency.

Islam is about submitting to God as God sees fit, not as we see fit. The toughest thing to overcome is our own opinion of ourself. We tend to think that if we think God loves us then it's true or that if we think God hates us then it's true, but that's not how it works at all. Likewise, the test of life isn't a numbers game about the quantity of good deeds one has, it's the quality that matters most. Another trap we tend to fall for is that we think we can continue living the way we are and march right into paradise. In reality we might have to change a few things about ourselves in order to enter paradise. The test of life is stressful but we must do whatever it takes to pass. God didn't promise mankind that passing the test of life would be easy, but he did promise that it's worth it and we can do it. What's certain, aside from our death, is that in order to enter paradise we have to believe what God wants, go where God wants us to go, stay where God wants us to stay, do what God wants us to do and don't do what God doesn't want us to do. This is how we should live every moment of every day. Every day is different and requires us to act accordingly. We should truly treat every day as a new day without thinking we have stored up any good deeds for the afterlife and treat it as though today is the only day we have in our life to do good deeds and avoid bad deeds. We don't want to get complacent or despair and let our past make us think we are either guaranteed or permanently prohibited from paradise.  The past is the past, don't waste your present by dwelling on it.  This would be like the person taking a test spending their time thinking about how good or bad they did on the earlier portions of the test and not proceeding to try to get more points.  We'd say that's foolish regardless whether they did good or bad earlier, they should just keep going and try their best every moment.  The road to paradise isn't the shortest or the easiest but it is the only one we want to finish traveling.  The sinful roads seem fun in the beginning but the further you get to the end the worse it gets, and both the road to paradise and the roads to hell result in the travelers residing forever at their final destination.  Allah helps those travelers who sincerely want to travel the road to paradise, because realistically we aren't going to be able to travel it without his help.  We just have to take one step at a time up the incline and before we know it, we'll be there God-willing.  Don't look back at your previous footprints, what's important is where you put the next step.  It's not about whether you think you are making progress or not, or if you think you are passing or failing and similarly it doesn't matter what you think of others.  For instance, you may think this book may be good or bad, but my book of deeds is what's important.  It would be stupid for me to delete a good sentence, paragraph or chapter of this book but it's even dumber for me to erase good deeds from my book of deeds by doing bad deeds.  Instead I should do good deeds which can cancel out the bad that I've done in the past.  You have a book of deeds too, which may well be better than mine.  You are writing your book of deeds at this time and will continue as long as you are alive.  Regarding your book of deeds, there is only one review and opinion that matters; the opinion of the Creator of all things.  Everyone is an author currently writing and revising their book of deeds before it gets published on the Day of Judgement.  This is why dwelling on the past is pointless for us to do just as it would be stupid for an author to dwell on how good or bad their earlier pages were.  If their book was good, you'd say, "don't stop keep writing" and if it was bad you'd tell them to fix it and keep writing.  But the advantage our book of deeds has over regular books is that in order to fix what we've done in the past we simply do good stuff in the present and then God will erase our mistakes or turn them into good deeds.  Thus, we should have very good books once they are published since we've been working on them our entire lives.  However, every book gets rated differently depending on who is reading it.  To be rated highly an author would write according to the criteria their reader uses to judge a book. For our book of deeds to be a prize winner and not tossed into the book burning pile we should write it/ live according to God's criteria, because if we live trying to please any other being, such as ourself, then we won't be getting those prizes from God which we desire. So, keep your eyes on the prizes, but more importantly focus on the opinion of the Divine Judge who gives out the prizes. Although unlike worldly writing competitions, our book of deeds gets better if we help others to improve their book of deeds. So, the human species is on a team. The problem is some of us are working for Satan, or for selfish interests which end up hurting our team. Also, some make their book of deeds a horror story or a true crime book without realizing it and others just want to have a fun time writing an adventure book. But only a Muslim author who presents a book from the Islamic genre will get rewarded by the Creator. God will let people write whatever they want in their book of deeds, just as a teacher will let a student write whatever they want for their assignment, but what we've been told to do is clear and if we want to pass the test of life we must obey the Creator without fear of anything other than our divine Maker who is merciful in forgiveness while simultaneously powerful in punishment.

Sincere repentance means you don't do that sin again. Repentance is not something where you just cry your eyes out and profusely apologize to God and promise and promise and promise not to do X sin ever again. True sincere repentance is a lifelong struggle, and this is why one typically only knows whether they are forgiven by God when they die. Repentance is a form of Jihad. True repentance doesn't only mean you don't do that sin anymore, it means you don't even want to do that sin anymore and no longer desire to do it. Acknowledgment of the sin, Regret of the sin, Apologizing to God and asking forgiveness for the sin is just 3/4 parts of repentance. Now there is no such thing as 75% forgiveness. Eventually when all is settled you are either forgiven 100% or 0%. Even if you are a believer, if you only do those 3 things when you repent then you will not be forgiven for your sins. The 4th part of promising never to do those sins again is a major determining factor as to whether one will be forgiven. The Quran teaches that those who believe AND do good deeds will be forgiven. It doesn't say those who believe and say sorry will be forgiven. It teaches those who <u>believe, repent and do good deeds</u> will be forgiven. The key to repentance is keeping your promise as best as possible to not do those sins again. Since if you really do know X is wrong, why would you do it?

If you really regret doing X in the past would you do it again?  If you really regret a sin then how could you ever desire to do it again?  This is why an addict is not someone who has fully repented, an addict could be forgiven but for an addict to still desire the sin indicates their repentance is not fully completed.  If you told God you were sincerely sorry for X sin, why would you want to do it again?  The reason is because we are humans and as such we are not always sincere.  Many think repentance just means not doing the sin again but true repentance involves not even having that sinful desire.  We might be sincerely sorry and sincerely repent soon after committing the sin yet some minutes, days, weeks, months, years or decades later we might lose that sincerity and do X sin again or desire to do X sin again.  Simply to have a desire to do a particular sin again after repenting is a sign of an insincere repentance.  Thus, we should repent not just from our deeds but our sinful desires and our lack of repentance as well as our laxity in repenting after sinning.  For example, if you commit X sin and then an hour later you repent, that is 2 sins there.  First you did X sin and then you did another sin by waiting a whole hour to repent.  Yet how many of us repent for laziness in repenting?  This is how Satan traps many people, because while we can get forgiven for sins we commit if we repent, we have to first actually repent from doing them.  To delay repentance is a sin which many of us rarely consider major, regret, apologize for or avoid and truly repent from.  If you are doing X sin then repent immediately, even if you do X repent do X again and repent and do X over and over in a very short period of time, you'd be half as sinful if you repented for X sin immediately after doing it rather than repenting later.  Hence sinful as you may be, you can be 50% less sinful just by repenting sooner than you currently do.  If you mess up and do a sin then do the repentance as soon as possible, don't mess up the repentance as well because the sin in delaying repentance could result in a punishment greater than the punishment you'd get for X sin you are repenting from doing.  These are the games Satan plays where people think they're doing good but remain sinful and unrepentant by not repenting for their flaws, insincerity and delay in repenting.  When many repent from X sin they should really do 2 types of repentance, one for X sin and another for their poor repentance.  Those who "repent" rarely do it enough or sincerely and this is why we persist in committing the same sins consistently, because our "repentance" has lots of problems with it.  We must ask forgiveness for the faults we have in our laxity in asking for forgiveness.  We might be forgiven for the sins we repent from but end up getting punished for making a lousy delayed repentance. Satan not only tries to get us to sin, but also wants to make our repentance insincere, delayed, deficient and incomplete. Such is the test of life, just as a test taker can always change their answers until the test is over, we can always have our bad deeds turn into good deeds or vice versa. We don't just want to give the correct answers to our test of life but want complete credit for our correct answers and to correct our mistakes fully in the best manner. Sincere repentance consists of a lifelong attitude and lifelong action. This is why God commands us to not just believe but to do good deeds as well in abundance, because God knows that the only way for us to stop doing bad sins is if we use our time, energy, etc. to do the good deeds instead. The point is our test is not over yet, God has deliberately given us this moment to continue taking the test. We have this moment to do better before our time is gone and our test score becomes permanent for all eternity. Whatever your score on the test of life is at this moment, it is not your final score. The stakes are high, the time is nearly over. What are you currently doing to do better on your test? What will you do tomorrow to do better on your test of life? Always remember that one day you will plan to do better tomorrow and time will be up and you will die with whatever score you have at that moment. Soon your current score on the test of life and your current relationship with God will be your eternal score and your eternal relationship with God. Are you satisfied to die this second and have your current relationship with God be the same for all eternity? If you get another second to live then it means God wants you to have a better score on the test of life and a better relationship than the one you have now. It doesn't matter whether you think you are doing good or if you are doing so bad you just wish it were over, you don't know what your score is at this moment and you don't know whether it will improve or get worse should your life be extended. Yet whoever you are, God wants you to be better. So, believe, repent and do good deeds; repeatedly until death. Fear the worst, hope for the best, follow the prophets and ask God for true success. At one time or another we've all been sinners, but Godwilling we can die as sincere believers. Every time you've sinned that is a sign from God that you have something that you should fix in your life and change, where if you do so then you've learned and improved. Being a human is a very unique experience, humans are special creatures who are made to live a life where they never stop improving their relationship with their Creator and Master. Your whole life amounts to answering 3 questions in the grave. If you don't answer correctly you lose the test of life. God has told us the answers and told us why to answer and how we will be able to answer the way God desires us to. The key is to live the right answers for the right reasons in this test of life. Of all who are asked the 3 questions in the grave, the few who pass are those whom when the questions are asked they are only asked because God has promised they'd be asked. In reality the 3 questions are rhetorical. Even though the questions will be verbally responded to, our lifetime of actions will speak a far louder answer than our words. The believer is asked the 3 questions in their grave by the angels Munkar and Nakir, "**Who is your Lord? What religion did you practice? Who is the man that was sent to you?**" After the believer correctly answers each ultimate question correctly by truthfully saying *"My Lord is Allah, the religion I practiced was Islam,"* and then citing the Muslim prophet of their era that was sent to instruct them, they will be asked a fourth question, "**How do you know this?**" This fourth question will only be asked to a believer and only true believers will answer correctly and honestly with confidence saying: ***"I read Allah's book, believed in it, obeyed it and applied it."***

Then Allah will call out: "*My slave has spoken the truth, so prepare for him a bed from Paradise and clothe him from Paradise, and open for him a gate to Paradise."* Then the believer will smell a sweet fragrance better than anything they ever smelled before, their grave will be filled with light and made wide as far as they can see. The good deeds of the believer will come to them in the grave in the form of a beautiful person with fine clothes and a sweet smell. Then they will ask Allah to hasten the Day of Resurrection/Judgement with anticipation for the rewards awaiting them. Will you be able to answer the questions in the grave correctly and quickly with confidence and sincerity? You could be asked these questions in the grave today. Will you pass the test? The rest of this book contains the Quranic verses of Allah and prophetic hadith of Muhammad that relate to our lifelong quest of sincere repentance.

A reader familiar with some of my previous books will notice I copied and pasted much of the aforementioned insights from books I previously wrote and the following remainder is mostly copy and pasted Quran and hadith, thus it's a rather copy pasted book. However, you can never copy and paste your sincerity nor your sincere repentance. Every time you sin and cry over it you have to be genuine in the regret, humility, desperation, shame, and motivation to never return to the sin again. And even if you eventually return to that sin, just as you underwent a thorough change from repentance mode to sin mode you have to undergo a thorough change again to repentance mode for it to stick.  This is why Muslim Scholars have said it is easier to avoid the sin in the first place than it is to repent from the sin afterwards.  And especially if you are so deluded into thinking that you can just sin and repent afterwards habitually, this is a type of abuse of God's forgiveness in some regard.  Such a creature that thinks and assumes God will forgive you, before you even asked for forgiveness, and that you are guaranteed to be forgiven so much so that you can sin in the future and feel confident in a further post-sin future repentance where you will be forgiven is certifiably crazy.  Truly consider a criminal who plans to compulsively rob or kill and confides in their heinous plan to you, telling you they know they will be caught 100% and brought to Court but they feel the Judge will let them go unpunished because they will apologize and promise not to do it anymore; and on top of this they have done this before where they have premeditated a long series of crimes and then apologized and were free to go on continuing to commit crimes.  We would say either they never truly been to Court or such a Judge is beyond comprehension.  Whereas truly God is beyond comprehension and truly none of us has been in God's Court yet.  But for all we know none of our sins might have been forgiven and we are planning more crimes until we finally die and then find out all those times we assumed forgiveness for we never got the ticket to paradise we imagined we had in store for us but had we stopped one crime less than our grand total then we might have been granted leniency.  So never be like the brothers of Prophet Joseph who premeditated their crimes against him planning to repent afterwards because such a repentance is guaranteed to be insincere.  For instance, in the above example of the criminal who confided their plans in you, what if the Judge asked you as a character witness whether the criminal had previously planned to give a repentful speech in Court before committing the crime and you said that indeed the Criminal did prewrite their repentance speech prior to committing the crime? You yourself as such a witness to the pre-concocted repentance would doubt the Judge should forgive that type of repentance because the likelihood of it being sincere is unlikely because it was premeditated.  Basically, if you are truly sorry for the sin that is one thing, however if you are planning to be truly sorry for a sin that you haven't yet done then if you were truly sorry you wouldn't follow through and do the sin would you? No.  So, it is extremely extreme for us to plan a repentance prior to sinning. Then we expect it to be automatically accepted as legit.  But with that said, even if you fall into this compound sin of sinning by planning a repentance that you expect to make prior to another sin, it is still possible to repent but it's a whole lot harder because now you have to reform yourself better than you planned.  If you said before you did the sin you would cry and promise and do X good deeds to make up for the sin, then you got to do that just to be honest; but to truly repent you have to do extra crying and reformation.  In actuality you have to repent regardless of whether you planned to repent before the sin or not.  The truly stupid would be the one who plans to repent then sins then doesn't repent at all.  That would be the destroyed person for whom we fear got lost in the sin entirely.  Yet what I'm focusing on is that instead of thinking our pre-planned repentances are valid we should actually be repenting for those plans too along with the sins, but oftentimes we just follow through with the sin and the pre-planned repentance as a lipservice habitual routine because it unfortunately becomes a habit to repent from habitual sins.  While it should be a habit to repent, since it is the key to salvation, we should not be habitually sinning to be habitually repenting in the first place.  The point is you should always repent no matter what as soon as possible without delay. And if you already expect to repent then don't do the sin and save yourself the trouble because you don't know if such a sin would be forgiven if you did it and repented.  To pre-plan repentance means you are suspect as to the sincerity of your repentance and it will be scrutinized more by God because God knows you already planned the sin and the sorry part afterwards.  God knows you were intending to say sorry to him before doing the sins and then hears the sorry but how do you know whether God is going to accept such an act?  You don't.  So, you got to stop acting like a criminal whether that's a career criminal who plans crimes or a plain criminal who messes up unintentionally without premediated atrocities.  But if we truly examine who has more right to feel assured of forgiveness it would be the occasional criminal rather than the pre-meditating criminal because of the possibility of sincerity being with the one who didn't pre-compose their repentance speech prior to committing crimes.  Sadly, many of us are in the latter category where we are criminal masterminds accustomed to habitually sinning and pre-planning how we will get away with it by pre-planning essentially a fun sinful path to paradise where we can play with the devils in this life and retire to be served by angels after death.  It's possible for some but most criminal masterminds are only fooling themselves prior to God punishing them with a dose of reality. So be realistically repentful. Increase your odds by decreasing your sins and adding good deeds continuously. At this moment God has destined for you to be alive. No matter what has past, God wants you alive now in the present to do proper monotheistic goodness, so do it. If you do what you are supposed to do from now on, why would God punish you? Even if insincere perhaps God will forgive you for good behavior in the present. Never lose hope in the mercy of God but don't play games either trying to be a criminal mastermind by planning repentance prior to committing crimes. Yet even criminal masterminds can sincerely repent and if you are smart enough to be a criminal mastermind then you can be a repenting Muslim more easily, all things considered. And that is the true reality of the repentful, is that we are in actuality criminal masterminds but we have changed and chosen the life of obedience to the prophetic guidance of monotheism vowing to oppose the criminal culture until we die in the process of continuous repentance coming close to goodness hoping to die upon a good deed. God knows what you did and what you could do better so rather than show God how much worse you can get by doing more sins with your life, instead show God how much better you can do by improving yourself and the relationship with your Maker. It's rarely ever about can or can't, it's if you want to then your desires will cause you to find a way to make it happen and God will help. Just consider the power of your desires. If a tiny part of you wants to sin then how often does that tiny desire get you into sinful trouble? If a tiny desire to sin can result in sin, then imagine what a pure sincere knowledgeable intention and major desire to do good and simultaneously avoid evil will result in?

Perfection in every aspect may be impossible, but the realistic definition of perfection is to always strive for perfection. As with the roads in this life the road to paradise has a speed limit, if you travel on it faster than you can handle you may crash and burn. Also, if Satan persuades you to go too slow out of fear, or laziness, you will run out of fuel before you reach your destination and also crash and burn for a different reason. The most important thing is to be on the road to paradise and not on one of the many roads to hell. If you can't travel on it at the same speed as others, that's okay you don't have to, but you do have to get on the road to paradise. Just try to practice Islam as much as you can, that's all God wants you to do. God will never punish you for not doing something which

God knows you can't do. Yet to be a Muslim hero you need extra stuff the "practicing Muslim" doesn't have/do. You don't have to be a Muslim hero if you don't want to, but why not try? Truly if you sincerely ask God to help you and put in some effort then God can help you become a Muslim hero. Again, God defines Muslim heroes, not people, there might be some super-Muslim doing all kinds of great deeds but another person who struggles to do a few mandatory deeds could well be vastly superior to the Muslim who everyone else thinks is the hero of the Muslim world. There are many different types of Muslim heroes.

I hope you or someone who reads this or is indirectly influenced by it can become such a Muslim hero so I may benefit for whatever role I played in aiding their victories Godwilling. Yet even then aid only comes from Allah, I just hope to be a slave that Allah uses to improve his other slaves. Doctors get ill too, but just because they may be sick doesn't mean that they quit advising others because of being unhealthy themselves. Sometimes after committing a sin, I end up condemning that sin or sins to someone else, which is hypocritical but in reality I may not have done so if I wasn't trying to condemn the sins I was guilty of in order to help myself repent. Whereas by me hypocritically remorsefully condemning what I'm guilty of to others it might just be exactly what they needed to hear and God may have used my speech at that moment to stop someone else from sinning. Likewise, it may be that when I get good advice, the other person may have only done that to recompense for their sins. Hence while God hates our sins, the effects of our sins or rather our repentance can lead us to help each other to stop doing sins. This doesn't mean you should sin thinking it's okay, because Satan will try to tell people that, but it does mean that even if you are sinful and hypocritical one still must talk the talk because God wants us to, even though we may not practice what we preach.

Though God knows all our sins before we do them, we are still fully responsible for them, and our sins displease God despite his foreknowledge of them. God simply knows the mistakes we will make before they happen, they are still mistakes. Those who think God knowing our sins before we do them somehow means they aren't sinful or that God is responsible are believing exactly what Satan believed and said when Satan blamed God for his sins. It's not God's fault we sin, it's our fault and all our sins are wrong, however sometimes the long-term consequences of our sins can result in great things such as life-changing improvements so this is why God allows some sins to occur. God hates our sins but can love the way we repent from sins. What I'm saying is don't do any sins but if/when you do then don't despair or stop doing good deeds just because you messed up a little (or a lot). You and I will never be 100% perfect, but that's no reason not to try. The goal isn't for us to be perfect, the goal God set for us is to be like the prophets. In order for you to obtain the love of Allah, his friendship and paradise you have to die trying. If you don't even try to obey the divine law, it's disrespectful to the Creator of us all. Never stop doing good no matter how sinful you are. <u>It is sinful to have no fear when doing sins and then have such fear doing good actions that you fail to do them. How dare you be fearless when doing sins and then have fear when doing something good that God desires?</u> Such a satanic fear is something to fear afflicting us. The more good deeds you do the less you will fear doing them and the more sins you do the less you will fear doing those. While the more sins you do the more you will fear doing good deeds, and the more good deeds you do the more you will fear doing sins. Thus stop your sins and increase your good deeds, but even if you struggle to stop sinning always try to do more good deeds because eventually they will cure you Godwilling. We may be hypocrites but a sinful hypocrite who does good deeds is far better than a sinful hypocrite who doesn't. A single good deed can give God an excuse to forgive all your sins. Good deeds are more precious than time itself, always do good. Even if you have to die to do a good deed it's worth it. Whereas if you have to die in the effort of avoiding sin, that too is worth dying for. Live/Die doing good sincerely for God's sake, without fear.

A Muslim does not have "bad days" because for the Muslim every day is a good day. Every day we have a chance to worship, repent and please our Creator is a good day because we can still do good deeds. Every day is a good opportunity we shouldn't waste, especially when so many have already died who wish they could have the opportunities we now have. Also, by not doing bad deeds we get good credit as well. When a difficulty or hardship comes their way, the Muslim is patient, praises Allah and is grateful, never bitter or in despair. The prophets were tested with the hardest tests mankind has ever faced and Allah loves them the most. Being tested is a sign that Allah loves you. On the other hand, it could also be preemptory punishment for disbelievers when hardships come their way, or an opportunity sent for them to change, or a way for them to be guided. Getting a flat tire when traveling on the road to hell is a good thing because it stops your sinful progression. We are tested so it can be made clear who is wicked and who is good, so that no one will be able to make excuses and think Allah has treated people unjustly on the Day of Judgment. The harder the test the greater the reward for passing. The more tests one passes the higher the level in paradise one will have, just like climbing a steep mountain, it's easy at the bottom. The road to paradise is steep, not cheap. Do not think you will say, "*I believe*" and then will be left alone without being tested. Allah has promised mankind that they will be tested, so whether we want it or not we are going to get it. You might as well get rewarded for the suffering by enduring it as a patient grateful believer. While our purpose in life is to be constantly tested, there is Satan who has made it his goal to try to make us fail. Although Allah has promised that we will never be burdened with something greater than we can bear, which includes addictions. So, if you got a burden, whatever it is, you can handle it. Maybe you can't handle it too well at this minute, but that's why Allah allows you to be burdened because Allah wants to help you out. You see the reason Allah says people are never given a burden that's greater than they can bear is because they always have Allah to help them out and lighten the burden for them. If we would just ask as a devout slave and do what's needed for

Allah's friendship, we will get that help. Asking isn't enough, action is commanded as well because Allah doesn't want to pamper us and turn into our slave. We are the slave and Allah is the master, as the slave we don't ask and wait for help from the master because that's not how a master operates. A master gives the slave the tools first then the advice then maybe more tools and then after the slave does all they can possibly do the master helps them finish. The means we take to get a cure are not the cure themselves, because 2 people can have identical conditions, make identical requests and take identical actions but one gets cured and the other doesn't. The cure is with Allah alone. Our battles are not won by our worldly weapons, strategy, support, efforts or experience. The outcome rests with God. To trust in the means is to not trust in God. The only reason we use means to an end is because God commands it, it's not because they can actually help us achieve our goal. It might appear that way to the ignorant but that's not the reality. The means we take are just another test to see that when God helps us after taking actions are we going to think our actions had something to do with success? Or will we give our Creator 100% of the credit? This applies to all actions, even prayer. Prayer itself is not a means to success; it can only lead to success if our Creator makes it be successful.

Many people pray to no avail, many do good deeds but go to hell. It's important to remember your goal is to play a role as a slave, your action doesn't truly affect the outcome, Allah just wants you to do good deeds and live a certain way to prove your commitment. Basically, the Creator wants to know if you will work hard as he commands even when you know it won't determine the outcome, or will you work hard as he commands and then think your efforts had something to do with your results. If you do the good deeds and avoid the evil, God will cause results and even may give you success; but that degree of success will be different depending on why you did what you did. Thus, it comes down to true sincerity. When you do something, whatever it is whether it's eating, sleeping, etc., are you doing it to please God, or come closer to God, or for yourself? If for yourself then that's selfish and wrong to do. Yet in the Quran Allah says to save yourself from the hellfire? But why should we save ourself from the hellfire? Because it hurts? NO. Because Allah said so that's why. Why do we do good deeds and strive for paradise? For eternal pleasure? Because Allah says we'll enjoy it? NO. Because Allah said to do that and he knows what's best for us. We are supposed to just enjoy doing what our Creator wants us to do. That's how we were designed. We shouldn't enjoy paradise because it's fun, we should enjoy it because it makes God happy if we enjoy it. Thus, even if God wanted us to be in hellfire, we should enjoy that, if it's what God wanted. God doesn't want anyone to be in hellfire, yet he is just, so people will be there forever and it will make God even more upset with them that they are there because it displeases God to punish his creation. But rules are rules so God will do so if we don't follow the rules which have been given to us. The rules are there, what's truth and falsehood are made clear, we've been taught right from wrong by the prophets and given our one time try on the test of life. A main part of that test is living it correctly, avoiding errors and fixing our mistakes before we die. However, when living this test the reason why we try to pass and do our best is part of that test. Some get good grades to please their parents, some to please themselves, some because good grades are better than bad grades, some because they want the reward whereas some simply try to get good grades to please the one who gave them the test. We should be of those who pass our test of life with this singular purpose of passing because the test giver wants us to. What is done with us after that we just hope it is what pleases our Creator. God will keep his promise of paradise to those who pass but even if theoretically he didn't we shouldn't care because we should want what God wants. Hate and Fear to be in hell because God wants you to feel that way. Love and Desire Paradise because God wants you to. Live for God and Die for God as a slave, the only reason we should try to be God's friend is because God tells us to do so.

Try to always be aware that every second of every day you are being tested and that Satan is there trying to make you fail every single test. Satan is patient too and has short-term, mid-term and long-term plots and has more plans than there are letters in all the alphabets. Satan uses sneakier strategies and more dangerous weapons as we develop so we can never let our guard down. Time is running out, soon we will no longer be tested and will receive the results of whether we passed or failed. Remember we are in a lifelong competition and Satan won't quit. God-willing we shall pass and our enemy Satan will fail. God-willing I will be someone who follows my own advice. May Allah protect us all from disbelief, hypocrisy and every type of sin. God tells us that Satan is our enemy and commands us to take him as our enemy. Satan will disavow us in the afterlife so why wait? Let's disavow him in this life and reject his offer of friendship so that we can be God's friend instead. God wants you to be his friend. It's the toughest type of friendship of all to maintain and billions will try to break it up, ourselves included, but it's the best type of friendship to live with and die with. We're just trying our best, it's all we can do. Every day a Muslim prays, we ask Allah a minimum of 17 times a day to: *"guide us to the straight path, the path of those who are blessed, not the path of those who have earned your wrath nor of those who have gone astray"*. Every one of us needs constant guidance more and more, should that guidance leave us then surely we would go astray and become evildoers. I can't guide anyone, trust me I've tried and tried and tried and tried and tried, I need guidance myself. It's easy to preach, it's harder to practice, God-willing preaching will help me practice. If Allah doesn't guide me, I'd be demonic. Truly if Allah doesn't protect me every second from my evil intentions and evil actions, I'd be the most evil hypocritical person of all time. Just take the people of Moses as an example, Moses left them for only 40 days and they ended up worshipping a golden calf despite all their prior guidance, good deeds and struggles to believe in the face of severe persecution. They believed through years of hardship but disbelieved in less than 40 days after their prophet left them to go get more guidance from God for them. Many books exist where those who read it are better than the one who wrote it. Even if theoretically someone writes a good book that does not mean they're a good person, writing a good book doesn't even mean they got credit for doing a good deed. Our good deeds will be weighed, not counted. One sincere great deed can easily outweigh a lifetime's worth of good deeds. While one bad deed can destroy a lifetime of great deeds.

Unlike all other religions, when accepting Islam and becoming a Muslim, you only become qualified to enter paradise. It's not as if one becomes Muslim then they are done, get a ticket to paradise with a receipt and don't have to worry about the hellfire anymore. Because all of us sin we also qualify to be punished if Allah doesn't forgive us. Being a Muslim qualifies one to be forgiven if you repent, while dying upon any other religion besides Islam disqualifies one from forgiveness no matter how much they repent or how many good deeds they may do. Becoming a Muslim is not a guarantee of paradise because one could become a Muslim and then die upon a religion other than Islam, which would make them worse than those disbelievers who never became Muslim. Or a Muslim could die as a hypocrite, whereas the Muslim hypocrites are in a lower position in the hellfire than the disbelievers, for faking it and not sincerely acting upon the knowledge which Allah blessed them with. Becoming a Muslim only qualifies one for paradise, but if a person is sincere and practices

Islam in the right prophetic manner wholeheartedly to the best of their abilities and dies in such a state as a Muslim, then paradise will await them guaranteed. However, if someone learns about Islam and rejects it after knowing what it is about and they die in that condition, then there is absolutely no way they will ever be taken out of the hellfire, they will never have the privilege of seeing their Creator and such a person will remain in miserable torment forever without end, despite their wishes and pleas to be ended and obliterated. May Allah help us to die as sincere grateful obedient believers and grant us the worldly benefits and eternal rewards they are entitled to and protect us from disbelief, hypocrisy, despair, sin, religious innovations, ignorance, arrogance and the consequences thereof. Most importantly we must recognize the value of the knowledge God gave us which others have been deprived of and that we benefit ourselves and others with that knowledge through our intentions and deeds. We frequently forget our blessings and fall into folly. Yet we then remember to repent to right our relationship and obtain rewards that are unmatched. There are no more words I can give to introduce the blessed information that follows except the admonition that repentance is an obligatory deed and beloved action of God so hasten to do it as soon as you can and then be firm strictly safe from sin afterwards never quitting in such a quest of following the prophets to paradise upon the path the salaf amongst their followers. In reality we need better role models to compete with instead of our contemporaries and the examples of the Salafis are the non-prophetic role models in every aspect of religion. So, seek wisdom on how to repent from the followers of such a blessed creed and methodology to attain success. I mention one wise quote of merely one member of the Muslim Salafi community, the 4th caliph and companion of Muhammad, his cousin Ali ibn Abi Talib when he was asked about the topic of repentance.

It is reported that a man came to Ali and asked, *What do you think about a man who committed a sin?*

He replied, *He must seek Allah's forgiveness and repent to Him.*

The man said, *He did that, but then sinned again?*

Ali said, *He must seek Allah's forgiveness and repent to Him.*

The man again said, *He did that, but returned to sin.*

Ali said, *He must seek Allah's forgiveness and repent to Him.*

The man said for the fourth time, *He did, but then sinned again.*

Ali then said, *Until when?* Then he said, *He must seek Allah's forgiveness and repent to Him; and not give up until it is Shaytan who is defeated [overcome].*

Source: Hunād bin Al-Sarī, Kitāb Al-Zuhd 910

Reflect on how every time you repent it may be that you have defeated the Shaitan if you stick to it and it is accepted by God. Yes, Shaitan defeated you when you sinned, that is known, but Shaitan doesn't want you to know that every time you repent correctly with the prophetic beliefs and correct intentions and actions then you in fact defeat Shaitan right back. So never beat yourself up over how many times you were defeated by sinning, rather consider every good deed you do a victory + every time you repent you are defeating Shaitan. With such a mindset no matter how many times we lose our ways we will recover. So do good deeds and continue until death for if you die while truly repentant then you have won against your enemy. Always seek God's forgiveness as fast as possible and sob your way to salvation and even if you have no tears to cry due to spiritual diseases just do what you are supposed to do and you will succeed. Allah sent the Quran and Sunnah for you to successfully repent and achieve alleviation from all woes so remember the odds are in your favor. It's not a numbers game but it's insane not to leverage the favorable odds in your favor by performing large quantities of high-quality good deeds. You got a book from God, a prophet to instruct you, the lessons preserved and the recipe to repent from any mistakes along the way. Surely those who go to hell in such a case deserve it right? So don't do wrong and you will be alongside the champions of the Creator.

Don't let guilt over a sin push you to commit more sins desperately trying incorrectly to drive the guilt away. This is like someone who sipped poison drinking more poison instead of spitting out the poison, or drinking the antidote. Don't let past good deeds distract you from the present or future possibilities by thinking you've done something great in the past when you haven't yet secured your future home in heaven. That is like climbing a mountain and thinking you are special for having almost made it to the top which causes you to stumble and fall off the mountain entirely via corrupted intentions, sins or wasted time. Repentance is the recipe for you and the best thing to do. It's not a one-hour act, or a lip service recitation. True repentance is a lifestyle. So, no matter what sins you did before you can live differently and get more mercy. No matter what kind of criminal mastermind you have become, to choose the right road after all that has occurred is truly noble and the purpose for which God placed you in this universe. So repent with more than just a two-rakat Salat of Taubah. Make good life changes that make a lasting difference and keep going learning as you go towards the goals. We all have a chance to get safety from a horrific hellfire and rewarded with a perfect paradise. The prophets proved clearly that God blesses those who follow the Islamic monotheistic guidance so follow it faithfully and when you die you shall have no fear. Truly the mercy of our Creator, Allah, is miraculous and available for you. That you exist on earth is already an evidence that mercy has been granted to you since you have time to live still while billions of others do not have that opportunity to strive. If you are alive then it's proven to you that God wants you to successfully strive or else you would be dead already. Go, strive in goodness as long as you are alive because when you die you get no extra tries. You get no redo and cannot go backwards. Time is running out, use your lifespan well.

Regarding time many Muslim criminal masterminds abuse the concept thinking that since Allah promised to eventually enter every Muslim soul into paradise then they are okay with enjoying sins in this life, doing their time in hellfire after punishment in the grave and then going to paradise. Satan deceives them into thinking it will be a short time so they gamble their afterlife for a few seconds of earthly pleasure. Many fall into this basic trap.

So to combat this we will mention a hadith mentioned in **Tafseer Ibn Katheer (4/425) via Miskeen Abu Faatimah: al-Yamaan ibn Yazeed told me, from Muhammad ibn Himyar, from Muhammad ibn 'Ali, from his father, from his grandfather, that the Prophet said:**

*"Those who commit major sins, among the people of Tawheed of all nations, if they die whilst still committing their sins, without regretting it or repenting – whoever among them enters the Fire, through the first gate of Hell, their eyes will not turn blue and their faces will not turn black, and they will not be paired with the devils, tied up in chains, or be given boiling water to drink or clothed in (garments of) pitch from the Fire. Allah will forbid their bodies to abide therein forever because of Tawheed, and He will forbid their faces to the Fire because of their prostration. Some of them will be seized by the Fire up to their feet; some of them will be seized by the Fire up to the waist and some of them will be seized by the fire up to the neck, according to their sins and actions. Some of them will remain there for one month, then be brought out; some will remain there for one year,*

*then be brought out of it; those who remain there for the longest time will remain as long as this world existed, from the day it was created until it ceased to be…"*

The key part of that hadith is that some will remain one month, some one year and others as long as the world existed, note that's not as long as humanity existed but as long as the world existed which is a much longer time. So perhaps you are thinking you will be of the blessed to only be sentenced to one month? Well one month in hellfire time is not the same as earth time. Hasan Al-Basri and Ali ibn Abi Talib and others amongst the Muslim scholars have mentioned that each month is of thirty "days" but each day in Hellfire as compared to earth time is 1,000 years in our time. So if we take the minimum sentence mentioned in Tafsir Ibn Kathir of one "month" then combine it with the linguistic and scholastic explanations that is a minimum sentence of 30,000 years in the painful punishment of Hellfire for those sinful Muslims who do not get forgiven for their crimes in this life before death via repentance or good deeds, nor in the punishment in the grave, nor through Allah's mercy on Judgment Day. For those sentenced to one "year" that's equal to 360,000 years in our time. Then there are the transgressors who transgress Allah's limits whether in private doing secret sins which only God knows of or those who do it publicly. Basically for those who think they will do the sin today and burn for it tomorrow for a bit then go to paradise later feeling they won enjoyment by sinning and still achieving salvation, they are signing up for a whole long time of hurt.  Only Allah knows which is worse concerning private or public transgressions as it depends on numerous factors.  The transgressors get sentenced to "ages" in hellfire before entry into paradise.  The word "ages" has been calculated as 80 "years" per age with each year of 12 months of 30 days of hellfire time.  So that "year" in hell of 360,000 years of our time multiplied by 80 equals 28,800,000 years in hell.  So, I ask you now if you are transgressing the limits of Allah, whether in private or public, by doing sins as a Muslim who knows better, do you really want to risk a potential 28 million year sentence in hellfire for that sin?  Isn't it easier to do whatever you need to do to avoid that sin and repent?  Is any sin worth Allah punishing you for 28 million years+ before you get let into paradise?  So, remember this lesson the next time you are tempted to sin and reflect on the value of obedience to Allah.  No matter what the sin you have problems with is, it's not worth it.

The Consequences of sin and misspent time foolishly malinvested gaining poisonous debt rather than profit is still to be regretted even if forgiveness is achieved.  Every deed we do every second is a step toward being a friend of Allah or an enemy of Allah. You currently are either one or the other, with steps left to go to further develop and improve that relationship. Remember even if forgiveness is granted the consequences of those steps add up. Missteps can make you miss out and are costly to afford even if forgiven and if not forgiven such results are worse than fatal. Never voluntarily choose to decrease your faith by committing sins. Rather than be worse than people think of you by performing secret sins, instead be better than people think of you by having many secret sincere good deeds done according to the Sunnah. Secrecy is what differentiates the truthful from the hypocrite. There is nothing better than doing good deeds secretly with sincerity according to the Sunnah while the secret sins show lack of sincerity while public sins show lack of shame. All sins are bad but some are worse than others. You likely won't be sinless after the first step on the road to repentance and salvation. It's truly a lifelong journey from which you could misstep at any time. Repentance is actually a very dangerous risky road to travel upon. Yet the rewards are worth it. No matter what always repent. God does not punish those who repent correctly. So always repent. But since you don't know if you got what it takes to repent correctly the safest position is to avoid sins as much as possible just in case you fail the test of repentance. Heed this advice and you will achieve success even if it is after a long time of struggles. You cannot assess your success yourself but you can sometimes know what you need to improve. This is because God wants us to constantly improve because that is the recipe for success and God doesn't want us to gloat or be complacent over past successes. Go strive despite your past sins, as long as you are alive. Striving is not a suggestion from Allah, it is an obligation. Whatever you truly seek sincerely you will find and keep for eternity.

# AYAT of MIRACULOUS MERCY

## Quran 1:2-4

ٱلْحَمْدُ لِلَّهِ رَبِّ ٱلْعَٰلَمِينَ (٢) ٱلرَّحْمَٰنِ ٱلرَّحِيمِ (٣) مَٰلِكِ يَوْمِ ٱلدِّينِ (٤)

[All] praise is [due] to Allah, Lord of the worlds - (2) The Entirely Merciful, the Especially Merciful, (3) Sovereign of the Day of Recompense. (4)

## Quran 2:25

وَبَشِّرِ ٱلَّذِينَ ءَامَنُوا۟ وَعَمِلُوا۟ ٱلصَّٰلِحَٰتِ أَنَّ لَهُمْ جَنَّٰتٍ تَجْرِى مِن تَحْتِهَا ٱلْأَنْهَٰرُ ۖ كُلَّمَا رُزِقُوا۟ مِنْهَا مِن ثَمَرَةٍ رِّزْقًا ۙ قَالُوا۟ هَٰذَا ٱلَّذِى رُزِقْنَا مِن قَبْلُ ۖ وَأُتُوا۟ بِهِۦ مُتَشَٰبِهًا ۖ وَلَهُمْ فِيهَآ أَزْوَٰجٌ مُّطَهَّرَةٌ ۖ وَهُمْ فِيهَا خَٰلِدُونَ (٢٥)

And give good tidings to those who believe and do righteous deeds that they will have gardens [in Paradise] beneath which rivers flow. Whenever they are provided with a provision of fruit therefrom, they will say, "This is what we were provided with before." And it is given to them in likeness. And they will have therein purified spouses, and they will abide therein eternally. (25)

## Quran 2:30-38

وَإِذْ قَالَ رَبُّكَ لِلْمَلَٰٓئِكَةِ إِنِّى جَاعِلٌ فِى ٱلْأَرْضِ خَلِيفَةً ۖ قَالُوٓا۟ أَتَجْعَلُ فِيهَا مَن يُفْسِدُ فِيهَا وَيَسْفِكُ ٱلدِّمَآءَ وَنَحْنُ نُسَبِّحُ بِحَمْدِكَ وَنُقَدِّسُ لَكَ ۖ قَالَ إِنِّىٓ أَعْلَمُ مَا لَا تَعْلَمُونَ (٣٠) وَعَلَّمَ ءَادَمَ ٱلْأَسْمَآءَ كُلَّهَا ثُمَّ عَرَضَهُمْ عَلَى ٱلْمَلَٰٓئِكَةِ فَقَالَ أَنۢبِـُٔونِى بِأَسْمَآءِ هَٰٓؤُلَآءِ إِن كُنتُمْ صَٰدِقِينَ (٣١) قَالُوا۟ سُبْحَٰنَكَ لَا عِلْمَ لَنَآ إِلَّا مَا عَلَّمْتَنَآ ۖ إِنَّكَ أَنتَ ٱلْعَلِيمُ ٱلْحَكِيمُ (٣٢) قَالَ يَٰٓـَٔادَمُ أَنۢبِئْهُم بِأَسْمَآئِهِمْ ۖ فَلَمَّآ أَنۢبَأَهُم بِأَسْمَآئِهِمْ قَالَ أَلَمْ أَقُل لَّكُمْ إِنِّىٓ أَعْلَمُ غَيْبَ ٱلسَّمَٰوَٰتِ وَٱلْأَرْضِ وَأَعْلَمُ مَا تُبْدُونَ وَمَا كُنتُمْ تَكْتُمُونَ (٣٣) وَإِذْ قُلْنَا لِلْمَلَٰٓئِكَةِ ٱسْجُدُوا۟ لِـَٔادَمَ فَسَجَدُوٓا۟ إِلَّآ إِبْلِيسَ أَبَىٰ وَٱسْتَكْبَرَ وَكَانَ مِنَ ٱلْكَٰفِرِينَ (٣٤) وَقُلْنَا يَٰٓـَٔادَمُ ٱسْكُنْ أَنتَ وَزَوْجُكَ ٱلْجَنَّةَ

وَكُلَا مِنْهَا رَغَدًا حَيْثُ شِئْتُمَا وَلَا تَقْرَبَا هَٰذِهِ ٱلشَّجَرَةَ فَتَكُونَا مِنَ ٱلظَّٰلِمِينَ (٣٥) فَأَزَلَّهُمَا ٱلشَّيْطَٰنُ عَنْهَا فَأَخْرَجَهُمَا مِمَّا كَانَا فِيهِ ۖ وَقُلْنَا ٱهْبِطُوا۟ بَعْضُكُمْ لِبَعْضٍ عَدُوٌّ ۖ وَلَكُمْ فِى ٱلْأَرْضِ مُسْتَقَرٌّ وَمَتَٰعٌ إِلَىٰ حِينٍ (٣٦) فَتَلَقَّىٰٓ ءَادَمُ مِن رَّبِّهِۦ كَلِمَٰتٍ فَتَابَ عَلَيْهِ ۚ إِنَّهُۥ هُوَ ٱلتَّوَّابُ ٱلرَّحِيمُ (٣٧) قُلْنَا ٱهْبِطُوا۟ مِنْهَا جَمِيعًا ۖ فَإِمَّا يَأْتِيَنَّكُم مِّنِّى هُدًى فَمَن تَبِعَ هُدَاىَ فَلَا خَوْفٌ عَلَيْهِمْ وَلَا هُمْ يَحْزَنُونَ (٣٨)

And [mention], when your Lord said to the angels, "Indeed, I will make upon the earth a successive authority." They said, "Will You place upon it one who causes corruption therein and sheds blood, while we declare Your praise and sanctify You?" Allah said, "Indeed, I know that which you do not know." (30) And He taught Adam the names - all of them. Then He showed them to the angels and said, "Inform Me of the names of these, if you are truthful." (31) They said, "Exalted are You; we have no knowledge except what You have taught us. Indeed, it is You who is the Knowing, the Wise." (32) He said, "O Adam, inform them of their names." And when he had informed them of their names, He said, "Did I not tell you that I know the unseen [aspects] of the heavens and the earth? And I know what you reveal and what you have concealed." (33) And [mention] when We said to the angels, "Prostrate before Adam"; so, they prostrated, except for Iblees (of the jinn). He refused and was arrogant and became of the disbelievers. (34) And We said, "O Adam, dwell, you and your wife, in Paradise and eat therefrom in [ease and] abundance from wherever you will. But do not approach this tree, lest you be among the wrongdoers." (35) But Satan caused them to slip out of it and removed them from that [condition] in which they had been. And We said, "Go down, [all of you], as enemies to one another, and you will have upon the earth a place of settlement and provision for a time." (36) Then Adam received from his Lord [some] words, and He accepted his repentance. Indeed, it is He who is the Accepting of repentance, the Merciful. (37) We said, "Go down from it, all of you. And when guidance comes to you from Me, whoever follows My guidance - there will be no fear concerning them, nor will they grieve. (38)

## Quran 2:51-54

وَإِذْ وَاعَدْنَا مُوسَىٰ أَرْبَعِينَ لَيْلَةً ثُمَّ اتَّخَذْتُمُ ٱلْعِجْلَ مِنۢ بَعْدِهِۦ وَأَنتُمْ ظَٰلِمُونَ (٥١) ثُمَّ عَفَوْنَا عَنكُم مِّنۢ بَعْدِ ذَٰلِكَ لَعَلَّكُمْ تَشْكُرُونَ (٥٢) وَإِذْ ءَاتَيْنَا مُوسَى ٱلْكِتَٰبَ وَٱلْفُرْقَانَ لَعَلَّكُمْ تَهْتَدُونَ (٥٣) وَإِذْ قَالَ مُوسَىٰ لِقَوْمِهِۦ يَٰقَوْمِ إِنَّكُمْ ظَلَمْتُمْ أَنفُسَكُم بِٱتِّخَاذِكُمُ ٱلْعِجْلَ فَتُوبُوٓا۟ إِلَىٰ بَارِئِكُمْ فَٱقْتُلُوٓا۟ أَنفُسَكُمْ ذَٰلِكُمْ خَيْرٌ لَّكُمْ عِندَ بَارِئِكُمْ فَتَابَ عَلَيْكُمْ إِنَّهُۥ هُوَ ٱلتَّوَّابُ ٱلرَّحِيمُ (٥٤)

And (remember) when We appointed for Mûsa (Moses) forty nights, and (in his absence) you took the calf (for worship), and you were Zâlimûn (polytheists and wrongdoers,) (51) Then after that We forgave you so that you might be grateful. (52) And (remember) when We gave Mûsa (Moses) the Scripture [the Taurât (Torah)] and the criterion (of right and wrong) so that you may be guided aright. (53) And (remember) when Mûsa (Moses) said to his people: "O my people! Verily, you have wronged yourselves by worshipping the calf. So turn in repentance to your Creator and kill yourselves (the innocent kill the wrongdoers among you), that will be better for you with your Creator." Then He accepted your repentance. Truly, He is the One Who accepts repentance, the Most Merciful. (54)

## Quran 2:58-59

وَإِذْ قُلْنَا ٱدْخُلُواْ هَـٰذِهِ ٱلْقَرْيَةَ فَكُلُواْ مِنْهَا حَيْثُ شِئْتُمْ رَغَدًا وَٱدْخُلُواْ ٱلْبَابَ سُجَّدًا وَقُولُواْ حِطَّةٌ نَغْفِرْ لَكُمْ خَطَـٰيَـٰكُمْ ۚ وَسَنَزِيدُ ٱلْمُحْسِنِينَ (٥٨) فَبَدَّلَ ٱلَّذِينَ ظَلَمُواْ قَوْلًا غَيْرَ ٱلَّذِى قِيلَ لَهُمْ فَأَنزَلْنَا عَلَى ٱلَّذِينَ ظَلَمُواْ رِجْزًا مِّنَ ٱلسَّمَآءِ بِمَا كَانُواْ يَفْسُقُونَ (٥٩)

And (remember) when We said: "Enter this town (Jerusalem) and eat bountifully therein with pleasure and delight wherever you wish, and enter the gate in prostration (or bowing with humility) and say: 'Forgive us,' and We shall forgive you your sins and shall increase (reward) for the good-doers." (58) But those who did wrong changed the word from that which had been told to them for another, so We sent upon the wrong-doers Rijzan (a punishment) from the heaven because of their rebelling against Allâh's Obedience. (59)

## Quran 2:105

مَّا يَوَدُّ ٱلَّذِينَ كَفَرُواْ مِنْ أَهْلِ ٱلْكِتَـٰبِ وَلَا ٱلْمُشْرِكِينَ أَن يُنَزَّلَ عَلَيْكُم مِّنْ خَيْرٍ مِّن رَّبِّكُمْ ۗ وَٱللَّهُ يَخْتَصُّ بِرَحْمَتِهِ مَن يَشَآءُ ۚ وَٱللَّهُ ذُو ٱلْفَضْلِ ٱلْعَظِيمِ (١٠٥)

Neither those who disbelieve from the People of the Scripture nor the polytheists wish that any good should be sent down to you from your Lord. But Allah selects for

His mercy whom He wills, and Allah is the possessor of great bounty. (105)

## Quran 2:159-160

إِنَّ ٱلَّذِينَ يَكْتُمُونَ مَآ أَنزَلْنَا مِنَ ٱلْبَيِّنَٰتِ وَٱلْهُدَىٰ مِنۢ بَعْدِ مَا بَيَّنَّٰهُ لِلنَّاسِ فِى ٱلْكِتَٰبِ أُو۟لَٰٓئِكَ يَلْعَنُهُمُ ٱللَّهُ وَيَلْعَنُهُمُ ٱللَّٰعِنُونَ (١٥٩) إِلَّا ٱلَّذِينَ تَابُوا۟ وَأَصْلَحُوا۟ وَبَيَّنُوا۟ فَأُو۟لَٰٓئِكَ أَتُوبُ عَلَيْهِمْ وَأَنَا ٱلتَّوَّابُ ٱلرَّحِيمُ (١٦٠)

Indeed, those who conceal what We sent down of clear proofs and guidance after We made it clear for the people in the Scripture - those are cursed by Allah and cursed by those who curse, (159) Except for those who repent and correct themselves and make evident [what they concealed]. Those - I will accept their repentance, and I am the Accepting of repentance, the Merciful. (160)

## Quran 2:172-173

يَٰٓأَيُّهَا ٱلَّذِينَ ءَامَنُوا۟ كُلُوا۟ مِن طَيِّبَٰتِ مَا رَزَقْنَٰكُمْ وَٱشْكُرُوا۟ لِلَّهِ إِن كُنتُمْ إِيَّاهُ تَعْبُدُونَ (١٧٢) إِنَّمَا حَرَّمَ عَلَيْكُمُ ٱلْمَيْتَةَ وَٱلدَّمَ وَلَحْمَ ٱلْخِنزِيرِ وَمَآ أُهِلَّ بِهِۦ لِغَيْرِ ٱللَّهِ فَمَنِ ٱضْطُرَّ غَيْرَ بَاغٍ وَلَا عَادٍ فَلَآ إِثْمَ عَلَيْهِ إِنَّ ٱللَّهَ غَفُورٌ رَّحِيمٌ (١٧٣)

O you who have believed, eat from the good things which We have provided for you and be grateful to Allah if it is [indeed] Him that you worship. (172) He has only forbidden to you dead animals, blood, the flesh of swine, and that which has been dedicated to other than Allah. But whoever is forced [by necessity], neither desiring [it] nor transgressing [its limit], there is no sin upon him. Indeed, Allah is Forgiving and Merciful. (173)

## Quran 2:186-187

وَإِذَا سَأَلَكَ عِبَادِى عَنِّى فَإِنِّى قَرِيبٌ أُجِيبُ دَعْوَةَ ٱلدَّاعِ إِذَا دَعَانِ فَلْيَسْتَجِيبُواْ لِى وَلْيُؤْمِنُواْ بِى لَعَلَّهُمْ يَرْشُدُونَ (١٨٦) أُحِلَّ لَكُمْ لَيْلَةَ ٱلصِّيَامِ ٱلرَّفَثُ إِلَىٰ نِسَآئِكُمْ هُنَّ لِبَاسٌ لَّكُمْ وَأَنتُمْ لِبَاسٌ لَّهُنَّ عَلِمَ ٱللَّهُ أَنَّكُمْ كُنتُمْ تَخْتَانُونَ أَنفُسَكُمْ فَتَابَ عَلَيْكُمْ وَعَفَا عَنكُمْ فَٱلْـَٔـٰنَ بَـٰشِرُوهُنَّ وَٱبْتَغُواْ مَا كَتَبَ ٱللَّهُ لَكُمْ وَكُلُواْ وَٱشْرَبُواْ حَتَّىٰ يَتَبَيَّنَ لَكُمُ ٱلْخَيْطُ ٱلْأَبْيَضُ مِنَ ٱلْخَيْطِ ٱلْأَسْوَدِ مِنَ ٱلْفَجْرِ ثُمَّ أَتِمُّواْ ٱلصِّيَامَ إِلَى ٱلَّيْلِ وَلَا تُبَـٰشِرُوهُنَّ وَأَنتُمْ عَـٰكِفُونَ فِى ٱلْمَسَـٰجِدِ تِلْكَ حُدُودُ ٱللَّهِ فَلَا تَقْرَبُوهَا كَذَٰلِكَ يُبَيِّنُ ٱللَّهُ ءَايَـٰتِهِۦ لِلنَّاسِ لَعَلَّهُمْ يَتَّقُونَ (١٨٧)

*And when My servants ask you, [O Muhammad], concerning Me - indeed I am near.* **<u>I respond to the invocation of the supplicant when he calls upon Me</u>**. *So let them respond to Me [by obedience] and believe in Me that they may be [rightly] guided. (186) It has been made permissible for you the night preceding fasting to go to your wives [for sexual relations]. They are clothing for you and you are clothing for them. Allah knows that you used to deceive yourselves, so He accepted your repentance and forgave you. So now, have relations with them and seek that which Allah has decreed for you. And eat and drink until the white thread of dawn becomes distinct to you from the black thread [of night]. Then complete the fast until the sunset. And do not have relations with them as long as you are staying for worship in the mosques. These are the limits [set by] Allah, so do not approach them. Thus does Allah make clear His ordinances to the people that they may become righteous. (187)*

## Quran 2:190-195

وَقَاتِلُواْ فِى سَبِيلِ ٱللَّهِ ٱلَّذِينَ يُقَاتِلُونَكُمْ وَلَا تَعْتَدُوٓاْ إِنَّ ٱللَّهَ لَا يُحِبُّ ٱلْمُعْتَدِينَ (١٩٠) وَٱقْتُلُوهُمْ حَيْثُ ثَقِفْتُمُوهُمْ وَأَخْرِجُوهُم مِّنْ حَيْثُ أَخْرَجُوكُمْ وَٱلْفِتْنَةُ أَشَدُّ مِنَ ٱلْقَتْلِ وَلَا تُقَاتِلُوهُمْ عِندَ ٱلْمَسْجِدِ ٱلْحَرَامِ حَتَّىٰ يُقَاتِلُوكُمْ فِيهِ فَإِن قَاتَلُوكُمْ فَٱقْتُلُوهُمْ كَذَٰلِكَ جَزَآءُ ٱلْكَافِرِينَ (١٩١) فَإِنِ ٱنتَهَوْاْ فَإِنَّ ٱللَّهَ غَفُورٌ رَّحِيمٌ (١٩٢) وَقَاتِلُوهُمْ حَتَّىٰ لَا تَكُونَ فِتْنَةٌ وَيَكُونَ ٱلدِّينُ لِلَّهِ فَإِنِ ٱنتَهَوْاْ فَلَا عُدْوَانَ إِلَّا عَلَى ٱلظَّالِمِينَ (١٩٣) ٱلشَّهْرُ ٱلْحَرَامُ بِٱلشَّهْرِ ٱلْحَرَامِ وَٱلْحُرُمَاتُ قِصَاصٌ فَمَنِ ٱعْتَدَىٰ عَلَيْكُمْ فَٱعْتَدُواْ عَلَيْهِ بِمِثْلِ مَا ٱعْتَدَىٰ عَلَيْكُمْ وَٱتَّقُواْ ٱللَّهَ وَٱعْلَمُوٓاْ أَنَّ ٱللَّهَ مَعَ ٱلْمُتَّقِينَ (١٩٤) وَأَنفِقُواْ فِى سَبِيلِ ٱللَّهِ وَلَا تُلْقُواْ بِأَيْدِيكُمْ إِلَى ٱلتَّهْلُكَةِ وَأَحْسِنُوٓاْ إِنَّ ٱللَّهَ يُحِبُّ ٱلْمُحْسِنِينَ (١٩٥)

Fight in the way of Allah those who fight you but do not transgress. Indeed. Allah does not like transgressors. (190) And kill them wherever you overtake them and expel them from wherever they have expelled you, and fitnah is worse than killing. And do not fight them at al- Masjid al- Haram until they fight you there. But if they fight you, then kill them. Such is the recompense of the disbelievers. (191) And if they cease, then indeed, Allah is Forgiving and Merciful. (192) Fight them until there is no [more] fitnah and [until] worship is [acknowledged to be] for Allah. But if they cease, then there is to be no aggression except against the oppressors. (193) [Fighting in] the sacred month is for [aggression committed in] the sacred month, and for [all] violations is legal retribution. So whoever has assaulted you, then assault him in the same way that he has assaulted you. And fear Allah and know that Allah is with those who fear Him. (194) And spend in the way of Allah and do not throw [yourselves] with your [own] hands into destruction [by refraining]. And do good; indeed, Allah loves the doers of good. (195)

## Quran 2:198-202

لَيْسَ عَلَيْكُمْ جُنَاحٌ أَن تَبْتَغُواْ فَضْلًا مِّن رَّبِّكُمْ فَإِذَآ أَفَضْتُم مِّنْ عَرَفَٰتٍ فَٱذْكُرُواْ ٱللَّهَ عِندَ ٱلْمَشْعَرِ ٱلْحَرَامِ وَٱذْكُرُوهُ كَمَا هَدَىٰكُمْ وَإِن كُنتُم مِّن قَبْلِهِۦ لَمِنَ ٱلضَّآلِّينَ (١٩٨) ثُمَّ أَفِيضُواْ مِنْ حَيْثُ أَفَاضَ ٱلنَّاسُ وَٱسْتَغْفِرُواْ ٱللَّهَ إِنَّ ٱللَّهَ غَفُورٌ رَّحِيمٌ (١٩٩) فَإِذَا قَضَيْتُم مَّنَٰسِكَكُمْ فَٱذْكُرُواْ ٱللَّهَ كَذِكْرِكُمْ ءَابَآءَكُمْ أَوْ أَشَدَّ ذِكْرًا فَمِنَ ٱلنَّاسِ مَن يَقُولُ رَبَّنَآ ءَاتِنَا فِى ٱلدُّنْيَا وَمَا لَهُۥ فِى ٱلْأَخِرَةِ مِنْ خَلَٰقٍ (٢٠٠) وَمِنْهُم مَّن يَقُولُ رَبَّنَآ ءَاتِنَا فِى ٱلدُّنْيَا حَسَنَةً وَفِى ٱلْأَخِرَةِ حَسَنَةً وَقِنَا عَذَابَ ٱلنَّارِ (٢٠١) أُوْلَٰٓئِكَ لَهُمْ نَصِيبٌ مِّمَّا كَسَبُواْ وَٱللَّهُ سَرِيعُ ٱلْحِسَابِ (٢٠٢)

*There is no blame upon you for seeking bounty from your Lord [during Hajj]. But when you depart from 'Arafat, remember Allah at al- Mash'ar al-Haram. And remember Him, as He has guided you, for indeed, you were before that among those astray. (198) Then depart from the place from where [all] the people depart and ask forgiveness of Allah. Indeed, Allah is Forgiving and Merciful. (199) And when you have completed your rites, remember Allah like your [previous] remembrance of your fathers or with [much] greater remembrance. And among the people is he who says, "Our Lord, give us in this world," and he will have in the Hereafter no share. (200) But among them is he who says, "Our Lord, give us in this world [that which is] good and in the Hereafter [that which is] good and protect us from the punishment of the Fire." (201) Those will have a share of what they have earned, and Allah is swift in account. (202)*

## Quran 2:222

وَيَسْـَٔلُونَكَ عَنِ ٱلْمَحِيضِ ۖ قُلْ هُوَ أَذًى فَٱعْتَزِلُوا۟ ٱلنِّسَآءَ فِى ٱلْمَحِيضِ ۖ وَلَا تَقْرَبُوهُنَّ حَتَّىٰ يَطْهُرْنَ ۖ فَإِذَا تَطَهَّرْنَ فَأْتُوهُنَّ مِنْ حَيْثُ أَمَرَكُمُ ٱللَّهُ ۚ إِنَّ ٱللَّهَ يُحِبُّ ٱلتَّوَّٰبِينَ وَيُحِبُّ ٱلْمُتَطَهِّرِينَ (٢٢٢)

And they ask you about menstruation. Say, "It is harm, so keep away from wives during menstruation. And do not approach them until they are pure. And when they have purified themselves, then come to them from where Allah has ordained for you. Indeed, Allah loves those who are constantly repentant and loves those who purify themselves." (222)

## Quran 2:225-226

لَّا يُؤَاخِذُكُمُ ٱللَّهُ بِٱللَّغْوِ فِىٓ أَيْمَٰنِكُمْ وَلَٰكِن يُؤَاخِذُكُم بِمَا كَسَبَتْ قُلُوبُكُمْ ۗ وَٱللَّهُ غَفُورٌ حَلِيمٌ (٢٢٥) لِّلَّذِينَ يُؤْلُونَ مِن نِّسَآئِهِمْ تَرَبُّصُ أَرْبَعَةِ أَشْهُرٍ ۖ فَإِنْ فَآءُو فَإِنَّ ٱللَّهَ غَفُورٌ رَّحِيمٌ (٢٢٦)

Allah does not impose blame upon you for what is unintentional in your oaths, but He imposes blame upon you for what your hearts have earned. And Allah is Forgiving and Forbearing. (225) For those who swear not to have sexual relations with their wives is a waiting time of four months, but if they return [to normal relations] - then indeed, Allah is Forgiving and Merciful. (226)

## Quran 2:268

ٱلشَّيْطَٰنُ يَعِدُكُمُ ٱلْفَقْرَ وَيَأْمُرُكُم بِٱلْفَحْشَآءِ ۖ وَٱللَّهُ يَعِدُكُم مَّغْفِرَةً مِّنْهُ وَفَضْلًا ۗ وَٱللَّهُ وَٰسِعٌ عَلِيمٌ (٢٦٨)

Satan threatens you with poverty and orders you to immorality, while Allah promises you forgiveness from

Him and bounty. And Allah is all-Encompassing and Knowing. (268)

## Quran 2:284-286

لِّلَّهِ مَا فِى ٱلسَّمَٰوَٰتِ وَمَا فِى ٱلْأَرْضِ ۗ وَإِن تُبْدُوا۟ مَا فِىٓ أَنفُسِكُمْ أَوْ تُخْفُوهُ يُحَاسِبْكُم بِهِ ٱللَّهُ ۖ فَيَغْفِرُ لِمَن يَشَآءُ وَيُعَذِّبُ مَن يَشَآءُ ۗ وَٱللَّهُ عَلَىٰ كُلِّ شَىْءٍ قَدِيرٌ (٢٨٤) ءَامَنَ ٱلرَّسُولُ بِمَآ أُنزِلَ إِلَيْهِ مِن رَّبِّهِۦ وَٱلْمُؤْمِنُونَ ۚ كُلٌّ ءَامَنَ بِٱللَّهِ وَمَلَٰٓئِكَتِهِۦ وَكُتُبِهِۦ وَرُسُلِهِۦ لَا نُفَرِّقُ بَيْنَ أَحَدٍ مِّن رُّسُلِهِۦ ۚ وَقَالُوا۟ سَمِعْنَا وَأَطَعْنَا ۖ غُفْرَانَكَ رَبَّنَا وَإِلَيْكَ ٱلْمَصِيرُ (٢٨٥) لَا يُكَلِّفُ ٱللَّهُ نَفْسًا إِلَّا وُسْعَهَا ۚ لَهَا مَا كَسَبَتْ وَعَلَيْهَا مَا ٱكْتَسَبَتْ ۗ رَبَّنَا لَا تُؤَاخِذْنَآ إِن نَّسِينَآ أَوْ أَخْطَأْنَا ۚ رَبَّنَا وَلَا تَحْمِلْ عَلَيْنَآ إِصْرًا كَمَا حَمَلْتَهُۥ عَلَى ٱلَّذِينَ مِن قَبْلِنَا ۚ رَبَّنَا وَلَا تُحَمِّلْنَا مَا لَا طَاقَةَ لَنَا بِهِۦ ۖ وَٱعْفُ عَنَّا وَٱغْفِرْ لَنَا وَٱرْحَمْنَآ ۚ أَنتَ مَوْلَىٰنَا فَٱنصُرْنَا عَلَى ٱلْقَوْمِ ٱلْكَٰفِرِينَ (٢٨٦)

To Allah belongs whatever is in the heavens and whatever is in the earth. Whether you show what is within yourselves or conceal it, Allah will bring you to account for it. Then He will forgive whom He wills and punish whom He wills, and Allah is over all things competent. (284) The Messenger has believed in what was revealed to him from his Lord, and [so have] the believers. All of them have believed in Allah and His angels and His books and His messengers, [saying], "We make no distinction between any of His messengers." And they say, "We hear and we obey. [We seek] Your forgiveness, our Lord, and to You is the [final] destination." (285) Allah does not charge a soul except [with that within] its capacity. It will have [the consequence of] what [good] it has gained, and it will bear [the consequence of] what [evil] it has earned. "Our

Lord, do not impose blame upon us if we have forgotten or erred. Our Lord, and lay not upon us a burden like that which You laid upon those before us. Our Lord, and burden us not with that which we have no ability to bear. And pardon us; and forgive us; and have mercy upon us. You are our protector, so give us victory over the disbelieving people." (286)

## Quran 3:30-31

يَوْمَ تَجِدُ كُلُّ نَفْسٍ مَّا عَمِلَتْ مِنْ خَيْرٍ مُّحْضَرًا وَمَا عَمِلَتْ مِن سُوءٍ تَوَدُّ لَوْ أَنَّ بَيْنَهَا وَبَيْنَهُ أَمَدًا بَعِيدًا ۗ وَيُحَذِّرُكُمُ ٱللَّهُ نَفْسَهُ ۗ وَٱللَّهُ رَءُوفٌ بِٱلْعِبَادِ (٣٠) قُلْ إِن كُنتُمْ تُحِبُّونَ ٱللَّهَ فَٱتَّبِعُونِى يُحْبِبْكُمُ ٱللَّهُ وَيَغْفِرْ لَكُمْ ذُنُوبَكُمْ ۗ وَٱللَّهُ غَفُورٌ رَّحِيمٌ (٣١)

On the Day when every person will be confronted with all the good he has done, and all the evil he has done, he will wish that there were a great distance between him and his evil. And Allâh warns you against Himself (His Punishment) and Allâh is full of Kindness to the (His) slaves. (30) Say (O Muhammad to mankind): "If you (really) love Allâh then follow me ( accept Islâmic Monotheism, follow the Qur'ân and the Sunnah), Allâh will love you and forgive you your sins. And Allâh is Oft-Forgiving, Most Merciful." (31)

## Quran 3:89

إِلَّا ٱلَّذِينَ تَابُوا۟ مِنۢ بَعْدِ ذَٰلِكَ وَأَصْلَحُوا۟ فَإِنَّ ٱللَّهَ غَفُورٌ رَّحِيمٌ (٨٩)

Except for those who repent after that and do righteous deeds. Verily, Allâh is Oft-Forgiving, Most Merciful. (89)

# Quran 3:103-108

وَٱعْتَصِمُوا۟ بِحَبْلِ ٱللَّهِ جَمِيعًا وَلَا تَفَرَّقُوا۟ وَٱذْكُرُوا۟ نِعْمَتَ ٱللَّهِ عَلَيْكُمْ إِذْ كُنتُمْ أَعْدَآءً فَأَلَّفَ بَيْنَ قُلُوبِكُمْ فَأَصْبَحْتُم بِنِعْمَتِهِۦٓ إِخْوَٰنًا وَكُنتُمْ عَلَىٰ شَفَا حُفْرَةٍ مِّنَ ٱلنَّارِ فَأَنقَذَكُم مِّنْهَا ۗ كَذَٰلِكَ يُبَيِّنُ ٱللَّهُ لَكُمْ ءَايَٰتِهِۦ لَعَلَّكُمْ تَهْتَدُونَ (١٠٣) وَلْتَكُن مِّنكُمْ أُمَّةٌ يَدْعُونَ إِلَى ٱلْخَيْرِ وَيَأْمُرُونَ بِٱلْمَعْرُوفِ وَيَنْهَوْنَ عَنِ ٱلْمُنكَرِ ۚ وَأُو۟لَٰٓئِكَ هُمُ ٱلْمُفْلِحُونَ (١٠٤) وَلَا تَكُونُوا۟ كَٱلَّذِينَ تَفَرَّقُوا۟ وَٱخْتَلَفُوا۟ مِنۢ بَعْدِ مَا جَآءَهُمُ ٱلْبَيِّنَٰتُ ۚ وَأُو۟لَٰٓئِكَ لَهُمْ عَذَابٌ عَظِيمٌ (١٠٥) يَوْمَ تَبْيَضُّ وُجُوهٌ وَتَسْوَدُّ وُجُوهٌ ۚ فَأَمَّا ٱلَّذِينَ ٱسْوَدَّتْ وُجُوهُهُمْ أَكَفَرْتُم بَعْدَ إِيمَٰنِكُمْ فَذُوقُوا۟ ٱلْعَذَابَ بِمَا كُنتُمْ تَكْفُرُونَ (١٠٦) وَأَمَّا ٱلَّذِينَ ٱبْيَضَّتْ وُجُوهُهُمْ فَفِى رَحْمَةِ ٱللَّهِ هُمْ فِيهَا خَٰلِدُونَ (١٠٧) تِلْكَ ءَايَٰتُ ٱللَّهِ نَتْلُوهَا عَلَيْكَ بِٱلْحَقِّ ۗ وَمَا ٱللَّهُ يُرِيدُ ظُلْمًا لِّلْعَٰلَمِينَ (١٠٨)

*And hold firmly to the rope of Allah all together and do not become divided. And remember the favor of Allah upon you - when you were enemies and He brought your hearts together and you became, by His favor, brothers. And you were on the edge of a pit of the Fire, and He saved you from it. Thus does Allah make clear to you His verses that you may be guided. (103) And let there be [arising] from you a nation inviting to [all that is] good, enjoining what is right and forbidding what is wrong, and those will be the successful. (104) And do not be like the ones who became divided and differed after the clear proofs had come to them. And those will have a great punishment. (105) On the Day [some] faces will turn white and [some] faces will turn black. As for those whose faces turn black, [to them it will be said], "Did you disbelieve after your belief? Then taste the punishment for what you used to reject." (106) But as for those whose faces will turn white, [they will be] within the mercy of*

Allah. They will abide therein eternally. (107) These are the verses of Allah. We recite them to you, in truth; and Allah wants no injustice to the worlds. (108)

## Quran 3:132-136

وَأَطِيعُوا۟ ٱللَّهَ وَٱلرَّسُولَ لَعَلَّكُمْ تُرْحَمُونَ (١٣٢) ۞ وَسَارِعُوٓا۟ إِلَىٰ مَغْفِرَةٍ مِّن رَّبِّكُمْ وَجَنَّةٍ عَرْضُهَا ٱلسَّمَـٰوَٰتُ وَٱلْأَرْضُ أُعِدَّتْ لِلْمُتَّقِينَ (١٣٣) ٱلَّذِينَ يُنفِقُونَ فِى ٱلسَّرَّآءِ وَٱلضَّرَّآءِ وَٱلْكَـٰظِمِينَ ٱلْغَيْظَ وَٱلْعَافِينَ عَنِ ٱلنَّاسِ ۗ وَٱللَّهُ يُحِبُّ ٱلْمُحْسِنِينَ (١٣٤) وَٱلَّذِينَ إِذَا فَعَلُوا۟ فَـٰحِشَةً أَوْ ظَلَمُوٓا۟ أَنفُسَهُمْ ذَكَرُوا۟ ٱللَّهَ فَٱسْتَغْفَرُوا۟ لِذُنُوبِهِمْ وَمَن يَغْفِرُ ٱلذُّنُوبَ إِلَّا ٱللَّهُ وَلَمْ يُصِرُّوا۟ عَلَىٰ مَا فَعَلُوا۟ وَهُمْ يَعْلَمُونَ (١٣٥) أُو۟لَـٰٓئِكَ جَزَآؤُهُم مَّغْفِرَةٌ مِّن رَّبِّهِمْ وَجَنَّـٰتٌ تَجْرِى مِن تَحْتِهَا ٱلْأَنْهَـٰرُ خَـٰلِدِينَ فِيهَا ۚ وَنِعْمَ أَجْرُ ٱلْعَـٰمِلِينَ (١٣٦)

And obey Allah and the Messenger that you may obtain mercy. (132) And hasten to forgiveness from your Lord and a garden as wide as the heavens and earth, prepared for the righteous (133) Who spend [in the cause of Allah] during ease and hardship and who restrain anger and who pardon the people - and Allah loves the doers of good; (134) And those who, when they commit an immorality or wrong themselves [by transgression], remember Allah and seek forgiveness for their sins - and who can forgive sins except Allah? - and [who] do not persist in what they have done while they know. (135) Those - their reward is forgiveness from their Lord and gardens beneath which rivers flow [in Paradise], wherein they will abide eternally; and excellent is the reward of the [righteous] workers. (136)

## Quran 3:145-148

وَمَا كَانَ لِنَفْسٍ أَن تَمُوتَ إِلَّا بِإِذْنِ ٱللَّهِ كِتَٰبًا مُّؤَجَّلًا ۗ وَمَن يُرِدْ ثَوَابَ ٱلدُّنْيَا نُؤْتِهِۦ مِنْهَا وَمَن يُرِدْ ثَوَابَ ٱلْءَاخِرَةِ نُؤْتِهِۦ مِنْهَا ۚ وَسَنَجْزِى ٱلشَّٰكِرِينَ (١٤٥) وَكَأَيِّن مِّن نَّبِىٍّ قَٰتَلَ مَعَهُۥ رِبِّيُّونَ كَثِيرٌ فَمَا وَهَنُوا۟ لِمَآ أَصَابَهُمْ فِى سَبِيلِ ٱللَّهِ وَمَا ضَعُفُوا۟ وَمَا ٱسْتَكَانُوا۟ ۗ وَٱللَّهُ يُحِبُّ ٱلصَّٰبِرِينَ (١٤٦) وَمَا كَانَ قَوْلَهُمْ إِلَّآ أَن قَالُوا۟ رَبَّنَا ٱغْفِرْ لَنَا ذُنُوبَنَا وَإِسْرَافَنَا فِىٓ أَمْرِنَا وَثَبِّتْ أَقْدَامَنَا وَٱنصُرْنَا عَلَى ٱلْقَوْمِ ٱلْكَٰفِرِينَ (١٤٧) فَـَٔاتَىٰهُمُ ٱللَّهُ ثَوَابَ ٱلدُّنْيَا وَحُسْنَ ثَوَابِ ٱلْءَاخِرَةِ ۗ وَٱللَّهُ يُحِبُّ ٱلْمُحْسِنِينَ (١٤٨)

And it is not [possible] for one to die except by permission of Allah at a decree determined. And whoever desires the reward of this world - We will give him thereof; and whoever desires the reward of the Hereafter - We will give him thereof. And we will reward the grateful. (145) And how many a prophet [fought and] with him fought many religious scholars. But they never lost assurance due to what afflicted them in the cause of Allah, nor did they weaken or submit. And Allah loves the steadfast. (146) And their words were not but that they said, "Our Lord, forgive us our sins and the excess [committed] in our affairs and plant firmly our feet and give us victory over the disbelieving people." (147) So Allah gave them the reward of this world and the good reward of the Hereafter. And Allah loves the doers of good. (148)

**Quran 3:155**

إِنَّ ٱلَّذِينَ تَوَلَّوْا۟ مِنكُمْ يَوْمَ ٱلْتَقَى ٱلْجَمْعَانِ إِنَّمَا ٱسْتَزَلَّهُمُ ٱلشَّيْطَٰنُ بِبَعْضِ مَا كَسَبُوا۟ ۖ وَلَقَدْ عَفَا ٱللَّهُ عَنْهُمْ ۗ إِنَّ ٱللَّهَ غَفُورٌ حَلِيمٌ (١٥٥)

Indeed, those of you who turned back on the day the two armies met, it was Satan who caused them to slip because of some [blame] they had earned. But Allah has already forgiven them. Indeed, Allah is Forgiving and Forbearing. (155)

## Quran 3:157

وَلَئِن قُتِلْتُمْ فِى سَبِيلِ ٱللَّهِ أَوْ مُتُّمْ لَمَغْفِرَةٌ مِّنَ ٱللَّهِ وَرَحْمَةٌ خَيْرٌ مِّمَّا يَجْمَعُونَ (١٥٧)

And if you are killed in the cause of Allah or die - then forgiveness from Allah and mercy are better than whatever they accumulate [in this world]. (157)

## Quran 3:190-195

إِنَّ فِى خَلْقِ ٱلسَّمَـٰوَٰتِ وَٱلْأَرْضِ وَٱخْتِلَـٰفِ ٱلَّيْلِ وَٱلنَّهَارِ لَـَٔايَـٰتٍ لِّأُو۟لِى ٱلْأَلْبَـٰبِ (١٩٠) ٱلَّذِينَ يَذْكُرُونَ ٱللَّهَ قِيَـٰمًا وَقُعُودًا وَعَلَىٰ جُنُوبِهِمْ وَيَتَفَكَّرُونَ فِى خَلْقِ ٱلسَّمَـٰوَٰتِ وَٱلْأَرْضِ رَبَّنَا مَا خَلَقْتَ هَـٰذَا بَـٰطِلًا سُبْحَـٰنَكَ فَقِنَا عَذَابَ ٱلنَّارِ (١٩١) رَبَّنَا إِنَّكَ مَن تُدْخِلِ ٱلنَّارَ فَقَدْ أَخْزَيْتَهُۥ ۖ وَمَا لِلظَّـٰلِمِينَ مِنْ أَنصَارٍ (١٩٢) رَبَّنَا إِنَّنَا سَمِعْنَا مُنَادِيًا يُنَادِى لِلْإِيمَـٰنِ أَنْ ءَامِنُوا۟ بِرَبِّكُمْ فَـَٔامَنَّا ۚ رَبَّنَا فَٱغْفِرْ لَنَا ذُنُوبَنَا وَكَفِّرْ عَنَّا سَيِّـَٔاتِنَا وَتَوَفَّنَا مَعَ ٱلْأَبْرَارِ (١٩٣) رَبَّنَا وَءَاتِنَا مَا وَعَدتَّنَا عَلَىٰ رُسُلِكَ وَلَا تُخْزِنَا يَوْمَ ٱلْقِيَـٰمَةِ ۗ إِنَّكَ لَا تُخْلِفُ ٱلْمِيعَادَ (١٩٤) فَٱسْتَجَابَ لَهُمْ رَبُّهُمْ أَنِّى لَا أُضِيعُ عَمَلَ عَـٰمِلٍ مِّنكُم مِّن ذَكَرٍ أَوْ أُنثَىٰ ۖ بَعْضُكُم مِّنۢ بَعْضٍ ۖ فَٱلَّذِينَ هَاجَرُوا۟ وَأُخْرِجُوا۟ مِن دِيَـٰرِهِمْ وَأُوذُوا۟ فِى سَبِيلِى وَقَـٰتَلُوا۟ وَقُتِلُوا۟ لَأُكَفِّرَنَّ عَنْهُمْ سَيِّـَٔاتِهِمْ وَلَأُدْخِلَنَّهُمْ جَنَّـٰتٍ تَجْرِى مِن تَحْتِهَا ٱلْأَنْهَـٰرُ ثَوَابًا مِّنْ عِندِ ٱللَّهِ ۗ وَٱللَّهُ عِندَهُۥ حُسْنُ ٱلثَّوَابِ (١٩٥)

Indeed, in the creation of the heavens and the earth and the alternation of the night and the day are signs for those of understanding. (190) Who remember Allah while standing or sitting or [lying] on their sides and give thought to the creation of the heavens and the earth, [saying], "Our Lord, You did not create this aimlessly;

exalted are You [above such a thing]; then protect us from the punishment of the Fire. (191) Our Lord, indeed whoever You admit to the Fire - You have disgraced him, and for the wrongdoers there are no helpers. (192) Our Lord, indeed we have heard a caller calling to faith, [saying], 'Believe in your Lord,' and we have believed. Our Lord, so forgive us our sins and remove from us our misdeeds and cause us to die with the righteous. (193) Our Lord, and grant us what You promised us through Your messengers and do not disgrace us on the Day of Resurrection. Indeed, You do not fail in [Your] promise." (194) And their Lord responded to them, "Never will I allow to be lost the work of [any] worker among you, whether male or female; you are of one another. So those who emigrated or were evicted from their homes or were harmed in My cause or fought or were killed - I will surely remove from them their misdeeds, and I will surely admit them to gardens beneath which rivers flow as reward from Allah, and Allah has with Him the best reward." (195)

## Quran 4:16-19

وَٱللَّذَانِ يَأْتِيَٰنِهَا مِنكُمْ فَـَٔاذُوهُمَا ۖ فَإِن تَابَا وَأَصْلَحَا فَأَعْرِضُوا۟ عَنْهُمَآ ۗ إِنَّ ٱللَّهَ كَانَ تَوَّابًا رَّحِيمًا (١٦) إِنَّمَا ٱلتَّوْبَةُ عَلَى ٱللَّهِ لِلَّذِينَ يَعْمَلُونَ ٱلسُّوٓءَ بِجَهَٰلَةٍ ثُمَّ يَتُوبُونَ مِن قَرِيبٍ فَأُو۟لَٰٓئِكَ يَتُوبُ ٱللَّهُ عَلَيْهِمْ ۗ وَكَانَ ٱللَّهُ عَلِيمًا حَكِيمًا (١٧) وَلَيْسَتِ ٱلتَّوْبَةُ لِلَّذِينَ يَعْمَلُونَ ٱلسَّيِّـَٔاتِ حَتَّىٰٓ إِذَا حَضَرَ أَحَدَهُمُ ٱلْمَوْتُ قَالَ إِنِّى تُبْتُ ٱلْـَٰٔنَ وَلَا ٱلَّذِينَ يَمُوتُونَ وَهُمْ كُفَّارٌ ۚ أُو۟لَٰٓئِكَ أَعْتَدْنَا لَهُمْ عَذَابًا أَلِيمًا (١٨)

*And the two who commit it among you, dishonor them both. But if they repent and correct themselves, leave them alone. Indeed, Allah is ever Accepting of repentance and Merciful. (16) The repentance accepted by Allah is only for those who do wrong in ignorance [or carelessness] and then repent soon after. It is those to whom Allah will turn in forgiveness, and Allah is ever Knowing and Wise. (17) But repentance is not [accepted] of those who [continue to] do evil deeds up until, when death comes to one of them, he says, "Indeed, I have repented now," or of those who die while they are disbelievers. For them We have prepared a painful punishment. (18)*

## Quran 4:25-29

وَمَن لَّمْ يَسْتَطِعْ مِنكُمْ طَوْلًا أَن يَنكِحَ ٱلْمُحْصَنَٰتِ ٱلْمُؤْمِنَٰتِ فَمِن مَّا مَلَكَتْ أَيْمَٰنُكُم مِّن فَتَيَٰتِكُمُ ٱلْمُؤْمِنَٰتِ وَٱللَّهُ أَعْلَمُ بِإِيمَٰنِكُم بَعْضُكُم مِّنۢ بَعْضٍۢ فَٱنكِحُوهُنَّ بِإِذْنِ أَهْلِهِنَّ وَءَاتُوهُنَّ أُجُورَهُنَّ بِٱلْمَعْرُوفِ مُحْصَنَٰتٍ غَيْرَ مُسَٰفِحَٰتٍ وَلَا مُتَّخِذَٰتِ أَخْدَانٍۢ فَإِذَآ أُحْصِنَّ فَإِنْ أَتَيْنَ بِفَٰحِشَةٍۢ فَعَلَيْهِنَّ نِصْفُ مَا عَلَى ٱلْمُحْصَنَٰتِ مِنَ ٱلْعَذَابِ ذَٰلِكَ لِمَنْ خَشِىَ ٱلْعَنَتَ مِنكُمْ وَأَن تَصْبِرُوا۟ خَيْرٌۭ لَّكُمْ وَٱللَّهُ غَفُورٌۭ رَّحِيمٌۭ (٢٥) يُرِيدُ ٱللَّهُ لِيُبَيِّنَ لَكُمْ وَيَهْدِيَكُمْ سُنَنَ ٱلَّذِينَ مِن قَبْلِكُمْ وَيَتُوبَ عَلَيْكُمْ وَٱللَّهُ عَلِيمٌ حَكِيمٌ (٢٦) وَٱللَّهُ يُرِيدُ أَن يَتُوبَ عَلَيْكُمْ وَيُرِيدُ ٱلَّذِينَ يَتَّبِعُونَ ٱلشَّهَوَٰتِ أَن تَمِيلُوا۟ مَيْلًا عَظِيمًۭا (٢٧) يُرِيدُ ٱللَّهُ أَن يُخَفِّفَ عَنكُمْ وَخُلِقَ ٱلْإِنسَٰنُ ضَعِيفًۭا (٢٨) يَٰٓأَيُّهَا ٱلَّذِينَ ءَامَنُوا۟ لَا تَأْكُلُوٓا۟ أَمْوَٰلَكُم بَيْنَكُم بِٱلْبَٰطِلِ إِلَّآ أَن تَكُونَ تِجَٰرَةً عَن تَرَاضٍۢ مِّنكُمْ وَلَا تَقْتُلُوٓا۟ أَنفُسَكُمْ إِنَّ ٱللَّهَ كَانَ بِكُمْ رَحِيمًۭا (٢٩)

*And whoever among you cannot [find] the means to marry free, believing women, then [he may marry] from those whom your right hands possess of believing slave* girls. And Allah is most knowing about your faith. You [believers] are of one another. So marry them with the permission of their people and give them their due compensation according to what is acceptable. [They should be] chaste, neither [of] those who commit unlawful intercourse randomly nor those who take [secret] lovers. But once they are sheltered in marriage, if they should commit adultery, then for them is half the punishment for free [unmarried] women. This [allowance] is for him among you who fears sin, but to be patient is better for you. And Allah is Forgiving and Merciful. (25) Allah wants to make clear to you [the lawful from the unlawful] and guide you to the [good] practices of those before you and to accept your repentance. And Allah is Knowing and Wise. (26) Allah wants to accept your repentance, but those who follow [their] passions want you to digress [into] a great deviation. (27) And Allah wants to lighten for you [your difficulties]; and mankind was created weak. (28) O you who have believed, do not consume one another's wealth unjustly but only [in lawful] business by mutual consent. And do not kill yourselves [or one another]. Indeed, Allah is to you ever Merciful. (29)

**Quran 4:31**

إِن تَجْتَنِبُواْ كَبَآئِرَ مَا تُنْهَوْنَ عَنْهُ نُكَفِّرْ عَنكُمْ سَيِّـَٔاتِكُمْ وَنُدْخِلْكُم مُّدْخَلاً كَرِيمًا (٣١)

*If you avoid the major sins which you are forbidden, We will remove from you your lesser sins and admit you to a noble entrance [into Paradise]. (31)*

## Quran 4:48

إِنَّ ٱللَّهَ لَا يَغْفِرُ أَن يُشْرَكَ بِهِۦ وَيَغْفِرُ مَا دُونَ ذَٰلِكَ لِمَن يَشَآءُ وَمَن يُشْرِكْ بِٱللَّهِ فَقَدِ ٱفْتَرَىٰٓ إِثْمًا عَظِيمًا (٤٨)

*Indeed, Allah does not forgive association with Him, but He forgives what is less than that for whom He wills. And he who associates others with Allah has certainly fabricated a tremendous sin. (48)*

## Quran 4:64

وَمَآ أَرْسَلْنَا مِن رَّسُولٍ إِلَّا لِيُطَاعَ بِإِذْنِ ٱللَّهِ وَلَوْ أَنَّهُمْ إِذ ظَّلَمُوٓاْ أَنفُسَهُمْ جَآءُوكَ فَٱسْتَغْفَرُواْ ٱللَّهَ وَٱسْتَغْفَرَ لَهُمُ ٱلرَّسُولُ لَوَجَدُواْ ٱللَّهَ تَوَّابًا رَّحِيمًا (٦٤)

*And We did not send any messenger except to be obeyed by permission of Allah. And if, when they wronged themselves, they had come to you, [O Muhammad], and asked forgiveness of Allah and the Messenger had asked forgiveness for them, they would have found Allah Accepting of repentance and Merciful. (64)*

## Quran 4:67-70

وَإِذًا لَّأَتَيْنَٰهُم مِّن لَّدُنَّآ أَجْرًا عَظِيمًا (٦٧) وَلَهَدَيْنَٰهُمْ صِرَٰطًا مُّسْتَقِيمًا (٦٨) وَمَن يُطِعِ ٱللَّهَ وَٱلرَّسُولَ فَأُوْلَٰٓئِكَ مَعَ ٱلَّذِينَ أَنْعَمَ ٱللَّهُ عَلَيْهِم مِّنَ ٱلنَّبِيِّـۧنَ وَٱلصِّدِّيقِينَ وَٱلشُّهَدَآءِ وَٱلصَّٰلِحِينَ وَحَسُنَ أُوْلَٰٓئِكَ رَفِيقًا (٦٩) ذَٰلِكَ ٱلْفَضْلُ مِنَ ٱللَّهِ وَكَفَىٰ بِٱللَّهِ عَلِيمًا (٧٠)

*And then We would have given them from Us a great reward. (67) And We would have guided them to a* straight path. (68) And whoever obeys Allah and the Messenger - those will be with the ones upon whom Allah has bestowed favor of the prophets, the steadfast affirmers of truth, the martyrs and the righteous. And excellent are those as companions. (69) That is the bounty from Allah, and sufficient is Allah as Knower. (70)

## Quran 4:79

مَّا أَصَابَكَ مِنْ حَسَنَةٍ فَمِنَ ٱللَّهِ ۖ وَمَا أَصَابَكَ مِن سَيِّئَةٍ فَمِن نَّفْسِكَ ۚ وَأَرْسَلْنَٰكَ لِلنَّاسِ رَسُولًا ۚ وَكَفَىٰ بِٱللَّهِ شَهِيدًا (٧٩)

What comes to you of good is from Allah, but what comes to you of evil, [O man], is from yourself. And We have sent you, [O Muhammad], to the people as a messenger, and sufficient is Allah as Witness. (79)

## Quran 4:95-100

لَّا يَسْتَوِى ٱلْقَٰعِدُونَ مِنَ ٱلْمُؤْمِنِينَ غَيْرُ أُو۟لِى ٱلضَّرَرِ وَٱلْمُجَٰهِدُونَ فِى سَبِيلِ ٱللَّهِ بِأَمْوَٰلِهِمْ وَأَنفُسِهِمْ ۚ فَضَّلَ ٱللَّهُ ٱلْمُجَٰهِدِينَ بِأَمْوَٰلِهِمْ وَأَنفُسِهِمْ عَلَى ٱلْقَٰعِدِينَ دَرَجَةً ۚ وَكُلًّا وَعَدَ ٱللَّهُ ٱلْحُسْنَىٰ ۚ وَفَضَّلَ ٱللَّهُ ٱلْمُجَٰهِدِينَ عَلَى ٱلْقَٰعِدِينَ أَجْرًا عَظِيمًا (٩٥) دَرَجَٰتٍ مِّنْهُ وَمَغْفِرَةً وَرَحْمَةً ۚ وَكَانَ ٱللَّهُ غَفُورًا رَّحِيمًا (٩٦) إِنَّ ٱلَّذِينَ تَوَفَّىٰهُمُ ٱلْمَلَٰٓئِكَةُ ظَالِمِىٓ أَنفُسِهِمْ قَالُوا۟ فِيمَ كُنتُمْ ۖ قَالُوا۟ كُنَّا مُسْتَضْعَفِينَ فِى ٱلْأَرْضِ ۚ قَالُوٓا۟ أَلَمْ تَكُنْ أَرْضُ ٱللَّهِ وَٰسِعَةً فَتُهَاجِرُوا۟ فِيهَا ۚ فَأُو۟لَٰٓئِكَ مَأْوَىٰهُمْ جَهَنَّمُ ۖ وَسَآءَتْ مَصِيرًا (٩٧) إِلَّا ٱلْمُسْتَضْعَفِينَ مِنَ ٱلرِّجَالِ وَٱلنِّسَآءِ وَٱلْوِلْدَٰنِ لَا يَسْتَطِيعُونَ حِيلَةً وَلَا يَهْتَدُونَ سَبِيلًا (٩٨) فَأُو۟لَٰٓئِكَ عَسَى ٱللَّهُ أَن يَعْفُوَ عَنْهُمْ ۚ وَكَانَ ٱللَّهُ عَفُوًّا غَفُورًا (٩٩) ۞ وَمَن يُهَاجِرْ فِى سَبِيلِ ٱللَّهِ يَجِدْ فِى ٱلْأَرْضِ مُرَٰغَمًا كَثِيرًا وَسَعَةً ۚ وَمَن يَخْرُجْ مِنۢ بَيْتِهِۦ مُهَاجِرًا إِلَى ٱللَّهِ وَرَسُولِهِۦ ثُمَّ يُدْرِكْهُ ٱلْمَوْتُ فَقَدْ وَقَعَ أَجْرُهُۥ عَلَى ٱللَّهِ ۗ وَكَانَ ٱللَّهُ غَفُورًا رَّحِيمًا (١٠٠)

*Not equal are those believers remaining [at home] - other than the disabled - and the mujahideen, [who strive and fight] in the cause of Allah with their wealth and their lives. Allah has preferred the mujahideen through their wealth and their lives over those who remain [behind], by degrees. And to both Allah has promised the best [reward]. But Allah has preferred the mujahideen over those who remain [behind] with a great reward - (95) Degrees [of high position] from Him and forgiveness and mercy. And Allah is ever Forgiving and Merciful. (96) Indeed, those whom the angels take [in death] while wronging themselves - [the angels] will say, "In what [condition] were you?" They will say, "We were oppressed in the land." The angels will say, "Was not the earth of Allah spacious [enough] for you to emigrate therein?" For those, their refuge is Hell - and evil it is as a destination. (97) Except for the oppressed among men, women and children who cannot devise a plan nor are they directed to a way - (98) For those it is expected that Allah will pardon them, and Allah is ever Pardoning and Forgiving. (99) And whoever emigrates for the cause of Allah will find on the earth many [alternative] locations and abundance. And whoever leaves his home as an emigrant to Allah and His Messenger and then death overtakes him - his reward has already become incumbent upon Allah. And Allah is ever Forgiving and Merciful. (100)*

**Quran 4:106**

وَٱسْتَغْفِرِ ٱللَّهَ إِنَّ ٱللَّهَ كَانَ غَفُورًا رَّحِيمًا (١٠٦)

And seek forgiveness of Allah. Indeed, Allah is ever Forgiving and Merciful. (106)

## Quran 4:110-114

وَمَن يَعْمَلْ سُوٓءًا أَوْ يَظْلِمْ نَفْسَهُۥ ثُمَّ يَسْتَغْفِرِ ٱللَّهَ يَجِدِ ٱللَّهَ غَفُورًا رَّحِيمًا (١١٠) وَمَن يَكْسِبْ إِثْمًا فَإِنَّمَا يَكْسِبُهُۥ عَلَىٰ نَفْسِهِۦ ۚ وَكَانَ ٱللَّهُ عَلِيمًا حَكِيمًا (١١١) وَمَن يَكْسِبْ خَطِيٓـَٔةً أَوْ إِثْمًا ثُمَّ يَرْمِ بِهِۦ بَرِيٓـًٔا فَقَدِ ٱحْتَمَلَ بُهْتَٰنًا وَإِثْمًا مُّبِينًا (١١٢) وَلَوْلَا فَضْلُ ٱللَّهِ عَلَيْكَ وَرَحْمَتُهُۥ لَهَمَّت طَّآئِفَةٌ مِّنْهُمْ أَن يُضِلُّوكَ وَمَا يُضِلُّونَ إِلَّآ أَنفُسَهُمْ ۖ وَمَا يَضُرُّونَكَ مِن شَىْءٍ ۚ وَأَنزَلَ ٱللَّهُ عَلَيْكَ ٱلْكِتَٰبَ وَٱلْحِكْمَةَ وَعَلَّمَكَ مَا لَمْ تَكُن تَعْلَمُ ۚ وَكَانَ فَضْلُ ٱللَّهِ عَلَيْكَ عَظِيمًا (١١٣) ۞ لَّا خَيْرَ فِى كَثِيرٍ مِّن نَّجْوَىٰهُمْ إِلَّا مَنْ أَمَرَ بِصَدَقَةٍ أَوْ مَعْرُوفٍ أَوْ إِصْلَٰحٍۭ بَيْنَ ٱلنَّاسِ ۚ وَمَن يَفْعَلْ ذَٰلِكَ ٱبْتِغَآءَ مَرْضَاتِ ٱللَّهِ فَسَوْفَ نُؤْتِيهِ أَجْرًا عَظِيمًا (١١٤)

And whoever does a wrong or wrongs himself but then seeks forgiveness of Allah will find Allah Forgiving and Merciful. (110) And whoever commits a sin only earns it against himself. And Allah is ever Knowing and Wise. (111) But whoever earns an offense or a sin and then blames it on an innocent [person] has taken upon himself a slander and manifest sin. (112) And if it was not for the favor of Allah upon you, [O Muhammad], and His mercy, a group of them would have determined to mislead you. But they do not mislead except themselves, and they will not harm you at all. And Allah has revealed to you the Book and wisdom and has taught you that which you did not know. And ever has the favor of Allah upon you been great. (113) No good is there in much of their private conversation, except for those who enjoin charity or that which is right or conciliation between people. And whoever does that seeking means to the approval of Allah - then We are going to give him a great reward. (114)

## Quran 4:120-124

يَعِدُهُمْ وَيُمَنِّيهِمْ ۖ وَمَا يَعِدُهُمُ ٱلشَّيْطَٰنُ إِلَّا غُرُورًا (١٢٠) أُو۟لَٰٓئِكَ مَأْوَىٰهُمْ جَهَنَّمُ وَلَا يَجِدُونَ عَنْهَا مَحِيصًا (١٢١) وَٱلَّذِينَ ءَامَنُوا۟ وَعَمِلُوا۟ ٱلصَّٰلِحَٰتِ سَنُدْخِلُهُمْ جَنَّٰتٍ تَجْرِى مِن تَحْتِهَا ٱلْأَنْهَٰرُ خَٰلِدِينَ فِيهَآ أَبَدًا ۖ وَعْدَ ٱللَّهِ حَقًّا ۚ وَمَنْ أَصْدَقُ مِنَ ٱللَّهِ قِيلًا (١٢٢) لَّيْسَ بِأَمَانِيِّكُمْ وَلَآ أَمَانِىِّ أَهْلِ ٱلْكِتَٰبِ ۗ مَن يَعْمَلْ سُوٓءًا يُجْزَ بِهِۦ وَلَا يَجِدْ لَهُۥ مِن دُونِ ٱللَّهِ وَلِيًّا وَلَا نَصِيرًا (١٢٣) وَمَن يَعْمَلْ مِنَ ٱلصَّٰلِحَٰتِ مِن ذَكَرٍ أَوْ أُنثَىٰ وَهُوَ مُؤْمِنٌ فَأُو۟لَٰٓئِكَ يَدْخُلُونَ ٱلْجَنَّةَ وَلَا يُظْلَمُونَ نَقِيرًا (١٢٤)

Satan promises them and arouses desire in them. But Satan does not promise them except delusion. (120) The refuge of those will be Hell, and they will not find from it an escape. (121) But the ones who believe and do righteous deeds - We will admit them to gardens beneath which rivers flow, wherein they will abide forever. [It is] the promise of Allah, [which is] truth, and who is more truthful than Allah in statement. (122) Paradise is not [obtained] by your wishful thinking nor by that of the People of the Scripture. Whoever does a wrong will be recompensed for it, and he will not find besides Allah a protector or a helper. (123) And whoever does righteous deeds, whether male or female, while being a believer - those will enter Paradise and will not be wronged, [even as much as] the speck on a date seed. (124)

## Quran 4:144-149

يَـٰٓأَيُّهَا ٱلَّذِينَ ءَامَنُوا۟ لَا تَتَّخِذُوا۟ ٱلْكَـٰفِرِينَ أَوْلِيَآءَ مِن دُونِ ٱلْمُؤْمِنِينَ أَتُرِيدُونَ أَن تَجْعَلُوا۟ لِلَّهِ عَلَيْكُمْ سُلْطَـٰنًا مُّبِينًا (١٤٤) إِنَّ ٱلْمُنَـٰفِقِينَ فِى ٱلدَّرْكِ ٱلْأَسْفَلِ مِنَ ٱلنَّارِ وَلَن تَجِدَ لَهُمْ نَصِيرًا (١٤٥) إِلَّا ٱلَّذِينَ تَابُوا۟ وَأَصْلَحُوا۟ وَٱعْتَصَمُوا۟ بِٱللَّهِ وَأَخْلَصُوا۟ دِينَهُمْ لِلَّهِ فَأُو۟لَـٰٓئِكَ مَعَ ٱلْمُؤْمِنِينَ وَسَوْفَ يُؤْتِ ٱللَّهُ ٱلْمُؤْمِنِينَ أَجْرًا عَظِيمًا (١٤٦) مَّا يَفْعَلُ ٱللَّهُ بِعَذَابِكُمْ إِن شَكَرْتُمْ وَءَامَنتُمْ وَكَانَ ٱللَّهُ شَاكِرًا عَلِيمًا (١٤٧) ۞ لَّا يُحِبُّ ٱللَّهُ ٱلْجَهْرَ بِٱلسُّوٓءِ مِنَ ٱلْقَوْلِ إِلَّا مَن ظُلِمَ وَكَانَ ٱللَّهُ سَمِيعًا عَلِيمًا (١٤٨) إِن تُبْدُوا۟ خَيْرًا أَوْ تُخْفُوهُ أَوْ تَعْفُوا۟ عَن سُوٓءٍ فَإِنَّ ٱللَّهَ كَانَ عَفُوًّا قَدِيرًا (١٤٩)

O you who have believed, do not take the disbelievers as allies instead of the believers. Do you wish to give Allah against yourselves a clear case? (144) Indeed, the hypocrites will be in the lowest depths of the Fire - and never will you find for them a helper - (145) Except for those who repent, correct themselves, hold fast to Allah, and are sincere in their religion for Allah, for those will be with the believers. And Allah is going to give the believers a great reward. (146) What would Allah do with your punishment if you are grateful and believe? And ever is Allah Appreciative and Knowing. (147) Allah does not like the public mention of evil except by one who has been wronged. And ever is Allah Hearing and Knowing. (148) If [instead] you show [some] good or conceal it or pardon an offense - indeed, Allah is ever Pardoning and Competent. (149)

## Quran 4:173-175

فَأَمَّا ٱلَّذِينَ ءَامَنُوا۟ وَعَمِلُوا۟ ٱلصَّـٰلِحَـٰتِ فَيُوَفِّيهِمْ أُجُورَهُمْ وَيَزِيدُهُم مِّن فَضْلِهِۦ وَأَمَّا ٱلَّذِينَ ٱسْتَنكَفُوا۟ وَٱسْتَكْبَرُوا۟ فَيُعَذِّبُهُمْ عَذَابًا أَلِيمًا وَلَا يَجِدُونَ لَهُم مِّن دُونِ ٱللَّهِ وَلِيًّا وَلَا نَصِيرًا (١٧٣) يَـٰٓأَيُّهَا ٱلنَّاسُ قَدْ جَآءَكُم بُرْهَـٰنٌ مِّن رَّبِّكُمْ وَأَنزَلْنَآ

إِلَيْكُمْ نُورًا مُبِينًا (١٧٤) فَأَمَّا ٱلَّذِينَ ءَامَنُوا بِٱللَّهِ وَٱعْتَصَمُوا بِهِۦ فَسَيُدْخِلُهُمْ فِى رَحْمَةٍ مِّنْهُ وَفَضْلٍ وَيَهْدِيهِمْ إِلَيْهِ صِرَٰطًا مُّسْتَقِيمًا (١٧٥)

And as for those who believed and did righteous deeds, He will give them in full their rewards and grant them extra from His bounty. But as for those who disdained and were arrogant, He will punish them with a painful punishment, and they will not find for themselves besides Allah any protector or helper. (173) O mankind, there has come to you a conclusive proof from your Lord, and We have sent down to you a clear light. (174) So those who believe in Allah and hold fast to Him - He will admit them to mercy from Himself and bounty and guide them to Himself on a straight path. (175)

## Quran 5:9

وَعَدَ ٱللَّهُ ٱلَّذِينَ ءَامَنُوا وَعَمِلُوا ٱلصَّٰلِحَٰتِ لَهُم مَّغْفِرَةٌ وَأَجْرٌ عَظِيمٌ (٩)

Allah has promised those who believe and do righteous deeds [that] for them there is forgiveness and great reward. (9)

## Quran 5:34-35

إِلَّا ٱلَّذِينَ تَابُوا مِن قَبْلِ أَن تَقْدِرُوا عَلَيْهِمْ فَٱعْلَمُوا أَنَّ ٱللَّهَ غَفُورٌ رَّحِيمٌ (٣٤) يَٰٓأَيُّهَا ٱلَّذِينَ ءَامَنُوا ٱتَّقُوا ٱللَّهَ وَٱبْتَغُوا إِلَيْهِ ٱلْوَسِيلَةَ وَجَٰهِدُوا فِى سَبِيلِهِۦ لَعَلَّكُمْ تُفْلِحُونَ (٣٥)

Except for those who return [repenting] before you apprehend them. And know that Allah is Forgiving and Merciful. (34) O you who have believed, fear Allah and seek the means [of nearness] to Him and strive in His cause that you may succeed. (35)

## Quran 5:39-40

فَمَن تَابَ مِنۢ بَعْدِ ظُلْمِهِۦ وَأَصْلَحَ فَإِنَّ ٱللَّهَ يَتُوبُ عَلَيْهِ ۗ إِنَّ ٱللَّهَ غَفُورٌ رَّحِيمٌ (٣٩) أَلَمْ تَعْلَمْ أَنَّ ٱللَّهَ لَهُۥ مُلْكُ ٱلسَّمَٰوَٰتِ وَٱلْأَرْضِ يُعَذِّبُ مَن يَشَآءُ وَيَغْفِرُ لِمَن يَشَآءُ ۗ وَٱللَّهُ عَلَىٰ كُلِّ شَىْءٍ قَدِيرٌ (٤٠)

But whoever repents after his wrongdoing and reforms, indeed, Allah will turn to him in forgiveness. Indeed, Allah is Forgiving and Merciful. (39) Do you not know that to Allah belongs the dominion of the heavens and the earth? He punishes whom He wills and forgives whom He wills, and Allah is over all things competent. (40)

## Quran 5:74

أَفَلَا يَتُوبُونَ إِلَى ٱللَّهِ وَيَسْتَغْفِرُونَهُۥ ۚ وَٱللَّهُ غَفُورٌ رَّحِيمٌ (٧٤)

So will they not repent to Allah and seek His forgiveness? And Allah is Forgiving and Merciful. (74)

## Quran 5:98

ٱعْلَمُوٓاْ أَنَّ ٱللَّهَ شَدِيدُ ٱلْعِقَابِ وَأَنَّ ٱللَّهَ غَفُورٌ رَّحِيمٌ (٩٨)

Know that Allah is severe in penalty and that Allah is Forgiving and Merciful. (98)

## Quran 5:101

يَٰٓأَيُّهَا ٱلَّذِينَ ءَامَنُواْ لَا تَسْـَٔلُواْ عَنْ أَشْيَآءَ إِن تُبْدَ لَكُمْ تَسُؤْكُمْ وَإِن تَسْـَٔلُواْ عَنْهَا حِينَ يُنَزَّلُ ٱلْقُرْءَانُ تُبْدَ لَكُمْ عَفَا ٱللَّهُ عَنْهَا ۗ وَٱللَّهُ غَفُورٌ حَلِيمٌ (١٠١)

*O you who have believed, do not ask about things which, if they are shown to you, will distress you. But if you ask about them while the Qur'an is being revealed, they will be shown to you. Allah has pardoned that which is past; and Allah is Forgiving and Forbearing. (101)*

## Quran 6:12

قُل لِّمَن مَّا فِى ٱلسَّمَـٰوَٰتِ وَٱلْأَرْضِ ۖ قُل لِّلَّهِ ۚ كَتَبَ عَلَىٰ نَفْسِهِ ٱلرَّحْمَةَ ۚ لَيَجْمَعَنَّكُمْ إِلَىٰ يَوْمِ ٱلْقِيَـٰمَةِ لَا رَيْبَ فِيهِ ۚ ٱلَّذِينَ خَسِرُوٓا۟ أَنفُسَهُمْ فَهُمْ لَا يُؤْمِنُونَ (١٢)

*Say, "To whom belongs whatever is in the heavens and earth?" Say, "To Allah." He has decreed upon Himself mercy. He will surely assemble you for the Day of Resurrection, about which there is no doubt. Those who will lose themselves [that Day] do not believe. (12)*

## Quran 6:15-19

قُلْ إِنِّىٓ أَخَافُ إِنْ عَصَيْتُ رَبِّى عَذَابَ يَوْمٍ عَظِيمٍ (١٥) مَّن يُصْرَفْ عَنْهُ يَوْمَئِذٍ فَقَدْ رَحِمَهُ ۚ وَذَٰلِكَ ٱلْفَوْزُ ٱلْمُبِينُ (١٦) وَإِن يَمْسَسْكَ ٱللَّهُ بِضُرٍّ فَلَا كَاشِفَ لَهُۥٓ إِلَّا هُوَ ۖ وَإِن يَمْسَسْكَ بِخَيْرٍ فَهُوَ عَلَىٰ كُلِّ شَىْءٍ قَدِيرٌ (١٧) وَهُوَ ٱلْقَاهِرُ فَوْقَ عِبَادِهِ ۚ وَهُوَ ٱلْحَكِيمُ ٱلْخَبِيرُ (١٨) قُلْ أَىُّ شَىْءٍ أَكْبَرُ شَهَـٰدَةً ۖ قُلِ ٱللَّهُ ۖ شَهِيدٌۢ بَيْنِى وَبَيْنَكُمْ ۚ وَأُوحِىَ إِلَىَّ هَـٰذَا ٱلْقُرْءَانُ لِأُنذِرَكُم بِهِۦ وَمَنۢ بَلَغَ ۚ أَئِنَّكُمْ لَتَشْهَدُونَ أَنَّ مَعَ ٱللَّهِ ءَالِهَةً أُخْرَىٰ ۚ قُل لَّآ أَشْهَدُ ۚ قُلْ إِنَّمَا هُوَ إِلَـٰهٌ وَٰحِدٌ وَإِنَّنِى بَرِىٓءٌ مِّمَّا تُشْرِكُونَ (١٩)

*Say, "Indeed I fear, if I should disobey my Lord, the punishment of a tremendous Day." (15) He from whom it is averted that Day - [Allah] has granted him mercy. And that is the clear attainment. (16) And if Allah should touch you with adversity, there is no remover of it except Him. And if He touches you with good - then He* is over all things competent. (17) And He is the subjugator over His servants. And He is the Wise, the Acquainted [with all]. (18) Say, "What thing is greatest in testimony?" Say, "Allah is witness between me and you. And this Qur'an was revealed to me that I may warn you thereby and whomever it reaches. Do you [truly] testify that with Allah there are other deities?" Say, "I will not testify [with you]." Say, "Indeed, He is but one God, and indeed, I am free of what you associate [with Him]." (19)

## Quran 6:133

وَرَبُّكَ ٱلْغَنِيُّ ذُو ٱلرَّحْمَةِ إِن يَشَأْ يُذْهِبْكُمْ وَيَسْتَخْلِفْ مِنۢ بَعْدِكُم مَّا يَشَآءُ كَمَآ أَنشَأَكُم مِّن ذُرِّيَّةِ قَوْمٍ ءَاخَرِينَ (١٣٣)

And your Lord is the Free of need, the possessor of mercy. If He wills, he can do away with you and give succession after you to whomever He wills, just as He produced you from the descendants of another people. (133)

## Quran 6:145

قُل لَّآ أَجِدُ فِى مَآ أُوحِىَ إِلَىَّ مُحَرَّمًا عَلَىٰ طَاعِمٍ يَطْعَمُهُۥٓ إِلَّآ أَن يَكُونَ مَيْتَةً أَوْ دَمًا مَّسْفُوحًا أَوْ لَحْمَ خِنزِيرٍ فَإِنَّهُۥ رِجْسٌ أَوْ فِسْقًا أُهِلَّ لِغَيْرِ ٱللَّهِ بِهِۦ ۚ فَمَنِ ٱضْطُرَّ غَيْرَ بَاغٍ وَلَا عَادٍ فَإِنَّ رَبَّكَ غَفُورٌ رَّحِيمٌ (١٤٥)

Say, "I do not find within that which was revealed to me [anything] forbidden to one who would eat it unless it be a dead animal or blood spilled out or the flesh of swine - for indeed, it is impure - or it be [that slaughtered in] disobedience, dedicated to other than Allah. But whoever is forced [by necessity], neither desiring [it] nor transgressing [its limit], then indeed, your Lord is Forgiving and Merciful." (145)

## Quran 6:160

مَن جَاءَ بِٱلْحَسَنَةِ فَلَهُ عَشْرُ أَمْثَالِهَا ۖ وَمَن جَاءَ بِٱلسَّيِّئَةِ فَلَا يُجْزَىٰ إِلَّا مِثْلَهَا وَهُمْ لَا يُظْلَمُونَ (١٦٠)

*Whoever comes [on the Day of Judgement] with a good deed will have ten times the like thereof [to his credit], and whoever comes with an evil deed will not be recompensed except the like thereof; and they will not be wronged. (160)*

## Quran 6:164-165

قُلْ أَغَيْرَ ٱللَّهِ أَبْغِى رَبًّا وَهُوَ رَبُّ كُلِّ شَىْءٍ ۚ وَلَا تَكْسِبُ كُلُّ نَفْسٍ إِلَّا عَلَيْهَا ۚ وَلَا تَزِرُ وَازِرَةٌ وِزْرَ أُخْرَىٰ ۚ ثُمَّ إِلَىٰ رَبِّكُم مَّرْجِعُكُمْ فَيُنَبِّئُكُم بِمَا كُنتُمْ فِيهِ تَخْتَلِفُونَ (١٦٤) وَهُوَ ٱلَّذِى جَعَلَكُمْ خَلَٰئِفَ ٱلْأَرْضِ وَرَفَعَ بَعْضَكُمْ فَوْقَ بَعْضٍ دَرَجَٰتٍ لِّيَبْلُوَكُمْ فِى مَا ءَاتَىٰكُمْ ۗ إِنَّ رَبَّكَ سَرِيعُ ٱلْعِقَابِ وَإِنَّهُ لَغَفُورٌ رَّحِيمٌ (١٦٥)

*Say, "Is it other than Allah I should desire as a lord while He is the Lord of all things? And every soul earns not [blame] except against itself, and no bearer of burdens will bear the burden of another. Then to your Lord is your return, and He will inform you concerning that over which you used to differ." (164) And it is He who has made you successors upon the earth and has raised some of you above others in degrees [of rank] that He may try you through what He has given you. Indeed, your Lord is swift in penalty; but indeed, He is Forgiving and Merciful. (165)*

## Quran 7:35

يَـٰبَنِىٓ ءَادَمَ إِمَّا يَأْتِيَنَّكُمْ رُسُلٌ مِّنكُمْ يَقُصُّونَ عَلَيْكُمْ ءَايَـٰتِى ۙ فَمَنِ ٱتَّقَىٰ وَأَصْلَحَ فَلَا خَوْفٌ عَلَيْهِمْ وَلَا هُمْ يَحْزَنُونَ (٣٥)

*O children of Adam, if there come to you messengers from among you relating to you My verses, then whoever fears Allah and reforms - there will be no fear concerning them, nor will they grieve. (35)*

## Quran 7:42-49

وَٱلَّذِينَ ءَامَنُوا۟ وَعَمِلُوا۟ ٱلصَّـٰلِحَـٰتِ لَا نُكَلِّفُ نَفْسًا إِلَّا وُسْعَهَآ أُو۟لَـٰٓئِكَ أَصْحَـٰبُ ٱلْجَنَّةِ ۖ هُمْ فِيهَا خَـٰلِدُونَ (٤٢) وَنَزَعْنَا مَا فِى صُدُورِهِم مِّنْ غِلٍّ تَجْرِى مِن تَحْتِهِمُ ٱلْأَنْهَـٰرُ ۖ وَقَالُوا۟ ٱلْحَمْدُ لِلَّهِ ٱلَّذِى هَدَىٰنَا لِهَـٰذَا وَمَا كُنَّا لِنَهْتَدِىَ لَوْلَآ أَنْ هَدَىٰنَا ٱللَّهُ ۖ لَقَدْ جَآءَتْ رُسُلُ رَبِّنَا بِٱلْحَقِّ ۖ وَنُودُوٓا۟ أَن تِلْكُمُ ٱلْجَنَّةُ أُورِثْتُمُوهَا بِمَا كُنتُمْ تَعْمَلُونَ (٤٣) وَنَادَىٰٓ أَصْحَـٰبُ ٱلْجَنَّةِ أَصْحَـٰبَ ٱلنَّارِ أَن قَدْ وَجَدْنَا مَا وَعَدَنَا رَبُّنَا حَقًّا فَهَلْ وَجَدتُّم مَّا وَعَدَ رَبُّكُمْ حَقًّا ۖ قَالُوا۟ نَعَمْ ۚ فَأَذَّنَ مُؤَذِّنٌۢ بَيْنَهُمْ أَن لَّعْنَةُ ٱللَّهِ عَلَى ٱلظَّـٰلِمِينَ (٤٤) ٱلَّذِينَ يَصُدُّونَ عَن سَبِيلِ ٱللَّهِ وَيَبْغُونَهَا عِوَجًا وَهُم بِٱلْءَاخِرَةِ كَـٰفِرُونَ (٤٥) وَبَيْنَهُمَا حِجَابٌ ۚ وَعَلَى ٱلْأَعْرَافِ رِجَالٌ يَعْرِفُونَ كُلًّۢا بِسِيمَىٰهُمْ ۚ وَنَادَوْا۟ أَصْحَـٰبَ ٱلْجَنَّةِ أَن سَلَـٰمٌ عَلَيْكُمْ ۚ لَمْ يَدْخُلُوهَا وَهُمْ يَطْمَعُونَ (٤٦) ۞ وَإِذَا صُرِفَتْ أَبْصَـٰرُهُمْ تِلْقَآءَ أَصْحَـٰبِ ٱلنَّارِ قَالُوا۟ رَبَّنَا لَا تَجْعَلْنَا مَعَ ٱلْقَوْمِ ٱلظَّـٰلِمِينَ (٤٧) وَنَادَىٰٓ أَصْحَـٰبُ ٱلْأَعْرَافِ رِجَالًا يَعْرِفُونَهُم بِسِيمَىٰهُمْ قَالُوا۟ مَآ أَغْنَىٰ عَنكُمْ جَمْعُكُمْ وَمَا كُنتُمْ تَسْتَكْبِرُونَ (٤٨) أَهَـٰٓؤُلَآءِ ٱلَّذِينَ أَقْسَمْتُمْ لَا يَنَالُهُمُ ٱللَّهُ بِرَحْمَةٍ ۚ ٱدْخُلُوا۟ ٱلْجَنَّةَ لَا خَوْفٌ عَلَيْكُمْ وَلَآ أَنتُمْ تَحْزَنُونَ (٤٩)

*But those who believed and did righteous deeds - We charge no soul except [within] its capacity. Those are the companions of Paradise; they will abide therein eternally. (42) And We will have removed whatever is within their breasts of resentment, [while] flowing beneath them are rivers. And they will say, "Praise to Allah, who has guided us to this; and we would never have been guided if Allah had not guided us. Certainly the messengers of our Lord had come with the truth." And they will be called, "This is Paradise, which you have been made to inherit for what you used to do." (43) And the companions of Paradise will call out to the companions of the Fire, "We have already found what our Lord promised us to be true. Have you found what your Lord promised to be true?" They will say, "Yes." Then an announcer will announce among them, "The curse of Allah shall be upon the wrongdoers." (44) Who averted [people] from the way of Allah and sought to make it [seem] deviant while they were, concerning the Hereafter, disbelievers. (45) And between them will be a partition, and on [its] elevations are men who recognize all by their mark. And they call out to the companions of Paradise, "Peace be upon you." They have not [yet] entered it, but they long intensely. (46) And when their eyes are turned toward the companions of the Fire, they say, "Our Lord, do not place us with the wrongdoing people." (47) And the companions of the Elevations will call to men [within Hell] whom they recognize by their mark, saying, "Of no avail to you was your gathering and [the fact] that you were arrogant." (48) [Allah will say], "Are these the ones whom you [inhabitants of Hell] swore that Allah would never offer them mercy? Enter Paradise, [O People of the Elevations]. No fear will there be concerning you, nor will you grieve." (49)*

**Quran 7:52**

وَلَقَدْ جِئْنَـٰهُم بِكِتَـٰبٍ فَصَّلْنَـٰهُ عَلَىٰ عِلْمٍ هُدًى وَرَحْمَةً لِّقَوْمٍ يُؤْمِنُونَ (٥٢)

And We had certainly brought them a Book which We detailed by knowledge - as guidance and mercy to a people who believe. (52)

## Quran 7:55-57

ٱدْعُوا۟ رَبَّكُمْ تَضَرُّعًا وَخُفْيَةً ۚ إِنَّهُ ۥ لَا يُحِبُّ ٱلْمُعْتَدِينَ (٥٥) وَلَا تُفْسِدُوا۟ فِى ٱلْأَرْضِ بَعْدَ إِصْلَـٰحِهَا وَٱدْعُوهُ خَوْفًا وَطَمَعًا ۚ إِنَّ رَحْمَتَ ٱللَّهِ قَرِيبٌ مِّنَ ٱلْمُحْسِنِينَ (٥٦) وَهُوَ ٱلَّذِى يُرْسِلُ ٱلرِّيَـٰحَ بُشْرًۢا بَيْنَ يَدَىْ رَحْمَتِهِۦ ۖ حَتَّىٰٓ إِذَآ أَقَلَّتْ سَحَابًا ثِقَالًا سُقْنَـٰهُ لِبَلَدٍ مَّيِّتٍ فَأَنزَلْنَا بِهِ ٱلْمَآءَ فَأَخْرَجْنَا بِهِۦ مِن كُلِّ ٱلثَّمَرَٰتِ ۚ كَذَٰلِكَ نُخْرِجُ ٱلْمَوْتَىٰ لَعَلَّكُمْ تَذَكَّرُونَ (٥٧)

Call upon your Lord in humility and privately; indeed, He does not like transgressors. (55) And cause not corruption upon the earth after its reformation. And invoke Him in fear and aspiration. Indeed, the mercy of Allah is near to the doers of good. (56) And it is He who sends the winds as good tidings before His mercy until, when they have carried heavy rainclouds, We drive them to a dead land and We send down rain therein and bring forth thereby [some] of all the fruits. Thus will We bring forth the dead; perhaps you may be reminded. (57)

## Quran 7:61-63

قَالَ يَـٰقَوْمِ لَيْسَ بِى ضَلَـٰلَةٌ وَلَـٰكِنِّى رَسُولٌ مِّن رَّبِّ ٱلْعَـٰلَمِينَ (٦١) أُبَلِّغُكُمْ رِسَـٰلَـٰتِ رَبِّى وَأَنصَحُ لَكُمْ وَأَعْلَمُ مِنَ ٱللَّهِ مَا لَا تَعْلَمُونَ (٦٢) أَوَعَجِبْتُمْ أَن جَآءَكُمْ ذِكْرٌ مِّن رَّبِّكُمْ عَلَىٰ رَجُلٍ مِّنكُمْ لِيُنذِرَكُمْ وَلِتَتَّقُوا۟ وَلَعَلَّكُمْ تُرْحَمُونَ (٦٣)

[Noah] said, "O my people, there is not error in me, but I am a messenger from the Lord of the worlds." (61) I convey to you the messages of my Lord and advise you; and I know from Allah what you do not know. (62) Then do you wonder that there has come to you a reminder from your Lord through a man from among you, that he may warn you and that you may fear Allah so you might receive mercy." (63)

## Quran 7:153-157

وَٱلَّذِينَ عَمِلُوا۟ ٱلسَّيِّـَٔاتِ ثُمَّ تَابُوا۟ مِنۢ بَعْدِهَا وَءَامَنُوٓا۟ إِنَّ رَبَّكَ مِنۢ بَعْدِهَا لَغَفُورٌ رَّحِيمٌ (١٥٣) وَلَمَّا سَكَتَ عَن مُّوسَى ٱلْغَضَبُ أَخَذَ ٱلْأَلْوَاحَ ۖ وَفِى نُسْخَتِهَا هُدًى وَرَحْمَةٌ لِّلَّذِينَ هُمْ لِرَبِّهِمْ يَرْهَبُونَ (١٥٤) وَٱخْتَارَ مُوسَىٰ قَوْمَهُۥ سَبْعِينَ رَجُلًا لِّمِيقَـٰتِنَا ۖ فَلَمَّآ أَخَذَتْهُمُ ٱلرَّجْفَةُ قَالَ رَبِّ لَوْ شِئْتَ أَهْلَكْتَهُم مِّن قَبْلُ وَإِيَّـٰىَ ۖ أَتُهْلِكُنَا بِمَا فَعَلَ ٱلسُّفَهَآءُ مِنَّآ ۖ إِنْ هِىَ إِلَّا فِتْنَتُكَ تُضِلُّ بِهَا مَن تَشَآءُ وَتَهْدِى مَن تَشَآءُ ۖ أَنتَ وَلِيُّنَا فَٱغْفِرْ لَنَا وَٱرْحَمْنَا ۖ وَأَنتَ خَيْرُ ٱلْغَـٰفِرِينَ (١٥٥) وَٱكْتُبْ لَنَا فِى هَـٰذِهِ ٱلدُّنْيَا حَسَنَةً وَفِى ٱلْـَٔاخِرَةِ إِنَّا هُدْنَآ إِلَيْكَ ۚ قَالَ عَذَابِىٓ أُصِيبُ بِهِۦ مَنْ أَشَآءُ ۖ وَرَحْمَتِى وَسِعَتْ كُلَّ شَىْءٍ ۚ فَسَأَكْتُبُهَا لِلَّذِينَ يَتَّقُونَ وَيُؤْتُونَ ٱلزَّكَوٰةَ وَٱلَّذِينَ هُم بِـَٔايَـٰتِنَا يُؤْمِنُونَ (١٥٦) ٱلَّذِينَ يَتَّبِعُونَ ٱلرَّسُولَ ٱلنَّبِىَّ ٱلْأُمِّىَّ ٱلَّذِى يَجِدُونَهُۥ مَكْتُوبًا عِندَهُمْ فِى ٱلتَّوْرَىٰةِ وَٱلْإِنجِيلِ يَأْمُرُهُم بِٱلْمَعْرُوفِ وَيَنْهَىٰهُمْ عَنِ ٱلْمُنكَرِ وَيُحِلُّ لَهُمُ ٱلطَّيِّبَـٰتِ وَيُحَرِّمُ عَلَيْهِمُ ٱلْخَبَـٰٓئِثَ وَيَضَعُ عَنْهُمْ إِصْرَهُمْ وَٱلْأَغْلَـٰلَ ٱلَّتِى كَانَتْ عَلَيْهِمْ ۚ فَٱلَّذِينَ ءَامَنُوا۟ بِهِۦ وَعَزَّرُوهُ وَنَصَرُوهُ وَٱتَّبَعُوا۟ ٱلنُّورَ ٱلَّذِىٓ أُنزِلَ مَعَهُۥٓ ۙ أُو۟لَـٰٓئِكَ هُمُ ٱلْمُفْلِحُونَ (١٥٧)

But those who committed misdeeds and then repented after them and believed - indeed your Lord, thereafter, is Forgiving and Merciful. (153) And when the anger subsided in Moses, he took up the tablets; and in their inscription was guidance and mercy for those who are fearful of their Lord. (154) And Moses chose from his people seventy men for Our appointment. And when the earthquake seized them, he said, "My Lord, if You had willed, You could have destroyed them before and me [as well]. Would You destroy us for what the foolish among us have done? This is not but Your trial by which You send astray whom You will and guide whom You will. You are our Protector, so forgive us and have mercy upon us; and You are the best of forgivers. (155) And decree for us in this world [that which is] good and [also] in the Hereafter; indeed, we have turned back to You." [Allah] said, "My punishment - I afflict with it whom I will, but My mercy encompasses all things." So I will decree it [especially] for those who fear Me and give zakah and those who believe in Our verses - (156) Those who follow the Messenger, the unlettered prophet, whom they find written in what they have of the Torah and the Injeel, who enjoins upon them what is right and forbids them what is wrong and makes lawful for them the good things and prohibits for them the evil and relieves them of their burden and the shackles which were upon them. So they who have believed in him, honored him, supported him and followed the light which was sent down with him - it is those who will be the successful. (157)

## Quran 7:161

وَإِذْ قِيلَ لَهُمُ ٱسْكُنُواْ هَٰذِهِ ٱلْقَرْيَةَ وَكُلُواْ مِنْهَا حَيْثُ شِئْتُمْ وَقُولُواْ حِطَّةٌ وَٱدْخُلُواْ ٱلْبَابَ سُجَّدًا نَّغْفِرْ لَكُمْ خَطِيٓـَٰتِكُمْ سَنَزِيدُ ٱلْمُحْسِنِينَ (١٦١)

And [mention, O Muhammad], when it was said to them, "Dwell in this city and eat from it wherever you will and say, 'Relieve us of our burdens,' and enter the gate bowing humbly; We will [then] forgive you your sins. We will increase the doers of good [in goodness and reward]." (161)

## Quran 7:167

وَإِذْ تَأَذَّنَ رَبُّكَ لَيَبْعَثَنَّ عَلَيْهِمْ إِلَىٰ يَوْمِ ٱلْقِيَٰمَةِ مَن يَسُومُهُمْ سُوٓءَ ٱلْعَذَابِ ۗ إِنَّ رَبَّكَ لَسَرِيعُ ٱلْعِقَابِ ۖ وَإِنَّهُۥ لَغَفُورٌ رَّحِيمٌ (١٦٧)

And [mention] when your Lord declared that He would surely [continue to] send upon them until the Day of Resurrection those who would afflict them with the worst torment. Indeed, your Lord is swift in penalty; but indeed, He is Forgiving and Merciful. (167)

## Quran 7:203-204

وَإِذَا لَمْ تَأْتِهِم بِـَٔايَةٍ قَالُوا۟ لَوْلَا ٱجْتَبَيْتَهَا ۚ قُلْ إِنَّمَآ أَتَّبِعُ مَا يُوحَىٰٓ إِلَىَّ مِن رَّبِّىٓ ۚ هَٰذَا بَصَآئِرُ مِن رَّبِّكُمْ وَهُدًى وَرَحْمَةٌ لِّقَوْمٍ يُؤْمِنُونَ (٢٠٣) وَإِذَا قُرِئَ ٱلْقُرْءَانُ فَٱسْتَمِعُوا۟ لَهُۥ وَأَنصِتُوا۟ لَعَلَّكُمْ تُرْحَمُونَ (٢٠٤)

And when you, [O Muhammad], do not bring them a sign, they say, "Why have you not contrived it?" Say, "I only follow what is revealed to me from my Lord. This [Qur'an] is enlightenment from your Lord and guidance and mercy for a people who believe." (203) So when the Qur'an is recited, then listen to it and pay attention that you may receive mercy. (204)

## Quran 8:2-4

إِنَّمَا ٱلْمُؤْمِنُونَ ٱلَّذِينَ إِذَا ذُكِرَ ٱللَّهُ وَجِلَتْ قُلُوبُهُمْ وَإِذَا تُلِيَتْ عَلَيْهِمْ ءَايَٰتُهُۥ زَادَتْهُمْ إِيمَٰنًا وَعَلَىٰ رَبِّهِمْ يَتَوَكَّلُونَ (٢) ٱلَّذِينَ يُقِيمُونَ ٱلصَّلَوٰةَ وَمِمَّا رَزَقْنَٰهُمْ يُنفِقُونَ (٣) أُو۟لَٰٓئِكَ هُمُ ٱلْمُؤْمِنُونَ حَقًّا ۚ لَّهُمْ دَرَجَٰتٌ عِندَ رَبِّهِمْ وَمَغْفِرَةٌ وَرِزْقٌ كَرِيمٌ (٤)

*The believers are only those who, when Allah is mentioned, their hearts become fearful, and when His verses are recited to them, it increases them in faith; and upon their Lord they rely - (2) The ones who establish prayer, and from what We have provided them, they spend. (3) Those are the believers, truly. For them are degrees [of high position] with their Lord and forgiveness and noble provision. (4)*

## Quran 8:69-70

فَكُلُواْ مِمَّا غَنِمْتُمْ حَلَـٰلًا طَيِّبًا ۚ وَٱتَّقُواْ ٱللَّهَ ۚ إِنَّ ٱللَّهَ غَفُورٌ رَّحِيمٌ (٦٩) يَـٰٓأَيُّهَا ٱلنَّبِىُّ قُل لِّمَن فِىٓ أَيْدِيكُم مِّنَ ٱلْأَسْرَىٰٓ إِن يَعْلَمِ ٱللَّهُ فِى قُلُوبِكُمْ خَيْرًا يُؤْتِكُمْ خَيْرًا مِّمَّآ أُخِذَ مِنكُمْ وَيَغْفِرْ لَكُمْ ۗ وَٱللَّهُ غَفُورٌ رَّحِيمٌ (٧٠)

*So consume what you have taken of war booty [as being] lawful and good, and fear Allah. Indeed, Allah is Forgiving and Merciful. (69) O Prophet, say to whoever is in your hands of the captives, "If Allah knows [any] good in your hearts, He will give you [something] better than what was taken from you, and He will forgive you; and Allah is Forgiving and Merciful." (70)*

## Quran 8:74

وَٱلَّذِينَ ءَامَنُواْ وَهَاجَرُواْ وَجَـٰهَدُواْ فِى سَبِيلِ ٱللَّهِ وَٱلَّذِينَ ءَاوَواْ وَّنَصَرُوٓاْ أُوْلَـٰٓئِكَ هُمُ ٱلْمُؤْمِنُونَ حَقًّا ۚ لَّهُم مَّغْفِرَةٌ وَرِزْقٌ كَرِيمٌ (٧٤)

*But those who have believed and emigrated and fought in the cause of Allah and those who gave shelter and aided - it is they who are the believers, truly. For them is forgiveness and noble provision. (74)*

## Quran 9:5

فَإِذَا ٱنسَلَخَ ٱلْأَشْهُرُ ٱلْحُرُمُ فَٱقْتُلُوا۟ ٱلْمُشْرِكِينَ حَيْثُ وَجَدتُّمُوهُمْ وَخُذُوهُمْ وَٱحْصُرُوهُمْ وَٱقْعُدُوا۟ لَهُمْ كُلَّ مَرْصَدٍ ۚ فَإِن تَابُوا۟ وَأَقَامُوا۟ ٱلصَّلَوٰةَ وَءَاتَوُا۟ ٱلزَّكَوٰةَ فَخَلُّوا۟ سَبِيلَهُمْ ۚ إِنَّ ٱللَّهَ غَفُورٌ رَّحِيمٌ (٥)

And when the sacred months have passed, then kill the polytheists wherever you find them and capture them and besiege them and sit in wait for them at every place of ambush. But if they should repent, establish prayer, and give zakah, let them [go] on their way. Indeed, Allah is Forgiving and Merciful. (5)

## Quran 9:11

فَإِن تَابُوا۟ وَأَقَامُوا۟ ٱلصَّلَوٰةَ وَءَاتَوُا۟ ٱلزَّكَوٰةَ فَإِخْوَٰنُكُمْ فِى ٱلدِّينِ ۗ وَنُفَصِّلُ ٱلْءَايَٰتِ لِقَوْمٍ يَعْلَمُونَ (١١)

But if they repent, establish prayer, and give zakah, then they are your brothers in religion; and We detail the verses for a people who know. (11)

## Quran 9:14-15

قَٰتِلُوهُمْ يُعَذِّبْهُمُ ٱللَّهُ بِأَيْدِيكُمْ وَيُخْزِهِمْ وَيَنصُرْكُمْ عَلَيْهِمْ وَيَشْفِ صُدُورَ قَوْمٍ مُّؤْمِنِينَ (١٤) وَيُذْهِبْ غَيْظَ قُلُوبِهِمْ ۗ وَيَتُوبُ ٱللَّهُ عَلَىٰ مَن يَشَآءُ ۗ وَٱللَّهُ عَلِيمٌ حَكِيمٌ (١٥)

Fight them; Allah will punish them by your hands and will disgrace them and give you victory over them and satisfy the breasts of a believing people (14) And remove the fury in the believers' hearts. And Allah turns in forgiveness to whom He wills; and Allah is Knowing and Wise. (15)

## Quran 9:26-27

ثُمَّ أَنزَلَ ٱللَّهُ سَكِينَتَهُۥ عَلَىٰ رَسُولِهِۦ وَعَلَى ٱلْمُؤْمِنِينَ وَأَنزَلَ جُنُودًا لَّمْ تَرَوْهَا وَعَذَّبَ ٱلَّذِينَ كَفَرُوا۟ وَذَٰلِكَ جَزَآءُ ٱلْكَٰفِرِينَ (٢٦) ثُمَّ يَتُوبُ ٱللَّهُ مِنۢ بَعْدِ ذَٰلِكَ عَلَىٰ مَن يَشَآءُ وَٱللَّهُ غَفُورٌ رَّحِيمٌ (٢٧)

Then Allah sent down His tranquility upon His Messenger and upon the believers and sent down soldiers; angels whom you did not see and punished those who disbelieved. And that is the recompense of the disbelievers. (26) Then Allah will accept repentance after that for whom He wills; and Allah is Forgiving and Merciful. (27)

## Quran 9:71-72

وَٱلْمُؤْمِنُونَ وَٱلْمُؤْمِنَٰتُ بَعْضُهُمْ أَوْلِيَآءُ بَعْضٍ يَأْمُرُونَ بِٱلْمَعْرُوفِ وَيَنْهَوْنَ عَنِ ٱلْمُنكَرِ وَيُقِيمُونَ ٱلصَّلَوٰةَ وَيُؤْتُونَ ٱلزَّكَوٰةَ وَيُطِيعُونَ ٱللَّهَ وَرَسُولَهُۥٓ أُو۟لَٰٓئِكَ سَيَرْحَمُهُمُ ٱللَّهُ إِنَّ ٱللَّهَ عَزِيزٌ حَكِيمٌ (٧١) وَعَدَ ٱللَّهُ ٱلْمُؤْمِنِينَ وَٱلْمُؤْمِنَٰتِ جَنَّٰتٍ تَجْرِى مِن تَحْتِهَا ٱلْأَنْهَٰرُ خَٰلِدِينَ فِيهَا وَمَسَٰكِنَ طَيِّبَةً فِى جَنَّٰتِ عَدْنٍ وَرِضْوَٰنٌ مِّنَ ٱللَّهِ أَكْبَرُ ذَٰلِكَ هُوَ ٱلْفَوْزُ ٱلْعَظِيمُ (٧٢)

The believing men and believing women are allies of one another. They enjoin what is right and forbid what is wrong and establish prayer and give zakah and obey Allah and His Messenger. Those - Allah will have mercy upon them. Indeed, Allah is Exalted in Might and Wise. (71) Allah has promised the believing men and believing women gardens beneath which rivers flow, wherein they abide eternally, and pleasant dwellings in gardens of perpetual residence; but approval from Allah is greater. It is that which is the great attainment. (72)

## Quran 9:74

يَحْلِفُونَ بِٱللَّهِ مَا قَالُوا۟ وَلَقَدْ قَالُوا۟ كَلِمَةَ ٱلْكُفْرِ وَكَفَرُوا۟ بَعْدَ إِسْلَٰمِهِمْ وَهَمُّوا۟ بِمَا لَمْ يَنَالُوا۟ ۚ وَمَا نَقَمُوٓا۟ إِلَّآ أَنْ أَغْنَىٰهُمُ ٱللَّهُ وَرَسُولُهُۥ مِن فَضْلِهِۦ ۚ فَإِن يَتُوبُوا۟ يَكُ خَيْرًا لَّهُمْ ۖ وَإِن يَتَوَلَّوْا۟ يُعَذِّبْهُمُ ٱللَّهُ عَذَابًا أَلِيمًا فِى ٱلدُّنْيَا وَٱلْءَاخِرَةِ ۚ وَمَا لَهُمْ فِى ٱلْأَرْضِ مِن وَلِىٍّ وَلَا نَصِيرٍ (٧٤)

They swear by Allah that they did not say [anything against the Prophet] while they had said the word of disbelief and disbelieved after their [pretense of] Islam and planned that which they were not to attain. And they were not resentful except [for the fact] that Allah and His Messenger had enriched them of His bounty. So if they repent, it is better for them; but if they turn away, Allah will punish them with a painful punishment in this world and the Hereafter. And there will not be for them on earth any protector or helper. (74)

## Quran 9:91

لَّيْسَ عَلَى ٱلضُّعَفَآءِ وَلَا عَلَى ٱلْمَرْضَىٰ وَلَا عَلَى ٱلَّذِينَ لَا يَجِدُونَ مَا يُنفِقُونَ حَرَجٌ إِذَا نَصَحُوا۟ لِلَّهِ وَرَسُولِهِۦ ۚ مَا عَلَى ٱلْمُحْسِنِينَ مِن سَبِيلٍ ۚ وَٱللَّهُ غَفُورٌ رَّحِيمٌ (٩١)

There is not upon the weak or upon the ill or upon those who do not find anything to spend any discomfort when they are sincere to Allah and His Messenger. There is not upon the doers of good any cause [for blame]. And Allah is Forgiving and Merciful. (91)

## Quran 9:99-100

وَمِنَ ٱلْأَعْرَابِ مَن يُؤْمِنُ بِٱللَّهِ وَٱلْيَوْمِ ٱلْءَاخِرِ وَيَتَّخِذُ مَا يُنفِقُ قُرُبَٰتٍ عِندَ ٱللَّهِ وَصَلَوَٰتِ ٱلرَّسُولِ ۚ أَلَآ إِنَّهَا قُرْبَةٌ لَّهُمْ ۚ سَيُدْخِلُهُمُ ٱللَّهُ فِى رَحْمَتِهِۦٓ ۗ إِنَّ ٱللَّهَ غَفُورٌ

رَّحِيمٌ (٩٩) وَٱلسَّٰبِقُونَ ٱلْأَوَّلُونَ مِنَ ٱلْمُهَٰجِرِينَ وَٱلْأَنصَارِ وَٱلَّذِينَ ٱتَّبَعُوهُم بِإِحْسَٰنٍ رَّضِىَ ٱللَّهُ عَنْهُمْ وَرَضُوا۟ عَنْهُ وَأَعَدَّ لَهُمْ جَنَّٰتٍ تَجْرِى تَحْتَهَا ٱلْأَنْهَٰرُ خَٰلِدِينَ فِيهَآ أَبَدًا ذَٰلِكَ ٱلْفَوْزُ ٱلْعَظِيمُ (١٠٠)

But among the bedouins are some who believe in Allah and the Last Day and consider what they spend as means of nearness to Allah and of [obtaining] invocations of the Messenger. Unquestionably, it is a means of nearness for them. Allah will admit them to His mercy. Indeed, Allah is Forgiving and Merciful. (99) And the first forerunners [in the faith] among the Muhajireen and the Ansar and those who followed them with good conduct - Allah is pleased with them and they are pleased with Him, and He has prepared for them gardens beneath which rivers flow, wherein they will abide forever. That is the great attainment. (100)

## Quran 9:102-106

وَءَاخَرُونَ ٱعْتَرَفُوا۟ بِذُنُوبِهِمْ خَلَطُوا۟ عَمَلًا صَٰلِحًا وَءَاخَرَ سَيِّئًا عَسَى ٱللَّهُ أَن يَتُوبَ عَلَيْهِمْ إِنَّ ٱللَّهَ غَفُورٌ رَّحِيمٌ (١٠٢) خُذْ مِنْ أَمْوَٰلِهِمْ صَدَقَةً تُطَهِّرُهُمْ وَتُزَكِّيهِم بِهَا وَصَلِّ عَلَيْهِمْ إِنَّ صَلَوٰتَكَ سَكَنٌ لَّهُمْ وَٱللَّهُ سَمِيعٌ عَلِيمٌ (١٠٣) أَلَمْ يَعْلَمُوٓا۟ أَنَّ ٱللَّهَ هُوَ يَقْبَلُ ٱلتَّوْبَةَ عَنْ عِبَادِهِۦ وَيَأْخُذُ ٱلصَّدَقَٰتِ وَأَنَّ ٱللَّهَ هُوَ ٱلتَّوَّابُ ٱلرَّحِيمُ (١٠٤) وَقُلِ ٱعْمَلُوا۟ فَسَيَرَى ٱللَّهُ عَمَلَكُمْ وَرَسُولُهُۥ وَٱلْمُؤْمِنُونَ وَسَتُرَدُّونَ إِلَىٰ عَٰلِمِ ٱلْغَيْبِ وَٱلشَّهَٰدَةِ فَيُنَبِّئُكُم بِمَا كُنتُمْ تَعْمَلُونَ (١٠٥) وَءَاخَرُونَ مُرْجَوْنَ لِأَمْرِ ٱللَّهِ إِمَّا يُعَذِّبُهُمْ وَإِمَّا يَتُوبُ عَلَيْهِمْ وَٱللَّهُ عَلِيمٌ حَكِيمٌ (١٠٦)

And [there are] others who have acknowledged their sins. They had mixed a righteous deed with another that was bad. Perhaps Allah will turn to them in forgiveness. Indeed, Allah is Forgiving and Merciful. (102) Take, [O,

Muhammad], from their wealth a charity by which you purify them and cause them increase, and invoke [Allah's blessings] upon them. Indeed, your invocations are reassurance for them. And Allah is Hearing and Knowing. (103) Do they not know that it is Allah who accepts repentance from His servants and receives charities and that it is Allah who is the Accepting of repentance, the Merciful? (104) And say, "Do [as you will], for Allah will see your deeds, and [so, will] His Messenger and the believers. And you will be returned to the Knower of the unseen and the witnessed, and He will inform you of what you used to do." (105) And [there are] others deferred until the command of Allah - whether He will punish them or whether He will forgive them. And Allah is Knowing and Wise. (106)

## Quran 9:112

ٱلتَّٰٓئِبُونَ ٱلۡعَٰبِدُونَ ٱلۡحَٰمِدُونَ ٱلسَّٰٓئِحُونَ ٱلرَّٰكِعُونَ ٱلسَّٰجِدُونَ ٱلۡءَامِرُونَ بِٱلۡمَعۡرُوفِ وَٱلنَّاهُونَ عَنِ ٱلۡمُنكَرِ وَٱلۡحَٰفِظُونَ لِحُدُودِ ٱللَّهِۗ وَبَشِّرِ ٱلۡمُؤۡمِنِينَ (١١٢)

[Such believers are] the repentant, the worshippers, the praisers [of Allah], the travelers [for His cause], those who bow and prostrate [in prayer], those who enjoin what is right and forbid what is wrong, and those who observe the limits [set by] Allah. And give good tidings to the believers. (112)

## Quran 9:117-119

لَقَد تَّابَ ٱللَّهُ عَلَى ٱلنَّبِيِّ وَٱلْمُهَٰجِرِينَ وَٱلْأَنصَارِ ٱلَّذِينَ ٱتَّبَعُوهُ فِى سَاعَةِ ٱلْعُسْرَةِ مِنۢ بَعْدِ مَا كَادَ يَزِيغُ قُلُوبُ فَرِيقٍ مِّنْهُمْ ثُمَّ تَابَ عَلَيْهِمْ ۚ إِنَّهُۥ بِهِمْ رَءُوفٌ رَّحِيمٌ (١١٧) وَعَلَى ٱلثَّلَٰثَةِ ٱلَّذِينَ خُلِّفُوا۟ حَتَّىٰٓ إِذَا ضَاقَتْ عَلَيْهِمُ ٱلْأَرْضُ بِمَا رَحُبَتْ وَضَاقَتْ عَلَيْهِمْ أَنفُسُهُمْ وَظَنُّوٓا۟ أَن لَّا مَلْجَأَ مِنَ ٱللَّهِ إِلَّآ إِلَيْهِ ثُمَّ تَابَ عَلَيْهِمْ لِيَتُوبُوٓا۟ ۚ إِنَّ ٱللَّهَ هُوَ ٱلتَّوَّابُ ٱلرَّحِيمُ (١١٨) يَٰٓأَيُّهَا ٱلَّذِينَ ءَامَنُوا۟ ٱتَّقُوا۟ ٱللَّهَ وَكُونُوا۟ مَعَ ٱلصَّٰدِقِينَ (١١٩)

*Allah has already forgiven the Prophet and the Muhajireen and the Ansar who followed him in the hour of difficulty after the hearts of a party of them had almost inclined [to doubt], and then He forgave them. Indeed, He was to them Kind and Merciful. (117) And [He also forgave] the three who were left behind [and regretted their error] to the point that the earth closed in on them in spite of its vastness and their souls confined them and they were certain that there is no refuge from Allah except in Him. Then He turned to them so they could repent. Indeed, Allah is the Accepting of repentance, the Merciful. (118) O you who have believed, fear Allah and be with those who are true. (119)*

## Quran 10:21

وَإِذَآ أَذَقْنَا ٱلنَّاسَ رَحْمَةً مِّنۢ بَعْدِ ضَرَّآءَ مَسَّتْهُمْ إِذَا لَهُم مَّكْرٌ فِىٓ ءَايَاتِنَا ۚ قُلِ ٱللَّهُ أَسْرَعُ مَكْرًا ۚ إِنَّ رُسُلَنَا يَكْتُبُونَ مَا تَمْكُرُونَ (٢١)

*And when We give the people a taste of mercy after adversity has touched them, at once they conspire against Our verses. Say, "Allah is swifter in strategy." Indeed, Our messengers record that which you conspire (21)*

## Quran 10:57-58

يَٰٓأَيُّهَا ٱلنَّاسُ قَدْ جَآءَتْكُم مَّوْعِظَةٌ مِّن رَّبِّكُمْ وَشِفَآءٌ لِّمَا فِى ٱلصُّدُورِ وَهُدًى وَرَحْمَةٌ لِّلْمُؤْمِنِينَ (٥٧) قُلْ بِفَضْلِ ٱللَّهِ وَبِرَحْمَتِهِۦ فَبِذَٰلِكَ فَلْيَفْرَحُوا۟ هُوَ خَيْرٌ مِّمَّا يَجْمَعُونَ (٥٨)

O mankind, there has to come to you instruction from your Lord and healing for what is in the breasts and guidance and mercy for the believers. (57) Say, "In the bounty of Allah and in His mercy - in that let them rejoice; it is better than what they accumulate." (58)

## Quran 10:107

وَإِن يَمْسَسْكَ ٱللَّهُ بِضُرٍّ فَلَا كَاشِفَ لَهُۥٓ إِلَّا هُوَ ۖ وَإِن يُرِدْكَ بِخَيْرٍ فَلَا رَآدَّ لِفَضْلِهِۦ ۚ يُصِيبُ بِهِۦ مَن يَشَآءُ مِنْ عِبَادِهِۦ ۚ وَهُوَ ٱلْغَفُورُ ٱلرَّحِيمُ (١٠٧)

And if Allah should touch you with adversity, there is no remover of it except Him; and if He intends for you good, then there is no repeller of His bounty. He causes it to reach whom He wills of His servants. And He is the Forgiving, the Merciful (107)

## Quran 11:3-4

وَأَنِ ٱسْتَغْفِرُوا۟ رَبَّكُمْ ثُمَّ تُوبُوٓا۟ إِلَيْهِ يُمَتِّعْكُم مَّتَٰعًا حَسَنًا إِلَىٰٓ أَجَلٍ مُّسَمًّى وَيُؤْتِ كُلَّ ذِى فَضْلٍ فَضْلَهُۥ ۖ وَإِن تَوَلَّوْا۟ فَإِنِّىٓ أَخَافُ عَلَيْكُمْ عَذَابَ يَوْمٍ كَبِيرٍ (٣) إِلَى ٱللَّهِ مَرْجِعُكُمْ ۖ وَهُوَ عَلَىٰ كُلِّ شَىْءٍ قَدِيرٌ (٤)

And [saying], "Seek forgiveness of your Lord and repent to Him, [and] He will let you enjoy a good provision for a specified term and give every doer of favor his favor. But if you turn away, then indeed, I fear for you the punishment of a great Day. (3) To Allah is your return, and He is over all things competent." (4)

## Quran 11:8-11

وَلَئِنْ أَخَّرْنَا عَنْهُمُ ٱلْعَذَابَ إِلَىٰٓ أُمَّةٍ مَّعْدُودَةٍ لَّيَقُولُنَّ مَا يَحْبِسُهُۥٓ ۗ أَلَا يَوْمَ يَأْتِيهِمْ لَيْسَ مَصْرُوفًا عَنْهُمْ وَحَاقَ بِهِم مَّا كَانُوا۟ بِهِۦ يَسْتَهْزِءُونَ (٨) وَلَئِنْ أَذَقْنَا ٱلْإِنسَٰنَ مِنَّا رَحْمَةً ثُمَّ نَزَعْنَٰهَا مِنْهُ إِنَّهُۥ لَيَـُٔوسٌ كَفُورٌ (٩) وَلَئِنْ أَذَقْنَٰهُ نَعْمَآءَ بَعْدَ ضَرَّآءَ مَسَّتْهُ لَيَقُولَنَّ ذَهَبَ ٱلسَّيِّـَٔاتُ عَنِّىٓ ۚ إِنَّهُۥ لَفَرِحٌ فَخُورٌ (١٠) إِلَّا ٱلَّذِينَ صَبَرُوا۟ وَعَمِلُوا۟ ٱلصَّٰلِحَٰتِ أُو۟لَٰٓئِكَ لَهُم مَّغْفِرَةٌ وَأَجْرٌ كَبِيرٌ (١١)

*And if We hold back from them the punishment for a limited time, they will surely say, "What detains it?" Unquestionably, on the Day it comes to them, it will not be averted from them, and they will be enveloped by what they used to ridicule. (8) And if We give man a taste of mercy from Us and then We withdraw it from him, indeed, he is despairing and ungrateful. (9) But if We give him a taste of favor after hardship has touched him, he will surely say, "Bad times have left me." Indeed, he is exultant and boastful - (10) Except for those who are patient and do righteous deeds; those will have forgiveness and great reward. (11)*

## Quran 11:47-48

قَالَ رَبِّ إِنِّىٓ أَعُوذُ بِكَ أَنْ أَسْـَٔلَكَ مَا لَيْسَ لِى بِهِۦ عِلْمٌ ۖ وَإِلَّا تَغْفِرْ لِى وَتَرْحَمْنِىٓ أَكُن مِّنَ ٱلْخَٰسِرِينَ (٤٧) قِيلَ يَٰنُوحُ ٱهْبِطْ بِسَلَٰمٍ مِّنَّا وَبَرَكَٰتٍ عَلَيْكَ وَعَلَىٰٓ أُمَمٍ مِّمَّن مَّعَكَ ۚ وَأُمَمٌ سَنُمَتِّعُهُمْ ثُمَّ يَمَسُّهُم مِّنَّا عَذَابٌ أَلِيمٌ (٤٨)

*[Noah] said, "My Lord, I seek refuge in You from asking that of which I have no knowledge. And unless You forgive me and have mercy upon me, I will be among the losers." (47) It was said, "O Noah, disembark in security*

from Us and blessings upon you and upon nations [descending] from those with you. But other nations [of them] We will grant enjoyment; then there will touch them from Us a painful punishment." (48)

## Quran 11:50-52

وَإِلَىٰ عَادٍ أَخَاهُمْ هُودًا ۚ قَالَ يَٰقَوْمِ ٱعْبُدُوا۟ ٱللَّهَ مَا لَكُم مِّنْ إِلَٰهٍ غَيْرُهُۥ ۖ إِنْ أَنتُمْ إِلَّا مُفْتَرُونَ (٥٠) يَٰقَوْمِ لَآ أَسْـَٔلُكُمْ عَلَيْهِ أَجْرًا ۖ إِنْ أَجْرِىَ إِلَّا عَلَى ٱلَّذِى فَطَرَنِىٓ ۚ أَفَلَا تَعْقِلُونَ (٥١) وَيَٰقَوْمِ ٱسْتَغْفِرُوا۟ رَبَّكُمْ ثُمَّ تُوبُوٓا۟ إِلَيْهِ يُرْسِلِ ٱلسَّمَآءَ عَلَيْكُم مِّدْرَارًا وَيَزِدْكُمْ قُوَّةً إِلَىٰ قُوَّتِكُمْ وَلَا تَتَوَلَّوْا۟ مُجْرِمِينَ (٥٢)

And to 'Aad [We sent] their brother Hud. He said, "O my people, worship Allah; you have no deity other than Him. You are not but inventors [of falsehood]. (50) O my people, I do not ask you for it any reward. My reward is only from the one who created me. Then will you not reason? (51) And O my people, ask forgiveness of your Lord and then repent to Him. He will send [rain from] the sky upon you in showers and increase you in strength [added] to your strength. And do not turn away, [being] criminals." (52)

## Quran 11:61

وَإِلَىٰ ثَمُودَ أَخَاهُمْ صَٰلِحًا ۚ قَالَ يَٰقَوْمِ ٱعْبُدُوا۟ ٱللَّهَ مَا لَكُم مِّنْ إِلَٰهٍ غَيْرُهُۥ ۖ هُوَ أَنشَأَكُم مِّنَ ٱلْأَرْضِ وَٱسْتَعْمَرَكُمْ فِيهَا فَٱسْتَغْفِرُوهُ ثُمَّ تُوبُوٓا۟ إِلَيْهِ ۚ إِنَّ رَبِّى قَرِيبٌ مُّجِيبٌ (٦١)

And to Thamud [We sent] their brother Salih. He said, "O my people, worship Allah; you have no deity other than Him. He has produced you from the earth and settled you in it, so ask forgiveness of Him and then repent to Him. Indeed, my Lord is near and responsive." (61)

## Quran 11:66

فَلَمَّا جَآءَ أَمْرُنَا نَجَّيْنَا صَٰلِحًا وَٱلَّذِينَ ءَامَنُوا۟ مَعَهُۥ بِرَحْمَةٍ مِّنَّا وَمِنْ خِزْىِ يَوْمِئِذٍ إِنَّ رَبَّكَ هُوَ ٱلْقَوِىُّ ٱلْعَزِيزُ (٦٦)

So when Our command came, We saved Salih and those who believed with him, by mercy from Us, and [saved them] from the disgrace of that day. Indeed, it is your Lord who is the Powerful, the Exalted in Might. (66)

## Quran 11:90

وَٱسْتَغْفِرُوا۟ رَبَّكُمْ ثُمَّ تُوبُوٓا۟ إِلَيْهِ إِنَّ رَبِّى رَحِيمٌ وَدُودٌ (٩٠)

And ask forgiveness of your Lord and then repent to Him. Indeed, my Lord is Merciful and Affectionate." (90)

## Quran 12:53

۞ وَمَآ أُبَرِّئُ نَفْسِىٓ إِنَّ ٱلنَّفْسَ لَأَمَّارَةٌۢ بِٱلسُّوٓءِ إِلَّا مَا رَحِمَ رَبِّىٓ إِنَّ رَبِّى غَفُورٌ رَّحِيمٌ (٥٣)

And I do not acquit myself. Indeed, the soul is a persistent enjoiner of evil, except those upon which my Lord has mercy. Indeed, my Lord is Forgiving and Merciful." (53)

## Quran 12:64

قَالَ هَلْ ءَامَنُكُمْ عَلَيْهِ إِلَّا كَمَآ أَمِنتُكُمْ عَلَىٰٓ أَخِيهِ مِن قَبْلُ فَٱللَّهُ خَيْرٌ حَٰفِظًا وَهُوَ أَرْحَمُ ٱلرَّٰحِمِينَ (٦٤)

He said, "Should I entrust you with him except [under coercion] as I entrusted you with his brother before? But Allah is the best guardian, and He is the most merciful of the merciful." (64)

## Quran 12:90-92

قَالُوٓاْ أَءِنَّكَ لَأَنتَ يُوسُفُۖ قَالَ أَنَا۠ يُوسُفُ وَهَٰذَآ أَخِيۖ قَدْ مَنَّ ٱللَّهُ عَلَيْنَآۖ إِنَّهُۥ مَن يَتَّقِ وَيَصْبِرْ فَإِنَّ ٱللَّهَ لَا يُضِيعُ أَجْرَ ٱلْمُحْسِنِينَ (٩٠) قَالُواْ تَٱللَّهِ لَقَدْ ءَاثَرَكَ ٱللَّهُ عَلَيْنَا وَإِن كُنَّا لَخَٰطِـِٔينَ (٩١) قَالَ لَا تَثْرِيبَ عَلَيْكُمُ ٱلْيَوْمَۖ يَغْفِرُ ٱللَّهُ لَكُمْۖ وَهُوَ أَرْحَمُ ٱلرَّٰحِمِينَ (٩٢)

They said, "Are you indeed Joseph?" He said "I am Joseph, and this is my brother. Allah has certainly favored us. Indeed, he who fears Allah and is patient, then indeed, Allah does not allow to be lost the reward of those who do good." (90) They said, "By Allah, certainly has Allah preferred you over us, and indeed, we have been sinners." (91) He said, "No blame will there be upon you today. Allah will forgive you; and He is the most merciful of the merciful." (92)

## Quran 12:97-98

قَالُواْ يَٰٓأَبَانَا ٱسْتَغْفِرْ لَنَا ذُنُوبَنَآ إِنَّا كُنَّا خَٰطِـِٔينَ (٩٧) قَالَ سَوْفَ أَسْتَغْفِرُ لَكُمْ رَبِّيٓۖ إِنَّهُۥ هُوَ ٱلْغَفُورُ ٱلرَّحِيمُ (٩٨)

They said, "O our father, ask for us forgiveness of our sins; indeed, we have been sinners." (97) He (Prophet Jacob) said, "I will ask forgiveness for you from my Lord. Indeed, it is He who is the Forgiving, the Merciful." (98)

## Quran 12:111

لَقَدْ كَانَ فِى قَصَصِهِمْ عِبْرَةٌ لِّأُوْلِى ٱلْأَلْبَٰبِ ۗ مَا كَانَ حَدِيثًا يُفْتَرَىٰ وَلَٰكِن تَصْدِيقَ ٱلَّذِى بَيْنَ يَدَيْهِ وَتَفْصِيلَ كُلِّ شَىْءٍ وَهُدًى وَرَحْمَةً لِّقَوْمٍ يُؤْمِنُونَ (١١١)

There was certainly in their stories a lesson for those of understanding. Never was the Qur'an a narration invented, but a confirmation of what was before it and a detailed explanation of all things and guidance and mercy for a people who believe. (111)

## Quran 13:6

وَيَسْتَعْجِلُونَكَ بِٱلسَّيِّئَةِ قَبْلَ ٱلْحَسَنَةِ وَقَدْ خَلَتْ مِن قَبْلِهِمُ ٱلْمَثُلَٰتُ ۗ وَإِنَّ رَبَّكَ لَذُو مَغْفِرَةٍ لِّلنَّاسِ عَلَىٰ ظُلْمِهِمْ ۖ وَإِنَّ رَبَّكَ لَشَدِيدُ ٱلْعِقَابِ (٦)

They impatiently urge you to bring about evil before good, while there has already occurred before them similar punishments [to what they demand]. And indeed, your Lord is full of forgiveness for the people despite their wrongdoing, and indeed, your Lord is severe in penalty. (6)

## Quran 13:11

لَهُۥ مُعَقِّبَٰتٌ مِّنۢ بَيْنِ يَدَيْهِ وَمِنْ خَلْفِهِۦ يَحْفَظُونَهُۥ مِنْ أَمْرِ ٱللَّهِ ۗ إِنَّ ٱللَّهَ لَا يُغَيِّرُ مَا بِقَوْمٍ حَتَّىٰ يُغَيِّرُوا۟ مَا بِأَنفُسِهِمْ ۗ وَإِذَآ أَرَادَ ٱللَّهُ بِقَوْمٍ سُوٓءًا فَلَا مَرَدَّ لَهُۥ ۚ وَمَا لَهُم مِّن دُونِهِۦ مِن وَالٍ (١١)

For each one are successive [angels] before and behind him who protect him by the decree of Allah. Indeed, Allah will not change the condition of a people until they change what is in themselves. And when Allah intends for a people ill, there is no repelling it. And there is not for them besides Him any patron. (11)

# Quran 13:27-31

وَيَقُولُ ٱلَّذِينَ كَفَرُواْ لَوْلَآ أُنزِلَ عَلَيْهِ ءَايَةٌ مِّن رَّبِّهِۦ ۗ قُلْ إِنَّ ٱللَّهَ يُضِلُّ مَن يَشَآءُ وَيَهْدِىٓ إِلَيْهِ مَنْ أَنَابَ (٢٧) ٱلَّذِينَ ءَامَنُواْ وَتَطْمَئِنُّ قُلُوبُهُم بِذِكْرِ ٱللَّهِ ۗ أَلَا بِذِكْرِ ٱللَّهِ تَطْمَئِنُّ ٱلْقُلُوبُ (٢٨) ٱلَّذِينَ ءَامَنُواْ وَعَمِلُواْ ٱلصَّٰلِحَٰتِ طُوبَىٰ لَهُمْ وَحُسْنُ مَـَٔابٍ (٢٩) كَذَٰلِكَ أَرْسَلْنَٰكَ فِىٓ أُمَّةٍ قَدْ خَلَتْ مِن قَبْلِهَآ أُمَمٌ لِّتَتْلُوَاْ عَلَيْهِمُ ٱلَّذِىٓ أَوْحَيْنَآ إِلَيْكَ وَهُمْ يَكْفُرُونَ بِٱلرَّحْمَٰنِ ۚ قُلْ هُوَ رَبِّى لَآ إِلَٰهَ إِلَّا هُوَ عَلَيْهِ تَوَكَّلْتُ وَإِلَيْهِ مَتَابِ (٣٠) وَلَوْ أَنَّ قُرْءَانًا سُيِّرَتْ بِهِ ٱلْجِبَالُ أَوْ قُطِّعَتْ بِهِ ٱلْأَرْضُ أَوْ كُلِّمَ بِهِ ٱلْمَوْتَىٰ ۗ بَل لِّلَّهِ ٱلْأَمْرُ جَمِيعًا ۗ أَفَلَمْ يَاْيْـَٔسِ ٱلَّذِينَ ءَامَنُوٓاْ أَن لَّوْ يَشَآءُ ٱللَّهُ لَهَدَى ٱلنَّاسَ جَمِيعًا ۗ وَلَا يَزَالُ ٱلَّذِينَ كَفَرُواْ تُصِيبُهُم بِمَا صَنَعُواْ قَارِعَةٌ أَوْ تَحُلُّ قَرِيبًا مِّن دَارِهِمْ حَتَّىٰ يَأْتِىَ وَعْدُ ٱللَّهِ ۚ إِنَّ ٱللَّهَ لَا يُخْلِفُ ٱلْمِيعَادَ (٣١)

And those who disbelieved say, "Why has a sign not been sent down to him from his Lord?" Say, [O Muhammad], "Indeed, Allah leaves astray whom He wills and guides to Himself whoever turns back [to Him] - (27) Those who have believed and whose hearts are assured by the remembrance of Allah. Unquestionably, by the remembrance of Allah hearts are assured." (28) Those who have believed and done righteous deeds - a good state is theirs and a good return. (29) Thus have We sent you to a community before which [other] communities have passed on so you might recite to them that which We revealed to you, while they disbelieve in the Most Merciful. Say, "He is my Lord; there is no deity except Him. Upon Him I rely, and to Him is my return." (30) And if there was any Qur'an by which the mountains would be removed or the earth would be broken apart or the dead would be made to speak, [it would be this Qur'an], but to Allah belongs the affair entirely. Then have those who believed not accepted that had Allah willed, He would have guided the people, all of them? And those who disbelieve do not cease to be struck, for what they have done, by calamity - or it will descend near their home - until there comes the promise of Allah. Indeed, Allah does not fail in [His] promise. (31)

## Quran 14:22-27

وَقَالَ ٱلشَّيْطَٰنُ لَمَّا قُضِىَ ٱلْأَمْرُ إِنَّ ٱللَّهَ وَعَدَكُمْ وَعْدَ ٱلْحَقِّ وَوَعَدتُّكُمْ فَأَخْلَفْتُكُمْ ۖ وَمَا كَانَ لِىَ عَلَيْكُم مِّن سُلْطَٰنٍ إِلَّآ أَن دَعَوْتُكُمْ فَٱسْتَجَبْتُمْ لِى ۖ فَلَا تَلُومُونِى وَلُومُوٓا۟ أَنفُسَكُم ۖ مَّآ أَنَا۠ بِمُصْرِخِكُمْ وَمَآ أَنتُم بِمُصْرِخِىَّ ۖ إِنِّى كَفَرْتُ بِمَآ أَشْرَكْتُمُونِ مِن قَبْلُ ۗ إِنَّ ٱلظَّٰلِمِينَ لَهُمْ عَذَابٌ أَلِيمٌ (٢٢) وَأُدْخِلَ ٱلَّذِينَ ءَامَنُوا۟ وَعَمِلُوا۟ ٱلصَّٰلِحَٰتِ جَنَّٰتٍ تَجْرِى مِن تَحْتِهَا ٱلْأَنْهَٰرُ خَٰلِدِينَ فِيهَا بِإِذْنِ رَبِّهِمْ ۖ تَحِيَّتُهُمْ فِيهَا سَلَٰمٌ (٢٣) أَلَمْ تَرَ كَيْفَ ضَرَبَ ٱللَّهُ مَثَلًا كَلِمَةً طَيِّبَةً كَشَجَرَةٍ طَيِّبَةٍ أَصْلُهَا ثَابِتٌ وَفَرْعُهَا فِى ٱلسَّمَآءِ (٢٤) تُؤْتِىٓ أُكُلَهَا كُلَّ حِينٍۭ بِإِذْنِ رَبِّهَا ۗ وَيَضْرِبُ ٱللَّهُ ٱلْأَمْثَالَ لِلنَّاسِ لَعَلَّهُمْ يَتَذَكَّرُونَ (٢٥) وَمَثَلُ كَلِمَةٍ خَبِيثَةٍ كَشَجَرَةٍ خَبِيثَةٍ ٱجْتُثَّتْ مِن فَوْقِ ٱلْأَرْضِ مَا لَهَا مِن قَرَارٍ (٢٦) يُثَبِّتُ ٱللَّهُ ٱلَّذِينَ ءَامَنُوا۟ بِٱلْقَوْلِ ٱلثَّابِتِ فِى ٱلْحَيَوٰةِ ٱلدُّنْيَا وَفِى ٱلْءَاخِرَةِ ۖ وَيُضِلُّ ٱللَّهُ ٱلظَّٰلِمِينَ ۚ وَيَفْعَلُ ٱللَّهُ مَا يَشَآءُ (٢٧)

And Satan will say when the matter has been concluded, "Indeed, Allah had promised you the promise of truth. And I promised you, but I betrayed you. But I had no authority over you except that I invited you, and you responded to me. So do not blame me; but blame yourselves. I cannot be called to your aid, nor can you be called to my aid. Indeed, I deny your association of me [with Allah] before. Indeed, for the wrongdoers is a painful punishment." (22) And those who believed and did righteous deeds will be admitted to gardens beneath which rivers flow, abiding eternally therein by permission of their Lord; and their greeting therein will be, "Peace!" (23) Have you not considered how Allah presents an example, [making] a good word like a good tree, whose root is firmly fixed and its branches [high] in the sky? (24) It produces its fruit all the time, by permission of its Lord. And Allah presents examples for the people that perhaps they will be reminded. (25) And the example of a bad word is like a bad tree, uprooted from the surface of the earth, not having any stability. (26) Allah keeps firm those who believe, with the firm word, in worldly life and in the Hereafter. And Allah sends astray the wrongdoers. And Allah does what He wills. (27)

## Quran 14:31-36

قُل لِّعِبَادِىَ ٱلَّذِينَ ءَامَنُوا۟ يُقِيمُوا۟ ٱلصَّلَوٰةَ وَيُنفِقُوا۟ مِمَّا رَزَقْنَـٰهُمْ سِرًّا وَعَلَانِيَةً مِّن قَبْلِ أَن يَأْتِىَ يَوْمٌ لَّا بَيْعٌ فِيهِ وَلَا خِلَـٰلٌ (٣١) ٱللَّهُ ٱلَّذِى خَلَقَ ٱلسَّمَـٰوَٰتِ وَٱلْأَرْضَ وَأَنزَلَ مِنَ ٱلسَّمَآءِ مَآءً فَأَخْرَجَ بِهِۦ مِنَ ٱلثَّمَرَٰتِ رِزْقًا لَّكُمْ ۖ وَسَخَّرَ لَكُمُ ٱلْفُلْكَ لِتَجْرِىَ فِى ٱلْبَحْرِ بِأَمْرِهِۦ ۖ وَسَخَّرَ لَكُمُ ٱلْأَنْهَـٰرَ (٣٢) وَسَخَّرَ لَكُمُ ٱلشَّمْسَ وَٱلْقَمَرَ دَآئِبَيْنِ ۖ وَسَخَّرَ لَكُمُ ٱلَّيْلَ وَٱلنَّهَارَ (٣٣) وَءَاتَىٰكُم مِّن كُلِّ مَا سَأَلْتُمُوهُ ۚ وَإِن تَعُدُّوا۟ نِعْمَتَ ٱللَّهِ لَا تُحْصُوهَآ ۗ إِنَّ ٱلْإِنسَـٰنَ لَظَلُومٌ كَفَّارٌ (٣٤) وَإِذْ قَالَ إِبْرَٰهِيمُ رَبِّ ٱجْعَلْ هَـٰذَا ٱلْبَلَدَ ءَامِنًا وَٱجْنُبْنِى وَبَنِىَّ أَن نَّعْبُدَ ٱلْأَصْنَامَ (٣٥) رَبِّ إِنَّهُنَّ أَضْلَلْنَ كَثِيرًا مِّنَ ٱلنَّاسِ ۖ فَمَن تَبِعَنِى فَإِنَّهُۥ مِنِّى ۖ وَمَنْ عَصَانِى فَإِنَّكَ غَفُورٌ رَّحِيمٌ (٣٦)

[O Muhammad], tell My servants who have believed to establish prayer and spend from what We have provided them, secretly and publicly, before a Day comes in which there will be no exchange, nor any friendships. (31) It is

Allah who created the heavens and the earth and sent down rain from the sky and produced thereby some fruits as provision for you and subjected for you the ships to sail through the sea by His command and subjected for you the rivers. (32) And He subjected for you the sun and the moon, continuous [in orbit], and subjected for you the night and the day. (33) And He gave you from all you asked of Him. And if you should count the favor of Allah, you could not enumerate them. Indeed, mankind is [generally] most unjust and ungrateful. (34) And [mention, O Muhammad], when Abraham said, "My Lord, make this city [Makkah] secure and keep me and my sons away from worshipping idols. (35) My Lord, indeed they have led astray many among the people. So whoever follows me - then he is of me; and whoever disobeys me - indeed, You are [yet] Forgiving and Merciful. (36)

## Quran 15:55-56

قَالُوا۟ بَشَّرْنَـٰكَ بِٱلْحَقِّ فَلَا تَكُن مِّنَ ٱلْقَـٰنِطِينَ (٥٥) قَالَ وَمَن يَقْنَطُ مِن رَّحْمَةِ رَبِّهِۦٓ إِلَّا ٱلضَّآلُّونَ (٥٦)

They said, "We have given you good tidings in truth, so do not be of the despairing." (55) He said, "And who despairs of the mercy of his Lord except for those astray?" (56)

## Quran 16:1-7

أَتَىٰٓ أَمْرُ ٱللَّهِ فَلَا تَسْتَعْجِلُوهُ ۚ سُبْحَـٰنَهُۥ وَتَعَـٰلَىٰ عَمَّا يُشْرِكُونَ (١) يُنَزِّلُ ٱلْمَلَـٰٓئِكَةَ بِٱلرُّوحِ مِنْ أَمْرِهِۦ عَلَىٰ مَن يَشَآءُ مِنْ عِبَادِهِۦٓ أَنْ أَنذِرُوٓا۟ أَنَّهُۥ لَآ إِلَـٰهَ إِلَّآ أَنَا۠

فَأَتَّقُونِ (٢) خَلَقَ ٱلسَّمَٰوَٰتِ وَٱلْأَرْضَ بِٱلْحَقِّ تَعَٰلَىٰ عَمَّا يُشْرِكُونَ (٣) خَلَقَ ٱلْإِنسَٰنَ مِن نُّطْفَةٍ فَإِذَا هُوَ خَصِيمٌ مُّبِينٌ (٤) وَٱلْأَنْعَٰمَ خَلَقَهَا لَكُمْ فِيهَا دِفْءٌ وَمَنَٰفِعُ وَمِنْهَا تَأْكُلُونَ (٥) وَلَكُمْ فِيهَا جَمَالٌ حِينَ تُرِيحُونَ وَحِينَ تَسْرَحُونَ (٦) وَتَحْمِلُ أَثْقَالَكُمْ إِلَىٰ بَلَدٍ لَّمْ تَكُونُوا۟ بَٰلِغِيهِ إِلَّا بِشِقِّ ٱلْأَنفُسِ إِنَّ رَبَّكُمْ لَرَءُوفٌ رَّحِيمٌ (٧)

*The command of Allah is coming, so be not impatient for it. Exalted is He and high above what they associate with Him. (1) He sends down the angels, with the inspiration of His command, upon whom He wills of His servants, [telling them], "Warn that there is no deity except Me; so fear Me." (2) He created the heavens and earth in truth. High is He above what they associate with Him. (3) He created man from a sperm-drop; then at once, he is a clear adversary. (4) And the grazing livestock He has created for you; in them is warmth and [numerous] benefits, and from them you eat. (5) And for you in them is [the enjoyment of] beauty when you bring them in [for the evening] and when you send them out [to pasture]. (6) And they carry your loads to a land you could not have reached except with difficulty to yourselves. Indeed, your Lord is Kind and Merciful. (7)*

## Quran 16:18

وَإِن تَعُدُّوا۟ نِعْمَةَ ٱللَّهِ لَا تُحْصُوهَا إِنَّ ٱللَّهَ لَغَفُورٌ رَّحِيمٌ (١٨)

*And if you should count the favors of Allah, you could not enumerate them. Indeed, Allah is Forgiving and Merciful. (18)*

## Quran 16:64

وَمَآ أَنزَلۡنَا عَلَيۡكَ ٱلۡكِتَٰبَ إِلَّا لِتُبَيِّنَ لَهُمُ ٱلَّذِى ٱخۡتَلَفُواْ فِيهِ وَهُدًى وَرَحۡمَةً لِّقَوۡمٍ يُؤۡمِنُونَ (٦٤)

And We have not revealed to you the Book, [O Muhammad], except for you to make clear to them that wherein they have differed and as guidance and mercy for a people who believe. (64)

## Quran 16:89

وَيَوۡمَ نَبۡعَثُ فِى كُلِّ أُمَّةٍ شَهِيدًا عَلَيۡهِم مِّنۡ أَنفُسِهِمۡ وَجِئۡنَا بِكَ شَهِيدًا عَلَىٰ هَٰٓؤُلَآءِ وَنَزَّلۡنَا عَلَيۡكَ ٱلۡكِتَٰبَ تِبۡيَٰنًا لِّكُلِّ شَىۡءٍ وَهُدًى وَرَحۡمَةً وَبُشۡرَىٰ لِلۡمُسۡلِمِينَ (٨٩)

And [mention] the Day when We will resurrect among every nation a witness over them from themselves. And We will bring you, [O Muhammad], as a witness over your nation. And We have sent down to you the Book as clarification for all things and as guidance and mercy and good tidings for the Muslims. (89)

## Quran 16:110-111

ثُمَّ إِنَّ رَبَّكَ لِلَّذِينَ هَاجَرُواْ مِنۢ بَعۡدِ مَا فُتِنُواْ ثُمَّ جَٰهَدُواْ وَصَبَرُوٓاْ إِنَّ رَبَّكَ مِنۢ بَعۡدِهَا لَغَفُورٌ رَّحِيمٌ (١١٠) ۞ يَوۡمَ تَأۡتِى كُلُّ نَفۡسٍ تُجَٰدِلُ عَن نَّفۡسِهَا وَتُوَفَّىٰ كُلُّ نَفۡسٍ مَّا عَمِلَتۡ وَهُمۡ لَا يُظۡلَمُونَ (١١١)

Then, indeed your Lord, to those who emigrated after they had been compelled [to renounce their religion] and thereafter fought [for the cause of Allah] and were patient - indeed, your Lord, after that, is Forgiving and Merciful (110) On the Day when every soul will come disputing for itself, and every soul will be fully compensated for what it did, and they will not be wronged. (111)

## Quran 16:115

إِنَّمَا حَرَّمَ عَلَيْكُمُ ٱلْمَيْتَةَ وَٱلدَّمَ وَلَحْمَ ٱلْخِنزِيرِ وَمَآ أُهِلَّ لِغَيْرِ ٱللَّهِ بِهِۦ ۖ فَمَنِ ٱضْطُرَّ غَيْرَ بَاغٍ وَلَا عَادٍ فَإِنَّ ٱللَّهَ غَفُورٌ رَّحِيمٌ (١١٥)

*He has only forbidden to you dead animals, blood, the flesh of swine, and that which has been dedicated to other than Allah. But whoever is forced [by necessity], neither desiring [it] nor transgressing [its limit] - then indeed, Allah is Forgiving and Merciful. (115)*

## Quran 16:119

ثُمَّ إِنَّ رَبَّكَ لِلَّذِينَ عَمِلُوا۟ ٱلسُّوٓءَ بِجَهَٰلَةٍ ثُمَّ تَابُوا۟ مِنۢ بَعْدِ ذَٰلِكَ وَأَصْلَحُوٓا۟ إِنَّ رَبَّكَ مِنۢ بَعْدِهَا لَغَفُورٌ رَّحِيمٌ (١١٩)

*Then, indeed your Lord, to those who have done wrong out of ignorance and then repent after that and correct themselves - indeed, your Lord, thereafter, is Forgiving and Merciful. (119)*

## Quran 17:8-9

عَسَىٰ رَبُّكُمْ أَن يَرْحَمَكُمْ ۚ وَإِنْ عُدتُّمْ عُدْنَا ۘ وَجَعَلْنَا جَهَنَّمَ لِلْكَٰفِرِينَ حَصِيرًا (٨) إِنَّ هَٰذَا ٱلْقُرْءَانَ يَهْدِى لِلَّتِى هِىَ أَقْوَمُ وَيُبَشِّرُ ٱلْمُؤْمِنِينَ ٱلَّذِينَ يَعْمَلُونَ ٱلصَّٰلِحَٰتِ أَنَّ لَهُمْ أَجْرًا كَبِيرًا (٩)

*[Then Allah said], "It is expected, [if you repent], that your Lord will have mercy upon you. But if you return [to sin], We will return [to punishment]. And We have made Hell, for the disbelievers, a prison-bed." (8) Indeed, this Qur'an guides to that which is most suitable and gives good tidings to the believers who do righteous deeds that they will have a great reward. (9)*

## Quran 17:13-15

وَكُلَّ إِنسَٰنٍ أَلْزَمْنَٰهُ طَٰٓئِرَهُۥ فِى عُنُقِهِۦ ۖ وَنُخْرِجُ لَهُۥ يَوْمَ ٱلْقِيَٰمَةِ كِتَٰبًا يَلْقَىٰهُ مَنشُورًا (١٣) ٱقْرَأْ كِتَٰبَكَ كَفَىٰ بِنَفْسِكَ ٱلْيَوْمَ عَلَيْكَ حَسِيبًا (١٤) مَّنِ ٱهْتَدَىٰ فَإِنَّمَا يَهْتَدِى لِنَفْسِهِۦ ۖ وَمَن ضَلَّ فَإِنَّمَا يَضِلُّ عَلَيْهَا ۚ وَلَا تَزِرُ وَازِرَةٌ وِزْرَ أُخْرَىٰ ۗ وَمَا كُنَّا مُعَذِّبِينَ حَتَّىٰ نَبْعَثَ رَسُولًا (١٥)

And [for] every person We have imposed his fate upon his neck, and We will produce for him on the Day of Resurrection a record which he will encounter spread open. (13) [It will be said], "Read your record. Sufficient is yourself against you this Day as accountant."
(14) Whoever is guided is only guided for [the benefit of] his soul. And whoever errs only errs against it. And no bearer of burdens will bear the burden of another. And never would We punish until We sent a messenger. (15)

## Quran 17:23-25

۞ وَقَضَىٰ رَبُّكَ أَلَّا تَعْبُدُوٓا۟ إِلَّآ إِيَّاهُ وَبِٱلْوَٰلِدَيْنِ إِحْسَٰنًا ۚ إِمَّا يَبْلُغَنَّ عِندَكَ ٱلْكِبَرَ أَحَدُهُمَآ أَوْ كِلَاهُمَا فَلَا تَقُل لَّهُمَآ أُفٍّ وَلَا تَنْهَرْهُمَا وَقُل لَّهُمَا قَوْلًا كَرِيمًا (٢٣) وَٱخْفِضْ لَهُمَا جَنَاحَ ٱلذُّلِّ مِنَ ٱلرَّحْمَةِ وَقُل رَّبِّ ٱرْحَمْهُمَا كَمَا رَبَّيَانِى صَغِيرًا (٢٤) رَّبُّكُمْ أَعْلَمُ بِمَا فِى نُفُوسِكُمْ ۚ إِن تَكُونُوا۟ صَٰلِحِينَ فَإِنَّهُۥ كَانَ لِلْأَوَّٰبِينَ غَفُورًا (٢٥)

And your Lord has decreed that you not worship except Him, and to parents, good treatment. Whether one or both of them reach old age [while] with you, say not to them [so much as], "uff," and do not repel them but speak to them a noble word. (23) And lower to them the wing of humility out of mercy and say, "My Lord, have mercy upon them as they brought me up [when I was] small." (24) Your Lord is most knowing of what is within yourselves. If you should be righteous [in intention] - then indeed He is ever, to the often returning [to Him], Forgiving. (25)

## Quran 17:28

وَإِمَّا تُعْرِضَنَّ عَنْهُمُ ٱبْتِغَاءَ رَحْمَةٍ مِّن رَّبِّكَ تَرْجُوهَا فَقُل لَّهُمْ قَوْلاً مَّيْسُورًا (٢٨)

And if you [must] turn away from the needy awaiting mercy from your Lord which you expect, then speak to them a gentle word. (28)

## Quran 17:53-54

وَقُل لِّعِبَادِى يَقُولُوا۟ ٱلَّتِى هِىَ أَحْسَنُ إِنَّ ٱلشَّيْطَٰنَ يَنزَغُ بَيْنَهُمْ إِنَّ ٱلشَّيْطَٰنَ كَانَ لِلْإِنسَٰنِ عَدُوًّا مُّبِينًا (٥٣) رَّبُّكُمْ أَعْلَمُ بِكُمْ إِن يَشَأْ يَرْحَمْكُمْ أَوْ إِن يَشَأْ يُعَذِّبْكُمْ وَمَآ أَرْسَلْنَٰكَ عَلَيْهِمْ وَكِيلًا (٥٤)

And tell My servants to say that which is best. Indeed, Satan induces [dissension] among them. Indeed Satan is ever, to mankind, a clear enemy. (53) Your Lord is most knowing of you. If He wills, He will have mercy upon you; or if He wills, He will punish you. And We have not sent you, [O Muhammad], over them as a manager. (54)

## Quran 17:57

أُو۟لَٰٓئِكَ ٱلَّذِينَ يَدْعُونَ يَبْتَغُونَ إِلَىٰ رَبِّهِمُ ٱلْوَسِيلَةَ أَيُّهُمْ أَقْرَبُ وَيَرْجُونَ رَحْمَتَهُۥ وَيَخَافُونَ عَذَابَهُۥٓ إِنَّ عَذَابَ رَبِّكَ كَانَ مَحْذُورًا (٥٧)

Those whom they invoke seek means of access to their Lord, [striving as to] which of them would be nearest, and they hope for His mercy and fear His punishment. Indeed, the punishment of your Lord is ever feared. (57)

## Quran 17:66

رَّبُّكُمُ ٱلَّذِى يُزْجِى لَكُمُ ٱلْفُلْكَ فِى ٱلْبَحْرِ لِتَبْتَغُوا۟ مِن فَضْلِهِۦٓ ۚ إِنَّهُۥ كَانَ بِكُمْ رَحِيمًا (٦٦)

It is your Lord who drives the ship for you through the sea that you may seek of His bounty. Indeed, He is ever, to you, Merciful. (66)

## Quran 17:82-83

وَنُنَزِّلُ مِنَ ٱلْقُرْءَانِ مَا هُوَ شِفَآءٌ وَرَحْمَةٌ لِّلْمُؤْمِنِينَ ۙ وَلَا يَزِيدُ ٱلظَّـٰلِمِينَ إِلَّا خَسَارًا (٨٢) وَإِذَآ أَنْعَمْنَا عَلَى ٱلْإِنسَـٰنِ أَعْرَضَ وَنَـَٔا بِجَانِبِهِۦ ۖ وَإِذَا مَسَّهُ ٱلشَّرُّ كَانَ يَـُٔوسًا (٨٣)

And We send down of the Qur'an that which is healing and mercy for the believers, but it does not increase the wrongdoers except in loss. (82) And when We bestow favor upon the disbeliever, he turns away and distances himself; and when evil touches him, he is ever despairing. (83)

## Quran 17:86-89

وَلَئِن شِئْنَا لَنَذْهَبَنَّ بِٱلَّذِىٓ أَوْحَيْنَآ إِلَيْكَ ثُمَّ لَا تَجِدُ لَكَ بِهِۦ عَلَيْنَا وَكِيلًا (٨٦) إِلَّا رَحْمَةً مِّن رَّبِّكَ ۚ إِنَّ فَضْلَهُۥ كَانَ عَلَيْكَ كَبِيرًا (٨٧) قُل لَّئِنِ ٱجْتَمَعَتِ ٱلْإِنسُ وَٱلْجِنُّ عَلَىٰٓ أَن يَأْتُوا۟ بِمِثْلِ هَـٰذَا ٱلْقُرْءَانِ لَا يَأْتُونَ بِمِثْلِهِۦ وَلَوْ كَانَ بَعْضُهُمْ لِبَعْضٍ ظَهِيرًا (٨٨) وَلَقَدْ صَرَّفْنَا لِلنَّاسِ فِى هَـٰذَا ٱلْقُرْءَانِ مِن كُلِّ مَثَلٍ فَأَبَىٰٓ أَكْثَرُ ٱلنَّاسِ إِلَّا كُفُورًا (٨٩)

And if We willed, We could surely do away with that which We revealed to you. Then you would not find for yourself concerning it an advocate against Us. (86) Except [We have left it with you] as a mercy from your Lord. Indeed, His favor upon you has ever been great. (87) Say, "If mankind and the jinn gathered in order to produce the like of this Qur'an, they could not produce the like of it, even if they were to each other assistants." (88) And We have certainly diversified for the people in this Qur'an from every [kind] of example, but most of the people refused [anything] except disbelief. (89)

## Quran 17:100

قُل لَّوْ أَنتُمْ تَمْلِكُونَ خَزَآئِنَ رَحْمَةِ رَبِّىٓ إِذًا لَّأَمْسَكْتُمْ خَشْيَةَ ٱلْإِنفَاقِۚ وَكَانَ ٱلْإِنسَٰنُ قَتُورًا (١٠٠)

Say [to them], "If you possessed the depositories of the mercy of my Lord, then you would withhold out of fear of spending." And ever has man been stingy. (100)

## Quran 17:110

قُلِ ٱدْعُواْ ٱللَّهَ أَوِ ٱدْعُواْ ٱلرَّحْمَٰنَۖ أَيًّا مَّا تَدْعُواْ فَلَهُ ٱلْأَسْمَآءُ ٱلْحُسْنَىٰۚ وَلَا تَجْهَرْ بِصَلَاتِكَ وَلَا تُخَافِتْ بِهَا وَٱبْتَغِ بَيْنَ ذَٰلِكَ سَبِيلًا (١١٠)

Say, "Call upon Allah or call upon the Most Merciful. Whichever [name] you call - to Him belong the best names." And do not recite [too] loudly in your prayer or [too] quietly but seek between that an [intermediate] way. (110)

## Quran 18:1-3

ٱلْحَمْدُ لِلَّهِ ٱلَّذِىٓ أَنزَلَ عَلَىٰ عَبْدِهِ ٱلْكِتَٰبَ وَلَمْ يَجْعَل لَّهُۥ عِوَجَا ۜ (١) قَيِّمًا لِّيُنذِرَ بَأْسًا شَدِيدًا مِّن لَّدُنْهُ وَيُبَشِّرَ ٱلْمُؤْمِنِينَ ٱلَّذِينَ يَعْمَلُونَ ٱلصَّٰلِحَٰتِ أَنَّ لَهُمْ أَجْرًا حَسَنًا (٢) مَّٰكِثِينَ فِيهِ أَبَدًا (٣)

[All] praise is [due] to Allah, who has sent down upon His Servant the Book and has not made therein any deviance. (1) [He has made it] straight, to warn of severe punishment from Him and to give good tidings to the believers who do righteous deeds that they will have a good reward (2) In which they will remain forever (3)

## Quran 18:10

إِذْ أَوَى ٱلْفِتْيَةُ إِلَى ٱلْكَهْفِ فَقَالُوا۟ رَبَّنَآ ءَاتِنَا مِن لَّدُنكَ رَحْمَةً وَهَيِّئْ لَنَا مِنْ أَمْرِنَا رَشَدًا (١٠)

[Mention] when the youths retreated to the cave and said, "Our Lord, grant us from Yourself mercy and prepare for us from our affair right guidance." (10)

## Quran 18:56-58

وَمَا نُرْسِلُ ٱلْمُرْسَلِينَ إِلَّا مُبَشِّرِينَ وَمُنذِرِينَ ۚ وَيُجَٰدِلُ ٱلَّذِينَ كَفَرُوا۟ بِٱلْبَٰطِلِ لِيُدْحِضُوا۟ بِهِ ٱلْحَقَّ ۖ وَٱتَّخَذُوٓا۟ ءَايَٰتِى وَمَآ أُنذِرُوا۟ هُزُوًا (٥٦) وَمَنْ أَظْلَمُ مِمَّن ذُكِّرَ بِـَٔايَٰتِ رَبِّهِۦ فَأَعْرَضَ عَنْهَا وَنَسِىَ مَا قَدَّمَتْ يَدَاهُ ۚ إِنَّا جَعَلْنَا عَلَىٰ قُلُوبِهِمْ أَكِنَّةً أَن يَفْقَهُوهُ وَفِىٓ ءَاذَانِهِمْ وَقْرًا ۖ وَإِن تَدْعُهُمْ إِلَى ٱلْهُدَىٰ فَلَن يَهْتَدُوٓا۟ إِذًا أَبَدًا (٥٧) وَرَبُّكَ ٱلْغَفُورُ ذُو ٱلرَّحْمَةِ ۖ لَوْ يُؤَاخِذُهُم بِمَا كَسَبُوا۟ لَعَجَّلَ لَهُمُ ٱلْعَذَابَ ۚ بَل لَّهُم مَّوْعِدٌ لَّن يَجِدُوا۟ مِن دُونِهِۦ مَوْئِلًا (٥٨)

And We send not the messengers except as bringers of good tidings and warners. And those who disbelieve dispute by [using] falsehood to [attempt to] invalidate thereby the truth and have taken My verses, and that of which they are warned, in ridicule. (56) And who is more unjust than one who is reminded of the verses of his Lord but turns away from them and forgets what his hands have put forth? Indeed, We have placed over their hearts coverings, lest they understand it, and in their ears deafness. And if you invite them to guidance - they will never be guided, then - ever. (57) And your Lord is the Forgiving, full of mercy. If He were to impose blame upon them for what they earned, He would have hastened for them the punishment. Rather, for them is an appointment from which they will never find an escape. (58)

## Quran 18:98

قَالَ هَٰذَا رَحْمَةٌ مِّن رَّبِّى ۖ فَإِذَا جَاءَ وَعْدُ رَبِّى جَعَلَهُۥ دَكَّاءَ ۖ وَكَانَ وَعْدُ رَبِّى حَقًّا (٩٨)

[Dhul-Qarnayn] said, "This is a mercy from my Lord; but when the promise of my Lord comes, He will make it level, and ever is the promise of my Lord true." (98)

## Quran 19:16-36

وَاذْكُرْ فِى ٱلْكِتَٰبِ مَرْيَمَ إِذِ ٱنتَبَذَتْ مِنْ أَهْلِهَا مَكَانًا شَرْقِيًّا (١٦) فَٱتَّخَذَتْ مِن دُونِهِمْ حِجَابًا فَأَرْسَلْنَآ إِلَيْهَا رُوحَنَا فَتَمَثَّلَ لَهَا بَشَرًا سَوِيًّا (١٧) قَالَتْ إِنِّىٓ أَعُوذُ بِٱلرَّحْمَٰنِ مِنكَ إِن كُنتَ تَقِيًّا (١٨) قَالَ إِنَّمَآ أَنَا۠ رَسُولُ رَبِّكِ لِأَهَبَ لَكِ غُلَٰمًا زَكِيًّا (١٩) قَالَتْ أَنَّىٰ يَكُونُ لِى غُلَٰمٌ وَلَمْ يَمْسَسْنِى بَشَرٌ وَلَمْ أَكُ بَغِيًّا (٢٠) قَالَ كَذَٰلِكِ قَالَ رَبُّكِ هُوَ عَلَىَّ هَيِّنٌ ۖ وَلِنَجْعَلَهُۥٓ ءَايَةً لِّلنَّاسِ وَرَحْمَةً مِّنَّا ۚ وَكَانَ أَمْرًا مَّقْضِيًّا (٢١) ۞ فَحَمَلَتْهُ فَٱنتَبَذَتْ بِهِۦ مَكَانًا قَصِيًّا (٢٢) فَأَجَآءَهَا ٱلْمَخَاضُ إِلَىٰ جِذْعِ ٱلنَّخْلَةِ قَالَتْ يَٰلَيْتَنِى مِتُّ قَبْلَ هَٰذَا وَكُنتُ نَسْيًا مَّنسِيًّا (٢٣) فَنَادَىٰهَا مِن تَحْتِهَآ أَلَّا تَحْزَنِى قَدْ جَعَلَ رَبُّكِ تَحْتَكِ سَرِيًّا (٢٤) وَهُزِّىٓ إِلَيْكِ بِجِذْعِ ٱلنَّخْلَةِ تُسَٰقِطْ عَلَيْكِ رُطَبًا جَنِيًّا (٢٥) فَكُلِى وَٱشْرَبِى وَقَرِّى عَيْنًا ۖ فَإِمَّا تَرَيِنَّ مِنَ ٱلْبَشَرِ أَحَدًا فَقُولِىٓ إِنِّى نَذَرْتُ لِلرَّحْمَٰنِ

صَوْمًا فَلَنْ أُكَلِّمَ ٱلْيَوْمَ إِنسِيًّا (٢٦) فَأَتَتْ بِهِ قَوْمَهَا تَحْمِلُهُ ۖ قَالُوا۟ يَٰمَرْيَمُ لَقَدْ جِئْتِ شَيْئًا فَرِيًّا (٢٧) يَٰٓأُخْتَ هَٰرُونَ مَا كَانَ أَبُوكِ ٱمْرَأَ سَوْءٍ وَمَا كَانَتْ أُمُّكِ بَغِيًّا (٢٨) فَأَشَارَتْ إِلَيْهِ ۖ قَالُوا۟ كَيْفَ نُكَلِّمُ مَن كَانَ فِى ٱلْمَهْدِ صَبِيًّا (٢٩) قَالَ إِنِّى عَبْدُ ٱللَّهِ ءَاتَىٰنِىَ ٱلْكِتَٰبَ وَجَعَلَنِى نَبِيًّا (٣٠) وَجَعَلَنِى مُبَارَكًا أَيْنَ مَا كُنتُ وَأَوْصَٰنِى بِٱلصَّلَوٰةِ وَٱلزَّكَوٰةِ مَا دُمْتُ حَيًّا (٣١) وَبَرًّۢا بِوَٰلِدَتِى وَلَمْ يَجْعَلْنِى جَبَّارًا شَقِيًّا (٣٢) وَٱلسَّلَٰمُ عَلَىَّ يَوْمَ وُلِدتُّ وَيَوْمَ أَمُوتُ وَيَوْمَ أُبْعَثُ حَيًّا (٣٣) ذَٰلِكَ عِيسَى ٱبْنُ مَرْيَمَ ۚ قَوْلَ ٱلْحَقِّ ٱلَّذِى فِيهِ يَمْتَرُونَ (٣٤) مَا كَانَ لِلَّهِ أَن يَتَّخِذَ مِن وَلَدٍ ۖ سُبْحَٰنَهُۥٓ ۚ إِذَا قَضَىٰٓ أَمْرًا فَإِنَّمَا يَقُولُ لَهُۥ كُن فَيَكُونُ (٣٥) وَإِنَّ ٱللَّهَ رَبِّى وَرَبُّكُمْ فَٱعْبُدُوهُ ۚ هَٰذَا صِرَٰطٌ مُّسْتَقِيمٌ (٣٦)

And mention, [O Muhammad], in the Book [the story of] Mary, when she withdrew from her family to a place toward the east. (16) And she took, in seclusion from them, a screen. Then We sent to her Our Angel, and he represented himself to her as a well-proportioned man. (17) She said, "Indeed, I seek refuge in the Most Merciful from you, [so leave me], if you should be fearing of Allah." (18) He said, "I am only the messenger of your Lord to give you [news of] a pure boy." (19) She said, "How can I have a boy while no man has touched me and I have not been unchaste?" (20) He said, "Thus [it will be]; your Lord says, 'It is easy for Me, and We will make him a sign to the people and a mercy from Us. And it is a matter [already] decreed.' " (21) So she conceived him, and she withdrew with him to a remote place. (22) And the pains of childbirth drove her to the trunk of a palm tree. She said, "Oh, I wish I had died before this and was in oblivion, forgotten." (23) But he called her from below her, "Do not grieve; your Lord has provided beneath you a stream. (24) And shake toward you the trunk of the palm tree; it will drop upon you ripe, fresh dates. (25) So eat and drink and be contented. And if you see from among humanity anyone, say, 'Indeed, I have vowed to the Most Merciful abstention, so I will not speak today to [any] man.' " (26) Then she brought him to her people, carrying him. They said, "O Mary, you have certainly done a thing unprecedented. (27) O sister of Aaron, your father was not a man of evil, nor was your mother unchaste." (28) So she pointed to him. They said, "How can we speak to one who is in the cradle a child?" (29) [Jesus] said, "Indeed, I am the servant of Allah. He has given me the Scripture and made me a prophet. (30) And He has made me blessed wherever I am and has enjoined upon me prayer and zakah as long as I remain alive (31) And [made me] dutiful to my mother, and He has not made me a wretched tyrant. (32) And peace is on me the day I was born and the day I will die and the day I am raised alive." (33) That is Jesus, the son of Mary - the word of truth about which they are in dispute. (34) It is not [befitting] for Allah to take a son; exalted is He! When He decrees an affair, He only says to it, "Be," and it is. (35) [Jesus said], "And indeed, Allah is my Lord and your Lord, so worship Him. That is a straight path." (36)

## Quran 19:41-54

وَاذْكُرْ فِى ٱلْكِتَٰبِ إِبْرَٰهِيمَ ۚ إِنَّهُۥ كَانَ صِدِّيقًا نَّبِيًّا (٤١) إِذْ قَالَ لِأَبِيهِ يَٰٓأَبَتِ لِمَ تَعْبُدُ مَا لَا يَسْمَعُ وَلَا يُبْصِرُ وَلَا يُغْنِى عَنكَ شَيْـًٔا (٤٢) يَٰٓأَبَتِ إِنِّى قَدْ جَآءَنِى مِنَ ٱلْعِلْمِ مَا لَمْ يَأْتِكَ فَٱتَّبِعْنِىٓ أَهْدِكَ صِرَٰطًا سَوِيًّا (٤٣) يَٰٓأَبَتِ لَا تَعْبُدِ ٱلشَّيْطَٰنَ ۖ إِنَّ ٱلشَّيْطَٰنَ كَانَ لِلرَّحْمَٰنِ عَصِيًّا (٤٤) يَٰٓأَبَتِ إِنِّىٓ أَخَافُ أَن يَمَسَّكَ

عَذَابٌ مِّنَ ٱلرَّحْمَٰنِ فَتَكُونَ لِلشَّيْطَٰنِ وَلِيًّا (٤٥) قَالَ أَرَاغِبٌ أَنتَ عَنْ ءَالِهَتِى يَٰٓإِبْرَٰهِيمُ ۖ لَئِن لَّمْ تَنتَهِ لَأَرْجُمَنَّكَ ۖ وَٱهْجُرْنِى مَلِيًّا (٤٦) قَالَ سَلَٰمٌ عَلَيْكَ ۖ سَأَسْتَغْفِرُ لَكَ رَبِّىٓ ۖ إِنَّهُۥ كَانَ بِى حَفِيًّا (٤٧) وَأَعْتَزِلُكُمْ وَمَا تَدْعُونَ مِن دُونِ ٱللَّهِ وَأَدْعُواْ رَبِّى عَسَىٰٓ أَلَّآ أَكُونَ بِدُعَآءِ رَبِّى شَقِيًّا (٤٨) فَلَمَّا ٱعْتَزَلَهُمْ وَمَا يَعْبُدُونَ مِن دُونِ ٱللَّهِ وَهَبْنَا لَهُۥٓ إِسْحَٰقَ وَيَعْقُوبَ ۖ وَكُلًّا جَعَلْنَا نَبِيًّا (٤٩) وَوَهَبْنَا لَهُم مِّن رَّحْمَتِنَا وَجَعَلْنَا لَهُمْ لِسَانَ صِدْقٍ عَلِيًّا (٥٠) وَٱذْكُرْ فِى ٱلْكِتَٰبِ مُوسَىٰٓ ۚ إِنَّهُۥ كَانَ مُخْلَصًا وَكَانَ رَسُولًا نَّبِيًّا (٥١) وَنَٰدَيْنَٰهُ مِن جَانِبِ ٱلطُّورِ ٱلْأَيْمَنِ وَقَرَّبْنَٰهُ نَجِيًّا (٥٢) وَوَهَبْنَا لَهُۥ مِن رَّحْمَتِنَآ أَخَاهُ هَٰرُونَ نَبِيًّا (٥٣) وَٱذْكُرْ فِى ٱلْكِتَٰبِ إِسْمَٰعِيلَ ۚ إِنَّهُۥ كَانَ صَادِقَ ٱلْوَعْدِ وَكَانَ رَسُولًا نَّبِيًّا (٥٤)

And mention in the Book [the story of] Abraham. Indeed, he was a man of truth and a prophet. (41) [Mention] when he said to his father, "O my father, why do you worship that which does not hear and does not see and will not benefit you at all? (42) O my father, indeed there has come to me of knowledge that which has not come to you, so follow me; I will guide you to an even path. (43) O my father, do not worship Satan. Indeed Satan has ever been, to the Most Merciful, disobedient. (44) O my father, indeed I fear that there will touch you a punishment from the Most Merciful so you would be to Satan a companion [in Hellfire]." (45) [His father] said, "Have you no desire for my gods, O Abraham? If you do not desist, I will surely stone you, so avoid me a prolonged time." (46) [Abraham] said, "Peace will be upon you. I will ask forgiveness for you of my Lord. Indeed, He is ever gracious to me. (47) And I will leave you and those you invoke other than Allah and will invoke my Lord. I expect that I will not be in invocation to my Lord unhappy." (48) So when he had left them and those they worshipped other than Allah, We gave him Isaac and Jacob, and each [of them] We made a prophet. (49) And We gave them of Our mercy, and we made for them a reputation of high honor. (50) And mention in the Book, Moses. Indeed, he was chosen, and he was a messenger and a prophet. (51) And We called him from the side of the mount at [his] right and brought him near, confiding [to him]. (52) And We gave him out of Our mercy his brother Aaron as a prophet. (53) And mention in the Book, Ishmael. Indeed, he was true to his promise, and he was a messenger and a prophet. (54)

## Quran 19:58-65

أُو۟لَٰٓئِكَ ٱلَّذِينَ أَنْعَمَ ٱللَّهُ عَلَيْهِم مِّنَ ٱلنَّبِيِّـۧنَ مِن ذُرِّيَّةِ ءَادَمَ وَمِمَّنْ حَمَلْنَا مَعَ نُوحٍ وَمِن ذُرِّيَّةِ إِبْرَٰهِيمَ وَإِسْرَٰٓءِيلَ وَمِمَّنْ هَدَيْنَا وَٱجْتَبَيْنَآ إِذَا تُتْلَىٰ عَلَيْهِمْ ءَايَٰتُ ٱلرَّحْمَٰنِ خَرُّوا۟ سُجَّدًا وَبُكِيًّا ۩ (٥٨) ۞ فَخَلَفَ مِنۢ بَعْدِهِمْ خَلْفٌ أَضَاعُوا۟ ٱلصَّلَوٰةَ وَٱتَّبَعُوا۟ ٱلشَّهَوَٰتِ فَسَوْفَ يَلْقَوْنَ غَيًّا (٥٩) إِلَّا مَن تَابَ وَءَامَنَ وَعَمِلَ صَٰلِحًا فَأُو۟لَٰٓئِكَ يَدْخُلُونَ ٱلْجَنَّةَ وَلَا يُظْلَمُونَ شَيْـًٔا (٦٠) جَنَّٰتِ عَدْنٍ ٱلَّتِى وَعَدَ ٱلرَّحْمَٰنُ عِبَادَهُۥ بِٱلْغَيْبِ إِنَّهُۥ كَانَ وَعْدُهُۥ مَأْتِيًّا (٦١) لَّا يَسْمَعُونَ فِيهَا لَغْوًا إِلَّا سَلَٰمًا وَلَهُمْ رِزْقُهُمْ فِيهَا بُكْرَةً وَعَشِيًّا (٦٢) تِلْكَ ٱلْجَنَّةُ ٱلَّتِى نُورِثُ مِنْ عِبَادِنَا مَن كَانَ تَقِيًّا (٦٣) وَمَا نَتَنَزَّلُ إِلَّا بِأَمْرِ رَبِّكَ لَهُۥ مَا بَيْنَ أَيْدِينَا وَمَا خَلْفَنَا وَمَا بَيْنَ ذَٰلِكَ وَمَا كَانَ رَبُّكَ نَسِيًّا (٦٤) رَّبُّ ٱلسَّمَٰوَٰتِ وَٱلْأَرْضِ وَمَا بَيْنَهُمَا فَٱعْبُدْهُ وَٱصْطَبِرْ لِعِبَٰدَتِهِۦ هَلْ تَعْلَمُ لَهُۥ سَمِيًّا (٦٥)

Those were the ones upon whom Allah bestowed favor from among the prophets of the descendants of Adam and of those We carried [in the ship] with Noah, and of the descendants of Abraham and Israel, and of those whom We guided and chose. When the verses of the Most

Merciful were recited to them, they fell in prostration and weeping. (58) But there came after them successors who neglected prayer and pursued desires; so they are going to meet evil - (59) Except those who repent, believe and do righteousness; for those will enter Paradise and will not be wronged at all. (60) [Therein are] gardens of perpetual residence which the Most Merciful has promised His servants in the unseen. Indeed, His promise has ever been coming. (61) They will not hear therein any ill speech - only [greetings of] peace - and they will have their provision therein, morning and afternoon. (62) That is Paradise, which We give as inheritance to those of Our servants who were fearing of Allah. (63) [Gabriel said], "And we [angels] descend not except by the order of your Lord. To Him belongs that before us and that behind us and what is in between. And never is your Lord forgetful - (64) Lord of the heavens and the earth and whatever is between them - so worship Him and have patience for His worship. Do you know of any similarity to Him?" (65)

## Quran 19:75

قُلْ مَن كَانَ فِى ٱلضَّلَـٰلَةِ فَلْيَمْدُدْ لَهُ ٱلرَّحْمَـٰنُ مَدًّا حَتَّىٰٓ إِذَا رَأَوْاْ مَا يُوعَدُونَ إِمَّا ٱلْعَذَابَ وَإِمَّا ٱلسَّاعَةَ فَسَيَعْلَمُونَ مَنْ هُوَ شَرٌّ مَّكَانًا وَأَضْعَفُ جُندًا (٧٥)

Say, "Whoever is in error - let the Most Merciful extend for him an extension [in wealth and time] until, when they see that which they were promised - either punishment [in this world] or the Hour [of resurrection]

- they will come to know who is worst in position and weaker in soldiers." (75)

## Quran 19:78

أَطَّلَعَ ٱلْغَيْبَ أَمِ ٱتَّخَذَ عِندَ ٱلرَّحْمَٰنِ عَهْدًا (٧٨)

Has he looked into the unseen, or has he taken from the Most Merciful a promise? (78)

## Quran 19:85-97

يَوْمَ نَحْشُرُ ٱلْمُتَّقِينَ إِلَى ٱلرَّحْمَٰنِ وَفْدًا (٨٥) وَنَسُوقُ ٱلْمُجْرِمِينَ إِلَىٰ جَهَنَّمَ وِرْدًا (٨٦) لَّا يَمْلِكُونَ ٱلشَّفَٰعَةَ إِلَّا مَنِ ٱتَّخَذَ عِندَ ٱلرَّحْمَٰنِ عَهْدًا (٨٧) وَقَالُوا۟ ٱتَّخَذَ ٱلرَّحْمَٰنُ وَلَدًا (٨٨) لَّقَدْ جِئْتُمْ شَيْـًٔا إِدًّا (٨٩) تَكَادُ ٱلسَّمَٰوَٰتُ يَتَفَطَّرْنَ مِنْهُ وَتَنشَقُّ ٱلْأَرْضُ وَتَخِرُّ ٱلْجِبَالُ هَدًّا (٩٠) أَن دَعَوْا۟ لِلرَّحْمَٰنِ وَلَدًا (٩١) وَمَا يَنۢبَغِى لِلرَّحْمَٰنِ أَن يَتَّخِذَ وَلَدًا (٩٢) إِن كُلُّ مَن فِى ٱلسَّمَٰوَٰتِ وَٱلْأَرْضِ إِلَّآ ءَاتِى ٱلرَّحْمَٰنِ عَبْدًا (٩٣) لَّقَدْ أَحْصَىٰهُمْ وَعَدَّهُمْ عَدًّا (٩٤) وَكُلُّهُمْ ءَاتِيهِ يَوْمَ ٱلْقِيَٰمَةِ فَرْدًا (٩٥) إِنَّ ٱلَّذِينَ ءَامَنُوا۟ وَعَمِلُوا۟ ٱلصَّٰلِحَٰتِ سَيَجْعَلُ لَهُمُ ٱلرَّحْمَٰنُ وُدًّا (٩٦) فَإِنَّمَا يَسَّرْنَٰهُ بِلِسَانِكَ لِتُبَشِّرَ بِهِ ٱلْمُتَّقِينَ وَتُنذِرَ بِهِۦ قَوْمًا لُّدًّا (٩٧)

On the Day We will gather the righteous to the Most Merciful as a delegation (85) And will drive the criminals to Hell in thirst (86) None will have [power of] intercession except he who had taken from the Most Merciful a covenant. (87) And they say, "The Most Merciful has taken [for Himself] a son." (88) You have done an atrocious thing. (89) The heavens almost rupture therefrom and the earth splits open and the mountains collapse in devastation (90) That they attribute to the Most Merciful a son. (91) And it is not appropriate for the Most Merciful that He should take a son. (92) There is no one in the heavens and earth but that he comes to the Most Merciful as a servant. (93) He has enumerated them and counted them a [full] counting. (94) And all of them are coming to Him on the Day of Resurrection alone. (95) Indeed, those who have believed and done righteous deeds - the Most Merciful will appoint for them affection. (96) So, [O Muhammad], We have only made Qur'an easy in the Arabic language that you may give good tidings thereby to the righteous and warn thereby a hostile people. (97)

## Quran 20:2-8

مَا أَنزَلْنَا عَلَيْكَ ٱلْقُرْءَانَ لِتَشْقَىٰ (٢) إِلَّا تَذْكِرَةً لِّمَن يَخْشَىٰ (٣) تَنزِيلًا مِّمَّنْ خَلَقَ ٱلْأَرْضَ وَٱلسَّمَٰوَٰتِ ٱلْعُلَى (٤) ٱلرَّحْمَٰنُ عَلَى ٱلْعَرْشِ ٱسْتَوَىٰ (٥) لَهُۥ مَا فِى ٱلسَّمَٰوَٰتِ وَمَا فِى ٱلْأَرْضِ وَمَا بَيْنَهُمَا وَمَا تَحْتَ ٱلثَّرَىٰ (٦) وَإِن تَجْهَرْ بِٱلْقَوْلِ فَإِنَّهُۥ يَعْلَمُ ٱلسِّرَّ وَأَخْفَىٰ (٧) ٱللَّهُ لَا إِلَٰهَ إِلَّا هُوَ ۖ لَهُ ٱلْأَسْمَآءُ ٱلْحُسْنَىٰ (٨)

We have not sent down to you the Qur'an that you be distressed (2) But only as a reminder for those who fear [Allah] - (3) A revelation from He who created the earth and highest heavens, (4) The Most Merciful [who is] above the Throne established. (5) To Him belongs what is in the heavens and what is on the earth and what is between them and what is under the soil. (6) And if you speak aloud - then indeed, He knows the secret and what is [even] more hidden. (7) Allah - there is no deity except Him. To Him belong the best names. (8)

## Quran 20:82

وَإِنِّى لَغَفَّارٌ لِّمَن تَابَ وَءَامَنَ وَعَمِلَ صَٰلِحًا ثُمَّ ٱهْتَدَىٰ (٨٢)

But indeed, I am the Perpetual Forgiver of whoever repents and believes and does righteousness and then continues in guidance. (82)

## Quran 20:108-123

يَوْمَئِذٍ يَتَّبِعُونَ ٱلدَّاعِىَ لَا عِوَجَ لَهُۥ ۖ وَخَشَعَتِ ٱلْأَصْوَاتُ لِلرَّحْمَٰنِ فَلَا تَسْمَعُ إِلَّا هَمْسًا (١٠٨) يَوْمَئِذٍ لَّا تَنفَعُ ٱلشَّفَٰعَةُ إِلَّا مَنْ أَذِنَ لَهُ ٱلرَّحْمَٰنُ وَرَضِىَ لَهُۥ قَوْلًا (١٠٩) يَعْلَمُ مَا بَيْنَ أَيْدِيهِمْ وَمَا خَلْفَهُمْ وَلَا يُحِيطُونَ بِهِۦ عِلْمًا (١١٠) ۞ وَعَنَتِ ٱلْوُجُوهُ لِلْحَىِّ ٱلْقَيُّومِ ۖ وَقَدْ خَابَ مَنْ حَمَلَ ظُلْمًا (١١١) وَمَن يَعْمَلْ مِنَ ٱلصَّٰلِحَٰتِ وَهُوَ مُؤْمِنٌ فَلَا يَخَافُ ظُلْمًا وَلَا هَضْمًا (١١٢) وَكَذَٰلِكَ أَنزَلْنَٰهُ قُرْءَانًا عَرَبِيًّا وَصَرَّفْنَا فِيهِ مِنَ ٱلْوَعِيدِ لَعَلَّهُمْ يَتَّقُونَ أَوْ يُحْدِثُ لَهُمْ ذِكْرًا (١١٣) فَتَعَٰلَى ٱللَّهُ ٱلْمَلِكُ ٱلْحَقُّ ۗ وَلَا تَعْجَلْ بِٱلْقُرْءَانِ مِن قَبْلِ أَن يُقْضَىٰ إِلَيْكَ وَحْيُهُۥ ۖ وَقُل رَّبِّ زِدْنِى عِلْمًا (١١٤) وَلَقَدْ عَهِدْنَآ إِلَىٰٓ ءَادَمَ مِن قَبْلُ فَنَسِىَ وَلَمْ نَجِدْ لَهُۥ عَزْمًا (١١٥) وَإِذْ قُلْنَا لِلْمَلَٰٓئِكَةِ ٱسْجُدُوا۟ لِـَٔادَمَ فَسَجَدُوٓا۟ إِلَّآ إِبْلِيسَ أَبَىٰ (١١٦) فَقُلْنَا يَٰٓـَٔادَمُ إِنَّ هَٰذَا عَدُوٌّ لَّكَ وَلِزَوْجِكَ فَلَا يُخْرِجَنَّكُمَا مِنَ ٱلْجَنَّةِ فَتَشْقَىٰٓ (١١٧) إِنَّ لَكَ أَلَّا تَجُوعَ فِيهَا وَلَا تَعْرَىٰ (١١٨) وَأَنَّكَ لَا تَظْمَؤُا۟ فِيهَا وَلَا تَضْحَىٰ (١١٩) فَوَسْوَسَ إِلَيْهِ ٱلشَّيْطَٰنُ قَالَ يَٰٓـَٔادَمُ هَلْ أَدُلُّكَ عَلَىٰ شَجَرَةِ ٱلْخُلْدِ وَمُلْكٍ لَّا يَبْلَىٰ (١٢٠) فَأَكَلَا مِنْهَا فَبَدَتْ لَهُمَا سَوْءَٰتُهُمَا وَطَفِقَا يَخْصِفَانِ عَلَيْهِمَا مِن وَرَقِ ٱلْجَنَّةِ ۚ وَعَصَىٰٓ ءَادَمُ رَبَّهُۥ فَغَوَىٰ (١٢١) ثُمَّ ٱجْتَبَٰهُ رَبُّهُۥ فَتَابَ عَلَيْهِ وَهَدَىٰ (١٢٢) قَالَ ٱهْبِطَا مِنْهَا جَمِيعًۢا ۖ بَعْضُكُمْ لِبَعْضٍ عَدُوٌّ ۖ فَإِمَّا يَأْتِيَنَّكُم مِّنِّى هُدًى فَمَنِ ٱتَّبَعَ هُدَاىَ فَلَا يَضِلُّ وَلَا يَشْقَىٰ (١٢٣)

That Day, everyone will follow [the call of] the Caller [with] no deviation therefrom, and [all] voices will be stilled before the Most Merciful, so you will not hear except a whisper [of footsteps]. (108) That Day, no intercession will benefit except [that of] one to whom the Most Merciful has given permission and has accepted his word. (109) Allah knows what is [presently] before them and what will be after them, but they do not encompass it in knowledge. (110) And [all] faces will be humbled before the Ever-Living, the Sustainer of existence. And he will have failed who carries injustice. (111) But he who does of righteous deeds while he is a believer - he will neither fear injustice nor deprivation. (112) And thus We have sent it down as an Arabic Qur'an and have diversified therein the warnings that perhaps they will avoid [sin] or it would cause them remembrance. (113) So high [above all] is Allah, the Sovereign, the Truth. And, [O Muhammad], do not hasten with [recitation of] the Qur'an before its revelation is completed to you, and say, "My Lord, increase me in knowledge." (114) And We had already taken a promise from Adam before, but he forgot; and We found not in him determination. (115) And [mention] when We said to the angels, "Prostrate to Adam," and they prostrated, except Iblees; he refused. (116) So We said, "O Adam, indeed this is an enemy to you and to your wife. Then let him not remove you from Paradise so you would suffer. (117) Indeed, it is [promised] for you not to be hungry therein or be unclothed. (118) And indeed, you will not be thirsty therein or be hot from the sun." (119) Then Satan whispered to him; he said, "O Adam, shall I direct you to the tree of eternity and possession that will not deteriorate?" (120) And Adam and his wife ate of it, and their private parts became apparent to them, and they began to fasten over themselves from the leaves of

Paradise. And Adam disobeyed his Lord and erred. (121) Then his Lord chose him and turned to him in forgiveness and guided [him]. (122) [Allah] said, "Descend from Paradise - all, [your descendants] being enemies to one another. And if there should come to you guidance from Me - then whoever follows My guidance will neither go astray [in the world] nor suffer [in the Hereafter]. (123)

## Quran 21:42

قُلْ مَن يَكْلَؤُكُم بِٱلَّيْلِ وَٱلنَّهَارِ مِنَ ٱلرَّحْمَـٰنِ ۗ بَلْ هُمْ عَن ذِكْرِ رَبِّهِم مُّعْرِضُونَ (٤٢)

Say, "Who can protect you at night or by day from the Most Merciful?" But they are, from the remembrance of their Lord, turning away. (42)

## Quran 21:83-90

۞ وَأَيُّوبَ إِذْ نَادَىٰ رَبَّهُۥٓ أَنِّى مَسَّنِىَ ٱلضُّرُّ وَأَنتَ أَرْحَمُ ٱلرَّٰحِمِينَ (٨٣) فَٱسْتَجَبْنَا لَهُۥ فَكَشَفْنَا مَا بِهِۦ مِن ضُرٍّ ۖ وَءَاتَيْنَـٰهُ أَهْلَهُۥ وَمِثْلَهُم مَّعَهُمْ رَحْمَةً مِّنْ عِندِنَا وَذِكْرَىٰ لِلْعَـٰبِدِينَ (٨٤) وَإِسْمَـٰعِيلَ وَإِدْرِيسَ وَذَا ٱلْكِفْلِ ۖ كُلٌّ مِّنَ ٱلصَّـٰبِرِينَ (٨٥) وَأَدْخَلْنَـٰهُمْ فِى رَحْمَتِنَآ ۖ إِنَّهُم مِّنَ ٱلصَّـٰلِحِينَ (٨٦) وَذَا ٱلنُّونِ إِذ ذَّهَبَ مُغَـٰضِبًا فَظَنَّ أَن لَّن نَّقْدِرَ عَلَيْهِ فَنَادَىٰ فِى ٱلظُّلُمَـٰتِ أَن لَّآ إِلَـٰهَ إِلَّآ أَنتَ سُبْحَـٰنَكَ إِنِّى كُنتُ مِنَ ٱلظَّـٰلِمِينَ (٨٧) فَٱسْتَجَبْنَا لَهُۥ وَنَجَّيْنَـٰهُ مِنَ ٱلْغَمِّ ۚ وَكَذَٰلِكَ نُـۨجِى ٱلْمُؤْمِنِينَ (٨٨) وَزَكَرِيَّآ إِذْ نَادَىٰ رَبَّهُۥ رَبِّ لَا تَذَرْنِى فَرْدًا وَأَنتَ خَيْرُ ٱلْوَٰرِثِينَ (٨٩) فَٱسْتَجَبْنَا لَهُۥ وَوَهَبْنَا لَهُۥ يَحْيَىٰ وَأَصْلَحْنَا لَهُۥ زَوْجَهُۥٓ ۚ إِنَّهُمْ كَانُوا۟ يُسَـٰرِعُونَ فِى ٱلْخَيْرَٰتِ وَيَدْعُونَنَا رَغَبًا وَرَهَبًا ۖ وَكَانُوا۟ لَنَا خَـٰشِعِينَ (٩٠)

And [mention] Job, when he called to his Lord, "Indeed, adversity has touched me, and you are the Most Merciful of the merciful." (83) So We responded to him and removed what afflicted him of adversity. And We gave him [back] his family and the like thereof with them as mercy from Us and a reminder for the worshippers [of Allah]. (84) And [mention] Ishmael and Idrees and Dhul-Kifl; all were of the patient. (85) And We admitted them into Our mercy. Indeed, they were of the righteous. (86) And [mention] the man of the fish, when he went off in anger and thought that We would not decree [anything] upon him. And he called out within the darknesses, "There is no deity except You; exalted are You. Indeed, I have been of the wrongdoers." (87) So We responded to him and saved him from the distress. And thus do We save the believers. (88) And [mention] Zechariah, when he called to his Lord, "My Lord, do not leave me alone [with no heir], while you are the best of inheritors." (89) So We responded to him, and We gave to him John, and amended for him his wife. Indeed, they used to hasten to good deeds and supplicate Us in hope and fear, and they were to Us humbly submissive. (90)

## Quran 21:106-108

إِنَّ فِى هَٰذَا لَبَلَٰغًا لِّقَوْمٍ عَٰبِدِينَ (١٠٦) وَمَآ أَرْسَلْنَٰكَ إِلَّا رَحْمَةً لِّلْعَٰلَمِينَ (١٠٧) قُلْ إِنَّمَا يُوحَىٰ إِلَىَّ أَنَّمَآ إِلَٰهُكُمْ إِلَٰهٌ وَٰحِدٌ ۖ فَهَلْ أَنتُم مُّسْلِمُونَ (١٠٨)

Indeed, in this [Qur'an] is notification for a worshipping people. (106) And We have not sent you, [Muhammad], except as a mercy to the worlds. (107) Say, "It is only revealed to me that your god is but one God; so will you be Muslims [in submission to Him]?" (108)

## Quran 21:112

قَـٰلَ رَبِّ ٱحْكُم بِٱلْحَقِّ ۗ وَرَبُّنَا ٱلرَّحْمَـٰنُ ٱلْمُسْتَعَانُ عَلَىٰ مَا تَصِفُونَ (١١٢)

[The Prophet] has said, "My Lord, judge [between us] in truth. And our Lord is the Most Merciful, the one whose help is sought against that which you describe." (112)

## Quran 22:58-66

وَٱلَّذِينَ هَاجَرُوا۟ فِى سَبِيلِ ٱللَّهِ ثُمَّ قُتِلُوٓا۟ أَوْ مَاتُوا۟ لَيَرْزُقَنَّهُمُ ٱللَّهُ رِزْقًا حَسَنًا ۚ وَإِنَّ ٱللَّهَ لَهُوَ خَيْرُ ٱلرَّٰزِقِينَ (٥٨) لَيُدْخِلَنَّهُم مُّدْخَلًا يَرْضَوْنَهُۥ ۗ وَإِنَّ ٱللَّهَ لَعَلِيمٌ حَلِيمٌ (٥٩) ۞ ذَٰلِكَ وَمَنْ عَاقَبَ بِمِثْلِ مَا عُوقِبَ بِهِۦ ثُمَّ بُغِىَ عَلَيْهِ لَيَنصُرَنَّهُ ٱللَّهُ ۗ إِنَّ ٱللَّهَ لَعَفُوٌّ غَفُورٌ (٦٠) ذَٰلِكَ بِأَنَّ ٱللَّهَ يُولِجُ ٱلَّيْلَ فِى ٱلنَّهَارِ وَيُولِجُ ٱلنَّهَارَ فِى ٱلَّيْلِ وَأَنَّ ٱللَّهَ سَمِيعٌۢ بَصِيرٌ (٦١) ذَٰلِكَ بِأَنَّ ٱللَّهَ هُوَ ٱلْحَقُّ وَأَنَّ مَا يَدْعُونَ مِن دُونِهِۦ هُوَ ٱلْبَـٰطِلُ وَأَنَّ ٱللَّهَ هُوَ ٱلْعَلِىُّ ٱلْكَبِيرُ (٦٢) أَلَمْ تَرَ أَنَّ ٱللَّهَ أَنزَلَ مِنَ ٱلسَّمَآءِ مَآءً فَتُصْبِحُ ٱلْأَرْضُ مُخْضَرَّةً ۗ إِنَّ ٱللَّهَ لَطِيفٌ خَبِيرٌ (٦٣) لَّهُۥ مَا فِى ٱلسَّمَـٰوَٰتِ وَمَا فِى ٱلْأَرْضِ ۗ وَإِنَّ ٱللَّهَ لَهُوَ ٱلْغَنِىُّ ٱلْحَمِيدُ (٦٤) أَلَمْ تَرَ أَنَّ ٱللَّهَ سَخَّرَ لَكُم مَّا فِى ٱلْأَرْضِ وَٱلْفُلْكَ تَجْرِى فِى ٱلْبَحْرِ بِأَمْرِهِۦ وَيُمْسِكُ ٱلسَّمَآءَ أَن تَقَعَ عَلَى ٱلْأَرْضِ إِلَّا بِإِذْنِهِۦٓ ۗ إِنَّ ٱللَّهَ بِٱلنَّاسِ لَرَءُوفٌ رَّحِيمٌ (٦٥) وَهُوَ ٱلَّذِىٓ أَحْيَاكُمْ ثُمَّ يُمِيتُكُمْ ثُمَّ يُحْيِيكُمْ ۗ إِنَّ ٱلْإِنسَـٰنَ لَكَفُورٌ (٦٦)

And those who emigrated for the cause of Allah and then were killed or died - Allah will surely provide for them a good provision. And indeed, it is Allah who is the best of providers. (58) He will surely cause them to enter an entrance with which they will be pleased, and indeed, Allah is Knowing and Forbearing. (59) That [is so]. And whoever responds [to injustice] with the equivalent of that with which he was harmed and then is tyrannized - Allah will surely aid him. Indeed, Allah is Pardoning and Forgiving. (60) That is because Allah causes the night to enter the day and causes the day to enter the night and because Allah is Hearing and Seeing. (61) That is because Allah is the Truth, and that which they call upon other than Him is falsehood, and because Allah is the Most High, the Grand. (62) Do you not see that Allah has sent down rain from the sky and the earth becomes green? Indeed, Allah is Subtle and Acquainted. (63) To Him belongs what is in the heavens and what is on the earth. And indeed, Allah is the Free of need, the Praiseworthy. (64) Do you not see that Allah has subjected to you whatever is on the earth and the ships which run through the sea by His command? And He restrains the sky from falling upon the earth, unless by His permission. Indeed Allah, to the people, is Kind and Merciful. (65) And He is the one who gave you life; then He causes you to die and then will [again] give you life. Indeed, mankind is ungrateful. (66)

## Quran 23:109-111

إِنَّهُۥ كَانَ فَرِيقٌ مِّنْ عِبَادِى يَقُولُونَ رَبَّنَآ ءَامَنَّا فَٱغْفِرْ لَنَا وَٱرْحَمْنَا وَأَنتَ خَيْرُ ٱلرَّٰحِمِينَ (١٠٩) فَٱتَّخَذْتُمُوهُمْ سِخْرِيًّا حَتَّىٰٓ أَنسَوْكُمْ ذِكْرِى وَكُنتُم مِّنْهُمْ تَضْحَكُونَ (١١٠) إِنِّى جَزَيْتُهُمُ ٱلْيَوْمَ بِمَا صَبَرُوٓاْ أَنَّهُمْ هُمُ ٱلْفَآئِزُونَ (١١١)

Indeed, there was a party of My servants who said, 'Our Lord, we have believed, so forgive us and have mercy upon us, and You are the best of the merciful.' (109) But you took them in mockery to the point that they made you forget My remembrance, and you used to laugh at them. (110) Indeed, I have rewarded them this Day for their patient endurance - that they are the attainers [of success]." (111)

## Quran 23:118

وَقُل رَّبِّ ٱغْفِرْ وَٱرْحَمْ وَأَنتَ خَيْرُ ٱلرَّٰحِمِينَ (١١٨)

And say, "My Lord, forgive and have mercy, and You are the best of the merciful." (118)

## Quran 24:5

إِلَّا ٱلَّذِينَ تَابُوا۟ مِنۢ بَعْدِ ذَٰلِكَ وَأَصْلَحُوا۟ فَإِنَّ ٱللَّهَ غَفُورٌ رَّحِيمٌ (٥)

Except for those who repent thereafter and reform, for indeed, Allah is Forgiving and Merciful. (5)

## Quran 24:10

وَلَوْلَا فَضْلُ ٱللَّهِ عَلَيْكُمْ وَرَحْمَتُهُۥ وَأَنَّ ٱللَّهَ تَوَّابٌ حَكِيمٌ (١٠)

And if not for the favor of Allah upon you and His mercy... and because Allah is Accepting of repentance and Wise. (10)

## Quran 24:14

وَلَوْلَا فَضْلُ ٱللَّهِ عَلَيْكُمْ وَرَحْمَتُهُۥ فِى ٱلدُّنْيَا وَٱلْءَاخِرَةِ لَمَسَّكُمْ فِى مَآ أَفَضْتُمْ فِيهِ عَذَابٌ عَظِيمٌ (١٤)

And if it had not been for the favor of Allah upon you and His mercy in this world and the Hereafter, you would have been touched for that [lie] in which you were involved by a great punishment (14)

## Quran 24:20-22

وَلَوْلَا فَضْلُ اللَّهِ عَلَيْكُمْ وَرَحْمَتُهُ وَأَنَّ اللَّهَ رَءُوفٌ رَّحِيمٌ (٢٠) يَـٰٓأَيُّهَا ٱلَّذِينَ ءَامَنُوا۟ لَا تَتَّبِعُوا۟ خُطُوَٰتِ ٱلشَّيْطَـٰنِ وَمَن يَتَّبِعْ خُطُوَٰتِ ٱلشَّيْطَـٰنِ فَإِنَّهُۥ يَأْمُرُ بِٱلْفَحْشَآءِ وَٱلْمُنكَرِ ۚ وَلَوْلَا فَضْلُ ٱللَّهِ عَلَيْكُمْ وَرَحْمَتُهُۥ مَا زَكَىٰ مِنكُم مِّنْ أَحَدٍ أَبَدًا وَلَـٰكِنَّ ٱللَّهَ يُزَكِّى مَن يَشَآءُ ۗ وَٱللَّهُ سَمِيعٌ عَلِيمٌ (٢١) وَلَا يَأْتَلِ أُو۟لُوا۟ ٱلْفَضْلِ مِنكُمْ وَٱلسَّعَةِ أَن يُؤْتُوٓا۟ أُو۟لِى ٱلْقُرْبَىٰ وَٱلْمَسَـٰكِينَ وَٱلْمُهَـٰجِرِينَ فِى سَبِيلِ ٱللَّهِ ۖ وَلْيَعْفُوا۟ وَلْيَصْفَحُوٓا۟ ۗ أَلَا تُحِبُّونَ أَن يَغْفِرَ ٱللَّهُ لَكُمْ ۗ وَٱللَّهُ غَفُورٌ رَّحِيمٌ (٢٢)

And if it had not been for the favor of Allah upon you and His mercy... and because Allah is Kind and Merciful. (20) O you who have believed, do not follow the footsteps of Satan. And whoever follows the footsteps of Satan - indeed, he enjoins immorality and wrongdoing. And if not for the favor of Allah upon you and His mercy, not one of you would have been pure, ever, but Allah purifies whom He wills, and Allah is Hearing and Knowing. (21) And let not those of virtue among you and wealth swear not to give [aid] to their relatives and the needy and the emigrants for the cause of Allah, and let them pardon and overlook. Would you not like that Allah should forgive you? And Allah is Forgiving and Merciful. (22)

## Quran 24:26

ٱلْخَبِيثَـٰتُ لِلْخَبِيثِينَ وَٱلْخَبِيثُونَ لِلْخَبِيثَـٰتِ ۖ وَٱلطَّيِّبَـٰتُ لِلطَّيِّبِينَ وَٱلطَّيِّبُونَ لِلطَّيِّبَـٰتِ ۚ أُو۟لَـٰٓئِكَ مُبَرَّءُونَ مِمَّا يَقُولُونَ ۖ لَهُم مَّغْفِرَةٌ وَرِزْقٌ كَرِيمٌ (٢٦)

Evil words are for evil men, and evil men are [subjected] to evil words. And good words are for good men, and good men are [an object] of good words. Those [good people] are declared innocent of what the slanderers say. For them is forgiveness and noble provision. (26)

## Quran 24:30-33

قُل لِّلْمُؤْمِنِينَ يَغُضُّوا۟ مِنْ أَبْصَـٰرِهِمْ وَيَحْفَظُوا۟ فُرُوجَهُمْ ۚ ذَٰلِكَ أَزْكَىٰ لَهُمْ ۗ إِنَّ ٱللَّهَ خَبِيرٌۢ بِمَا يَصْنَعُونَ (٣٠) وَقُل لِّلْمُؤْمِنَـٰتِ يَغْضُضْنَ مِنْ أَبْصَـٰرِهِنَّ وَيَحْفَظْنَ فُرُوجَهُنَّ وَلَا يُبْدِينَ زِينَتَهُنَّ إِلَّا مَا ظَهَرَ مِنْهَا ۖ وَلْيَضْرِبْنَ بِخُمُرِهِنَّ عَلَىٰ جُيُوبِهِنَّ ۖ وَلَا يُبْدِينَ زِينَتَهُنَّ إِلَّا لِبُعُولَتِهِنَّ أَوْ ءَابَآئِهِنَّ أَوْ ءَابَآءِ بُعُولَتِهِنَّ أَوْ أَبْنَآئِهِنَّ أَوْ أَبْنَآءِ بُعُولَتِهِنَّ أَوْ إِخْوَٰنِهِنَّ أَوْ بَنِىٓ إِخْوَٰنِهِنَّ أَوْ بَنِىٓ أَخَوَٰتِهِنَّ أَوْ نِسَآئِهِنَّ أَوْ مَا مَلَكَتْ أَيْمَـٰنُهُنَّ أَوِ ٱلتَّـٰبِعِينَ غَيْرِ أُو۟لِى ٱلْإِرْبَةِ مِنَ ٱلرِّجَالِ أَوِ ٱلطِّفْلِ ٱلَّذِينَ لَمْ يَظْهَرُوا۟ عَلَىٰ عَوْرَٰتِ ٱلنِّسَآءِ ۖ وَلَا يَضْرِبْنَ بِأَرْجُلِهِنَّ لِيُعْلَمَ مَا يُخْفِينَ مِن زِينَتِهِنَّ ۚ وَتُوبُوٓا۟ إِلَى ٱللَّهِ جَمِيعًا أَيُّهَ ٱلْمُؤْمِنُونَ لَعَلَّكُمْ تُفْلِحُونَ (٣١) وَأَنكِحُوا۟ ٱلْأَيَـٰمَىٰ مِنكُمْ وَٱلصَّـٰلِحِينَ مِنْ عِبَادِكُمْ وَإِمَآئِكُمْ ۚ إِن يَكُونُوا۟ فُقَرَآءَ يُغْنِهِمُ ٱللَّهُ مِن فَضْلِهِۦ ۗ وَٱللَّهُ وَٰسِعٌ عَلِيمٌ (٣٢) وَلْيَسْتَعْفِفِ ٱلَّذِينَ لَا يَجِدُونَ نِكَاحًا حَتَّىٰ يُغْنِيَهُمُ ٱللَّهُ مِن فَضْلِهِۦ ۗ وَٱلَّذِينَ يَبْتَغُونَ ٱلْكِتَـٰبَ مِمَّا مَلَكَتْ أَيْمَـٰنُكُمْ فَكَاتِبُوهُمْ إِنْ عَلِمْتُمْ فِيهِمْ خَيْرًا ۖ وَءَاتُوهُم مِّن مَّالِ ٱللَّهِ ٱلَّذِىٓ ءَاتَىٰكُمْ ۚ وَلَا تُكْرِهُوا۟ فَتَيَـٰتِكُمْ عَلَى ٱلْبِغَآءِ إِنْ أَرَدْنَ تَحَصُّنًا لِّتَبْتَغُوا۟ عَرَضَ ٱلْحَيَوٰةِ ٱلدُّنْيَا ۚ وَمَن يُكْرِههُّنَّ فَإِنَّ ٱللَّهَ مِنۢ بَعْدِ إِكْرَٰهِهِنَّ غَفُورٌ رَّحِيمٌ (٣٣)

Tell the believing men to reduce [some] of their vision and guard their private parts. That is purer for them. Indeed, Allah is Acquainted with what they do. (30) And tell the believing women to reduce [some] of their vision and guard their private parts and not expose their adornment except that which [necessarily] appears thereof and to wrap [a portion of] their headcovers over their chests and not expose their adornment except to their husbands, their fathers, their husbands' fathers, their sons, their husbands' sons, their brothers, their brothers' sons, their sisters' sons, their women, that which their right hands possess, or those male attendants having no physical desire, or children who are not yet aware of the private aspects of women. And let them not stamp their feet to make known what they conceal of their adornment. And turn to Allah in repentance, all of you, O believers, that you might succeed. (31) And marry the unmarried among you and the righteous among your male slaves and female slaves. If they should be poor, Allah will enrich them from His bounty, and Allah is all-Encompassing and Knowing. (32) But let them who find not [the means for] marriage abstain [from sexual relations] until Allah enriches them from His bounty. And those who seek a contract [for eventual emancipation] from among whom your right hands possess - then make a contract with them if you know there is within them goodness and give them from the wealth of Allah which He has given you. And do not compel your slave girls to prostitution, if they desire chastity, to seek [thereby] the temporary interests of worldly life. And if someone should compel them, then indeed, Allah is [to them], after their compulsion, Forgiving and Merciful. (33)

## Quran 24:56

وَأَقِيمُوا۟ ٱلصَّلَوٰةَ وَءَاتُوا۟ ٱلزَّكَوٰةَ وَأَطِيعُوا۟ ٱلرَّسُولَ لَعَلَّكُمْ تُرْحَمُونَ (٥٦)

And establish prayer and give zakah and obey the Messenger - that you may receive mercy. (56)

## Quran 24:62

إِنَّمَا ٱلْمُؤْمِنُونَ ٱلَّذِينَ ءَامَنُوا۟ بِٱللَّهِ وَرَسُولِهِۦ وَإِذَا كَانُوا۟ مَعَهُۥ عَلَىٰٓ أَمْرٍ جَامِعٍ لَّمْ يَذْهَبُوا۟ حَتَّىٰ يَسْتَـْٔذِنُوهُ إِنَّ ٱلَّذِينَ يَسْتَـْٔذِنُونَكَ أُو۟لَـٰٓئِكَ ٱلَّذِينَ يُؤْمِنُونَ بِٱللَّهِ وَرَسُولِهِۦ فَإِذَا ٱسْتَـْٔذَنُوكَ لِبَعْضِ شَأْنِهِمْ فَأْذَن لِّمَن شِئْتَ مِنْهُمْ وَٱسْتَغْفِرْ لَهُمُ ٱللَّهَ إِنَّ ٱللَّهَ غَفُورٌ رَّحِيمٌ (٦٢)

The believers are only those who believe in Allah and His Messenger and, when they are [meeting] with him for a matter of common interest, do not depart until they have asked his permission. Indeed, those who ask your permission, [O Muhammad] - those are the ones who believe in Allah and His Messenger. So when they ask your permission for something of their affairs, then give permission to whom you will among them and ask forgiveness for them of Allah. Indeed, Allah is Forgiving and Merciful. (62)

## Quran 25:6

قُلْ أَنزَلَهُ ٱلَّذِى يَعْلَمُ ٱلسِّرَّ فِى ٱلسَّمَـٰوَٰتِ وَٱلْأَرْضِ إِنَّهُۥ كَانَ غَفُورًا رَّحِيمًا (٦)

Say, [O Muhammad], "It has been revealed by He who knows [every] secret within the heavens and the earth. Indeed, He is ever Forgiving and Merciful." (6)

## Quran 25:26

ٱلْمُلْكُ يَوْمَئِذٍ ٱلْحَقُّ لِلرَّحْمَـٰنِ وَكَانَ يَوْمًا عَلَى ٱلْكَـٰفِرِينَ عَسِيرًا (٢٦)

True sovereignty, that Day, is for the Most Merciful. And it will be upon the disbelievers a difficult Day. (26)

## Quran 25:58-76

وَتَوَكَّلْ عَلَى ٱلْحَىِّ ٱلَّذِى لَا يَمُوتُ وَسَبِّحْ بِحَمْدِهِۦ ۚ وَكَفَىٰ بِهِۦ بِذُنُوبِ عِبَادِهِۦ خَبِيرًا (٥٨) ٱلَّذِى خَلَقَ ٱلسَّمَٰوَٰتِ وَٱلْأَرْضَ وَمَا بَيْنَهُمَا فِى سِتَّةِ أَيَّامٍ ثُمَّ ٱسْتَوَىٰ عَلَى ٱلْعَرْشِ ۚ ٱلرَّحْمَٰنُ فَسْـَٔلْ بِهِۦ خَبِيرًا (٥٩) وَإِذَا قِيلَ لَهُمُ ٱسْجُدُوا۟ لِلرَّحْمَٰنِ قَالُوا۟ وَمَا ٱلرَّحْمَٰنُ أَنَسْجُدُ لِمَا تَأْمُرُنَا وَزَادَهُمْ نُفُورًا ۩ (٦٠) تَبَارَكَ ٱلَّذِى جَعَلَ فِى ٱلسَّمَاءِ بُرُوجًا وَجَعَلَ فِيهَا سِرَٰجًا وَقَمَرًا مُّنِيرًا (٦١) وَهُوَ ٱلَّذِى جَعَلَ ٱلَّيْلَ وَٱلنَّهَارَ خِلْفَةً لِّمَنْ أَرَادَ أَن يَذَّكَّرَ أَوْ أَرَادَ شُكُورًا (٦٢) وَعِبَادُ ٱلرَّحْمَٰنِ ٱلَّذِينَ يَمْشُونَ عَلَى ٱلْأَرْضِ هَوْنًا وَإِذَا خَاطَبَهُمُ ٱلْجَٰهِلُونَ قَالُوا۟ سَلَٰمًا (٦٣) وَٱلَّذِينَ يَبِيتُونَ لِرَبِّهِمْ سُجَّدًا وَقِيَٰمًا (٦٤) وَٱلَّذِينَ يَقُولُونَ رَبَّنَا ٱصْرِفْ عَنَّا عَذَابَ جَهَنَّمَ ۖ إِنَّ عَذَابَهَا كَانَ غَرَامًا (٦٥) إِنَّهَا سَاءَتْ مُسْتَقَرًّا وَمُقَامًا (٦٦) وَٱلَّذِينَ إِذَا أَنفَقُوا۟ لَمْ يُسْرِفُوا۟ وَلَمْ يَقْتُرُوا۟ وَكَانَ بَيْنَ ذَٰلِكَ قَوَامًا (٦٧) وَٱلَّذِينَ لَا يَدْعُونَ مَعَ ٱللَّهِ إِلَٰهًا ءَاخَرَ وَلَا يَقْتُلُونَ ٱلنَّفْسَ ٱلَّتِى حَرَّمَ ٱللَّهُ إِلَّا بِٱلْحَقِّ وَلَا يَزْنُونَ ۚ وَمَن يَفْعَلْ ذَٰلِكَ يَلْقَ أَثَامًا (٦٨) يُضَٰعَفْ لَهُ ٱلْعَذَابُ يَوْمَ ٱلْقِيَٰمَةِ وَيَخْلُدْ فِيهِۦ مُهَانًا (٦٩) إِلَّا مَن تَابَ وَءَامَنَ وَعَمِلَ عَمَلًا صَٰلِحًا فَأُو۟لَٰٓئِكَ يُبَدِّلُ ٱللَّهُ سَيِّـَٔاتِهِمْ حَسَنَٰتٍ ۗ وَكَانَ ٱللَّهُ غَفُورًا رَّحِيمًا (٧٠) وَمَن تَابَ وَعَمِلَ صَٰلِحًا فَإِنَّهُۥ يَتُوبُ إِلَى ٱللَّهِ مَتَابًا (٧١) وَٱلَّذِينَ لَا يَشْهَدُونَ ٱلزُّورَ وَإِذَا مَرُّوا۟ بِٱللَّغْوِ مَرُّوا۟ كِرَامًا (٧٢) وَٱلَّذِينَ إِذَا ذُكِّرُوا۟ بِـَٔايَٰتِ رَبِّهِمْ لَمْ يَخِرُّوا۟ عَلَيْهَا صُمًّا وَعُمْيَانًا (٧٣) وَٱلَّذِينَ يَقُولُونَ رَبَّنَا هَبْ لَنَا مِنْ أَزْوَٰجِنَا وَذُرِّيَّٰتِنَا قُرَّةَ أَعْيُنٍ وَٱجْعَلْنَا لِلْمُتَّقِينَ إِمَامًا (٧٤) أُو۟لَٰٓئِكَ يُجْزَوْنَ ٱلْغُرْفَةَ بِمَا صَبَرُوا۟ وَيُلَقَّوْنَ فِيهَا تَحِيَّةً وَسَلَٰمًا (٧٥) خَٰلِدِينَ فِيهَا ۚ حَسُنَتْ مُسْتَقَرًّا وَمُقَامًا (٧٦)

*And rely upon the Ever-Living who does not die, and exalt [Allah] with His praise. And sufficient is He to be, with the sins of His servants, Acquainted - (58) He who created the heavens and the earth and what is between them in six days and then established Himself above the Throne - the Most Merciful, so ask about Him one well informed. (59) And when it is said to them, "Prostrate to the Most Merciful," they say, "And what is the Most Merciful? Should we prostrate to that which you order us?" And it increases them in aversion. (60) Blessed is*

*He who has placed in the sky great stars and placed therein a [burning] lamp and luminous moon. (61) And it is He who has made the night and the day in succession for whoever desires to remember or desires gratitude. (62) And the servants of the Most Merciful are those who walk upon the earth easily, and when the ignorant address them [harshly], they say [words of] peace, (63) And those who spend [part of] the night to their Lord prostrating and standing [in prayer] (64) And those who say, "Our Lord, avert from us the punishment of Hell. Indeed, its punishment is ever adhering; (65) Indeed, it is evil as a settlement and residence." (66) And [they are] those who, when they spend, do so not excessively or sparingly but are ever, between that, [justly] moderate (67) And those who do not invoke with Allah another deity or kill the soul which Allah has forbidden [to be killed], except by right, and do not commit unlawful sexual intercourse. And whoever should do that will meet a penalty. (68) Multiplied for him is the punishment on the Day of Resurrection, and he will abide therein humiliated - (69) Except for those who repent, believe and do righteous work. For them Allah will replace their evil deeds with good. And ever is Allah Forgiving and Merciful. (70) And he who repents and does righteousness does indeed turn to Allah with [accepted] repentance. (71) And [they are] those who do not testify to falsehood, and when they pass near ill speech, they pass by with dignity. (72) And those who, when reminded of the verses of their Lord, do not fall* upon them deaf and blind. (73) And those who say, "Our Lord, grant us from among our wives and offspring comfort to our eyes and make us an example for the righteous." (74) Those will be awarded the Chamber for what they patiently endured, and they will be received therein with greetings and [words of] peace. (75) Abiding eternally therein. Good is the settlement and residence. (76)

## Quran 26:5

وَمَا يَأْتِيهِم مِّن ذِكْرٍ مِّنَ ٱلرَّحْمَٰنِ مُحْدَثٍ إِلَّا كَانُوا۟ عَنْهُ مُعْرِضِينَ (٥)

And no revelation comes to them anew from the Most Merciful except that they turn away from it. (5)

## Quran 26:104

وَإِنَّ رَبَّكَ لَهُوَ ٱلْعَزِيزُ ٱلرَّحِيمُ (١٠٤)

And indeed, your Lord - He is the Exalted in Might, the Merciful. (104)

## Quran 26:122

وَإِنَّ رَبَّكَ لَهُوَ ٱلْعَزِيزُ ٱلرَّحِيمُ (١٢٢)

And indeed, your Lord - He is the Exalted in Might, the Merciful. (122)

## Quran 26:140

وَإِنَّ رَبَّكَ لَهُوَ ٱلْعَزِيزُ ٱلرَّحِيمُ (١٤٠)

And indeed, your Lord - He is the Exalted in Might, the Merciful. (140)

## Quran 26:191-197

وَإِنَّ رَبَّكَ لَهُوَ ٱلْعَزِيزُ ٱلرَّحِيمُ (١٩١) وَإِنَّهُۥ لَتَنزِيلُ رَبِّ ٱلْعَٰلَمِينَ (١٩٢) نَزَلَ بِهِ ٱلرُّوحُ ٱلْأَمِينُ (١٩٣) عَلَىٰ قَلْبِكَ لِتَكُونَ مِنَ ٱلْمُنذِرِينَ (١٩٤) بِلِسَانٍ عَرَبِيٍّ مُّبِينٍ (١٩٥) وَإِنَّهُۥ لَفِى زُبُرِ ٱلْأَوَّلِينَ (١٩٦) أَوَلَمْ يَكُن لَّهُمْ ءَايَةً أَن يَعْلَمَهُۥ عُلَمَٰٓؤُا۟ بَنِىٓ إِسْرَٰٓءِيلَ (١٩٧)

*And indeed, your Lord - He is the Exalted in Might, the Merciful. (191) And indeed, the Qur'an is the revelation of the Lord of the worlds. (192) The Trustworthy Spirit has brought it down (193) Upon your heart, [O Muhammad] - that you may be of the warners - (194) In a clear Arabic language. (195) And indeed, it is [mentioned] in the scriptures of former peoples. (196) And has it not been a sign to them that it is recognized by the scholars of the Children of Israel? (197)*

## Quran 27:11

إِلَّا مَن ظَلَمَ ثُمَّ بَدَّلَ حُسْنًۢا بَعْدَ سُوٓءٍ فَإِنِّى غَفُورٌ رَّحِيمٌ (١١)

*Otherwise, he who wrongs, then substitutes good after evil - indeed, I am Forgiving and Merciful. (11)*

## Quran 27:19

فَتَبَسَّمَ ضَاحِكًا مِّن قَوْلِهَا وَقَالَ رَبِّ أَوْزِعْنِىٓ أَنْ أَشْكُرَ نِعْمَتَكَ ٱلَّتِىٓ أَنْعَمْتَ عَلَىَّ وَعَلَىٰ وَٰلِدَىَّ وَأَنْ أَعْمَلَ صَٰلِحًا تَرْضَىٰهُ وَأَدْخِلْنِى بِرَحْمَتِكَ فِى عِبَادِكَ ٱلصَّٰلِحِينَ (١٩)

*So [Solomon] smiled, amused at her speech, and said, "My Lord, enable me to be grateful for Your favor which You have bestowed upon me and upon my parents and to do righteousness of which You approve. And admit me* by Your mercy into [the ranks of] Your righteous servants." (19)

## Quran 27:30-31

إِنَّهُ مِن سُلَيْمَٰنَ وَإِنَّهُ بِسْمِ ٱللَّهِ ٱلرَّحْمَٰنِ ٱلرَّحِيمِ (٣٠) أَلَّا تَعْلُوا۟ عَلَىَّ وَأْتُونِى مُسْلِمِينَ (٣١)

Indeed, it is from Solomon, and indeed, it reads: 'In the name of Allah, the Entirely Merciful, the Especially Merciful, (30) Be not haughty with me but come to me in submission [as Muslims].' " (31)

## Quran 27:46

قَالَ يَٰقَوْمِ لِمَ تَسْتَعْجِلُونَ بِٱلسَّيِّئَةِ قَبْلَ ٱلْحَسَنَةِ ۖ لَوْلَا تَسْتَغْفِرُونَ ٱللَّهَ لَعَلَّكُمْ تُرْحَمُونَ (٤٦)

He said, "O my people, why are you impatient for evil instead of good? Why do you not seek forgiveness of Allah that you may receive mercy?" (46)

## Quran 27:26-27

إِنَّ هَٰذَا ٱلْقُرْءَانَ يَقُصُّ عَلَىٰ بَنِىٓ إِسْرَٰٓءِيلَ أَكْثَرَ ٱلَّذِى هُمْ فِيهِ يَخْتَلِفُونَ (٧٦) وَإِنَّهُ لَهُدًى وَرَحْمَةٌ لِّلْمُؤْمِنِينَ (٧٧)

Indeed, this Qur'an relates to the Children of Israel most of that over which they disagree. (76) And indeed, it is guidance and mercy for the believers. (77)

## Quran 28:16-17

قَالَ رَبِّ إِنِّى ظَلَمْتُ نَفْسِى فَٱغْفِرْ لِى فَغَفَرَ لَهُۥٓ ۚ إِنَّهُۥ هُوَ ٱلْغَفُورُ ٱلرَّحِيمُ (١٦) قَالَ رَبِّ بِمَآ أَنْعَمْتَ عَلَىَّ فَلَنْ أَكُونَ ظَهِيرًا لِّلْمُجْرِمِينَ (١٧)

He said, "My Lord, indeed I have wronged myself, so forgive me," and He forgave him. Indeed, He is the Forgiving, the Merciful. (16) He said, "My Lord, for the favor You bestowed upon me, I will never be an assistant to the criminals." (17)

## Quran 28:46

وَمَا كُنتَ بِجَانِبِ ٱلطُّورِ إِذْ نَادَيْنَا وَلَٰكِن رَّحْمَةً مِّن رَّبِّكَ لِتُنذِرَ قَوْمًا مَّآ أَتَىٰهُم مِّن نَّذِيرٍ مِّن قَبْلِكَ لَعَلَّهُمْ يَتَذَكَّرُونَ (٤٦)

And you were not at the side of the mount when We called [Moses] but [were sent] as a mercy from your Lord to warn a people to whom no warner had come before you that they might be reminded. (46)

## Quran 28:67

فَأَمَّا مَن تَابَ وَءَامَنَ وَعَمِلَ صَٰلِحًا فَعَسَىٰٓ أَن يَكُونَ مِنَ ٱلْمُفْلِحِينَ (٦٧)

But as for one who had repented, believed, and done righteousness, it is promised by Allah that he will be among the successful. (67)

## Quran 28:72-73

قُلْ أَرَءَيْتُمْ إِن جَعَلَ ٱللَّهُ عَلَيْكُمُ ٱلنَّهَارَ سَرْمَدًا إِلَىٰ يَوْمِ ٱلْقِيَٰمَةِ مَنْ إِلَٰهٌ غَيْرُ ٱللَّهِ يَأْتِيكُم بِلَيْلٍ تَسْكُنُونَ فِيهِ أَفَلَا تُبْصِرُونَ (٧٢) وَمِن رَّحْمَتِهِۦ جَعَلَ لَكُمُ ٱلَّيْلَ وَٱلنَّهَارَ لِتَسْكُنُوا۟ فِيهِ وَلِتَبْتَغُوا۟ مِن فَضْلِهِۦ وَلَعَلَّكُمْ تَشْكُرُونَ (٧٣)

Say, "Have you considered: if Allah should make for you the day continuous until the Day of Resurrection, what deity other than Allah could bring you a night in which you may rest? Then will you not see?" (72) And out of His mercy He made for you the night and the day that you may rest therein and [by day] seek from His bounty and [that] perhaps you will be grateful. (73)

## Quran 28:86

وَمَا كُنتَ تَرْجُوٓاْ أَن يُلْقَىٰٓ إِلَيْكَ ٱلْكِتَٰبُ إِلَّا رَحْمَةً مِّن رَّبِّكَ ۖ فَلَا تَكُونَنَّ ظَهِيرًا لِّلْكَٰفِرِينَ (٨٦)

And you were not expecting that the Book would be conveyed to you, but [it is] a mercy from your Lord. So do not be an assistant to the disbelievers. (86)

## Quran 29:12-13

وَقَالَ ٱلَّذِينَ كَفَرُواْ لِلَّذِينَ ءَامَنُواْ ٱتَّبِعُواْ سَبِيلَنَا وَلْنَحْمِلْ خَطَٰيَٰكُمْ وَمَا هُم بِحَٰمِلِينَ مِنْ خَطَٰيَٰهُم مِّن شَىْءٍ ۖ إِنَّهُمْ لَكَٰذِبُونَ (١٢) وَلَيَحْمِلُنَّ أَثْقَالَهُمْ وَأَثْقَالًا مَّعَ أَثْقَالِهِمْ ۖ وَلَيُسْـَٔلُنَّ يَوْمَ ٱلْقِيَٰمَةِ عَمَّا كَانُواْ يَفْتَرُونَ (١٣)

And those who disbelieve say to those who believe, "Follow our way, and we will carry your sins." But they will not carry anything of their sins. Indeed, they are liars. (12) But they will surely carry their [own] burdens and [other] burdens along with their burdens, and they will surely be questioned on the Day of Resurrection about what they used to invent. (13)

## Quran 29:21-23

يُعَذِّبُ مَن يَشَآءُ وَيَرْحَمُ مَن يَشَآءُ ۖ وَإِلَيْهِ تُقْلَبُونَ (٢١) وَمَآ أَنتُم بِمُعْجِزِينَ فِى ٱلْأَرْضِ وَلَا فِى ٱلسَّمَآءِ ۖ وَمَا لَكُم مِّن دُونِ ٱللَّهِ مِن وَلِىٍّ وَلَا نَصِيرٍ (٢٢) وَٱلَّذِينَ كَفَرُواْ بِـَٔايَٰتِ ٱللَّهِ وَلِقَآئِهِۦٓ أُوْلَٰٓئِكَ يَئِسُواْ مِن رَّحْمَتِى وَأُوْلَٰٓئِكَ لَهُمْ عَذَابٌ أَلِيمٌ (٢٣)

He punishes whom He wills and has mercy upon whom He wills, and to Him you will be returned. (21) And you will not cause failure [to Allah] upon the earth or in the heaven. And you have not other than Allah any protector or any helper. (22) And the ones who disbelieve in the signs of Allah and the meeting with Him - those have despaired of My mercy, and they will have a painful punishment. (23)

## Quran 29:51

أَوَلَمْ يَكْفِهِمْ أَنَّا أَنزَلْنَا عَلَيْكَ ٱلْكِتَٰبَ يُتْلَىٰ عَلَيْهِمْ إِنَّ فِى ذَٰلِكَ لَرَحْمَةً وَذِكْرَىٰ لِقَوْمٍ يُؤْمِنُونَ (٥١)

And is it not sufficient for them that We revealed to you the Book which is recited to them? Indeed in that is a mercy and reminder for a people who believe. (51)

## Quran 30:21-34

وَمِنْ ءَايَٰتِهِۦٓ أَنْ خَلَقَ لَكُم مِّنْ أَنفُسِكُمْ أَزْوَٰجًا لِّتَسْكُنُوٓا۟ إِلَيْهَا وَجَعَلَ بَيْنَكُم مَّوَدَّةً وَرَحْمَةً إِنَّ فِى ذَٰلِكَ لَءَايَٰتٍ لِّقَوْمٍ يَتَفَكَّرُونَ (٢١) وَمِنْ ءَايَٰتِهِۦ خَلْقُ ٱلسَّمَٰوَٰتِ وَٱلْأَرْضِ وَٱخْتِلَٰفُ أَلْسِنَتِكُمْ وَأَلْوَٰنِكُمْ إِنَّ فِى ذَٰلِكَ لَءَايَٰتٍ لِّلْعَٰلِمِينَ (٢٢) وَمِنْ ءَايَٰتِهِۦ مَنَامُكُم بِٱلَّيْلِ وَٱلنَّهَارِ وَٱبْتِغَآؤُكُم مِّن فَضْلِهِۦٓ إِنَّ فِى ذَٰلِكَ لَءَايَٰتٍ لِّقَوْمٍ يَسْمَعُونَ (٢٣) وَمِنْ ءَايَٰتِهِۦ يُرِيكُمُ ٱلْبَرْقَ خَوْفًا وَطَمَعًا وَيُنَزِّلُ مِنَ ٱلسَّمَآءِ مَآءً فَيُحْىِۦ بِهِ ٱلْأَرْضَ بَعْدَ مَوْتِهَآ إِنَّ فِى ذَٰلِكَ لَءَايَٰتٍ لِّقَوْمٍ يَعْقِلُونَ (٢٤) وَمِنْ ءَايَٰتِهِۦٓ أَن تَقُومَ ٱلسَّمَآءُ وَٱلْأَرْضُ بِأَمْرِهِۦ ثُمَّ إِذَا دَعَاكُمْ دَعْوَةً مِّنَ ٱلْأَرْضِ إِذَآ أَنتُمْ تَخْرُجُونَ (٢٥) وَلَهُۥ مَن فِى ٱلسَّمَٰوَٰتِ وَٱلْأَرْضِ كُلٌّ لَّهُۥ قَٰنِتُونَ (٢٦) وَهُوَ ٱلَّذِى يَبْدَؤُا۟ ٱلْخَلْقَ ثُمَّ يُعِيدُهُۥ وَهُوَ أَهْوَنُ عَلَيْهِ وَلَهُ ٱلْمَثَلُ ٱلْأَعْلَىٰ فِى ٱلسَّمَٰوَٰتِ وَٱلْأَرْضِ وَهُوَ ٱلْعَزِيزُ ٱلْحَكِيمُ (٢٧) ضَرَبَ لَكُم مَّثَلًا مِّنْ أَنفُسِكُمْ هَل لَّكُم مِّن مَّا مَلَكَتْ أَيْمَٰنُكُم مِّن شُرَكَآءَ فِى مَا رَزَقْنَٰكُمْ فَأَنتُمْ فِيهِ سَوَآءٌ تَخَافُونَهُمْ كَخِيفَتِكُمْ أَنفُسَكُمْ كَذَٰلِكَ نُفَصِّلُ ٱلْءَايَٰتِ لِقَوْمٍ يَعْقِلُونَ (٢٨) بَلِ ٱتَّبَعَ ٱلَّذِينَ ظَلَمُوٓا۟ أَهْوَآءَهُم بِغَيْرِ عِلْمٍ فَمَن يَهْدِى مَنْ أَضَلَّ ٱللَّهُ وَمَا لَهُم مِّن نَّٰصِرِينَ (٢٩) فَأَقِمْ وَجْهَكَ لِلدِّينِ حَنِيفًا فِطْرَتَ ٱللَّهِ ٱلَّتِى فَطَرَ ٱلنَّاسَ عَلَيْهَا لَا تَبْدِيلَ لِخَلْقِ ٱللَّهِ ذَٰلِكَ ٱلدِّينُ ٱلْقَيِّمُ وَلَٰكِنَّ أَكْثَرَ ٱلنَّاسِ لَا يَعْلَمُونَ

(٣٠) مُنِيبِينَ إِلَيْهِ وَٱتَّقُوهُ وَأَقِيمُواْ ٱلصَّلَوٰةَ وَلَا تَكُونُواْ مِنَ ٱلْمُشْرِكِينَ (٣١) مِنَ ٱلَّذِينَ فَرَّقُواْ دِينَهُمْ وَكَانُواْ شِيَعًا كُلُّ حِزْبٍ بِمَا لَدَيْهِمْ فَرِحُونَ (٣٢) وَإِذَا مَسَّ ٱلنَّاسَ ضُرٌّ دَعَوْاْ رَبَّهُم مُّنِيبِينَ إِلَيْهِ ثُمَّ إِذَآ أَذَاقَهُم مِّنْهُ رَحْمَةً إِذَا فَرِيقٌ مِّنْهُم بِرَبِّهِمْ يُشْرِكُونَ (٣٣) لِيَكْفُرُواْ بِمَآ ءَاتَيْنَـٰهُمْ فَتَمَتَّعُواْ فَسَوْفَ تَعْلَمُونَ (٣٤)

And of His signs is that He created for you from yourselves mates that you may find tranquility in them; and He placed between you affection and mercy. Indeed in that are signs for a people who give thought. (21) And of His signs is the creation of the heavens and the earth and the diversity of your languages and your colors. Indeed in that are signs for those of knowledge. (22) And of His signs is your sleep by night and day and your seeking of His bounty. Indeed in that are signs for a people who listen. (23) And of His signs is [that] He shows you the lightning [causing] fear and aspiration, and He sends down rain from the sky by which He brings to life the earth after its lifelessness. Indeed in that are signs for a people who use reason. (24) And of His signs is that the heaven and earth remain by His command. Then when He calls you with a [single] call from the earth, immediately you will come forth. (25) And to Him belongs whoever is in the heavens and earth. All are to Him devoutly obedient. (26) And it is He who begins creation; then He repeats it, and that is [even] easier for Him. To Him belongs the highest attribute in the heavens and earth. And He is the Exalted in Might, the Wise. (27) He presents to you an example from yourselves. Do you have among those whom your right hands possess any partners in what We have provided for you so that you are equal therein [and] would fear them as your fear of one another [within a partnership]? Thus do We detail the verses for a people who use reason. (28) But those who wrong follow their [own] desires without knowledge. Then who can guide one whom Allah has sent astray? And for them there are no helpers. (29) So direct your face toward the religion, inclining to truth. [Adhere to] the fitrah of Allah upon which He has created [all] people. No change should there be in the creation of Allah. That is the correct religion, but most of the people do not know. (30) [Adhere to it], turning in repentance to Him, and fear Him and establish prayer and do not be of those who associate others with Allah (31) [Or] of those who have divided their religion and become sects, every faction rejoicing in what it has. (32) And when adversity touches the people, they call upon their Lord, turning in repentance to Him. Then when He lets them taste mercy from Him, at once a party of them associate others with their Lord, (33) So that they will deny what We have granted them. Then enjoy yourselves, for you are going to know. (34)

## Quran 30:36-38

وَإِذَآ أَذَقْنَا ٱلنَّاسَ رَحْمَةً فَرِحُوا۟ بِهَا ۖ وَإِن تُصِبْهُمْ سَيِّئَةٌۢ بِمَا قَدَّمَتْ أَيْدِيهِمْ إِذَا هُمْ يَقْنَطُونَ (٣٦) أَوَلَمْ يَرَوْا۟ أَنَّ ٱللَّهَ يَبْسُطُ ٱلرِّزْقَ لِمَن يَشَآءُ وَيَقْدِرُ ۚ إِنَّ فِى ذَٰلِكَ لَءَايَـٰتٍ لِّقَوْمٍ يُؤْمِنُونَ (٣٧) فَـَٔاتِ ذَا ٱلْقُرْبَىٰ حَقَّهُۥ وَٱلْمِسْكِينَ وَٱبْنَ ٱلسَّبِيلِ ۚ ذَٰلِكَ خَيْرٌ لِّلَّذِينَ يُرِيدُونَ وَجْهَ ٱللَّهِ ۖ وَأُو۟لَـٰٓئِكَ هُمُ ٱلْمُفْلِحُونَ (٣٨)

And when We let the people taste mercy, they rejoice therein, but if evil afflicts them for what their hands have put forth, immediately they despair. (36) Do they not see that Allah extends provision for whom He wills and restricts [it]? Indeed, in that are signs for a people who believe. (37) So give the relative his right, as well as the needy and the traveler. That is best for those who desire the countenance of Allah, and it is they who will be the successful. (38)

## Quran 30:46-50

وَمِنْ ءَايَٰتِهِۦٓ أَن يُرْسِلَ ٱلرِّيَاحَ مُبَشِّرَٰتٍ وَلِيُذِيقَكُم مِّن رَّحْمَتِهِۦ وَلِتَجْرِىَ ٱلْفُلْكُ بِأَمْرِهِۦ وَلِتَبْتَغُوا۟ مِن فَضْلِهِۦ وَلَعَلَّكُمْ تَشْكُرُونَ (٤٦) وَلَقَدْ أَرْسَلْنَا مِن قَبْلِكَ رُسُلًا إِلَىٰ قَوْمِهِمْ فَجَآءُوهُم بِٱلْبَيِّنَٰتِ فَٱنتَقَمْنَا مِنَ ٱلَّذِينَ أَجْرَمُوا۟ۖ وَكَانَ حَقًّا عَلَيْنَا نَصْرُ ٱلْمُؤْمِنِينَ (٤٧) ٱللَّهُ ٱلَّذِى يُرْسِلُ ٱلرِّيَٰحَ فَتُثِيرُ سَحَابًا فَيَبْسُطُهُۥ فِى ٱلسَّمَآءِ كَيْفَ يَشَآءُ وَيَجْعَلُهُۥ كِسَفًا فَتَرَى ٱلْوَدْقَ يَخْرُجُ مِنْ خِلَٰلِهِۦۖ فَإِذَآ أَصَابَ بِهِۦ مَن يَشَآءُ مِنْ عِبَادِهِۦٓ إِذَا هُمْ يَسْتَبْشِرُونَ (٤٨) وَإِن كَانُوا۟ مِن قَبْلِ أَن يُنَزَّلَ عَلَيْهِم مِّن قَبْلِهِۦ لَمُبْلِسِينَ (٤٩) فَٱنظُرْ إِلَىٰٓ ءَاثَٰرِ رَحْمَتِ ٱللَّهِ كَيْفَ يُحْىِ ٱلْأَرْضَ بَعْدَ مَوْتِهَآۚ إِنَّ ذَٰلِكَ لَمُحْىِ ٱلْمَوْتَىٰۖ وَهُوَ عَلَىٰ كُلِّ شَىْءٍ قَدِيرٌ (٥٠)

And of His signs is that He sends the winds as bringers of good tidings and to let you taste His mercy and so the ships may sail at His command and so you may seek of His bounty, and perhaps you will be grateful. (46) And We have already sent messengers before you to their peoples, and they came to them with clear evidences; then We took retribution from those who committed crimes, and incumbent upon Us was support of the believers. (47) It is Allah who sends the winds, and they stir the clouds and spread them in the sky however He wills, and He makes them fragments so you see the rain emerge from within them. And when He causes it to fall upon whom He wills of His servants, immediately they rejoice (48) Although they were, before it was sent down upon them - before that, in despair. (49) So observe the effects of the mercy of Allah - how He gives life to the earth after its lifelessness. Indeed, that [same one] will give life to the dead, and He is over all things competent. (50)

## Quran 31:2-5

تِلْكَ ءَايَـٰتُ ٱلْكِتَـٰبِ ٱلْحَكِيمِ (٢) هُدًى وَرَحْمَةً لِّلْمُحْسِنِينَ (٣) ٱلَّذِينَ يُقِيمُونَ ٱلصَّلَوٰةَ وَيُؤْتُونَ ٱلزَّكَوٰةَ وَهُم بِٱلْأَخِرَةِ هُمْ يُوقِنُونَ (٤) أُو۟لَـٰٓئِكَ عَلَىٰ هُدًى مِّن رَّبِّهِمْ ۖ وَأُو۟لَـٰٓئِكَ هُمُ ٱلْمُفْلِحُونَ (٥)

These are verses of the wise Book, (2) As guidance and mercy for the doers of good (3) Who establish prayer and give zakah, and they, of the Hereafter, are certain [in faith]. (4) Those are on [right] guidance from their Lord, and it is those who are the successful. (5)

## Quran 33:4-5

مَّا جَعَلَ ٱللَّهُ لِرَجُلٍ مِّن قَلْبَيْنِ فِى جَوْفِهِۦ ۚ وَمَا جَعَلَ أَزْوَٰجَكُمُ ٱلَّـٰٓـِٔى تُظَـٰهِرُونَ مِنْهُنَّ أُمَّهَـٰتِكُمْ ۚ وَمَا جَعَلَ أَدْعِيَآءَكُمْ أَبْنَآءَكُمْ ۚ ذَٰلِكُمْ قَوْلُكُم بِأَفْوَٰهِكُمْ ۖ وَٱللَّهُ يَقُولُ ٱلْحَقَّ وَهُوَ يَهْدِى ٱلسَّبِيلَ (٤) ٱدْعُوهُمْ لِـَٔابَآئِهِمْ هُوَ أَقْسَطُ عِندَ ٱللَّهِ ۚ فَإِن لَّمْ تَعْلَمُوٓا۟ ءَابَآءَهُمْ فَإِخْوَٰنُكُمْ فِى ٱلدِّينِ وَمَوَٰلِيكُمْ ۚ وَلَيْسَ عَلَيْكُمْ جُنَاحٌ فِيمَآ أَخْطَأْتُم بِهِۦ وَلَـٰكِن مَّا تَعَمَّدَتْ قُلُوبُكُمْ ۚ وَكَانَ ٱللَّهُ غَفُورًا رَّحِيمًا (٥)

Allah has not made for a man two hearts in his interior. And He has not made your wives whom you declare unlawful your mothers. And he has not made your adopted sons your [true] sons. That is [merely] your saying by your mouths, but Allah says the truth, and He guides to the [right] way. (4) Call them by [the names of] their fathers; it is more just in the sight of Allah. But if you do not know their fathers - then they are [still] your brothers in religion and those entrusted to you. And there is no blame upon you for that in which you have erred but [only for] what your hearts intended. And ever is Allah Forgiving and Merciful. (5)

## Quran 33:17

قُلْ مَن ذَا ٱلَّذِى يَعْصِمُكُم مِّنَ ٱللَّهِ إِنْ أَرَادَ بِكُمْ سُوٓءًا أَوْ أَرَادَ بِكُمْ رَحْمَةً ۚ وَلَا يَجِدُونَ لَهُم مِّن دُونِ ٱللَّهِ وَلِيًّا وَلَا نَصِيرًا (١٧)

Say, "Who is it that can protect you from Allah if He intends for you an ill or intends for you a mercy?" And they will not find for themselves besides Allah any protector or any helper. (17)

## Quran 33:21-24

لَّقَدْ كَانَ لَكُمْ فِى رَسُولِ ٱللَّهِ أُسْوَةٌ حَسَنَةٌ لِّمَن كَانَ يَرْجُواْ ٱللَّهَ وَٱلْيَوْمَ ٱلْءَاخِرَ وَذَكَرَ ٱللَّهَ كَثِيرًا (٢١) وَلَمَّا رَءَا ٱلْمُؤْمِنُونَ ٱلْأَحْزَابَ قَالُواْ هَٰذَا مَا وَعَدَنَا ٱللَّهُ وَرَسُولُهُۥ وَصَدَقَ ٱللَّهُ وَرَسُولُهُۥ ۚ وَمَا زَادَهُمْ إِلَّآ إِيمَٰنًا وَتَسْلِيمًا (٢٢) مِّنَ ٱلْمُؤْمِنِينَ رِجَالٌ صَدَقُواْ مَا عَٰهَدُواْ ٱللَّهَ عَلَيْهِ ۖ فَمِنْهُم مَّن قَضَىٰ نَحْبَهُۥ وَمِنْهُم مَّن يَنتَظِرُ ۖ وَمَا بَدَّلُواْ تَبْدِيلًا (٢٣) لِّيَجْزِىَ ٱللَّهُ ٱلصَّٰدِقِينَ بِصِدْقِهِمْ وَيُعَذِّبَ ٱلْمُنَٰفِقِينَ إِن شَآءَ أَوْ يَتُوبَ عَلَيْهِمْ ۚ إِنَّ ٱللَّهَ كَانَ غَفُورًا رَّحِيمًا (٢٤)

There has certainly been for you in the Messenger of Allah an excellent pattern for anyone whose hope is in Allah and the Last Day and [who] remembers Allah often. (21) And when the believers saw the companies, they said, "This is what Allah and His Messenger had promised us, and Allah and His Messenger spoke the truth." And it increased them only in faith and acceptance. (22) Among the believers are men true to what they promised Allah. Among them is he who has fulfilled his vow [to the death], and among them is he who awaits [his chance]. And they did not alter [the terms of their commitment] by any alteration - (23) That Allah may reward the truthful for their truth and punish the hypocrites if He wills or accept their repentance. Indeed, Allah is ever Forgiving and Merciful. (24)

## Quran 33:35-36

إِنَّ ٱلْمُسْلِمِينَ وَٱلْمُسْلِمَٰتِ وَٱلْمُؤْمِنِينَ وَٱلْمُؤْمِنَٰتِ وَٱلْقَٰنِتِينَ وَٱلْقَٰنِتَٰتِ وَٱلصَّٰدِقِينَ وَٱلصَّٰدِقَٰتِ وَٱلصَّٰبِرِينَ وَٱلصَّٰبِرَٰتِ وَٱلْخَٰشِعِينَ وَٱلْخَٰشِعَٰتِ وَٱلْمُتَصَدِّقِينَ وَٱلْمُتَصَدِّقَٰتِ وَٱلصَّٰٓئِمِينَ وَٱلصَّٰٓئِمَٰتِ وَٱلْحَٰفِظِينَ فُرُوجَهُمْ وَٱلْحَٰفِظَٰتِ وَٱلذَّٰكِرِينَ ٱللَّهَ كَثِيرًا وَٱلذَّٰكِرَٰتِ أَعَدَّ ٱللَّهُ لَهُم مَّغْفِرَةً وَأَجْرًا عَظِيمًا (٣٥) وَمَا كَانَ لِمُؤْمِنٍ وَلَا مُؤْمِنَةٍ إِذَا قَضَى ٱللَّهُ وَرَسُولُهُۥٓ أَمْرًا أَن يَكُونَ لَهُمُ ٱلْخِيَرَةُ مِنْ أَمْرِهِمْ ۗ وَمَن يَعْصِ ٱللَّهَ وَرَسُولَهُۥ فَقَدْ ضَلَّ ضَلَٰلًا مُّبِينًا (٣٦)

Indeed, the Muslim men and Muslim women, the believing men and believing women, the obedient men and obedient women, the truthful men and truthful women, the patient men and patient women, the humble men and humble women, the charitable men and charitable women, the fasting men and fasting women, the men who guard their private parts and the women who do so, and the men who remember Allah often and the women who do so - for them Allah has prepared forgiveness and a great reward. (35) It is not for a believing man or a believing woman, when Allah and His Messenger have decided a matter, that they should [thereafter] have any choice about their affair. And whoever disobeys Allah and His Messenger has certainly strayed into clear error. (36)

## Quran 33:41-47

يَـٰٓأَيُّهَا ٱلَّذِينَ ءَامَنُوا۟ ٱذْكُرُوا۟ ٱللَّهَ ذِكْرًا كَثِيرًا (٤١) وَسَبِّحُوهُ بُكْرَةً وَأَصِيلًا (٤٢) هُوَ ٱلَّذِى يُصَلِّى عَلَيْكُمْ وَمَلَـٰٓئِكَتُهُۥ لِيُخْرِجَكُم مِّنَ ٱلظُّلُمَـٰتِ إِلَى ٱلنُّورِ ۚ وَكَانَ بِٱلْمُؤْمِنِينَ رَحِيمًا (٤٣) تَحِيَّتُهُمْ يَوْمَ يَلْقَوْنَهُۥ سَلَـٰمٌ ۚ وَأَعَدَّ لَهُمْ أَجْرًا كَرِيمًا (٤٤) يَـٰٓأَيُّهَا ٱلنَّبِىُّ إِنَّآ أَرْسَلْنَـٰكَ شَـٰهِدًا وَمُبَشِّرًا وَنَذِيرًا (٤٥) وَدَاعِيًا إِلَى ٱللَّهِ بِإِذْنِهِۦ وَسِرَاجًا مُّنِيرًا (٤٦) وَبَشِّرِ ٱلْمُؤْمِنِينَ بِأَنَّ لَهُم مِّنَ ٱللَّهِ فَضْلًا كَبِيرًا (٤٧)

O you who have believed, remember Allah with much remembrance (41) And exalt Him morning and afternoon. (42) It is He who confers blessing upon you, and His angels [ask Him to do so] that He may bring you out from darknesses into the light. And ever is He, to the believers, Merciful. (43) Their greeting the Day they meet Him will be, "Peace." And He has prepared for them a noble reward. (44) O Prophet, indeed We have sent you as a witness and a bringer of good tidings and a warner. (45) And one who invites to Allah, by His permission, and an illuminating lamp. (46) And give good tidings to the believers that they will have from Allah great bounty. (47)

## Quran 33:50

يَـٰٓأَيُّهَا ٱلنَّبِىُّ إِنَّآ أَحْلَلْنَا لَكَ أَزْوَٰجَكَ ٱلَّـٰتِىٓ ءَاتَيْتَ أُجُورَهُنَّ وَمَا مَلَكَتْ يَمِينُكَ مِمَّآ أَفَآءَ ٱللَّهُ عَلَيْكَ وَبَنَاتِ عَمِّكَ وَبَنَاتِ عَمَّـٰتِكَ وَبَنَاتِ خَالِكَ وَبَنَاتِ خَـٰلَـٰتِكَ ٱلَّـٰتِى هَاجَرْنَ مَعَكَ وَٱمْرَأَةً مُّؤْمِنَةً إِن وَهَبَتْ نَفْسَهَا لِلنَّبِىِّ إِنْ أَرَادَ ٱلنَّبِىُّ أَن يَسْتَنكِحَهَا خَالِصَةً لَّكَ مِن دُونِ ٱلْمُؤْمِنِينَ قَدْ عَلِمْنَا مَا فَرَضْنَا عَلَيْهِمْ فِىٓ أَزْوَٰجِهِمْ وَمَا مَلَكَتْ أَيْمَـٰنُهُمْ لِكَيْلَا يَكُونَ عَلَيْكَ حَرَجٌ وَكَانَ ٱللَّهُ غَفُورًا رَّحِيمًا (٥٠)

*O Prophet, indeed We have made lawful to you your wives to whom you have given their due compensation and those your right hand possesses from what Allah has returned to you [of captives] and the daughters of your paternal uncles and the daughters of your paternal aunts and the daughters of your maternal uncles and the daughters of your maternal aunts who emigrated with you and a believing woman if she gives herself to the Prophet [and] if the Prophet wishes to marry her, [this is] only for you, excluding the [other] believers. We certainly know what We have made obligatory upon them concerning their wives and those their right hands possess, [but this is for you] in order that there will be upon you no discomfort. And ever is Allah Forgiving and Merciful. (50)*

## Quran 33:59

يَـٰٓأَيُّهَا ٱلنَّبِىُّ قُل لِّأَزْوَٰجِكَ وَبَنَاتِكَ وَنِسَآءِ ٱلْمُؤْمِنِينَ يُدْنِينَ عَلَيْهِنَّ مِن جَلَـٰبِيبِهِنَّ ذَٰلِكَ أَدْنَىٰٓ أَن يُعْرَفْنَ فَلَا يُؤْذَيْنَ وَكَانَ ٱللَّهُ غَفُورًا رَّحِيمًا (٥٩)

*O Prophet, tell your wives and your daughters and the women of the believers to bring down over themselves [part] of their outer garments. That is more suitable that* they will be known and not be abused. And ever is Allah Forgiving and Merciful. (59)

## Quran 33:70-73

يَٰٓأَيُّهَا ٱلَّذِينَ ءَامَنُوا۟ ٱتَّقُوا۟ ٱللَّهَ وَقُولُوا۟ قَوْلًا سَدِيدًا (٧٠) يُصْلِحْ لَكُمْ أَعْمَٰلَكُمْ وَيَغْفِرْ لَكُمْ ذُنُوبَكُمْ وَمَن يُطِعِ ٱللَّهَ وَرَسُولَهُۥ فَقَدْ فَازَ فَوْزًا عَظِيمًا (٧١) إِنَّا عَرَضْنَا ٱلْأَمَانَةَ عَلَى ٱلسَّمَٰوَٰتِ وَٱلْأَرْضِ وَٱلْجِبَالِ فَأَبَيْنَ أَن يَحْمِلْنَهَا وَأَشْفَقْنَ مِنْهَا وَحَمَلَهَا ٱلْإِنسَٰنُ إِنَّهُۥ كَانَ ظَلُومًا جَهُولًا (٧٢) لِّيُعَذِّبَ ٱللَّهُ ٱلْمُنَٰفِقِينَ وَٱلْمُنَٰفِقَٰتِ وَٱلْمُشْرِكِينَ وَٱلْمُشْرِكَٰتِ وَيَتُوبَ ٱللَّهُ عَلَى ٱلْمُؤْمِنِينَ وَٱلْمُؤْمِنَٰتِ وَكَانَ ٱللَّهُ غَفُورًا رَّحِيمًا (٧٣)

*O you who have believed, fear Allah and speak words of appropriate justice. (70) He will [then] amend for you your deeds and forgive you your sins. And whoever obeys Allah and His Messenger has certainly attained a great attainment. (71) Indeed, we offered the Trust to the heavens and the earth and the mountains, and they declined to bear it and feared it; but man [undertook to] bear it. Indeed, he was unjust and ignorant. (72) [It was] so that Allah may punish the hypocrite men and hypocrite women and the men and women who associate others with Him and that Allah may accept repentance from the believing men and believing women. And ever is Allah Forgiving and Merciful. (73)*

## Quran 34:1-2

ٱلْحَمْدُ لِلَّهِ ٱلَّذِى لَهُۥ مَا فِى ٱلسَّمَٰوَٰتِ وَمَا فِى ٱلْأَرْضِ وَلَهُ ٱلْحَمْدُ فِى ٱلْءَاخِرَةِ وَهُوَ ٱلْحَكِيمُ ٱلْخَبِيرُ (١) يَعْلَمُ مَا يَلِجُ فِى ٱلْأَرْضِ وَمَا يَخْرُجُ مِنْهَا وَمَا يَنزِلُ مِنَ ٱلسَّمَآءِ وَمَا يَعْرُجُ فِيهَا وَهُوَ ٱلرَّحِيمُ ٱلْغَفُورُ (٢)

[All] praise is [due] to Allah, to whom belongs whatever is in the heavens and whatever is in the earth, and to Him belongs [all] praise in the Hereafter. And He is the Wise, the Acquainted. (1) He knows what penetrates into the earth and what emerges from it and what descends from the heaven and what ascends therein. And He is the Merciful, the Forgiving. (2)

## Quran 34:4

لِيَجْزِىَ ٱلَّذِينَ ءَامَنُوا۟ وَعَمِلُوا۟ ٱلصَّٰلِحَٰتِ أُو۟لَٰٓئِكَ لَهُم مَّغْفِرَةٌ وَرِزْقٌ كَرِيمٌ (٤)

That He may reward those who believe and do righteous deeds. Those will have forgiveness and noble provision. (4)

## Quran 35:2-3

مَّا يَفْتَحِ ٱللَّهُ لِلنَّاسِ مِن رَّحْمَةٍ فَلَا مُمْسِكَ لَهَا ۖ وَمَا يُمْسِكْ فَلَا مُرْسِلَ لَهُۥ مِنۢ بَعْدِهِۦ ۚ وَهُوَ ٱلْعَزِيزُ ٱلْحَكِيمُ (٢) يَٰٓأَيُّهَا ٱلنَّاسُ ٱذْكُرُوا۟ نِعْمَتَ ٱللَّهِ عَلَيْكُمْ ۚ هَلْ مِنْ خَٰلِقٍ غَيْرُ ٱللَّهِ يَرْزُقُكُم مِّنَ ٱلسَّمَآءِ وَٱلْأَرْضِ ۚ لَآ إِلَٰهَ إِلَّا هُوَ ۖ فَأَنَّىٰ تُؤْفَكُونَ (٣)

Whatever Allah grants to people of mercy - none can withhold it; and whatever He withholds - none can release it thereafter. And He is the Exalted in Might, the Wise. (2) O mankind, remember the favor of Allah upon you. Is there any creator other than Allah who provides for you from the heaven and earth? There is no deity except Him, so how are you deluded? (3)

## Quran 35:28-30

وَمِنَ ٱلنَّاسِ وَٱلدَّوَابِّ وَٱلْأَنْعَٰمِ مُخْتَلِفٌ أَلْوَٰنُهُۥ ۗ كَذَٰلِكَ ۚ إِنَّمَا يَخْشَى ٱللَّهَ مِنْ عِبَادِهِ ٱلْعُلَمَٰٓؤُا۟ ۗ إِنَّ ٱللَّهَ عَزِيزٌ غَفُورٌ (٢٨) إِنَّ ٱلَّذِينَ يَتْلُونَ كِتَٰبَ ٱللَّهِ وَأَقَامُوا۟ ٱلصَّلَوٰةَ وَأَنفَقُوا۟ مِمَّا رَزَقْنَٰهُمْ سِرًّا وَعَلَانِيَةً يَرْجُونَ تِجَٰرَةً لَّن تَبُورَ (٢٩) لِيُوَفِّيَهُمْ أُجُورَهُمْ وَيَزِيدَهُم مِّن فَضْلِهِۦٓ ۚ إِنَّهُۥ غَفُورٌ شَكُورٌ (٣٠)

And among people and moving creatures and grazing livestock are various colors similarly. Only those fear Allah, from among His servants, who have knowledge. Indeed, Allah is Exalted in Might and Forgiving. (28) Indeed, those who recite the Book of Allah and establish prayer and spend [in His cause] out of what We have provided them, secretly and publicly, [can] expect a profit that will never perish - (29) That He may give them in full their rewards and increase for them of His bounty. Indeed, He is Forgiving and Appreciative. (30)

## Quran 35:32-35

ثُمَّ أَوْرَثْنَا ٱلْكِتَٰبَ ٱلَّذِينَ ٱصْطَفَيْنَا مِنْ عِبَادِنَا ۖ فَمِنْهُمْ ظَالِمٌ لِّنَفْسِهِۦ وَمِنْهُم مُّقْتَصِدٌ وَمِنْهُمْ سَابِقٌۢ بِٱلْخَيْرَٰتِ بِإِذْنِ ٱللَّهِ ۚ ذَٰلِكَ هُوَ ٱلْفَضْلُ ٱلْكَبِيرُ (٣٢) جَنَّٰتُ عَدْنٍ يَدْخُلُونَهَا يُحَلَّوْنَ فِيهَا مِنْ أَسَاوِرَ مِن ذَهَبٍ وَلُؤْلُؤًا ۖ وَلِبَاسُهُمْ فِيهَا حَرِيرٌ (٣٣) وَقَالُوا۟ ٱلْحَمْدُ لِلَّهِ ٱلَّذِىٓ أَذْهَبَ عَنَّا ٱلْحَزَنَ ۖ إِنَّ رَبَّنَا لَغَفُورٌ شَكُورٌ (٣٤) ٱلَّذِىٓ أَحَلَّنَا دَارَ ٱلْمُقَامَةِ مِن فَضْلِهِۦ لَا يَمَسُّنَا فِيهَا نَصَبٌ وَلَا يَمَسُّنَا فِيهَا لُغُوبٌ (٣٥)

Then we caused to inherit the Book those We have chosen of Our servants; and among them is he who wrongs himself, and among them is he who is moderate, and among them is he who is foremost in good deeds by permission of Allah. That [inheritance] is what is the great bounty. (32) [For them are] gardens of perpetual residence which they will enter. They will be adorned therein with bracelets of gold and pearls, and their garments therein will be silk. (33) And they will say, "Praise to Allah, who has removed from us [all] sorrow. Indeed, our Lord is Forgiving and Appreciative - (34) He who has settled us in the home of duration out of His bounty. There touches us not in it any fatigue, and there touches us not in it weariness [of mind]." (35)

## Quran 35:41

إِنَّ ٱللَّهَ يُمْسِكُ ٱلسَّمَٰوَٰتِ وَٱلْأَرْضَ أَن تَزُولَا وَلَئِن زَالَتَا إِنْ أَمْسَكَهُمَا مِنْ أَحَدٍ مِّنۢ بَعْدِهِۦٓ ۚ إِنَّهُۥ كَانَ حَلِيمًا غَفُورًا (٤١)

Indeed, Allah holds the heavens and the earth, lest they cease. And if they should cease, no one could hold them [in place] after Him. Indeed, He is Forbearing and Forgiving. (41)

## Quran 36:11

إِنَّمَا تُنذِرُ مَنِ ٱتَّبَعَ ٱلذِّكْرَ وَخَشِىَ ٱلرَّحْمَٰنَ بِٱلْغَيْبِ ۖ فَبَشِّرْهُ بِمَغْفِرَةٍ وَأَجْرٍ كَرِيمٍ (١١)

You can only warn one who follows the message and fears the Most Merciful unseen. So give him good tidings of forgiveness and noble reward. (11)

## Quran 36:23-24

ءَأَتَّخِذُ مِن دُونِهِۦٓ ءَالِهَةً إِن يُرِدْنِ ٱلرَّحْمَٰنُ بِضُرٍّ لَّا تُغْنِ عَنِّى شَفَٰعَتُهُمْ شَيْـًٔا وَلَا يُنقِذُونِ (٢٣) إِنِّىٓ إِذًا لَّفِى ضَلَٰلٍ مُّبِينٍ (٢٤)

Should I take other than Him [false] deities [while], if the Most Merciful intends for me some adversity, their intercession will not avail me at all, nor can they save me? (23) Indeed, I would then be in manifest error. (24)

## Quran 36:41-45

وَءَايَةٌ لَّهُمْ أَنَّا حَمَلْنَا ذُرِّيَّتَهُمْ فِى ٱلْفُلْكِ ٱلْمَشْحُونِ (٤١) وَخَلَقْنَا لَهُم مِّن مِّثْلِهِۦ مَا يَرْكَبُونَ (٤٢) وَإِن نَّشَأْ نُغْرِقْهُمْ فَلَا صَرِيخَ لَهُمْ وَلَا هُمْ يُنقَذُونَ (٤٣) إِلَّا رَحْمَةً مِّنَّا وَمَتَٰعًا إِلَىٰ حِينٍ (٤٤) وَإِذَا قِيلَ لَهُمُ ٱتَّقُوا۟ مَا بَيْنَ أَيْدِيكُمْ وَمَا خَلْفَكُمْ لَعَلَّكُمْ تُرْحَمُونَ (٤٥)

And a sign for them is that We carried their forefathers in a laden ship. (41) And We created for them from the likes of it that which they ride. (42) And if We should will, We could drown them; then no one responding to a cry would there be for them, nor would they be saved (43) Except as a mercy from Us and provision for a time. (44) But when it is said to them, "Beware of what is before you and what is behind you; perhaps you will receive mercy..." (45)

## Quran 36:51-59

وَنُفِخَ فِى ٱلصُّورِ فَإِذَا هُم مِّنَ ٱلْأَجْدَاثِ إِلَىٰ رَبِّهِمْ يَنسِلُونَ (٥١) قَالُوا۟ يَٰوَيْلَنَا مَنۢ بَعَثَنَا مِن مَّرْقَدِنَا ۜ ۗ هَٰذَا مَا وَعَدَ ٱلرَّحْمَٰنُ وَصَدَقَ ٱلْمُرْسَلُونَ (٥٢) إِن كَانَتْ إِلَّا صَيْحَةً وَٰحِدَةً فَإِذَا هُمْ جَمِيعٌ لَّدَيْنَا مُحْضَرُونَ (٥٣) فَٱلْيَوْمَ لَا تُظْلَمُ نَفْسٌ شَيْـًٔا وَلَا تُجْزَوْنَ إِلَّا مَا كُنتُمْ تَعْمَلُونَ (٥٤) إِنَّ أَصْحَٰبَ ٱلْجَنَّةِ ٱلْيَوْمَ فِى شُغُلٍ فَٰكِهُونَ (٥٥) هُمْ وَأَزْوَٰجُهُمْ فِى ظِلَٰلٍ عَلَى ٱلْأَرَآئِكِ مُتَّكِـُٔونَ (٥٦) لَهُمْ فِيهَا فَٰكِهَةٌ وَلَهُم مَّا يَدَّعُونَ (٥٧) سَلَٰمٌ قَوْلًا مِّن رَّبٍّ رَّحِيمٍ (٥٨) وَٱمْتَٰزُوا۟ ٱلْيَوْمَ أَيُّهَا ٱلْمُجْرِمُونَ (٥٩)

And the Horn will be blown; and at once from the graves to their Lord they will hasten. (51) They will say, "O woe to us! Who has raised us up from our sleeping place?"

[The reply will be], "This is what the Most Merciful had promised, and the messengers told the truth." (52) It will not be but one blast, and at once they are all brought present before Us. (53) So today no soul will be wronged at all, and you will not be recompensed except for what you used to do. (54) Indeed the companions of Paradise, that Day, will be amused in [joyful] occupation - (55) They and their spouses - in shade, reclining on adorned couches. (56) For them therein is fruit, and for them is whatever they request [or wish] (57) [And] "Peace," a word from a Merciful Lord. (58) [Then He will say], "But stand apart today, you criminals. (59)

## Quran 38:9-10

أَمْ عِندَهُمْ خَزَآئِنُ رَحْمَةِ رَبِّكَ ٱلْعَزِيزِ ٱلْوَهَّابِ (٩) أَمْ لَهُم مُّلْكُ ٱلسَّمَـٰوَٰتِ وَٱلْأَرْضِ وَمَا بَيْنَهُمَا فَلْيَرْتَقُوا۟ فِى ٱلْأَسْبَـٰبِ (١٠)

Or do they have the depositories of the mercy of your Lord, the Exalted in Might, the Bestower? (9) Or is theirs the dominion of the heavens and the earth and what is between them? Then let them ascend through [any] ways of access. (10)

## Quran 38:24-25

قَالَ لَقَدْ ظَلَمَكَ بِسُؤَالِ نَعْجَتِكَ إِلَىٰ نِعَاجِهِۦ ۖ وَإِنَّ كَثِيرًا مِّنَ ٱلْخُلَطَآءِ لَيَبْغِى بَعْضُهُمْ عَلَىٰ بَعْضٍ إِلَّا ٱلَّذِينَ ءَامَنُوا۟ وَعَمِلُوا۟ ٱلصَّـٰلِحَـٰتِ وَقَلِيلٌ مَّا هُمْ ۗ وَظَنَّ دَاوُۥدُ أَنَّمَا فَتَنَّـٰهُ فَٱسْتَغْفَرَ رَبَّهُۥ وَخَرَّ رَاكِعًا وَأَنَابَ ۩ (٢٤) فَغَفَرْنَا لَهُۥ ذَٰلِكَ ۖ وَإِنَّ لَهُۥ عِندَنَا لَزُلْفَىٰ وَحُسْنَ مَـَٔابٍ (٢٥)

[David] said, "He has certainly wronged you in demanding your ewe [in addition] to his ewes. And indeed, many associates oppress one another, except for those who believe and do righteous deeds - and few are they." And David became certain that We had tried him, and he asked forgiveness of his Lord and fell down bowing [in prostration] and turned in repentance [to Allah]. (24) So We forgave him that; and indeed, for him is nearness to Us and a good place of return. (25)

**Quran 38:28-35**

أَمْ نَجْعَلُ ٱلَّذِينَ ءَامَنُوا۟ وَعَمِلُوا۟ ٱلصَّٰلِحَٰتِ كَٱلْمُفْسِدِينَ فِى ٱلْأَرْضِ أَمْ نَجْعَلُ ٱلْمُتَّقِينَ كَٱلْفُجَّارِ (٢٨) كِتَٰبٌ أَنزَلْنَٰهُ إِلَيْكَ مُبَٰرَكٌ لِّيَدَّبَّرُوٓا۟ ءَايَٰتِهِۦ وَلِيَتَذَكَّرَ أُو۟لُوا۟ ٱلْأَلْبَٰبِ (٢٩) وَوَهَبْنَا لِدَاوُۥدَ سُلَيْمَٰنَ ۚ نِعْمَ ٱلْعَبْدُ ۖ إِنَّهُۥٓ أَوَّابٌ (٣٠) إِذْ عُرِضَ عَلَيْهِ بِٱلْعَشِىِّ ٱلصَّٰفِنَٰتُ ٱلْجِيَادُ (٣١) فَقَالَ إِنِّىٓ أَحْبَبْتُ حُبَّ ٱلْخَيْرِ عَن ذِكْرِ رَبِّى حَتَّىٰ تَوَارَتْ بِٱلْحِجَابِ (٣٢) رُدُّوهَا عَلَىَّ ۖ فَطَفِقَ مَسْحًۢا بِٱلسُّوقِ وَٱلْأَعْنَاقِ (٣٣) وَلَقَدْ فَتَنَّا سُلَيْمَٰنَ وَأَلْقَيْنَا عَلَىٰ كُرْسِيِّهِۦ جَسَدًا ثُمَّ أَنَابَ (٣٤) قَالَ رَبِّ ٱغْفِرْ لِى وَهَبْ لِى مُلْكًا لَّا يَنۢبَغِى لِأَحَدٍ مِّنۢ بَعْدِىٓ ۖ إِنَّكَ أَنتَ ٱلْوَهَّابُ (٣٥)

Or should we treat those who believe and do righteous deeds like corrupters in the land? Or should We treat those who fear Allah like the wicked? (28) [This is] a blessed Book which We have revealed to you, [O Muhammad], that they might reflect upon its verses and that those of understanding would be reminded. (29) And to David We gave Solomon. An excellent servant, indeed he was one repeatedly turning back [to Allah]. (30) [Mention] when there were exhibited before him in the afternoon the poised [standing] racehorses. (31) And he said, "Indeed, I gave preference to the love of good [things] over the remembrance of my Lord until the sun disappeared into the curtain [of darkness]." (32) [He said], "Return them to me," and set about striking [their] legs and necks. (33) And We certainly tried Solomon and placed on his throne a body; then he returned. (34) He said, "My Lord, forgive me and grant me a kingdom such as will not belong to anyone after me. Indeed, You are the Bestower." (35)

## Quran 39:5

خَلَقَ ٱلسَّمَٰوَٰتِ وَٱلْأَرْضَ بِٱلْحَقِّ يُكَوِّرُ ٱلَّيْلَ عَلَى ٱلنَّهَارِ وَيُكَوِّرُ ٱلنَّهَارَ عَلَى ٱلَّيْلِ وَسَخَّرَ ٱلشَّمْسَ وَٱلْقَمَرَ كُلٌّ يَجْرِى لِأَجَلٍ مُّسَمًّى أَلَا هُوَ ٱلْعَزِيزُ ٱلْغَفَّرُ (٥)

He created the heavens and earth in truth. He wraps the night over the day and wraps the day over the night and has subjected the sun and the moon, each running [its course] for a specified term. Unquestionably, He is the Exalted in Might, the Perpetual Forgiver. (5)

## Quran 39:9-10

أَمَّنْ هُوَ قَٰنِتٌ ءَانَآءَ ٱلَّيْلِ سَاجِدًا وَقَآئِمًا يَحْذَرُ ٱلْءَاخِرَةَ وَيَرْجُوا۟ رَحْمَةَ رَبِّهِ قُلْ هَلْ يَسْتَوِى ٱلَّذِينَ يَعْلَمُونَ وَٱلَّذِينَ لَا يَعْلَمُونَ إِنَّمَا يَتَذَكَّرُ أُو۟لُوا۟ ٱلْأَلْبَٰبِ (٩) قُلْ يَٰعِبَادِ ٱلَّذِينَ ءَامَنُوا۟ ٱتَّقُوا۟ رَبَّكُمْ لِلَّذِينَ أَحْسَنُوا۟ فِى هَٰذِهِ ٱلدُّنْيَا حَسَنَةٌ وَأَرْضُ ٱللَّهِ وَٰسِعَةٌ إِنَّمَا يُوَفَّى ٱلصَّٰبِرُونَ أَجْرَهُم بِغَيْرِ حِسَابٍ (١٠)

Is one who is devoutly obedient during periods of the night, prostrating and standing [in prayer], fearing the Hereafter and hoping for the mercy of his Lord, [like one who does not]? Say, "Are those who know equal to those who do not know?" Only they will remember [who are] people of understanding. (9) Say, "O My servants who have believed, fear your Lord. For those who do good in this world is good, and the earth of Allah is spacious. Indeed, the patient will be given their reward without account." (10)

## Quran 39:17-18

وَٱلَّذِينَ ٱجْتَنَبُوا۟ ٱلطَّٰغُوتَ أَن يَعْبُدُوهَا وَأَنَابُوٓا۟ إِلَى ٱللَّهِ لَهُمُ ٱلْبُشْرَىٰ ۚ فَبَشِّرْ عِبَادِ (١٧) ٱلَّذِينَ يَسْتَمِعُونَ ٱلْقَوْلَ فَيَتَّبِعُونَ أَحْسَنَهُۥٓ ۚ أُو۟لَٰٓئِكَ ٱلَّذِينَ هَدَىٰهُمُ ٱللَّهُ ۖ وَأُو۟لَٰٓئِكَ هُمْ أُو۟لُوا۟ ٱلْأَلْبَٰبِ (١٨)

Those who avoid At-Tâghût (false deities) by not worshipping them and turn to Allâh (in repentance), for them are glad tidings; so announce the good news to My slaves, – (17) Those who listen to the Word [good advice Lâ ilâha ill-allâh – (none has the right to be worshipped but Allâh) and Islâmic Monotheism] and follow the best thereof ( worship Allâh Alone, repent to Him and avoid Tâghût) those are (the ones) whom Allâh has guided and those are men of understanding. (18)

## Quran 39:20-23

لَٰكِنِ ٱلَّذِينَ ٱتَّقَوْا۟ رَبَّهُمْ لَهُمْ غُرَفٌ مِّن فَوْقِهَا غُرَفٌ مَّبْنِيَّةٌ تَجْرِى مِن تَحْتِهَا ٱلْأَنْهَٰرُ ۖ وَعْدَ ٱللَّهِ ۖ لَا يُخْلِفُ ٱللَّهُ ٱلْمِيعَادَ (٢٠) أَلَمْ تَرَ أَنَّ ٱللَّهَ أَنزَلَ مِنَ ٱلسَّمَآءِ مَآءً فَسَلَكَهُۥ يَنَٰبِيعَ فِى ٱلْأَرْضِ ثُمَّ يُخْرِجُ بِهِۦ زَرْعًا مُّخْتَلِفًا أَلْوَٰنُهُۥ ثُمَّ يَهِيجُ فَتَرَىٰهُ مُصْفَرًّا ثُمَّ يَجْعَلُهُۥ حُطَٰمًا ۚ إِنَّ فِى ذَٰلِكَ لَذِكْرَىٰ لِأُو۟لِى ٱلْأَلْبَٰبِ (٢١) أَفَمَن شَرَحَ ٱللَّهُ صَدْرَهُۥ لِلْإِسْلَٰمِ فَهُوَ عَلَىٰ نُورٍ مِّن رَّبِّهِۦ ۚ فَوَيْلٌ لِّلْقَٰسِيَةِ قُلُوبُهُم مِّن ذِكْرِ ٱللَّهِ ۚ أُو۟لَٰٓئِكَ فِى ضَلَٰلٍ مُّبِينٍ (٢٢) ٱللَّهُ نَزَّلَ أَحْسَنَ ٱلْحَدِيثِ كِتَٰبًا مُّتَشَٰبِهًا مَّثَانِىَ تَقْشَعِرُّ مِنْهُ جُلُودُ ٱلَّذِينَ يَخْشَوْنَ رَبَّهُمْ ثُمَّ تَلِينُ جُلُودُهُمْ وَقُلُوبُهُمْ إِلَىٰ ذِكْرِ ٱللَّهِ ۚ ذَٰلِكَ هُدَى ٱللَّهِ يَهْدِى بِهِۦ مَن يَشَآءُ ۚ وَمَن يُضْلِلِ ٱللَّهُ فَمَا لَهُۥ مِنْ هَادٍ (٢٣)

But those who have feared their Lord - for them are chambers, above them chambers built high, beneath which rivers flow. [This is] the promise of Allah. Allah does not fail in [His] promise. (20) Do you not see that Allah sends down rain from the sky and makes it flow as springs [and rivers] in the earth; then He produces thereby crops of varying colors; then they dry and you see them turned yellow; then He makes them [scattered] debris. Indeed in that is a reminder for those of understanding. (21) So is one whose breast Allah has expanded to [accept] Islam and he is upon a light from his Lord [like one whose heart rejects it]? Then woe to those whose hearts are hardened against the remembrance of Allah. Those are in manifest error. (22) Allah has sent down the best statement: a consistent Book wherein is reiteration. The skins shiver therefrom of those who fear their Lord; then their skins and their hearts relax at the remembrance of Allah. That is the guidance of Allah by which He guides whom He wills. And one whom Allah leaves astray - for him there is no guide. (23)

## Quran 39:27-28

وَلَقَدْ ضَرَبْنَا لِلنَّاسِ فِى هَٰذَا ٱلْقُرْءَانِ مِن كُلِّ مَثَلٍ لَّعَلَّهُمْ يَتَذَكَّرُونَ (٢٧) قُرْءَانًا عَرَبِيًّا غَيْرَ ذِى عِوَجٍ لَّعَلَّهُمْ يَتَّقُونَ (٢٨)

And We have certainly presented for the people in this Qur'an from every [kind of] example - that they might remember. (27) [It is] an Arabic Qur'an, without any deviance that they might become righteous. (28)

## Quran 39:33-35

وَٱلَّذِى جَآءَ بِٱلصِّدْقِ وَصَدَّقَ بِهِۦٓ ۙ أُو۟لَٰٓئِكَ هُمُ ٱلْمُتَّقُونَ (٣٣) لَهُم مَّا يَشَآءُونَ عِندَ رَبِّهِمْ ۚ ذَٰلِكَ جَزَآءُ ٱلْمُحْسِنِينَ (٣٤) لِيُكَفِّرَ ٱللَّهُ عَنْهُمْ أَسْوَأَ ٱلَّذِى عَمِلُوا۟ وَيَجْزِيَهُمْ أَجْرَهُم بِأَحْسَنِ ٱلَّذِى كَانُوا۟ يَعْمَلُونَ (٣٥)

And the one who has brought the truth and [they who] believed in it - those are the righteous. (33) They will have whatever they desire with their Lord. That is the reward of the doers of good - (34) That Allah may remove from them the worst of what they did and reward them their due for the best of what they used to do. (35)

## Quran 39:38

وَلَئِن سَأَلْتَهُم مَّنْ خَلَقَ ٱلسَّمَٰوَٰتِ وَٱلْأَرْضَ لَيَقُولُنَّ ٱللَّهُ ۚ قُلْ أَفَرَءَيْتُم مَّا تَدْعُونَ مِن دُونِ ٱللَّهِ إِنْ أَرَادَنِىَ ٱللَّهُ بِضُرٍّ هَلْ هُنَّ كَٰشِفَٰتُ ضُرِّهِۦٓ أَوْ أَرَادَنِى بِرَحْمَةٍ هَلْ هُنَّ مُمْسِكَٰتُ رَحْمَتِهِۦ ۚ قُلْ حَسْبِىَ ٱللَّهُ ۖ عَلَيْهِ يَتَوَكَّلُ ٱلْمُتَوَكِّلُونَ (٣٨)

And if you asked them, "Who created the heavens and the earth?" they would surely say, "Allah." Say, "Then have you considered what you invoke besides Allah? If Allah intended me harm, are they removers of His harm; or if He intended me mercy, are they withholders of His mercy?" Say, "Sufficient for me is Allah; upon Him [alone] rely the [wise] reliers." (38)

## Quran 39:53-58

۞ قُلْ يَٰعِبَادِىَ ٱلَّذِينَ أَسْرَفُوا۟ عَلَىٰٓ أَنفُسِهِمْ لَا تَقْنَطُوا۟ مِن رَّحْمَةِ ٱللَّهِ ۚ إِنَّ ٱللَّهَ يَغْفِرُ ٱلذُّنُوبَ جَمِيعًا ۚ إِنَّهُۥ هُوَ ٱلْغَفُورُ ٱلرَّحِيمُ (٥٣) وَأَنِيبُوٓا۟ إِلَىٰ رَبِّكُمْ وَأَسْلِمُوا۟ لَهُۥ مِن قَبْلِ أَن يَأْتِيَكُمُ ٱلْعَذَابُ ثُمَّ لَا تُنصَرُونَ (٥٤) وَٱتَّبِعُوٓا۟ أَحْسَنَ مَآ أُنزِلَ إِلَيْكُم مِّن رَّبِّكُم مِّن قَبْلِ أَن يَأْتِيَكُمُ ٱلْعَذَابُ بَغْتَةً وَأَنتُمْ لَا تَشْعُرُونَ (٥٥) أَن تَقُولَ نَفْسٌ يَٰحَسْرَتَىٰ عَلَىٰ مَا فَرَّطتُ فِى جَنۢبِ ٱللَّهِ وَإِن كُنتُ لَمِنَ

ٱلسَّٰخِرِينَ (٥٦) أَوْ تَقُولَ لَوْ أَنَّ ٱللَّهَ هَدَىٰنِى لَكُنتُ مِنَ ٱلْمُتَّقِينَ (٥٧) أَوْ تَقُولَ حِينَ تَرَى ٱلْعَذَابَ لَوْ أَنَّ لِى كَرَّةً فَأَكُونَ مِنَ ٱلْمُحْسِنِينَ (٥٨)

Say, "O My servants who have transgressed against themselves [by sinning], do not despair of the mercy of Allah. Indeed, Allah forgives all sins. Indeed, it is He who is the Forgiving, the Merciful." (53) And return [in repentance] to your Lord and submit to Him before the punishment comes upon you; then you will not be helped. (54) And follow the best of what was revealed to you from your Lord before the punishment comes upon you suddenly while you do not perceive, (55) Lest a soul should say, "Oh [how great is] my regret over what I neglected in regard to Allah and that I was among the mockers." (56) Or [lest] it say, "If only Allah had guided me, I would have been among the righteous." (57) Or [lest] it say when it sees the punishment, "If only I had another turn so I could be among the doers of good." (58)

## Quran 40:2-3

تَنزِيلُ ٱلْكِتَٰبِ مِنَ ٱللَّهِ ٱلْعَزِيزِ ٱلْعَلِيمِ (٢) غَافِرِ ٱلذَّنۢبِ وَقَابِلِ ٱلتَّوْبِ شَدِيدِ ٱلْعِقَابِ ذِى ٱلطَّوْلِ لَآ إِلَٰهَ إِلَّا هُوَ إِلَيْهِ ٱلْمَصِيرُ (٣)

The revelation of the Book is from Allah, the Exalted in Might, the Knowing. (2) The forgiver of sin, acceptor of repentance, severe in punishment, owner of abundance. There is no deity except Him; to Him is the destination. (3)

## Quran 40:7-9

ٱلَّذِينَ يَحْمِلُونَ ٱلْعَرْشَ وَمَنْ حَوْلَهُ يُسَبِّحُونَ بِحَمْدِ رَبِّهِمْ وَيُؤْمِنُونَ بِهِۦ وَيَسْتَغْفِرُونَ لِلَّذِينَ ءَامَنُوا۟ رَبَّنَا وَسِعْتَ كُلَّ شَىْءٍ رَّحْمَةً وَعِلْمًا فَٱغْفِرْ لِلَّذِينَ تَابُوا۟ وَٱتَّبَعُوا۟ سَبِيلَكَ وَقِهِمْ عَذَابَ ٱلْجَحِيمِ (٧) رَبَّنَا وَأَدْخِلْهُمْ جَنَّٰتِ عَدْنٍ ٱلَّتِى وَعَدتَّهُمْ وَمَن صَلَحَ مِنْ ءَابَآئِهِمْ وَأَزْوَٰجِهِمْ وَذُرِّيَّٰتِهِمْ إِنَّكَ أَنتَ ٱلْعَزِيزُ ٱلْحَكِيمُ (٨) وَقِهِمُ ٱلسَّيِّـَٔاتِ وَمَن تَقِ ٱلسَّيِّـَٔاتِ يَوْمَئِذٍ فَقَدْ رَحِمْتَهُۥ وَذَٰلِكَ هُوَ ٱلْفَوْزُ ٱلْعَظِيمُ (٩)

*Those [angels] who carry the Throne and those around it exalt [Allah] with praise of their Lord and believe in Him and ask forgiveness for those who have believed, [saying], "Our Lord, You have encompassed all things in mercy and knowledge, so forgive those who have repented and followed Your way and protect them from the punishment of Hellfire. (7) Our Lord, and admit them to gardens of perpetual residence which You have promised them and whoever was righteous among their fathers, their spouses and their offspring. Indeed, it is You who is the Exalted in Might, the Wise. (8) And protect them from the evil consequences [of their deeds]. And he whom You protect from evil consequences that Day - You will have given him mercy. And that is the great attainment." (9)*

## Quran 40:13

هُوَ ٱلَّذِى يُرِيكُمْ ءَايَٰتِهِۦ وَيُنَزِّلُ لَكُم مِّنَ ٱلسَّمَآءِ رِزْقًا وَمَا يَتَذَكَّرُ إِلَّا مَن يُنِيبُ (١٣)

*It is He who shows you His signs and sends down to you from the sky, provision. But none will remember except he who turns back [in repentance]. (13)*

## Quran 41:2-4

تَنزِيلٌ مِّنَ ٱلرَّحْمَٰنِ ٱلرَّحِيمِ (٢) كِتَٰبٌ فُصِّلَتْ ءَايَٰتُهُۥ قُرْءَانًا عَرَبِيًّا لِّقَوْمٍ يَعْلَمُونَ (٣) بَشِيرًا وَنَذِيرًا فَأَعْرَضَ أَكْثَرُهُمْ فَهُمْ لَا يَسْمَعُونَ (٤)

[This is] a revelation from the Entirely Merciful, the Especially Merciful - (2) A Book whose verses have been detailed, an Arabic Qur'an for a people who know, (3) As a giver of good tidings and a warner; but most of them turn away, so they do not hear. (4)

## Quran 41:6-8

قُلْ إِنَّمَآ أَنَا۠ بَشَرٌ مِّثْلُكُمْ يُوحَىٰٓ إِلَىَّ أَنَّمَآ إِلَٰهُكُمْ إِلَٰهٌ وَٰحِدٌ فَٱسْتَقِيمُوٓا۟ إِلَيْهِ وَٱسْتَغْفِرُوهُ وَوَيْلٌ لِّلْمُشْرِكِينَ (٦) ٱلَّذِينَ لَا يُؤْتُونَ ٱلزَّكَوٰةَ وَهُم بِٱلْءَاخِرَةِ هُمْ كَٰفِرُونَ (٧) إِنَّ ٱلَّذِينَ ءَامَنُوا۟ وَعَمِلُوا۟ ٱلصَّٰلِحَٰتِ لَهُمْ أَجْرٌ غَيْرُ مَمْنُونٍ (٨)

Say, O [Muhammad], "I am only a man like you to whom it has been revealed that your god is but one God; so take a straight course to Him and seek His forgiveness." And woe to those who associate others with Allah - (6) Those who do not give zakah, and in the Hereafter they are disbelievers. (7) Indeed, those who believe and do righteous deeds - for them is a reward uninterrupted. (8)

## Quran 41:30-36

إِنَّ ٱلَّذِينَ قَالُوا۟ رَبُّنَا ٱللَّهُ ثُمَّ ٱسْتَقَٰمُوا۟ تَتَنَزَّلُ عَلَيْهِمُ ٱلْمَلَٰٓئِكَةُ أَلَّا تَخَافُوا۟ وَلَا تَحْزَنُوا۟ وَأَبْشِرُوا۟ بِٱلْجَنَّةِ ٱلَّتِى كُنتُمْ تُوعَدُونَ (٣٠) نَحْنُ أَوْلِيَآؤُكُمْ فِى ٱلْحَيَوٰةِ ٱلدُّنْيَا وَفِى ٱلْءَاخِرَةِ وَلَكُمْ فِيهَا مَا تَشْتَهِىٓ أَنفُسُكُمْ وَلَكُمْ فِيهَا مَا تَدَّعُونَ (٣١) نُزُلًا مِّنْ غَفُورٍ رَّحِيمٍ (٣٢) وَمَنْ أَحْسَنُ قَوْلًا مِّمَّن دَعَآ إِلَى ٱللَّهِ وَعَمِلَ صَٰلِحًا وَقَالَ إِنَّنِى مِنَ ٱلْمُسْلِمِينَ (٣٣) وَلَا تَسْتَوِى ٱلْحَسَنَةُ وَلَا ٱلسَّيِّئَةُ ٱدْفَعْ بِٱلَّتِى هِىَ أَحْسَنُ فَإِذَا ٱلَّذِى بَيْنَكَ وَبَيْنَهُۥ عَدَٰوَةٌ كَأَنَّهُۥ وَلِىٌّ حَمِيمٌ (٣٤) وَمَا

يُلَقَّىٰهَآ إِلَّا ٱلَّذِينَ صَبَرُوا۟ وَمَا يُلَقَّىٰهَآ إِلَّا ذُو حَظٍّ عَظِيمٍ (٣٥) وَإِمَّا يَنزَغَنَّكَ مِنَ ٱلشَّيْطَٰنِ نَزْغٌ فَٱسْتَعِذْ بِٱللَّهِ ۚ إِنَّهُۥ هُوَ ٱلسَّمِيعُ ٱلْعَلِيمُ (٣٦)

Indeed, those who have said, "Our Lord is Allah " and then remained on a right course - the angels will descend upon them, [saying], "Do not fear and do not grieve but receive good tidings of Paradise, which you were promised. (30) We [angels] were your allies in worldly life and [are so] in the Hereafter. And you will have therein whatever your souls desire, and you will have therein whatever you request [or wish] (31) As accommodation from a [Lord who is] Forgiving and Merciful." (32) And who is better in speech than one who invites to Allah and does righteousness and says, "Indeed, I am of the Muslims." (33) And not equal are the good deed and the bad. Repel [evil] by that [deed] which is better; and thereupon the one whom between you and him is enmity [will become] as though he was a devoted friend. (34) But none is granted it except those who are patient, and none is granted it except one having a great portion [of good]. (35) And if there comes to you from Satan an evil suggestion, then seek refuge in Allah. Indeed, He is the Hearing, the Knowing. (36)

## Quran 41:43-46

مَّا يُقَالُ لَكَ إِلَّا مَا قَدْ قِيلَ لِلرُّسُلِ مِن قَبْلِكَ ۚ إِنَّ رَبَّكَ لَذُو مَغْفِرَةٍ وَذُو عِقَابٍ أَلِيمٍ (٤٣) وَلَوْ جَعَلْنَٰهُ قُرْءَانًا أَعْجَمِيًّا لَّقَالُوا۟ لَوْلَا فُصِّلَتْ ءَايَٰتُهُۥٓ ۖ ءَا۬عْجَمِيٌّ وَعَرَبِيٌّ ۗ قُلْ هُوَ لِلَّذِينَ ءَامَنُوا۟ هُدًى وَشِفَآءٌ ۖ وَٱلَّذِينَ لَا يُؤْمِنُونَ فِىٓ ءَاذَانِهِمْ وَقْرٌ وَهُوَ عَلَيْهِمْ عَمًى ۚ أُو۟لَٰٓئِكَ يُنَادَوْنَ مِن مَّكَانٍۭ بَعِيدٍ (٤٤) وَلَقَدْ ءَاتَيْنَا مُوسَى ٱلْكِتَٰبَ فَٱخْتُلِفَ فِيهِ ۗ وَلَوْلَا كَلِمَةٌ سَبَقَتْ مِن رَّبِّكَ لَقُضِىَ بَيْنَهُمْ ۚ وَإِنَّهُمْ لَفِى شَكٍّ

مِنْهُ مُرِيبٍ (٤٥) مَّنْ عَمِلَ صَٰلِحًا فَلِنَفْسِهِۦ ۖ وَمَنْ أَسَآءَ فَعَلَيْهَا ۗ وَمَا رَبُّكَ بِظَلَّٰمٍ لِّلْعَبِيدِ (٤٦)

Nothing is said to you, [O Muhammad], except what was already said to the messengers before you. Indeed, your Lord is a possessor of forgiveness and a possessor of painful penalty. (43) And if We had made it a non-Arabic Qur'an, they would have said, "Why are its verses not explained in detail [in our language]? Is it a foreign [recitation] and an Arab [messenger]?" Say, "It is, for those who believe, a guidance and cure." And those who do not believe - in their ears is deafness, and it is upon them blindness. Those are being called from a distant place. (44) And We had already given Moses the Scripture, but it came under disagreement. And if not for a word that preceded from your Lord, it would have been concluded between them. And indeed they are, concerning the Qur'an, in disquieting doubt.
(45) Whoever does righteousness - it is for his [own] soul; and whoever does evil [does so] against it. And your Lord is not ever unjust to [His] servants. (46)

## Quran 41:49-52

لَّا يَسْـَٔمُ ٱلْإِنسَٰنُ مِن دُعَآءِ ٱلْخَيْرِ وَإِن مَّسَّهُ ٱلشَّرُّ فَيَـُٔوسٌ قَنُوطٌ (٤٩) وَلَئِنْ أَذَقْنَٰهُ رَحْمَةً مِّنَّا مِنۢ بَعْدِ ضَرَّآءَ مَسَّتْهُ لَيَقُولَنَّ هَٰذَا لِى وَمَآ أَظُنُّ ٱلسَّاعَةَ قَآئِمَةً وَلَئِن رُّجِعْتُ إِلَىٰ رَبِّىٓ إِنَّ لِى عِندَهُۥ لَلْحُسْنَىٰ ۚ فَلَنُنَبِّئَنَّ ٱلَّذِينَ كَفَرُوا۟ بِمَا عَمِلُوا۟ وَلَنُذِيقَنَّهُم مِّنْ عَذَابٍ غَلِيظٍ (٥٠) وَإِذَآ أَنْعَمْنَا عَلَى ٱلْإِنسَٰنِ أَعْرَضَ وَنَـَٔا بِجَانِبِهِۦ وَإِذَا مَسَّهُ ٱلشَّرُّ فَذُو دُعَآءٍ عَرِيضٍ (٥١) قُلْ أَرَءَيْتُمْ إِن كَانَ مِنْ عِندِ ٱللَّهِ ثُمَّ كَفَرْتُم بِهِۦ مَنْ أَضَلُّ مِمَّنْ هُوَ فِى شِقَاقٍۭ بَعِيدٍ (٥٢)

Man is not weary of supplication for good [things], but if evil touches him, he is hopeless and despairing. (49) And if We let him taste mercy from Us after an adversity which has touched him, he will surely say, "This is [due] to me, and I do not think the Hour will occur; and [even] if I should be returned to my Lord, indeed, for me there will be with Him the best." But We will surely inform those who disbelieved about what they did, and We will surely make them taste a massive punishment. (50) And when We bestow favor upon man, he turns away and distances himself; but when evil touches him, then he is full of extensive supplication. (51) Say, "Have you considered: if the Qur'an is from Allah and you disbelieved in it, who would be more astray than one who is in extreme dissension?" (52)

## Quran 42:5

تَكَادُ ٱلسَّمَٰوَٰتُ يَتَفَطَّرْنَ مِن فَوْقِهِنَّ وَٱلْمَلَٰٓئِكَةُ يُسَبِّحُونَ بِحَمْدِ رَبِّهِمْ وَيَسْتَغْفِرُونَ لِمَن فِى ٱلْأَرْضِ أَلَآ إِنَّ ٱللَّهَ هُوَ ٱلْغَفُورُ ٱلرَّحِيمُ (٥)

The heavens almost break from above them, and the angels exalt [Allah] with praise of their Lord and ask forgiveness for those on earth. Unquestionably, it is Allah who is the Forgiving, the Merciful. (5)

## Quran 42:8-9

وَلَوْ شَآءَ ٱللَّهُ لَجَعَلَهُمْ أُمَّةً وَٰحِدَةً وَلَٰكِن يُدْخِلُ مَن يَشَآءُ فِى رَحْمَتِهِۦ وَٱلظَّٰلِمُونَ مَا لَهُم مِّن وَلِىٍّ وَلَا نَصِيرٍ (٨) أَمِ ٱتَّخَذُوا۟ مِن دُونِهِۦٓ أَوْلِيَآءَ فَٱللَّهُ هُوَ ٱلْوَلِىُّ وَهُوَ يُحْىِ ٱلْمَوْتَىٰ وَهُوَ عَلَىٰ كُلِّ شَىْءٍ قَدِيرٌ (٩)

And if Allah willed, He could have made them [of] one religion, but He admits whom He wills into His mercy. And the wrongdoers have not any protector or helper. (8) Or have they taken protectors [or allies] besides him? But Allah - He is the Protector, and He gives life to the dead, and He is over all things competent. (9)

## Quran 42:13

شَرَعَ لَكُم مِّنَ ٱلدِّينِ مَا وَصَّىٰ بِهِۦ نُوحًا وَٱلَّذِىٓ أَوْحَيْنَآ إِلَيْكَ وَمَا وَصَّيْنَا بِهِۦٓ إِبْرَٰهِيمَ وَمُوسَىٰ وَعِيسَىٰٓ أَنْ أَقِيمُوا۟ ٱلدِّينَ وَلَا تَتَفَرَّقُوا۟ فِيهِ كَبُرَ عَلَى ٱلْمُشْرِكِينَ مَا تَدْعُوهُمْ إِلَيْهِ ٱللَّهُ يَجْتَبِىٓ إِلَيْهِ مَن يَشَآءُ وَيَهْدِىٓ إِلَيْهِ مَن يُنِيبُ (١٣)

He has ordained for you of religion what He enjoined upon Noah and that which We have revealed to you, [O Muhammad], and what We enjoined upon Abraham and Moses and Jesus - to establish the religion and not be divided therein. Difficult for those who associate others with Allah is that to which you invite them. Allah chooses for Himself whom He wills and guides to Himself whoever turns back [to Him]. (13)

## Quran 42:25-40

وَهُوَ ٱلَّذِى يَقْبَلُ ٱلتَّوْبَةَ عَنْ عِبَادِهِۦ وَيَعْفُوا۟ عَنِ ٱلسَّيِّـَٔاتِ وَيَعْلَمُ مَا تَفْعَلُونَ (٢٥) وَيَسْتَجِيبُ ٱلَّذِينَ ءَامَنُوا۟ وَعَمِلُوا۟ ٱلصَّـٰلِحَـٰتِ وَيَزِيدُهُم مِّن فَضْلِهِۦ وَٱلْكَـٰفِرُونَ لَهُمْ عَذَابٌ شَدِيدٌ (٢٦) ۞ وَلَوْ بَسَطَ ٱللَّهُ ٱلرِّزْقَ لِعِبَادِهِۦ لَبَغَوْا۟ فِى ٱلْأَرْضِ وَلَـٰكِن يُنَزِّلُ بِقَدَرٍ مَّا يَشَآءُ إِنَّهُۥ بِعِبَادِهِۦ خَبِيرٌۢ بَصِيرٌ (٢٧) وَهُوَ ٱلَّذِى يُنَزِّلُ ٱلْغَيْثَ مِنۢ بَعْدِ مَا قَنَطُوا۟ وَيَنشُرُ رَحْمَتَهُۥ وَهُوَ ٱلْوَلِىُّ ٱلْحَمِيدُ (٢٨) وَمِنْ ءَايَـٰتِهِۦ خَلْقُ ٱلسَّمَـٰوَٰتِ وَٱلْأَرْضِ وَمَا بَثَّ فِيهِمَا مِن دَآبَّةٍ وَهُوَ عَلَىٰ جَمْعِهِمْ إِذَا يَشَآءُ قَدِيرٌ (٢٩) وَمَآ أَصَـٰبَكُم مِّن مُّصِيبَةٍ فَبِمَا كَسَبَتْ أَيْدِيكُمْ وَيَعْفُوا۟ عَن كَثِيرٍ (٣٠) وَمَآ أَنتُم بِمُعْجِزِينَ فِى ٱلْأَرْضِ وَمَا لَكُم مِّن

دُونِ ٱللَّهِ مِن وَلِىٍّ وَلَا نَصِيرٍ (٣١) وَمِنْ ءَايَـٰتِهِ ٱلْجَوَارِ فِى ٱلْبَحْرِ كَٱلْأَعْلَـٰمِ (٣٢) إِن يَشَأْ يُسْكِنِ ٱلرِّيحَ فَيَظْلَلْنَ رَوَاكِدَ عَلَىٰ ظَهْرِهِۦٓ ۚ إِنَّ فِى ذَٰلِكَ لَءَايَـٰتٍ لِّكُلِّ صَبَّارٍ شَكُورٍ (٣٣) أَوْ يُوبِقْهُنَّ بِمَا كَسَبُوا۟ وَيَعْفُ عَن كَثِيرٍ (٣٤) وَيَعْلَمَ ٱلَّذِينَ يُجَـٰدِلُونَ فِىٓ ءَايَـٰتِنَا مَا لَهُم مِّن مَّحِيصٍ (٣٥) فَمَآ أُوتِيتُم مِّن شَىْءٍ فَمَتَـٰعُ ٱلْحَيَوٰةِ ٱلدُّنْيَا ۖ وَمَا عِندَ ٱللَّهِ خَيْرٌ وَأَبْقَىٰ لِلَّذِينَ ءَامَنُوا۟ وَعَلَىٰ رَبِّهِمْ يَتَوَكَّلُونَ (٣٦) وَٱلَّذِينَ يَجْتَنِبُونَ كَبَـٰٓئِرَ ٱلْإِثْمِ وَٱلْفَوَٰحِشَ وَإِذَا مَا غَضِبُوا۟ هُمْ يَغْفِرُونَ (٣٧) وَٱلَّذِينَ ٱسْتَجَابُوا۟ لِرَبِّهِمْ وَأَقَامُوا۟ ٱلصَّلَوٰةَ وَأَمْرُهُمْ شُورَىٰ بَيْنَهُمْ وَمِمَّا رَزَقْنَـٰهُمْ يُنفِقُونَ (٣٨) وَٱلَّذِينَ إِذَآ أَصَابَهُمُ ٱلْبَغْىُ هُمْ يَنتَصِرُونَ (٣٩) وَجَزَٰٓؤُا۟ سَيِّئَةٍ سَيِّئَةٌ مِّثْلُهَا ۖ فَمَنْ عَفَا وَأَصْلَحَ فَأَجْرُهُۥ عَلَى ٱللَّهِ ۚ إِنَّهُۥ لَا يُحِبُّ ٱلظَّـٰلِمِينَ (٤٠)

And it is He who accepts repentance from his servants and pardons misdeeds, and He knows what you do. (25) And He answers [the supplication of] those who have believed and done righteous deeds and increases [for] them from His bounty. But the disbelievers will have a severe punishment. (26) And if Allah had extended [excessively] provision for His servants, they would have committed tyranny throughout the earth. But He sends [it] down in an amount which He wills. Indeed He is, of His servants, Acquainted and Seeing. (27) And it is He who sends down the rain after they had despaired and spreads His mercy. And He is the Protector, the Praiseworthy. (28) And of his signs is the creation of the heavens and earth and what He has dispersed throughout them of creatures. And He, for gathering them when He wills, is competent. (29) And whatever strikes you of disaster - it is for what your hands have earned; but He pardons much. (30) And you will not cause failure [to Allah] upon the earth. And you have not besides Allah any protector or helper. (31) And of His signs are the ships in the sea, like mountains. (32) If He willed, He could still the wind, and they would remain motionless on its surface. Indeed in that are signs for everyone patient and grateful. (33) Or He could destroy them for what they earned; but He pardons much. (34) And [that is so] those who dispute concerning Our signs may know that for them there is no place of escape. (35) So whatever thing you have been given - it is but [for] enjoyment of the worldly life. But what is with Allah is better and more lasting for those who have believed and upon their Lord rely (36) And those who avoid the major sins and immoralities, and when they are angry, they forgive, (37) And those who have responded to their lord and established prayer and whose affair is [determined by] consultation among themselves, and from what We have provided them, they spend. (38) And those who, when tyranny strikes them, they defend themselves, (39) And the retribution for an evil act is an evil one like it, but whoever pardons and makes reconciliation - his reward is [due] from Allah. Indeed, He does not like wrongdoers. (40)

## Quran 43:19-20

وَجَعَلُوا۟ ٱلْمَلَـٰٓئِكَةَ ٱلَّذِينَ هُمْ عِبَـٰدُ ٱلرَّحْمَـٰنِ إِنَـٰثًا ۚ أَشَهِدُوا۟ خَلْقَهُمْ ۚ سَتُكْتَبُ شَهَـٰدَتُهُمْ وَيُسْـَٔلُونَ (١٩) وَقَالُوا۟ لَوْ شَآءَ ٱلرَّحْمَـٰنُ مَا عَبَدْنَـٰهُم ۗ مَّا لَهُم بِذَٰلِكَ مِنْ عِلْمٍ ۖ إِنْ هُمْ إِلَّا يَخْرُصُونَ (٢٠)

And they have made the angels, who are servants of the Most Merciful, females. Did they witness their creation?

Their testimony will be recorded, and they will be questioned. (19) And they said, "If the Most Merciful had willed, we would not have worshipped them." They have of that no knowledge. They are not but falsifying. (20)

## Quran 43:32-37

أَهُمْ يَقْسِمُونَ رَحْمَتَ رَبِّكَ ۚ نَحْنُ قَسَمْنَا بَيْنَهُم مَّعِيشَتَهُمْ فِي ٱلْحَيَوٰةِ ٱلدُّنْيَا ۚ وَرَفَعْنَا بَعْضَهُمْ فَوْقَ بَعْضٍ دَرَجَـٰتٍ لِّيَتَّخِذَ بَعْضُهُم بَعْضًا سُخْرِيًّا ۗ وَرَحْمَتُ رَبِّكَ خَيْرٌ مِّمَّا يَجْمَعُونَ (٣٢) وَلَوْلَا أَن يَكُونَ ٱلنَّاسُ أُمَّةً وَٰحِدَةً لَّجَعَلْنَا لِمَن يَكْفُرُ بِٱلرَّحْمَـٰنِ لِبُيُوتِهِمْ سُقُفًا مِّن فِضَّةٍ وَمَعَارِجَ عَلَيْهَا يَظْهَرُونَ (٣٣) وَلِبُيُوتِهِمْ أَبْوَٰبًا وَسُرُرًا عَلَيْهَا يَتَّكِـُٔونَ (٣٤) وَزُخْرُفًا ۚ وَإِن كُلُّ ذَٰلِكَ لَمَّا مَتَـٰعُ ٱلْحَيَوٰةِ ٱلدُّنْيَا ۚ وَٱلْـَٔاخِرَةُ عِندَ رَبِّكَ لِلْمُتَّقِينَ (٣٥) وَمَن يَعْشُ عَن ذِكْرِ ٱلرَّحْمَـٰنِ نُقَيِّضْ لَهُۥ شَيْطَـٰنًا فَهُوَ لَهُۥ قَرِينٌ (٣٦) وَإِنَّهُمْ لَيَصُدُّونَهُمْ عَنِ ٱلسَّبِيلِ وَيَحْسَبُونَ أَنَّهُم مُّهْتَدُونَ (٣٧)

Do they distribute the mercy of your Lord? It is We who have apportioned among them their livelihood in the life of this world and have raised some of them above others in degrees [of rank] that they may make use of one another for service. But the mercy of your Lord is better than whatever they accumulate. (32) And if it were not that the people would become one community [of disbelievers], We would have made for those who disbelieve in the Most Merciful - for their houses - ceilings and stairways of silver upon which to mount (33) And for their houses - doors and couches [of silver] upon which to recline (34) And gold ornament. But all that is not but the enjoyment of worldly life. And the Hereafter with your Lord is for the righteous. (35) And whoever is blinded from remembrance of the Most Merciful - We appoint for him a devil, and he is to him a companion. (36) And indeed, the devils avert them from the way [of guidance] while they think that they are [rightly] guided (37)

## Quran 43:45

وَسْـَٔلْ مَنْ أَرْسَلْنَا مِن قَبْلِكَ مِن رُّسُلِنَآ أَجَعَلْنَا مِن دُونِ ٱلرَّحْمَـٰنِ ءَالِهَةً يُعْبَدُونَ (٤٥)

And ask those We sent before you of Our messengers; have We made besides the Most Merciful deities to be worshipped? (45)

## Quran 44:2-9

وَٱلْكِتَـٰبِ ٱلْمُبِينِ (٢) إِنَّآ أَنزَلْنَـٰهُ فِى لَيْلَةٍ مُّبَـٰرَكَةٍ إِنَّا كُنَّا مُنذِرِينَ (٣) فِيهَا يُفْرَقُ كُلُّ أَمْرٍ حَكِيمٍ (٤) أَمْرًا مِّنْ عِندِنَآ إِنَّا كُنَّا مُرْسِلِينَ (٥) رَحْمَةً مِّن رَّبِّكَ إِنَّهُۥ هُوَ ٱلسَّمِيعُ ٱلْعَلِيمُ (٦) رَبِّ ٱلسَّمَـٰوَٰتِ وَٱلْأَرْضِ وَمَا بَيْنَهُمَآ إِن كُنتُم مُّوقِنِينَ (٧) لَآ إِلَـٰهَ إِلَّا هُوَ يُحْىِۦ وَيُمِيتُ رَبُّكُمْ وَرَبُّ ءَابَآئِكُمُ ٱلْأَوَّلِينَ (٨) بَلْ هُمْ فِى شَكٍّ يَلْعَبُونَ (٩)

By the clear Book, (2) Indeed, We sent it down during a blessed night. Indeed, We were to warn [mankind]. (3) On that night is made distinct every precise matter - (4) [Every] matter [proceeding] from Us. Indeed, We were to send [a messenger] (5) As mercy from your Lord. Indeed, He is the Hearing, the Knowing. (6) Lord of the heavens and the earth and that between them, if you would be certain. (7) There is no deity except Him; He gives life and causes death. [He is] your Lord and the

Lord of your first forefathers. (8) But they are in doubt, amusing themselves. (9)

## Quran 44:40-42

إِنَّ يَوْمَ ٱلْفَصْلِ مِيقَٰتُهُمْ أَجْمَعِينَ (٤٠) يَوْمَ لَا يُغْنِى مَوْلًى عَن مَّوْلًى شَيْـًٔا وَلَا هُمْ يُنصَرُونَ (٤١) إِلَّا مَن رَّحِمَ ٱللَّهُ ۚ إِنَّهُۥ هُوَ ٱلْعَزِيزُ ٱلرَّحِيمُ (٤٢)

*Indeed, the Day of Judgement is the appointed time for them all - (40) The Day when no relation will avail a relation at all, nor will they be helped - (41) Except those [believers] on whom Allah has mercy. Indeed, He is the Exalted in Might, the Merciful. (42)*

## Quran 45:20

هَٰذَا بَصَٰٓئِرُ لِلنَّاسِ وَهُدًى وَرَحْمَةٌ لِّقَوْمٍ يُوقِنُونَ (٢٠)

*This [Qur'an] is enlightenment for mankind and guidance and mercy for a people who are certain [in faith]. (20)*

## Quran 45:26-30

قُلِ ٱللَّهُ يُحْيِيكُمْ ثُمَّ يُمِيتُكُمْ ثُمَّ يَجْمَعُكُمْ إِلَىٰ يَوْمِ ٱلْقِيَٰمَةِ لَا رَيْبَ فِيهِ وَلَٰكِنَّ أَكْثَرَ ٱلنَّاسِ لَا يَعْلَمُونَ (٢٦) وَلِلَّهِ مُلْكُ ٱلسَّمَٰوَٰتِ وَٱلْأَرْضِ ۚ وَيَوْمَ تَقُومُ ٱلسَّاعَةُ يَوْمَئِذٍ يَخْسَرُ ٱلْمُبْطِلُونَ (٢٧) وَتَرَىٰ كُلَّ أُمَّةٍ جَاثِيَةً ۚ كُلُّ أُمَّةٍ تُدْعَىٰٓ إِلَىٰ كِتَٰبِهَا ٱلْيَوْمَ تُجْزَوْنَ مَا كُنتُمْ تَعْمَلُونَ (٢٨) هَٰذَا كِتَٰبُنَا يَنطِقُ عَلَيْكُم بِٱلْحَقِّ ۚ إِنَّا كُنَّا نَسْتَنسِخُ مَا كُنتُمْ تَعْمَلُونَ (٢٩) فَأَمَّا ٱلَّذِينَ ءَامَنُوا۟ وَعَمِلُوا۟ ٱلصَّٰلِحَٰتِ فَيُدْخِلُهُمْ رَبُّهُمْ فِى رَحْمَتِهِۦ ۚ ذَٰلِكَ هُوَ ٱلْفَوْزُ ٱلْمُبِينُ (٣٠)

*Say, "Allah causes you to live, then causes you to die; then He will assemble you for the Day of Resurrection, about which there is no doubt, but most of the people do not know." (26) And to Allah belongs the dominion of* the heavens and the earth. And the Day the Hour appears - that Day the falsifiers will lose. (27) And you will see every nation kneeling [from fear]. Every nation will be called to its record [and told], "Today you will be recompensed for what you used to do. (28) This, Our record, speaks about you in truth. Indeed, We were having transcribed whatever you used to do." (29) So as for those who believed and did righteous deeds, their Lord will admit them into His mercy. That is what is the clear attainment. (30)

## Quran 46:8

أَمْ يَقُولُونَ ٱفْتَرَىٰهُ ۖ قُلْ إِنِ ٱفْتَرَيْتُهُۥ فَلَا تَمْلِكُونَ لِى مِنَ ٱللَّهِ شَيْـًٔا ۖ هُوَ أَعْلَمُ بِمَا تُفِيضُونَ فِيهِ ۖ كَفَىٰ بِهِۦ شَهِيدًۢا بَيْنِى وَبَيْنَكُمْ ۖ وَهُوَ ٱلْغَفُورُ ٱلرَّحِيمُ (٨)

Or do they say, "He has invented it?" Say, "If I have invented it, you will not possess for me [the power of protection] from Allah at all. He is most knowing of that in which you are involved. Sufficient is He as Witness between me and you, and He is the Forgiving the Merciful." (8)

## Quran 46:12-16

وَمِن قَبْلِهِۦ كِتَـٰبُ مُوسَىٰٓ إِمَامًا وَرَحْمَةً ۚ وَهَـٰذَا كِتَـٰبٌ مُّصَدِّقٌ لِّسَانًا عَرَبِيًّا لِّيُنذِرَ ٱلَّذِينَ ظَلَمُوا۟ وَبُشْرَىٰ لِلْمُحْسِنِينَ (١٢) إِنَّ ٱلَّذِينَ قَالُوا۟ رَبُّنَا ٱللَّهُ ثُمَّ ٱسْتَقَـٰمُوا۟ فَلَا خَوْفٌ عَلَيْهِمْ وَلَا هُمْ يَحْزَنُونَ (١٣) أُو۟لَـٰٓئِكَ أَصْحَـٰبُ ٱلْجَنَّةِ خَـٰلِدِينَ فِيهَا جَزَآءًۢ بِمَا كَانُوا۟ يَعْمَلُونَ (١٤) وَوَصَّيْنَا ٱلْإِنسَـٰنَ بِوَٰلِدَيْهِ إِحْسَـٰنًا ۖ حَمَلَتْهُ أُمُّهُۥ كُرْهًا وَوَضَعَتْهُ كُرْهًا ۖ وَحَمْلُهُۥ وَفِصَـٰلُهُۥ ثَلَـٰثُونَ شَهْرًا ۚ حَتَّىٰٓ إِذَا بَلَغَ أَشُدَّهُۥ وَبَلَغَ أَرْبَعِينَ سَنَةً قَالَ رَبِّ أَوْزِعْنِىٓ أَنْ أَشْكُرَ نِعْمَتَكَ ٱلَّتِىٓ أَنْعَمْتَ عَلَىَّ وَعَلَىٰ وَٰلِدَىَّ وَأَنْ أَعْمَلَ صَـٰلِحًا تَرْضَىٰهُ وَأَصْلِحْ لِى فِى ذُرِّيَّتِىٓ ۖ إِنِّى تُبْتُ إِلَيْكَ وَإِنِّى

مِنَ ٱلْمُسْلِمِينَ (١٥) أُو۟لَٰٓئِكَ ٱلَّذِينَ نَتَقَبَّلُ عَنْهُمْ أَحْسَنَ مَا عَمِلُوا۟ وَنَتَجَاوَزُ عَن سَيِّـَٔاتِهِمْ فِىٓ أَصْحَٰبِ ٱلْجَنَّةِ ۖ وَعْدَ ٱلصِّدْقِ ٱلَّذِى كَانُوا۟ يُوعَدُونَ (١٦)

And before it was the scripture of Moses to lead and as a mercy. And this is a confirming Book in an Arabic tongue to warn those who have wronged and as good tidings to the doers of good. (12) Indeed, those who have said, "Our Lord is Allah," and then remained on a right course - there will be no fear concerning them, nor will they grieve. (13) Those are the companions of Paradise, abiding eternally therein as reward for what they used to do. (14) And We have enjoined upon man, to his parents, good treatment. His mother carried him with hardship and gave birth to him with hardship, and his gestation and weaning [period] is thirty months. [He grows] until, when he reaches maturity and reaches [the age of] forty years, he says, "My Lord, enable me to be grateful for Your favor which You have bestowed upon me and upon my parents and to work righteousness of which You will approve and make righteous for me my offspring. Indeed, I have repented to You, and indeed, I am of the Muslims." (15) Those are the ones from whom We will accept the best of what they did and overlook their misdeeds, [their being] among the companions of Paradise. [That is] the promise of truth which they had been promised. (16)

## Quran 47:19

فَٱعْلَمْ أَنَّهُۥ لَآ إِلَٰهَ إِلَّا ٱللَّهُ وَٱسْتَغْفِرْ لِذَنۢبِكَ وَلِلْمُؤْمِنِينَ وَٱلْمُؤْمِنَٰتِ ۗ وَٱللَّهُ يَعْلَمُ مُتَقَلَّبَكُمْ وَمَثْوَىٰكُمْ (١٩)

So know, [O Muhammad], that there is no deity except Allah and ask forgiveness for your sin and for the believing men and believing women. And Allah knows of your movement and your resting place. (19)

## Quran 48:14

وَلِلَّهِ مُلْكُ ٱلسَّمَـٰوَٰتِ وَٱلْأَرْضِ يَغْفِرُ لِمَن يَشَآءُ وَيُعَذِّبُ مَن يَشَآءُ وَكَانَ ٱللَّهُ غَفُورًا رَّحِيمًا (١٤)

And to Allah belongs the dominion of the heavens and the earth. He forgives whom He wills and punishes whom He wills. And ever is Allah Forgiving and Merciful. (14)

## Quran 48:29

مُحَمَّدٌ رَّسُولُ ٱللَّهِ وَٱلَّذِينَ مَعَهُ أَشِدَّآءُ عَلَى ٱلْكُفَّارِ رُحَمَآءُ بَيْنَهُمْ تَرَىٰهُمْ رُكَّعًا سُجَّدًا يَبْتَغُونَ فَضْلًا مِّنَ ٱللَّهِ وَرِضْوَٰنًا سِيمَاهُمْ فِى وُجُوهِهِم مِّنْ أَثَرِ ٱلسُّجُودِ ذَٰلِكَ مَثَلُهُمْ فِى ٱلتَّوْرَىٰةِ وَمَثَلُهُمْ فِى ٱلْإِنجِيلِ كَزَرْعٍ أَخْرَجَ شَطْـَٔهُ فَـَٔازَرَهُ فَٱسْتَغْلَظَ فَٱسْتَوَىٰ عَلَىٰ سُوقِهِ يُعْجِبُ ٱلزُّرَّاعَ لِيَغِيظَ بِهِمُ ٱلْكُفَّارَ وَعَدَ ٱللَّهُ ٱلَّذِينَ ءَامَنُوا۟ وَعَمِلُوا۟ ٱلصَّـٰلِحَـٰتِ مِنْهُم مَّغْفِرَةً وَأَجْرًا عَظِيمًۢا (٢٩)

Muhammad is the Messenger of Allah; and those with him are forceful against the disbelievers, merciful among themselves. You see them bowing and prostrating [in prayer], seeking bounty from Allah and [His] pleasure. Their mark is on their faces from the trace of prostration. That is their description in the Torah. And their description in the Injeel is as a plant which produces its offshoots and strengthens them so they grow firm and stand upon their stalks, delighting the sowers - so that Allah may enrage by them the disbelievers. Allah has promised those who believe and do righteous deeds among them forgiveness and a great reward. (29)

## Quran 49:3

إِنَّ ٱلَّذِينَ يَغُضُّونَ أَصْوَٰتَهُمْ عِندَ رَسُولِ ٱللَّهِ أُو۟لَٰٓئِكَ ٱلَّذِينَ ٱمْتَحَنَ ٱللَّهُ قُلُوبَهُمْ لِلتَّقْوَىٰ ۚ لَهُم مَّغْفِرَةٌ وَأَجْرٌ عَظِيمٌ (٣)

*Indeed, those who lower their voices before the Messenger of Allah - they are the ones whose hearts Allah has tested for righteousness. For them is forgiveness and great reward. (3)*

## Quran 49:9-12

وَإِن طَآئِفَتَانِ مِنَ ٱلْمُؤْمِنِينَ ٱقْتَتَلُوا۟ فَأَصْلِحُوا۟ بَيْنَهُمَا ۖ فَإِنۢ بَغَتْ إِحْدَىٰهُمَا عَلَى ٱلْأُخْرَىٰ فَقَٰتِلُوا۟ ٱلَّتِى تَبْغِى حَتَّىٰ تَفِىٓءَ إِلَىٰٓ أَمْرِ ٱللَّهِ ۚ فَإِن فَآءَتْ فَأَصْلِحُوا۟ بَيْنَهُمَا بِٱلْعَدْلِ وَأَقْسِطُوٓا۟ ۖ إِنَّ ٱللَّهَ يُحِبُّ ٱلْمُقْسِطِينَ (٩) إِنَّمَا ٱلْمُؤْمِنُونَ إِخْوَةٌ فَأَصْلِحُوا۟ بَيْنَ أَخَوَيْكُمْ ۚ وَٱتَّقُوا۟ ٱللَّهَ لَعَلَّكُمْ تُرْحَمُونَ (١٠) يَٰٓأَيُّهَا ٱلَّذِينَ ءَامَنُوا۟ لَا يَسْخَرْ قَوْمٌ مِّن قَوْمٍ عَسَىٰٓ أَن يَكُونُوا۟ خَيْرًا مِّنْهُمْ وَلَا نِسَآءٌ مِّن نِّسَآءٍ عَسَىٰٓ أَن يَكُنَّ خَيْرًا مِّنْهُنَّ ۖ وَلَا تَلْمِزُوٓا۟ أَنفُسَكُمْ وَلَا تَنَابَزُوا۟ بِٱلْأَلْقَٰبِ ۖ بِئْسَ ٱلِٱسْمُ ٱلْفُسُوقُ بَعْدَ ٱلْإِيمَٰنِ ۚ وَمَن لَّمْ يَتُبْ فَأُو۟لَٰٓئِكَ هُمُ ٱلظَّٰلِمُونَ (١١) يَٰٓأَيُّهَا ٱلَّذِينَ ءَامَنُوا۟ ٱجْتَنِبُوا۟ كَثِيرًا مِّنَ ٱلظَّنِّ إِنَّ بَعْضَ ٱلظَّنِّ إِثْمٌ ۖ وَلَا تَجَسَّسُوا۟ وَلَا يَغْتَب بَّعْضُكُم بَعْضًا ۚ أَيُحِبُّ أَحَدُكُمْ أَن يَأْكُلَ لَحْمَ أَخِيهِ مَيْتًا فَكَرِهْتُمُوهُ ۚ وَٱتَّقُوا۟ ٱللَّهَ ۚ إِنَّ ٱللَّهَ تَوَّابٌ رَّحِيمٌ (١٢)

*And if two factions among the believers should fight, then make settlement between the two. But if one of them oppresses the other, then fight against the one that oppresses until it returns to the ordinance of Allah. And if it returns, then make settlement between them in justice and act justly. Indeed, Allah loves those who act justly. (9) The believers are but brothers, so make* settlement between your brothers. And fear Allah that you may receive mercy. (10) O you who have believed, let not a people ridicule [another] people; perhaps they may be better than them; nor let women ridicule [other] women; perhaps they may be better than them. And do not insult one another and do not call each other by [offensive] nicknames. Wretched is the name of disobedience after [one's] faith. And whoever does not repent - then it is those who are the wrongdoers. (11) O you who have believed, avoid much [negative] assumption. Indeed, some assumption is sin. And do not spy or backbite each other. Would one of you like to eat the flesh of his brother when dead? You would detest it. And fear Allah; indeed, Allah is Accepting of repentance and Merciful. (12)

## Quran 49:14

۞ قَالَتِ ٱلْأَعْرَابُ ءَامَنَّا ۖ قُل لَّمْ تُؤْمِنُوا۟ وَلَٰكِن قُولُوٓا۟ أَسْلَمْنَا وَلَمَّا يَدْخُلِ ٱلْإِيمَٰنُ فِى قُلُوبِكُمْ ۖ وَإِن تُطِيعُوا۟ ٱللَّهَ وَرَسُولَهُۥ لَا يَلِتْكُم مِّنْ أَعْمَٰلِكُمْ شَيْـًٔا ۚ إِنَّ ٱللَّهَ غَفُورٌ رَّحِيمٌ (١٤)

The bedouins say, "We have believed." Say, "You have not [yet] believed; but say [instead], 'We have submitted,' for faith has not yet entered your hearts. And if you obey Allah and His Messenger, He will not deprive you from your deeds of anything. Indeed, Allah is Forgiving and Merciful." (14)

## Quran 50:31-35

وَأُزْلِفَتِ ٱلْجَنَّةُ لِلْمُتَّقِينَ غَيْرَ بَعِيدٍ (٣١) هَٰذَا مَا تُوعَدُونَ لِكُلِّ أَوَّابٍ حَفِيظٍ (٣٢) مَنْ خَشِىَ ٱلرَّحْمَٰنَ بِٱلْغَيْبِ وَجَآءَ بِقَلْبٍ مُّنِيبٍ (٣٣) ٱدْخُلُوهَا بِسَلَٰمٍ ذَٰلِكَ يَوْمُ ٱلْخُلُودِ (٣٤) لَهُم مَّا يَشَآءُونَ فِيهَا وَلَدَيْنَا مَزِيدٌ (٣٥)

And Paradise will be brought near to the righteous, not far, (31) [It will be said], "This is what you were promised - for every returner [to Allah] and keeper [of His covenant] (32) Who feared the Most Merciful unseen and came with a heart returning [in repentance]. (33) Enter it in peace. This is the Day of Eternity." (34) They will have whatever they wish therein, and with Us is more. (35)

## Quran 52:26-28

قَالُوٓا۟ إِنَّا كُنَّا قَبْلُ فِىٓ أَهْلِنَا مُشْفِقِينَ (٢٦) فَمَنَّ ٱللَّهُ عَلَيْنَا وَوَقَىٰنَا عَذَابَ ٱلسَّمُومِ (٢٧) إِنَّا كُنَّا مِن قَبْلُ نَدْعُوهُ ۖ إِنَّهُۥ هُوَ ٱلْبَرُّ ٱلرَّحِيمُ (٢٨)

They will say, "Indeed, we were previously among our people fearful [of displeasing Allah]. (26) So Allah conferred favor upon us and protected us from the punishment of the Scorching Fire. (27) Indeed, we used to supplicate Him before. Indeed, it is He who is the Beneficent, the Merciful." (28)

## Quran 53:31-32

وَلِلَّهِ مَا فِى ٱلسَّمَٰوَٰتِ وَمَا فِى ٱلْأَرْضِ لِيَجْزِىَ ٱلَّذِينَ أَسَٰٓـُٔوا۟ بِمَا عَمِلُوا۟ وَيَجْزِىَ ٱلَّذِينَ أَحْسَنُوا۟ بِٱلْحُسْنَى (٣١) ٱلَّذِينَ يَجْتَنِبُونَ كَبَٰٓئِرَ ٱلْإِثْمِ وَٱلْفَوَٰحِشَ إِلَّا ٱللَّمَمَ ۚ إِنَّ رَبَّكَ وَٰسِعُ ٱلْمَغْفِرَةِ ۚ هُوَ أَعْلَمُ بِكُمْ إِذْ أَنشَأَكُم مِّنَ ٱلْأَرْضِ وَإِذْ أَنتُمْ أَجِنَّةٌ فِى بُطُونِ أُمَّهَٰتِكُمْ ۖ فَلَا تُزَكُّوٓا۟ أَنفُسَكُمْ ۖ هُوَ أَعْلَمُ بِمَنِ ٱتَّقَىٰٓ (٣٢)

And to Allah belongs whatever is in the heavens and whatever is in the earth - that He may recompense those who do evil with [the penalty of] what they have done and recompense those who do good with the best [reward] - (31) Those who avoid the major sins and immoralities, only [committing] slight ones. Indeed, your Lord is vast in forgiveness. He was most knowing of you when He produced you from the earth and when you were fetuses in the wombs of your mothers. So do not claim yourselves to be pure; He is most knowing of who fears Him. (32)

## Quran 55:1-4

ٱلرَّحۡمَـٰنُ (١) عَلَّمَ ٱلۡقُرۡءَانَ (٢) خَلَقَ ٱلۡإِنسَـٰنَ (٣) عَلَّمَهُ ٱلۡبَيَانَ (٤)

The Most Merciful (1) Taught the Qur'an, (2) Created man, (3) [And] taught him eloquence. (4)

## Quran 57:7-9

ءَامِنُوا۟ بِٱللَّهِ وَرَسُولِهِۦ وَأَنفِقُوا۟ مِمَّا جَعَلَكُم مُّسۡتَخۡلَفِينَ فِيهِۖ فَٱلَّذِينَ ءَامَنُوا۟ مِنكُمۡ وَأَنفَقُوا۟ لَهُمۡ أَجۡرٌ كَبِيرٌ (٧) وَمَا لَكُمۡ لَا تُؤۡمِنُونَ بِٱللَّهِۙ وَٱلرَّسُولُ يَدۡعُوكُمۡ لِتُؤۡمِنُوا۟ بِرَبِّكُمۡ وَقَدۡ أَخَذَ مِيثَـٰقَكُمۡ إِن كُنتُم مُّؤۡمِنِينَ (٨) هُوَ ٱلَّذِى يُنَزِّلُ عَلَىٰ عَبۡدِهِۦٓ ءَايَـٰتِۭ بَيِّنَـٰتٍ لِّيُخۡرِجَكُم مِّنَ ٱلظُّلُمَـٰتِ إِلَى ٱلنُّورِۚ وَإِنَّ ٱللَّهَ بِكُمۡ لَرَءُوفٌ رَّحِيمٌ (٩)

Believe in Allah and His Messenger and spend out of that in which He has made you successors. For those who have believed among you and spent, there will be a great reward. (7) And why do you not believe in Allah while the Messenger invites you to believe in your Lord and He has taken your covenant, if you should [truly] be believers? (8) It is He who sends down upon His Servant [Muhammad] verses of clear evidence that He may bring you out from darknesses into the light. And indeed, Allah is to you Kind and Merciful. (9)

## Quran 57:21

سَابِقُوٓا۟ إِلَىٰ مَغْفِرَةٍ مِّن رَّبِّكُمْ وَجَنَّةٍ عَرْضُهَا كَعَرْضِ ٱلسَّمَآءِ وَٱلْأَرْضِ أُعِدَّتْ لِلَّذِينَ ءَامَنُوا۟ بِٱللَّهِ وَرُسُلِهِۦ ۚ ذَٰلِكَ فَضْلُ ٱللَّهِ يُؤْتِيهِ مَن يَشَآءُ ۚ وَٱللَّهُ ذُو ٱلْفَضْلِ ٱلْعَظِيمِ (٢١)

*Race toward forgiveness from your Lord and a Garden whose width is like the width of the heavens and earth, prepared for those who believed in Allah and His messengers. That is the bounty of Allah which He gives to whom He wills, and Allah is the possessor of great bounty. (21)*

## Quran 57:28

يَـٰٓأَيُّهَا ٱلَّذِينَ ءَامَنُوا۟ ٱتَّقُوا۟ ٱللَّهَ وَءَامِنُوا۟ بِرَسُولِهِۦ يُؤْتِكُمْ كِفْلَيْنِ مِن رَّحْمَتِهِۦ وَيَجْعَل لَّكُمْ نُورًا تَمْشُونَ بِهِۦ وَيَغْفِرْ لَكُمْ ۚ وَٱللَّهُ غَفُورٌ رَّحِيمٌ (٢٨)

*O you who have believed, fear Allah and believe in His Messenger; He will [then] give you a double portion of His mercy and make for you a light by which you will walk and forgive you; and Allah is Forgiving and Merciful. (28)*

## Quran 58:1-2

قَدْ سَمِعَ ٱللَّهُ قَوْلَ ٱلَّتِى تُجَـٰدِلُكَ فِى زَوْجِهَا وَتَشْتَكِىٓ إِلَى ٱللَّهِ وَٱللَّهُ يَسْمَعُ تَحَاوُرَكُمَآ ۚ إِنَّ ٱللَّهَ سَمِيعٌۢ بَصِيرٌ (١) ٱلَّذِينَ يُظَـٰهِرُونَ مِنكُم مِّن نِّسَآئِهِم مَّا هُنَّ أُمَّهَـٰتِهِمْ ۖ إِنْ أُمَّهَـٰتُهُمْ إِلَّا ٱلَّـٰٓـِٔى وَلَدْنَهُمْ ۚ وَإِنَّهُمْ لَيَقُولُونَ مُنكَرًا مِّنَ ٱلْقَوْلِ وَزُورًا ۚ وَإِنَّ ٱللَّهَ لَعَفُوٌّ غَفُورٌ (٢)

Certainly has Allah heard the speech of the one who argues with you, [O Muhammad], concerning her husband and directs her complaint to Allah. And Allah hears your dialogue; indeed, Allah is Hearing and Seeing. (1) Those who pronounce thihar among you [to separate] from their wives - they are not [consequently] their mothers. Their mothers are none but those who gave birth to them. And indeed, they are saying an objectionable statement and a falsehood. But indeed, Allah is Pardoning and Forgiving. (2)

## Quran 58:12-13

يَـٰٓأَيُّهَا ٱلَّذِينَ ءَامَنُوٓاْ إِذَا نَـٰجَيْتُمُ ٱلرَّسُولَ فَقَدِّمُواْ بَيْنَ يَدَىْ نَجْوَىٰكُمْ صَدَقَةً ذَٰلِكَ خَيْرٌ لَّكُمْ وَأَطْهَرُ فَإِن لَّمْ تَجِدُواْ فَإِنَّ ٱللَّهَ غَفُورٌ رَّحِيمٌ (١٢) ءَأَشْفَقْتُمْ أَن تُقَدِّمُواْ بَيْنَ يَدَىْ نَجْوَىٰكُمْ صَدَقَـٰتٍ فَإِذْ لَمْ تَفْعَلُواْ وَتَابَ ٱللَّهُ عَلَيْكُمْ فَأَقِيمُواْ ٱلصَّلَوٰةَ وَءَاتُواْ ٱلزَّكَوٰةَ وَأَطِيعُواْ ٱللَّهَ وَرَسُولَهُۥ وَٱللَّهُ خَبِيرٌ بِمَا تَعْمَلُونَ (١٣)

O you who have believed, when you [wish to] privately consult the Messenger, present before your consultation a charity. That is better for you and purer. But if you find not [the means] - then indeed, Allah is Forgiving and Merciful. (12) Have you feared to present before your consultation charities? Then when you do not and Allah has forgiven you, then [at least] establish prayer and give zakah and obey Allah and His Messenger. And Allah is Acquainted with what you do. (13)

## Quran 59:10

وَٱلَّذِينَ جَآءُو مِنۢ بَعْدِهِمْ يَقُولُونَ رَبَّنَا ٱغْفِرْ لَنَا وَلِإِخْوَٰنِنَا ٱلَّذِينَ سَبَقُونَا بِٱلْإِيمَـٰنِ وَلَا تَجْعَلْ فِى قُلُوبِنَا غِلاًّ لِّلَّذِينَ ءَامَنُواْ رَبَّنَآ إِنَّكَ رَءُوفٌ رَّحِيمٌ (١٠)

And [there is a share for] those who came after them, saying, "Our Lord, forgive us and our brothers who preceded us in faith and put not in our hearts [any] resentment toward those who have believed. Our Lord, indeed You are Kind and Merciful." (10)

## Quran 59:21-24

لَوْ أَنزَلْنَا هَٰذَا ٱلْقُرْءَانَ عَلَىٰ جَبَلٍ لَّرَأَيْتَهُۥ خَٰشِعًا مُّتَصَدِّعًا مِّنْ خَشْيَةِ ٱللَّهِ ۚ وَتِلْكَ ٱلْأَمْثَٰلُ نَضْرِبُهَا لِلنَّاسِ لَعَلَّهُمْ يَتَفَكَّرُونَ (٢١) هُوَ ٱللَّهُ ٱلَّذِى لَا إِلَٰهَ إِلَّا هُوَ ۖ عَٰلِمُ ٱلْغَيْبِ وَٱلشَّهَٰدَةِ ۖ هُوَ ٱلرَّحْمَٰنُ ٱلرَّحِيمُ (٢٢) هُوَ ٱللَّهُ ٱلَّذِى لَا إِلَٰهَ إِلَّا هُوَ ٱلْمَلِكُ ٱلْقُدُّوسُ ٱلسَّلَٰمُ ٱلْمُؤْمِنُ ٱلْمُهَيْمِنُ ٱلْعَزِيزُ ٱلْجَبَّارُ ٱلْمُتَكَبِّرُ ۚ سُبْحَٰنَ ٱللَّهِ عَمَّا يُشْرِكُونَ (٢٣) هُوَ ٱللَّهُ ٱلْخَٰلِقُ ٱلْبَارِئُ ٱلْمُصَوِّرُ ۖ لَهُ ٱلْأَسْمَآءُ ٱلْحُسْنَىٰ ۚ يُسَبِّحُ لَهُۥ مَا فِى ٱلسَّمَٰوَٰتِ وَٱلْأَرْضِ ۖ وَهُوَ ٱلْعَزِيزُ ٱلْحَكِيمُ (٢٤)

If We had sent down this Qur'an upon a mountain, you would have seen it humbled and coming apart from fear of Allah. And these examples We present to the people that perhaps they will give thought. (21) He is Allah, other than whom there is no deity, Knower of the unseen and the witnessed. He is the Entirely Merciful, the Especially Merciful. (22) He is Allah, other than whom there is no deity, the Sovereign, the Pure, the Perfection, the Bestower of Faith, the Overseer, the Exalted in Might, the Compeller, the Superior. Exalted is Allah above whatever they associate with Him. (23) He is Allah, the Creator, the Inventor, the Fashioner; to Him belong the best names. Whatever is in the heavens and earth is exalting Him. And He is the Exalted in Might, the Wise. (24)

## Quran 60:7

۞ عَسَى ٱللَّهُ أَن يَجْعَلَ بَيْنَكُمْ وَبَيْنَ ٱلَّذِينَ عَادَيْتُم مِّنْهُم مَّوَدَّةً ۚ وَٱللَّهُ قَدِيرٌ ۚ وَٱللَّهُ غَفُورٌ رَّحِيمٌ (٧)

Perhaps Allah will put, between you and those to whom you have been enemies among them, affection. And Allah is competent, and Allah is Forgiving and Merciful. (7)

## Quran 60:12

يَـٰٓأَيُّهَا ٱلنَّبِىُّ إِذَا جَاءَكَ ٱلْمُؤْمِنَـٰتُ يُبَايِعْنَكَ عَلَىٰٓ أَن لَّا يُشْرِكْنَ بِٱللَّهِ شَيْـًٔا وَلَا يَسْرِقْنَ وَلَا يَزْنِينَ وَلَا يَقْتُلْنَ أَوْلَـٰدَهُنَّ وَلَا يَأْتِينَ بِبُهْتَـٰنٍ يَفْتَرِينَهُۥ بَيْنَ أَيْدِيهِنَّ وَأَرْجُلِهِنَّ وَلَا يَعْصِينَكَ فِى مَعْرُوفٍ ۙ فَبَايِعْهُنَّ وَٱسْتَغْفِرْ لَهُنَّ ٱللَّهَ ۖ إِنَّ ٱللَّهَ غَفُورٌ رَّحِيمٌ (١٢)

O Prophet, when the believing women come to you pledging to you that they will not associate anything with Allah, nor will they steal, nor will they commit unlawful sexual intercourse, nor will they kill their children, nor will they bring forth a slander they have invented between their arms and legs, nor will they disobey you in what is right - then accept their pledge and ask forgiveness for them of Allah. Indeed, Allah is Forgiving and Merciful. (12)

## Quran 64:14

يَـٰٓأَيُّهَا ٱلَّذِينَ ءَامَنُوٓا۟ إِنَّ مِنْ أَزْوَٰجِكُمْ وَأَوْلَـٰدِكُمْ عَدُوًّا لَّكُمْ فَٱحْذَرُوهُمْ ۚ وَإِن تَعْفُوا۟ وَتَصْفَحُوا۟ وَتَغْفِرُوا۟ فَإِنَّ ٱللَّهَ غَفُورٌ رَّحِيمٌ (١٤)

O you who have believed, indeed, among your wives and your children are enemies to you, so beware of them. But if you pardon and overlook and forgive - then indeed, Allah is Forgiving and Merciful. (14)

## Quran 64:16-17

فَٱتَّقُوا۟ ٱللَّهَ مَا ٱسْتَطَعْتُمْ وَٱسْمَعُوا۟ وَأَطِيعُوا۟ وَأَنفِقُوا۟ خَيْرًا لِّأَنفُسِكُمْ ۗ وَمَن يُوقَ شُحَّ نَفْسِهِۦ فَأُو۟لَـٰٓئِكَ هُمُ ٱلْمُفْلِحُونَ (١٦) إِن تُقْرِضُوا۟ ٱللَّهَ قَرْضًا حَسَنًا يُضَـٰعِفْهُ لَكُمْ وَيَغْفِرْ لَكُمْ ۚ وَٱللَّهُ شَكُورٌ حَلِيمٌ (١٧)

So fear Allah as much as you are able and listen and obey and spend [in the way of Allah]; it is better for yourselves. And whoever is protected from the stinginess of his soul - it is those who will be the successful. (16) If you loan Allah a goodly loan, He will multiply it for you and forgive you. And Allah is Most Appreciative and Forbearing. (17)

## Quran 66:1

يَـٰٓأَيُّهَا ٱلنَّبِىُّ لِمَ تُحَرِّمُ مَآ أَحَلَّ ٱللَّهُ لَكَ ۖ تَبْتَغِى مَرْضَاتَ أَزْوَٰجِكَ ۚ وَٱللَّهُ غَفُورٌ رَّحِيمٌ (١)

O Prophet, why do you prohibit [yourself from] what Allah has made lawful for you, seeking the approval of your wives? And Allah is Forgiving and Merciful. (1)

## Quran 66:8

يَـٰٓأَيُّهَا ٱلَّذِينَ ءَامَنُوا۟ تُوبُوٓا۟ إِلَى ٱللَّهِ تَوْبَةً نَّصُوحًا عَسَىٰ رَبُّكُمْ أَن يُكَفِّرَ عَنكُمْ سَيِّـَٔاتِكُمْ وَيُدْخِلَكُمْ جَنَّـٰتٍ تَجْرِى مِن تَحْتِهَا ٱلْأَنْهَـٰرُ يَوْمَ لَا يُخْزِى ٱللَّهُ ٱلنَّبِىَّ وَٱلَّذِينَ ءَامَنُوا۟ مَعَهُۥ ۖ نُورُهُمْ يَسْعَىٰ بَيْنَ أَيْدِيهِمْ وَبِأَيْمَـٰنِهِمْ يَقُولُونَ رَبَّنَآ أَتْمِمْ لَنَا نُورَنَا وَٱغْفِرْ لَنَآ ۖ إِنَّكَ عَلَىٰ كُلِّ شَىْءٍ قَدِيرٌ (٨)

O you who have believed, repent to Allah with sincere repentance. Perhaps your Lord will remove from you your misdeeds and admit you into gardens beneath which rivers flow [on] the Day when Allah will not disgrace the

Prophet and those who believed with him. Their light will proceed before them and on their right; they will say, "Our Lord, perfect for us our light and forgive us. Indeed, You are over all things competent." (8)

## Quran 67:1-3

تَبَارَكَ ٱلَّذِي بِيَدِهِ ٱلْمُلْكُ وَهُوَ عَلَىٰ كُلِّ شَيْءٍ قَدِيرٌ (١) ٱلَّذِي خَلَقَ ٱلْمَوْتَ وَٱلْحَيَوٰةَ لِيَبْلُوَكُمْ أَيُّكُمْ أَحْسَنُ عَمَلًا وَهُوَ ٱلْعَزِيزُ ٱلْغَفُورُ (٢) ٱلَّذِي خَلَقَ سَبْعَ سَمَٰوَٰتٍ طِبَاقًا مَّا تَرَىٰ فِي خَلْقِ ٱلرَّحْمَٰنِ مِن تَفَٰوُتٍ فَٱرْجِعِ ٱلْبَصَرَ هَلْ تَرَىٰ مِن فُطُورٍ (٣)

Blessed is He in whose hand is dominion, and He is over all things competent - (1) [He] who created death and life to test you [as to] which of you is best in deed - and He is the Exalted in Might, the Forgiving - (2) [And] who created seven heavens in layers. You do not see in the creation of the Most Merciful any inconsistency. So return [your] vision [to the sky]; do you see any breaks? (3)

## Quran 67:12

إِنَّ ٱلَّذِينَ يَخْشَوْنَ رَبَّهُم بِٱلْغَيْبِ لَهُم مَّغْفِرَةٌ وَأَجْرٌ كَبِيرٌ (١٢)

Indeed, those who fear their Lord unseen will have forgiveness and great reward. (12)

## Quran 67:19-20

أَوَلَمْ يَرَوْا إِلَى ٱلطَّيْرِ فَوْقَهُمْ صَٰٓفَّٰتٍ وَيَقْبِضْنَ مَا يُمْسِكُهُنَّ إِلَّا ٱلرَّحْمَٰنُ إِنَّهُۥ بِكُلِّ شَيْءٍ بَصِيرٌ (١٩) أَمَّنْ هَٰذَا ٱلَّذِي هُوَ جُندٌ لَّكُمْ يَنصُرُكُم مِّن دُونِ ٱلرَّحْمَٰنِ إِنِ ٱلْكَٰفِرُونَ إِلَّا فِي غُرُورٍ (٢٠)

Do they not see the birds above them with wings outspread and [sometimes] folded in? None holds them [aloft] except the Most Merciful. Indeed He is, of all things, Seeing. (19) Or who is it that could be an army for you to aid you other than the Most Merciful? The disbelievers are not but in delusion. (20)

### Quran 67:28-29

قُلْ أَرَءَيْتُمْ إِنْ أَهْلَكَنِيَ ٱللَّهُ وَمَن مَّعِىَ أَوْ رَحِمَنَا فَمَن يُجِيرُ ٱلْكَٰفِرِينَ مِنْ عَذَابٍ أَلِيمٍ (٢٨) قُلْ هُوَ ٱلرَّحْمَٰنُ ءَامَنَّا بِهِۦ وَعَلَيْهِ تَوَكَّلْنَا ۖ فَسَتَعْلَمُونَ مَنْ هُوَ فِى ضَلَٰلٍ مُّبِينٍ (٢٩)

Say, [O Muhammad], "Have you considered: whether Allah should cause my death and those with me or have mercy upon us, who can protect the disbelievers from a painful punishment?" (28) Say, "He is the Most Merciful; we have believed in Him, and upon Him we have relied. And you will [come to] know who it is that is in clear error." (29)

### Quran 71:1-4

إِنَّا أَرْسَلْنَا نُوحًا إِلَىٰ قَوْمِهِۦ أَنْ أَنذِرْ قَوْمَكَ مِن قَبْلِ أَن يَأْتِيَهُمْ عَذَابٌ أَلِيمٌ (١) قَالَ يَٰقَوْمِ إِنِّى لَكُمْ نَذِيرٌ مُّبِينٌ (٢) أَنِ ٱعْبُدُوا۟ ٱللَّهَ وَٱتَّقُوهُ وَأَطِيعُونِ (٣) يَغْفِرْ لَكُم مِّن ذُنُوبِكُمْ وَيُؤَخِّرْكُمْ إِلَىٰ أَجَلٍ مُّسَمًّى ۚ إِنَّ أَجَلَ ٱللَّهِ إِذَا جَآءَ لَا يُؤَخَّرُ ۖ لَوْ كُنتُمْ تَعْلَمُونَ (٤)

Indeed, We sent Noah to his people, [saying], "Warn your people before there comes to them a painful punishment." (1) He said, "O my people, indeed I am to you a clear warner, (2) [Saying], 'Worship Allah, fear Him and obey me. (3) Allah will forgive you of your sins and delay you for a specified term. Indeed, the time [set by] Allah, when it comes, will not be delayed, if you only knew.' " (4)

## Quran 71:10-13

فَقُلْتُ ٱسْتَغْفِرُوا۟ رَبَّكُمْ إِنَّهُ كَانَ غَفَّارًا (١٠) يُرْسِلِ ٱلسَّمَآءَ عَلَيْكُم مِّدْرَارًا (١١) وَيُمْدِدْكُم بِأَمْوَٰلٍ وَبَنِينَ وَيَجْعَل لَّكُمْ جَنَّـٰتٍ وَيَجْعَل لَّكُمْ أَنْهَـٰرًا (١٢) مَّا لَكُمْ لَا تَرْجُونَ لِلَّهِ وَقَارًا (١٣)

And said, 'Ask forgiveness of your Lord. Indeed, He is ever a Perpetual Forgiver. (10) He will send [rain from] the sky upon you in [continuing] showers (11) And give you increase in wealth and children and provide for you gardens and provide for you rivers. (12) What is [the matter] with you that you do not attribute to Allah [due] grandeur (13)

## Quran 73:20

۞ إِنَّ رَبَّكَ يَعْلَمُ أَنَّكَ تَقُومُ أَدْنَىٰ مِن ثُلُثَيِ ٱلَّيْلِ وَنِصْفَهُ وَثُلُثَهُ وَطَآئِفَةٌ مِّنَ ٱلَّذِينَ مَعَكَ ۚ وَٱللَّهُ يُقَدِّرُ ٱلَّيْلَ وَٱلنَّهَارَ ۚ عَلِمَ أَن لَّن تُحْصُوهُ فَتَابَ عَلَيْكُمْ ۖ فَٱقْرَءُوا۟ مَا تَيَسَّرَ مِنَ ٱلْقُرْءَانِ ۚ عَلِمَ أَن سَيَكُونُ مِنكُم مَّرْضَىٰ ۙ وَءَاخَرُونَ يَضْرِبُونَ فِى ٱلْأَرْضِ يَبْتَغُونَ مِن فَضْلِ ٱللَّهِ ۙ وَءَاخَرُونَ يُقَـٰتِلُونَ فِى سَبِيلِ ٱللَّهِ ۖ فَٱقْرَءُوا۟ مَا تَيَسَّرَ مِنْهُ ۚ وَأَقِيمُوا۟ ٱلصَّلَوٰةَ وَءَاتُوا۟ ٱلزَّكَوٰةَ وَأَقْرِضُوا۟ ٱللَّهَ قَرْضًا حَسَنًا ۚ وَمَا تُقَدِّمُوا۟ لِأَنفُسِكُم مِّنْ خَيْرٍ تَجِدُوهُ عِندَ ٱللَّهِ هُوَ خَيْرًا وَأَعْظَمَ أَجْرًا ۚ وَٱسْتَغْفِرُوا۟ ٱللَّهَ ۖ إِنَّ ٱللَّهَ غَفُورٌ رَّحِيمٌ (٢٠)

Indeed, your Lord knows, [O Muhammad], that you stand [in prayer] almost two thirds of the night or half of it or a third of it, and [so do] a group of those with you. And Allah determines [the extent of] the night and the day. He has known that you [Muslims] will not be able to do it and has turned to you in forgiveness, so recite what is easy [for you] of the Qur'an. He has known that there will be among you those who are ill and others traveling throughout the land seeking [something] of the bounty of Allah and others fighting for the cause of Allah. So recite what is easy from it and establish prayer and give zakah and loan Allah a goodly loan. And whatever good you put forward for yourselves - you will find it with Allah. It is better and greater in reward. And seek forgiveness of Allah. Indeed, Allah is Forgiving and Merciful. (20)

## Quran 74:54-56

كَلَّا إِنَّهُ تَذْكِرَةٌ (٥٤) فَمَن شَاءَ ذَكَرَهُ (٥٥) وَمَا يَذْكُرُونَ إِلَّا أَن يَشَاءَ ٱللَّهُ هُوَ أَهْلُ ٱلتَّقْوَىٰ وَأَهْلُ ٱلْمَغْفِرَةِ (٥٦)

No! Indeed, the Qur'an is a reminder (54) Then whoever wills will remember it. (55) And they will not remember except that Allah wills. He is worthy of fear and adequate for [granting] forgiveness. (56)

## Quran 76:29-31

إِنَّ هَـٰذِهِ تَذْكِرَةٌ فَمَن شَاءَ ٱتَّخَذَ إِلَىٰ رَبِّهِ سَبِيلًا (٢٩) وَمَا تَشَاءُونَ إِلَّا أَن يَشَاءَ ٱللَّهُ إِنَّ ٱللَّهَ كَانَ عَلِيمًا حَكِيمًا (٣٠) يُدْخِلُ مَن يَشَاءُ فِى رَحْمَتِهِ وَٱلظَّـٰلِمِينَ أَعَدَّ لَهُمْ عَذَابًا أَلِيمًا (٣١)

Indeed, this is a reminder, so he who wills may take to his Lord a way. (29) And you do not will except that Allah wills. Indeed, Allah is ever Knowing and Wise. (30) He admits whom He wills into His mercy; but the wrongdoers - He has prepared for them a painful punishment. (31)

## Quran 85:10-16

إِنَّ ٱلَّذِينَ فَتَنُواْ ٱلْمُؤْمِنِينَ وَٱلْمُؤْمِنَٰتِ ثُمَّ لَمْ يَتُوبُواْ فَلَهُمْ عَذَابُ جَهَنَّمَ وَلَهُمْ عَذَابُ ٱلْحَرِيقِ (١٠) إِنَّ ٱلَّذِينَ ءَامَنُواْ وَعَمِلُواْ ٱلصَّٰلِحَٰتِ لَهُمْ جَنَّٰتٌ تَجْرِى مِن تَحْتِهَا ٱلْأَنْهَٰرُ ذَٰلِكَ ٱلْفَوْزُ ٱلْكَبِيرُ (١١) إِنَّ بَطْشَ رَبِّكَ لَشَدِيدٌ (١٢) إِنَّهُۥ هُوَ يُبْدِئُ وَيُعِيدُ (١٣) وَهُوَ ٱلْغَفُورُ ٱلْوَدُودُ (١٤) ذُو ٱلْعَرْشِ ٱلْمَجِيدُ (١٥) فَعَّالٌ لِّمَا يُرِيدُ (١٦)

*Indeed, those who have tortured the believing men and believing women and then have not repented will have the punishment of Hell, and they will have the punishment of the Burning Fire. (10) Indeed, those who have believed and done righteous deeds will have gardens beneath which rivers flow. That is the great attainment. (11) Indeed, the vengeance of your Lord is severe. (12) Indeed, it is He who originates [creation] and repeats. (13) And He is the Forgiving, the Affectionate, (14) Honorable Owner of the Throne, (15) Effecter of what He intends. (16)*

## Quran 110:1-3

إِذَا جَآءَ نَصْرُ ٱللَّهِ وَٱلْفَتْحُ (١) وَرَأَيْتَ ٱلنَّاسَ يَدْخُلُونَ فِى دِينِ ٱللَّهِ أَفْوَاجًا (٢) فَسَبِّحْ بِحَمْدِ رَبِّكَ وَٱسْتَغْفِرْهُ ۚ إِنَّهُۥ كَانَ تَوَّابًۢا (٣)

*When the victory of Allah has come and the conquest, (1) And you see the people entering into the religion of Allah in multitudes, (2) Then exalt [Him] with praise of your Lord and ask forgiveness of Him. Indeed, He is ever Accepting of repentance. (3)*

**Quran 114:1-6**

قُلْ أَعُوذُ بِرَبِّ ٱلنَّاسِ (١) مَلِكِ ٱلنَّاسِ (٢) إِلَٰهِ ٱلنَّاسِ (٣) مِن شَرِّ ٱلْوَسْوَاسِ ٱلْخَنَّاسِ (٤) ٱلَّذِى يُوَسْوِسُ فِى صُدُورِ ٱلنَّاسِ (٥) مِنَ ٱلْجِنَّةِ وَٱلنَّاسِ (٦)

*Say, "I seek refuge in the Lord of mankind, (1) The King of mankind. (2) The God of mankind, (3) From the evil of the retreating whisperer (devil who whispers evil in the hearts of men) (4) Who whispers [evil] into the breasts of mankind - (5) From among the jinn and mankind." (6)*

# HADITH of MIRACULOUS MERCY

## A'isha reported:

*The Messenger of Allah (ﷺ) recited often these words: Hallowed be Allah and with His praise, I seek the forgiveness of Allah and return to Him. She said: I asked: Messenger of Allah, I see that you often repeat the saying" subhan allahi bihamdihi astag firullahi watubuilaih" whereupon he said: My Lord informed me that I would soon see a sign in my Ummah, so when I see it I often recite (these) words: Hallowed be Allah and with His Praise, I seek forgiveness of Allah and return to Him. Indeed I saw it (when this verse) was revealed:" When Allah's help and victory came, it marked the victory of Mecca, and you see people entering into Allah's religion in troops, celebrate the praise of Thy Lord and ask His forgiveness. Surely He is ever returning to Mercy."*

Source: Sahih Muslim 484d

## It was narrated from Abu Hurairah that the Messenger of Allah (ﷺ) said:

*"When the believer commits sin, a black spot appears on his heart. If he repents and gives up that sin and seeks forgiveness, his heart will be polished. But if (the sin) increases, (the black spot) increases. That is the Ran that Allah mentions in His Book: "Nay! But on their hearts is the Ran (covering of sins and evil deeds) which they used to earn." [83:14]*

Source: Sunan Ibn Majah 4244 Grade: Hasan

**Abu Hurairah reported:**

*The Prophet (ﷺ) said, "Allah, the Exalted, and Glorious said: 'A slave committed a sin and he said: O Allah, forgive my sin,' and Allah said: 'My slave committed a sin and then he realized that he has a Lord Who forgives the sins and punishes for the sin.' He then again committed a sin and said: 'My Lord, forgive my sin,' and Allah said: 'My slave committed a sin and then realized that he has a Lord Who forgives his sin and punishes for the sin.' He again committed a sin and said: 'My Lord, forgive my sin,' and Allah said: 'My slave has committed a sin and then realized that he has a Lord Who forgives the sin or takes (him) to account for sin. I have granted forgiveness to my slave. Let him do whatever he likes".*

Source: Riyad as-Saliheen 421 Grade: Sahih

**Anas reported:**

*Messenger of Allah (ﷺ) said, "Allah, the Exalted, has said: 'O son of Adam, I forgive you as long as you pray to Me and hope for My forgiveness, whatever sins you have committed. O son of 'Adam, I do not care if your sins reach the height of the heaven, then you ask for my forgiveness, I would forgive you. O son of 'Adam, if you come to Me with an earth load of sins, and meet Me associating nothing to Me, I would match it with an earthload of forgiveness."'*

Source: Riyad as-Saliheen 442 Grade: Hasan

**Abdullah ibn 'Amr was heard to say:**

*"Abu Bakr, may Allah be pleased with him, said to the Prophet, may Allah bless him and grant him peace, 'Teach me a supplication which I can use in my prayer.' He said, 'Say, "O Allah, I have wronged myself greatly. Only You forgive wrong actions. Forgive me with forgiveness directly from you. You are the Ever-Forgiving, Most Merciful."'"*

Source: Al-Adab Al-Mufrad 706 Grade: Sahih

**Thauban reported:**

*When the Messenger of Allah (ﷺ) finished his prayer. He begged forgiveness three times and said: O Allah! Thou art Peace, and peace comes from Thee; Blessed art Thou, O Possessor of Glory and Honour. Walid reported: I said to Auza'i: How is the seeking of forgiveness? He replied: You should say: I beg forgiveness from Allah, I beg forgiveness from Allah."*

Source: Sahih Muslim 591

**It was narrated from 'Aishah that she said:**

*"O Messenger of Allah, what do you think I should say in my supplication, if I come upon Laylatul-Qadr?" He said: "Say: 'Allahumma innaka 'afuwwun tuhibbul-'afwa, fa'fu 'anni (O Allah, You are Forgiving and love forgiveness, so forgive me).'"*

Source: Sunan Ibn Majah 3850 Grade: Sahih

**It was narrated from Hudhaifah:**

The Prophet (ﷺ) used to say between the two prostrations:

"Rabbighfir li, Rabbighfir li

(O Lord forgive me, O Lord forgive me)."

Source: Sunan Ibn Majah 897 Grade: Sahih

**Thauban reported:**

Whenever the Messenger of Allah (ﷺ) concluded his prayer, he would beg forgiveness from Allah thrice and then would recite: "Allahumma Antas- Salamu, wa minkas-salamu, tabarakta ya Dhal-Jalali wal-Ikram (O Allah, You are the Grantor of security, and security comes from You. You are Blessing, O You Who have majesty and nobility)!" (Imam) Al-Awza'i, one of the narrators of this Hadith, was asked: "How forgiveness is to be sought?" He answered: "The Messenger of Allah (ﷺ) used to say: 'Astaghfirullah! Astaghfirullah! (I beseech Allah for forgiveness, I beseech Allah for forgiveness)'."

Source: Riyad as-Salihin 1415 Grade: Sahih

**Narrated Abdullah ibn Umar:**

We counted that the Messenger of Allah (ﷺ) would say a hundred times during a meeting: "My Lord, forgive me and pardon me; Thou art the Pardoning and forgiving One".

Source: Sunan Abi Dawud 1516 Grade: Sahih

**It was narrated from Abu Hurairah that the Messenger of Allah (ﷺ) said:**

*"The pilgrims performing Hajj and 'Umrah are a delegation to Allah. If they call upon Him, He will answer them; and if they ask for His forgiveness, He will forgive them."*

Source: Sunan Ibn Majah 2892 Grade: Hasan

**It was narrated that Hudhaifah said:**

*"I was harsh in the way I spoke to my family, but not to others. I mentioned that to the Prophet and he said: 'Why don't you ask for forgiveness? Ask Allah to forgive you, seventy times each day.'"*

Source: Sunan Ibn Majah 3817 Grade: Hasan

**Narrated Abu Huraira:**

*The Prophet (ﷺ) said, "There was a merchant who used to lend the people, and whenever his debtor was in straitened circumstances, he would say to his employees, 'Forgive him so that Allah may forgive us.' So, Allah forgave him."*

Source: Sahih al-Bukhari 2078

**Ali said:**

*Abu Bakr told me - and Abu Bakr spoke the truth - he said: The Messenger of Allah (ﷺ) said: `There is no Muslim who commits a sin then does wudu' and prays two rak'ahs then asks Allah for forgiveness for that sin, but He will forgive him." And he recited these two verses: `And whoever does evil or wrongs himself but afterwards seeks Allah's forgiveness, he will find Allah Oft-Forgiving Most Merciful` [an-Nisa' 4:110] "And those who, when they have committed Fahishah (illegal sexual intercourse) or wronged themselves with evil, remember Allah and ask forgiveness for their sins;-and none can forgive sins but Allah - and do not persist in what (wrong) they have done, while they know` [Al 'Imran 3:135]*

Source: Musnad Ahmed 47 Grade: Sahih

**Abdullah ibn al-'As reported that the Prophet said:** "Show mercy and you will be shown mercy. Forgive and Allah will forgive you. Woe to the vessels that catch words ( the ears). Woe to those who persist and consciously continue in what they are doing."

Source: Al-Adab Al-Mufrad 380 Grade: Sahih

**Shaddad bin Aus narrated that the Messenger of Allah (ﷺ) said:**

*"The best manner of asking for forgiveness is to say: "O Allah! You are my Lord. None has the right to be worshipped except You. You created me and I am your servant and I abide by your covenant and promise as best*

I can. I seek refuge in you from the evil, which I have committed. I acknowledge your favor upon me and I acknowledge my sins, so forgive me, for verily none can forgive sin except you."

Source: Bulugh al Maram and Sahih Bukhari

**Shaddad ibn Aws reported that the Prophet said:**

"The best way of asking forgiveness is 'O Allah, You are my Lord. There is no god but You. You created me and I am Your slave. I follow Your covenant and promise as much as I can. I acknowledge Your blessing and I confess to my wrong actions, so forgive me. Only You can forgive wrong actions. I seek refuge with You from the evil of what I have done.' If he says it in the evening and then dies, he will enter the Garden - or he said that he will be one of the people of the Garden. If he says it in the morning and dies that day - it is the same."

Source: Al-Adab Al-Mufrad 617 Grade: Sahih

**Abu Musa reported the Prophet used to say this supplication**:

"O Allah, forgive my errors, my ignorance and my excess in all my affairs, and what You know better than me of these things. O Allah, forgive all my errors, what I do intentionally or out of my ignorance or in jest and in all that I do. O Allah, forgive me my past and future wrong actions, what I conceal of them and what I divulge. You are the One who puts things ahead and the One who delays them. You have power over all things."

Source: Al-Adab Al-Mufrad 688 Grade: Sahih

**Yahya related from Malik from Abu Zinad from al-Araj from Abu Huraira that the Messenger of Allah said:**

''When you are making dua do not say; 'O Allah, forgive me if You wish. O Allah, forgive me if you wish.' You should be firm in your asking, for there is no compelling Him."

Source: Muwatta Imam Malik

**Anas bin Malik narrated that:**

*The Messenger of Allah said regarding this Ayah: "He is the One deserving of the Taqwa, and He is the One Who forgives. – he said: 'Allah, Blessed is He and Most High, said: "I am the most worthy to have Taqwa of, so whoever has Taqwa of Me, not having any god besides Me, then I am most worthy that I forgive him."*

Source: Jami` at-Tirmidhi 3328 Grade: Daif

**Narrated Abu Burdah bin Abi Musa:**

*from his father, that the Messenger of Allah (ﷺ) said: "Allah sent down two guarantees of safety for the benefit of my Ummah: And Allah would not punish them while you are among them, nor will He punish them while they seek forgiveness (8:33). So when I pass, I leave seeking forgiveness among them until the Day of Resurrection."*

Source: Jami` at-Tirmidhi 3082 Grade: Daif

**It was narrated that Wathilah bin Asqa' said:**

*"The Messenger of Allah (ﷺ) offered the funeral prayer for a man among the Muslims and I heard him say: 'O Allah, so-and-so the son of so-and-so is in Your case and under Your protection. Protect him from the trial of the grave and the torment of the Fire, for You are the One Who keeps the promise and You are the Truth. Forgive him and have mercy on him, for You are the Oft-Forgiving, Most Merciful."*

Source: Sunan Ibn Majah 1499 Grade: Hasan

**Ibn `Umar narrated that one day:**

*The Messenger of Allah (ﷺ) said to his Companions: "Say 'Glory is to Allah and with His Praise (Subḥān Allāh, wa biḥamdih)' a hundred times. Whoever says [it] one time, it is written for him ten, and whoever says it ten (times), it is written for him a hundred, and whoever says it a hundred (times), it is written for him a thousand, and whoever increases, Allah will increase for him, and whoever seeks Allah's forgiveness, [Allah] will forgive him."*

Source: Jami` at-Tirmidhi 3470 Grade: Hasan

**It was narrated from 'Irbad bin Sariyah:**

*the Messenger of Allah (ﷺ) used to ask for forgiveness for the first row three times and for the second row twice.*

Source: Sunan Ibn Majah 996 Grade: Sahih

**Abu Qatadah narrated that:**

*the Prophet said: "Fast the Day of Ashura, for indeed I anticipate that Allah will forgive (the sins of) the year before it."*

Source: Jami` at-Tirmidhi 752 Grade: Sahih

**Abdullah bin Busr said that:**

*the Prophet said: "Glad tidings to those who find a lot of seeking forgiveness in the record of their deeds."*

Source: Sunan Ibn Majah 3818 Grade: Hasan

**Narrated Aisha, Ummul Mu'minin:**

*When the Prophet (ﷺ) came out of the privy, he used to say: "Grant me Thy forgiveness."*

Source: Sunan Abi Dawud 30 Grade: Sahih

**Bilal bin Yasar bin Zaid [the freed slave of the Prophet(ﷺ)] narrated:**

*"My father narrated to me, from my grandfather, that he heard the Prophet (ﷺ) say: 'Whoever says: "I seek forgiveness from Allah, the Magnificent, whom there is none worthy of worship but Him, the Living, Al-Qayyum, and I repent to him," (Astaghfirullāhal-`Aẓīm alladhī lā ilāha illā huwal-Ḥayyul-Qayyūmu wa atūbu*

ilaih) then Allah will forgive him, even if he fled from battle.'"

Source: Jami` at-Tirmidhi 3577 Grade: Hasan

**Narrated Al-Bara' ibn Azib:**

*The Prophet (ﷺ) said: If two Muslims meet, shake hands, praise Allah, and ask Him for forgiveness, they will be forgiven.*

Source: Sunan Abi Dawud 5211 Grade: Daif

**Abu Qatadah narrated that:**

*the Prophet said: "Fast the Day of Arafah, for indeed I anticipate that Allah will forgive (the sins) of the year after it, and the year before it."*

Source: Jami` at-Tirmidhi 749 Grade: Daif

**It was narrated that Abu Dharr said:**

*"I heard the Messenger of Allah say: 'Everyone in the universe, in the heavens and on earth, prays for forgiveness for the scholar, even the fish in the sea."*

Source: Sunan Ibn Majah 239 Grade: Daif

**It was narrated from Abu Hurairah that:**

*the Messenger of Allah said: 'I seek the forgiveness of Allah and repent to Him one hundred times each day.'*

Source: Sunan Ibn Majah 3815 Grade: Hasan

**It was narrated from Abu Hurairah that the Messenger of Allah (ﷺ) said:**

*Whoever agrees with a Muslim to cancel a transaction Allah will forgive his sins on the Day of Resurrection."*

Source: Sunan Ibn Majah 2199 Grade: Daif

**Narrated Abu Huraira:**

*The Prophet (ﷺ) said, "Allah forgives my followers those (evil deeds) their souls may whisper or suggest to them as long as they do not act (on it) or speak."*

Source: Sahih al-Bukhari 6664

**Abu Hurairah narrated the Messenger of Allah said:**

*"When a man was walking on the road, he found a thorny branch and removed it. Allah appreciated his action by forgiving him."*

Source: Jami` at-Tirmidhi 1958 Grade: Sahih

**Abu Huraira reported the Messenger of Allah (ﷺ) as saying:**

*"If a thorn pricks a Muslim in this world and he hopes for the reward against it then Allah forgives him his sins on the day of Resurrection".*

Source: Al-Adab Al-Mufrad 507 Grade: Sahih

**Abu Hurairah narrated:**

Messenger of Allah (ﷺ) said, "He who repents before the sun rises from the west, Allah will forgive him".

Source: Riyad as-Salihin 17 Grade: Sahih

**Narrated Ali ibn Abu Talib:**

Ali ibn Rabi'ah said: I was present with Ali while a beast was brought to him to ride. When he put his foot in the stirrup, he said: "In the name of Allah." Then when he sat on its back, he said: "Praise be to Allah." He then said: "Glory be to Him Who has made this subservient to us, for we had not the strength, and to our Lord do we return." He then said: "Praise be to Allah (thrice); Allah is Most Great (thrice): glory be to Thee, I have wronged myself, so forgive me, for only Thou forgivest sins." He then laughed. He was asked: At what did you laugh? He replied: I saw the Messenger of Allah (ﷺ) do as I have done, and laugh after that. I asked: Messenger of Allah, at what are you laughing? He replied: Your Lord, Most High, is pleased with His servant when he says: "Forgive me my sins." He knows that no one forgives sins except Him.

Source: Sunan Abi Dawud 2602 Grade: Sahih

**Abu Sa`eed narrated that:**

the Prophet (ﷺ) said: "Whoever says, when he goes to his bed: 'I seek forgiveness from Allah, [the Magnificent] the One whom there is none worthy of worship except for Him, the Living, the Sustainer, and I repent to Him

(Astaghfirullāha [al-`Aẓim] alladhi lā ilāha illā huw, al-Ḥayyul-Qayyūm, wa atūbu ilaihi)' three times, Allah shall forgive him his sins if they were like the foam of the sea, even if they were the number of leaves of the trees, even if they were the number of sand particles of `Alij, even if they were the number of the days of the world."

Source: Jami` at-Tirmidhi 3397 Grade: Daif

**Narrated Abdullah ibn Abbas:**

*The Prophet (ﷺ) used to say between the two prostrations: "O Allah, forgive me, have mercy on me, guide me, heal me, and provide for me."*

Source: Sunan Abi Dawud 850 Grade: Hasan

**It was narrated from Mu'adh bin Jabal that:**

*Messenger of Allah(ﷺ) said: "There is no soul that died bearing witness to La ilaha illallah, and that I am the Messenger of Allah, from the heart with certainty, but Allah will forgive it."*

Source: Sunan Ibn Majah 3796 Grade: Hasan

**It was narrated that Sulaim bin 'Amr said:**

*I heard Abu Umamah saying: I heard the Messenger of Allah (ﷺ) say: "The martyr at sea is like two martyrs on land, and the one who suffers seasickness is like one who gets drenched in his own blood on land. The time spent between one wave and the next is like a lifetime spent in obedience to Allah. Allah has appointed the Angel of*

Death to seize souls, except for the martyr at sea, for Allah Himself seizes their souls. He forgives the martyrs on land for all sins except debt, but (He forgives) the martyr at sea all his sins and his debt."

Source: Sunan Ibn Majah 2778 Grade: Daif

**It was narrated that Abu Hurairah said:**

"A man came to the Prophet (ﷺ) while he was delivering a Khutbah from the Minbar, and he said: 'If I fight in the cause of Allah with patience and seeking reward, facing the enemy and not running away, do you think that Allah will forgive my sins?' He said: 'Yes.' Then he fell silent for a while. Then he said: 'Where is the one who was asking just now?' The man said: 'Here I am.' He said: 'What did you say?' He said: 'What did you say?' He said: 'I said: I said: If I fight in the cause of Allah with patience and seeking reward, facing the enemy and not running away, do you think that Allah will forgive my sins?' He said: 'Yes, except for debt. Gabriel told me that just now.'"

Source: Sunan an-Nasa'i 3155 Grade: Sahih

**Abu Huraira reported:**

The Messenger of Allah (ﷺ) used to say while prostrating himself: O Lord, forgive me all my sins, small and great, first and last, open and secret.

Source: Sahih Muslim 483

**It was narrated from Abu Darda' that:**

*The Prophet said concerning the Verse: "Every day He is (engaged) in some affair." "His affairs include forgiving sins, relieving distress, raising some people and bringing others low."*

Source: Sunan Ibn Majah 202 Grade: Hasan

**Narrated Abu Huraira:**

*Allah's Messenger (ﷺ) said, "Say Ameen when the Imam says 'Ghairi l-maghdubi `alaihim wala d-daalleen' (not the path of those who earn Your Anger (such as Jews) nor of those who go astray (such as Christians)); all the past sins of the person whose saying (of Ameen) coincides with that of the angels, will be forgiven".*

Source: Sahih al-Bukhari 782

**Aishah said:**

*"I heard the Messenger of Allah (ﷺ) saying at his death: 'O Allah, forgive me and have mercy on me, and join me with the Highest Company (Allāhummaghfirlī warḥamnī wa alḥiqnī bir-rafīqil a`lā).'"*

Source: Jami` at-Tirmidhi 3496 Grade: Sahih

**It is narrated on the authority of Ibn 'Abbas that some persons amongst the polytheist had committed a large number of murders and had excessively indulged in fornication. Then they came to Muhammad (ﷺ) and said:**

*Whatever you assert and whatever you call to is indeed good. But if you inform us that there is atonement of our past deeds (then we would embrace Islam). Then it was revealed: And those who call not unto another god along with Allah and slay not any soul which Allah has forbidden except in the cause of justice, nor commit fornication; and he who does this shall meet the requital of sin. Multiplied for him shall be the torment on the Day of Resurrection, and he shall therein abide disgraced, except him who repents and believes and does good deeds. Then these! For the Allah shall change their vices into virtues. Verily Allah is Ever Forgiving, Merciful. Say thou: O my bondsmen who have committed extravagance against themselves despair not of the Mercy of Allah. Verily Allah will forgive the sins altogether. He is indeed the Forgiving, the Merciful.*

Source: Sahih Muslim 122

**Abu Dharr reported:**

*The Prophet (ﷺ) said, "Allah, the Almighty, says: 'Whosoever does a good deed, will have (reward) ten times like it and I add more; and whosoever does an evil, will have the punishment like it or I will forgive (him); and whosoever approaches Me by one span, I will approach him by one cubit; and whosoever approaches Me by one cubit, I approach him by one fathom, and whosoever comes to Me walking, I go to him running; and whosoever meets Me with an earth-load of sins without associating anything with Me, I meet him with forgiveness like that".*

Source: Riyad as-Salihin 413 Grade: Sahih

**Aisha reported:**

*The Messenger of Allah (ﷺ) said, "If a group of Muslims numbering a hundred perform funeral prayer over a dead person, and all of them ask Allah's forgiveness for him, their prayer for him will be accepted."*

Source: Riyad as-Salihin 932 Grade: Sahih

**Awf bin Malik said:**

*"I heard the Messenger of Allah (ﷺ) offering the (funeral) prayer for one who had died, and I heard him say in his supplication: 'Allahummaghfir lahu warhamhu wa 'afihi was a'fu 'anhu, wa akrim nuzulahu wa wassi' ,adkhalahu waghsilhu bil-ma'i wath-thalji wal-baradi wa naqqihi min al-khataya kama ynaqqath-thawb al-abyad min ad-danas. (O Allah, forgive him and have mercy on him, keep him safe and sound and forgive him, honor the place where he settles and make his entrance wide; wash him with water and snow and hail, and cleanse him of sin as a white garment is cleansed of dirt)."*

Source: Sunan an-Nasa'i 62 Grade: Sahih

**Adi ibn Arta' said:**

*"When one of the Companions of the Prophet, was praised, he said in supplication to Allah, 'Do not take me*

to task for what they say and forgive me for what they do not know.'"

Source: Al-Adab Al-Mufrad 761 Grade: Sahih

**Narrated Ibn `Abbas:**

*I heard the Prophet (ﷺ) saying, "If the son of Adam (the human being) had two valleys of money, he would wish for a third, for nothing can fill the belly of Adam's son except dust, and Allah forgives him who repents to Him."*

Source: Sahih al-Bukhari 6436

**Narrated Ubayy bin Ka'b:**

*that the Messenger of Allah (ﷺ) said to him: "Indeed Allah has ordered me to recite the Qur'an to you." So he recited to him: "Those who disbelieved were not going to... (98:1) and he recited in it: "Indeed the religion with Allah is that which is Hanafiyyah, Muslim, not Judaism, nor Christianity, nor Zoroastrian, whoever does good then it shall not be rejected from him." And he recited to him: "If the son of Adam had a valley of wealth he would seek a second, and if he had a second he would seek a third, and nothing fills the belly of the son of Adam except dirt. And Allah pardons those who repent."*

Source: Jami` at-Tirmidhi 3898 Grade: Hasan

**It was narrated from 'Abdullah bin 'Abbas that:**

the Messenger of Allah said: "Whoever persists in asking for forgiveness, Allah will grant him relief from every worry, and a way out from every hardship, and will grant him provision from (sources) he could never imagine."

Source: Sunan Ibn Majah 3819 Grade: Daif

**Narrated Umm Salamah, Ummul Mu'minin:**

The Messenger of Allah (ﷺ) taught me to say when the adhan for the sunset prayer was called; "O Allah, this is the time when Thy night comes on, Thy day retires, and the voices of Thy summoners are heard, so forgive me."

Source: Sunan Abi Dawud 530 Grade: Daif

**It was narrated that Umm 'Asim said:**

"Nubaishah, the freed slave of the Messenger of Allah (ﷺ), entered upon us when we were eating from a bowl. He said that the Messenger of Allah (ﷺ) said: "Whoever eats from a bowl and cleans it, the bowl will pray for forgiveness for him."

Source: Sunan Ibn Majah 3271 Grade: Daif

**It was narrated that Sa'sa'ah bin Mu'awiyah said:**

"I met Abu Dharr and said: 'Tell me a Hadith.' He said: the Messenger of Allah said: There are no two Muslims, three of whose children die before reaching puberty, but Allah will forgive them by virtue of His mercy towards them."'

Source: Sunan an-Nasa'i 1874 Grade: Sahih

**Abu Dharr reported that the Prophet reported that Allah, the Blessed and Exalted, said:**

*"My slaves! I have forbidden injustice for Myself and I have made it forbidden among you, so do not wrong one another. "My slaves! You err by night and day and I forgive wrong actions and do not care. Ask me for forgiveness and I will forgive you. "My slaves! All of you are hungry unless I have fed you, so ask Me to feed you, and I will feed you. All of you are naked unless I have clothed you, so ask Me to clothe you and I will clothe you. "My slaves! If all of you, the first of you and the last of you, the jinn among you and the men among you, were to be as godfearing as the most godfearing heart of any one of you, that would not add anything to My kingdom. If they were to be as corrupt as the most corrupt heart of any one of you, that would not decrease anything in My kingdom. If they were to join together in one place and then ask of Me, and I gave every man among them what he asked for that, that would not reduce My kingdom at all, except as the sea is decreased if a needle is dipped into it. "My slaves! It is only your actions which I have appointed for you. Whoever finds good should praise Allah. Whoever finds other than that should only blame himself.'"*

Source: Al-Adab Al-Mufrad 490 Grade: Sahih

**Abu Sa'id and Abu Huraira reported Allah's Messenger (ﷺ) as saying:**

*Allah waits till when one-third of the first part of the night is over; He descends to the lowest heaven and says: Is there any supplicator of forgiveness? Is there any penitent? Is there any petitioner (for mercy and favour)? Is there any solicitor? -till it is daybreak.*

Source: Sahih Muslim 758e

**It was narrated from Abu Hurairah that the Prophet (ﷺ) used to fast on Mondays and Thursdays. It was said:**

*"O Messenger of Allah, why do you fast on Mondays and Thursdays?" He said: "On Mondays and Thursdays Allah forgives every Muslim except two who have forsaken one another. He says: 'Leave these two until they reconcile.'"*

Source: Sunan Ibn Majah 1740 Grade: Hasan

**Narrated Abu Hurairah:**

*The Prophet (ﷺ) said: The mu'adhdhin will receive forgiveness to the extent to which his voice reaches, and every moist and dry place will testify on his behalf; and he who attends (the congregation of) prayer will have twenty-five prayers recorded for him and will have expiation for sins committed between every two times of prayer.*

Source: Sunan Abi Dawud 515 Grade: Sahih

**Narrated Uqbah ibn Amir:**

*I heard the Messenger of Allah (ﷺ) say: Allah is pleased with a shepherd of goats who calls to prayer at the peak of a mountain, and offers prayer, Allah, the Exalted, says: Look at this servant of Mine; he calls to prayer and offers it and he fears Me. So I forgive him and admit him to paradise.*

Source: Sunan Abi Dawud 1203 Grade: Sahih

**Ibn 'Abbas reported that the Prophet said:**

*"Three things are not concealed and He forgives everything else to whomever He wills:*

*the one who dies and has not associated anything with Allah, the one who was not a sorcerer nor a follower of the sorcerers, and the one who did not have rancour towards his brother."*

Source: Al-Adab Al-Mufrad 413 Grade: Daif

**Abu Hurairah narrated that:**

*Allah's Messenger said: "Qintar is twelve thousand 'Uqiyah, each 'Uqiyah of which is better than what is between heaven and earth." And the Messenger of Allah(ﷺ) said: "A man will be raised in status in Paradise and will say: 'Where did this come from?' And it will be said: 'From your son's praying for forgiveness for you.'"*

Source: Sunan Ibn Majah 3660 Grade: Hasan

**Abu Hurairah narrated that:**

*the Messenger of Allah said: "Verily, when the slave (of Allah) commits a sin, a black spot appears on his heart. When he refrains from it, seeks forgiveness and repents, his heart is polished clean. But if he returns, it increases until it covers his entire heart. And that is the 'Ran' which Allah mentioned: 'Nay, but on their hearts is the Ran which they used to earn.'"*

Source: Jami` at-Tirmidhi 3334 Grade: Hasan

**It was narrated from Abu Sa'eed Al-Khudri that the Prophet (ﷺ) said:**

*"The one who fights in the cause of Allah has a guarantee from Allah. Either He will raise him to His forgiveness and mercy, or He will send him back with reward and spoils of war. The likeness of the one who fights in the cause of Allah is that of one who fasts and prays at night without ceasing, until he returns."*

Source: Sunan Ibn Majah 2754 Grade: Hasan

**It has been reported on the authority of Abu Huraira that the Messenger of Allah (ﷺ) said:**

*God laughs at the two men one of whom kills the other; both of them will enter Paradise. They (the Companions) said: How, Messenger of Allah? He said: One is slain (in the way of Allah) and enters Paradise. Then God forgives the other and guides him to Islam; then he fights in the way of Allah and dies a martyr.*

Source: Sahih Muslim 1890c

**Jundub bin 'Abdullah reported:**

The Messenger of Allah (ﷺ) said, "Once someone said: 'By Allah! Allah will not forgive such and such (a person).' Thereupon Allah, the Exalted and the Glorious, said: 'Who is he who takes an oath in My Name that I will not grant pardon to so-and-so? I have granted pardon to so-and-so and rendered your good deeds fruitless.'"

Source: Riyad as-Salihin 1576 Grade: Sahih

**Narrated Ali bin Abu Talib:**

that the Prophet (ﷺ) said: "Whoever is penalized (for a crime) then his punishment has been hastened for him in the world, for Allah is more just than to double the punishment upon His slave in the Hereafter. And whoever does a punishable act and then Allah covers it for him and forgives him, then Allah is more kind than to recount something which He has already forgiven."

Source: Jami` at-Tirmidhi 2626 Grade: Daif

**Abdullah bin Kinanah bin 'Abbas bin Mirdas As-Sulami narrated that his father told him, from his father, that the Messenger of Allah (ﷺ) prayed for forgiveness for his nation one evening at 'Arafat, and the response came:**

"I have forgiven them, except for the wrongdoer, with whom I will settle the score in favor of the one whom he wronged." He said: "O Lord, if You will, then grant Paradise to the one who is wronged, and forgive the wrongdoer." No response came (that evening). The next day at Muzdalifah he repeated the supplication, and received a response to what he asked for. He (the narrator) said: "The Messenger of Allah (ﷺ) laughed," or he said, "He smiled. Abu Bakr and 'Umar said to him: 'May my father and mother be ransomed for you; this is not a time when you usually laugh. What made you laugh, may Allah make your years filled with laughter?' He said: 'The enemy of Allah, Iblis, when he came to know that Allah answered my prayer and forgiven my nation, took some dust and started to sprinkle it on his head, uttering cries of woe and doom, and what I saw of his anguish made me laugh.'"

Source: Sunan Ibn Majah 3013 Grade: Daif

**It was narrated that 'Ubadah bin Samit said:**

"I heard the Messenger of Allah (ﷺ) say: 'Five prayers that Allah has enjoined upon His slaves, so whoever does them, and does not omit anything out of negligence, on the Day of Resurrection Allah will make a covenant with him that He will admit him to Paradise. But whoever does them but omits something from them out of negligence, will not have such a covenant with Allah; if He wills He will punish him, and if He wills, He will forgive him.'"

Source: Sunan Ibn Majah 1401 Grade: Hasan

**It was narrated that Abu Sa'eed Al-Khudri said:**

"*The Messenger of Allah said: 'No one of you disputes more intensely for something that is rightly his in this world, than the believers will dispute with their Lord for their brothers who have entered the Fire. They will say: 'Our Lord, our brothers used to pray with us and fast with us, and perform Hajj with us, and you have caused them to enter the Fire?' He will say: 'Go and bring forth whomever you recognize among them.' So they will go to them, and will recognize them by their appearances. Among them will be those who have been seized by the Fire up to the middle of their shins, and some among them those whom it has taken up to his ankles. They will bring them forth, then they will say: 'Our Lord, we have brought forth those whom You commanded us (to bring forth).' He will say: 'Bring forth everyone in whose heart is faith the weight of a Dinar.' Then He will say: 'Everyone in whose heart is faith the weight of half a Dinar,' until He will say: 'In whose heart is faith the weight of the smallest speck.'*" Abu Sa'eed said: "*Whoever does not believe this, let him read the Verse: 'Verily, Allah forgives not that partners should be set up with Him (in worship), but He forgives except that (anything else) to whom He wills up to a tremendous (sin).'*"

Source: Sunan an-Nasa'i 5010 Grade: Sahih

**Ibn 'Umar reported:**

I heard Messenger of Allah (ﷺ) saying, "A believer will be brought close to his Lord on the Day of Resurrection and enveloping him in His Mercy, He will make him confess his sins by saying: 'Do you remember (doing) this sin and this sin?' He will reply: 'My Lord, I remember.' Then He will say: 'I covered it up for you in the life of world, and I forgive it for you today.' Then the record of his good deeds will be handed to him".

Source: Riyad as-Salihin 433 Grade: Sahih

**It was narrated that Abu Musa said:**

"There was an eclipse of the sun, and the Messenger of Allah (ﷺ) got up in a rush, fearing that it might be the Hour. He went to the masjid, where he stood and prayed, standing, bowing and prostrating for the longest time that I ever saw him do in prayer. Then he said: 'These signs that Allah sends do not occur for the death or birth of anyone, but Allah sends them to strike fear into His slaves. If you see any of these things, then hasten to remember Him, call upon Him supplicate and ask for His forgiveness.'"

Source: Sunan an-Nasa'i 1503 Grade: Sahih

**Abdullah ibn 'Umar said:**

"The sun was eclipsed one day in the era of Allah's Messenger so Allah's Messenger stood performing the ritual prayer, until he could hardly bow down, then he bowed down and could hardly raise his head, then he raised his head and could hardly prostrate himself, then *he prostrated himself and could hardly raise his head, so he began to gasp and weep, saying: 'O my Lord, have You not promised me that You will not torment them while I am among them? O my Lord, have You not promised me that You will not torment them while they and we are appealing to You for forgiveness?' Then, once he had performed two cycles of ritual prayer, the sun became visible, so he stood up, praised Allah (Exalted is He) and extolled Him. Then he said: 'The sun and the moon are among the signs of Allah. They are not eclipsed because of someone's death, nor because of his coming to life, so when they are eclipsed, you must seek refuge in the remembrance of Allah (Exalted is He)!'"*

Source: Shama'il Al-Muhammadiyah 323 Grade: Hasan

### A'isha reported Allah's Messenger (ﷺ) as saying:

*Every one of the children of Adam has been created with three hundred and sixty joints; so he who declares the Glory of Allah, praises Allah, declares Allah to be One, Glorifies Allah, and seeks forgiveness from Allah, and removes stone, or thorn, or bone from people's path, and enjoins what is good and forbids from evil, to the number of those three hundred and sixty joints, will walk that day having saved himself from the Fire.*

Source: Sahih Muslim 1007a

### It was narrated from 'Aishah that the Messenger of Allah (ﷺ) said:

*"Whoever loves to meet Allah, Allah loves to meet him, and whoever hates to meet Allah, Allah hates to meet him."* It was said to him: *"O Messenger of Allah, does hating to meet Allah mean hating to meet death? For all of us hate death."* He said: *"No. Rather that is only at the moment of death. But if he is given the glad tidings of the mercy and forgiveness of Allah, he loves to meet Allah and Allah loves to meet him; and if he is given the tidings of the punishment of Allah, he hates to meet Allah and Allah hates to meet him."*

Source: Sunan Ibn Majah 4264 Grade: Sahih

### Ali said:

*"The Messenger of Allah (ﷺ) said to me: 'Should I not teach you some words that if you say them, Allah will forgive you, even if you were already forgiven?' He said: 'Say: None has the right to be worshipped by Allah, the Most High, the Magnificent. None has the right to be worshipped by Allah, the Forbearing, the Generous. None has the right to be worshipped but Allah. Glory to Allah, the Lord of the Magnificent Throne. (Lā ilāha illallāhul-`aliyul-`aẓīm, lā ilāha illallāhul-ḥalīmul-karīm, lā ilāha illallāh, subḥān Allāhi rabbil-`arshil-`aẓīm.)'"*

Source: Jami` at-Tirmidhi 3504 Grade: Daif

### Aisha reported:

The Prophet (ﷺ) came in when a woman was sitting beside me. He asked me, "Who is she?" I said: "She is the one whose performance of Salat (prayer) has become the talk of the town." Addressing her, he (ﷺ) said, "(What is this!) You are required to take upon yourselves only what you can carry out easily. By Allah, Allah does not withhold His Mercy and forgiveness of you until you neglect and give up (good works). Allah likes the deeds best which a worshipper can carry out constantly".

Source: Riyad as-Salihin 142 Grade: Sahih

**Abud-Darda' reported:**

*I heard the Messenger of Allah (ﷺ) saying, "Whenever a Muslim supplicates for his (Muslim) brother in his absence, the angels say: 'May the same be for you too'."*

Source: Riyad as-Salihin 1494 Grade: Sahih

**It was narrated from Hudhaifah that the Messenger of Allah said:**

*"There was a man among those who came before you who thought badly of his deeds, so when death was approaching, he said to his family: 'When I am dead, burn my body and grind up my bones, then scatter me in the sea, for if Allah gets hold of me, He will never forgive me.' But Allah commanded the angels to seize his soul. He said to him: 'What made you do what you did?' He said: 'O Lord, I only did it because I feared You.' So Allah forgave him."*

Source: Sunan an-Nasa'i 2080 Grade: Sahih

**It was narrated that Ibn 'Abbas said:**

"A man from among the Ansar accepted Islam, then he apostatized and went back to Shirk. Then he regretted that, and sent word to his people (saying): 'Ask the Messenger of Allah, is there any repentance for me?' His people came to the Messenger of Allah and said: 'So and so regrets (what he did), and he has told us to ask you if there is any repentance for him?' Then the Verses: 'How shall Allah guide a people who disbelieved after their Belief up to His saying: Verily, Allah is Oft-Forgiving, Most Merciful' was revealed. So he sent word to him, and he accepted Islam."

Source: Sunan an-Nasa'i 4068 Grade: Sahih

**It was narrated that Abu Bakr bin Abi Zuhair said:**

*I was told that Abu Bakr said: O Messenger of Allah, how could we be in a good state after this verse: "It will not be in accordance with your desires (Muslims), nor those of the people of the Scripture (Jews and Christians), whosoever works evil, will have the recompense thereof [ 4:123]? Will we be punished for every bad deed we do? There Messenger of Allah (ﷺ) said: `May Allah forgive you, O Abu Bakr, do you not fall sick? Do you not get exhausted? Do you not feel sad? Don't calamities befall you?` He said: Of course. He said: `That is the recompense you are given.`*

Source: Musnad Ahmad 68 Grade: Sahih

**It is narrated on the authority of Abdullaah bin Umar that when the Messenger of Allah (ﷺ) was**

taken for the Night (mi'rāj) journey, he was taken to Sidrat al-Muntaha, which is situated on the sixth heaven, where terminates everything that ascends from the earth and is held there, and where terminates everything that descends from above it and is held there. (It is with reference to this that) Allah said (in the meaning of), "while the Lote Tree was overwhelmed with ˹heavenly˺ splendours" (53:16). The narrator said:

*(It was) gold moths. He also said: The Messenger of Allah (ﷺ) was given three things: "He was given the five daily prayers, he was given the concluding verses of Sūrah al-Baqarah (i.e., 285-286), and forgiveness of serious sins for those among his Ummah who do not associate partners with Allah."*

Source: Sahih Muslim 173

**Narrated Abu Hurairah:**

*A man from the Companions of the Prophet (ﷺ) passed by ravine containing a small spring of thirst-quenching water, so he was amazed by how pleasant it was. So he said: 'I should leave the people and stay in this ravine. But I will not do it until I seek permission from the Messenger of Allah (ﷺ).' So he mentioned that to the Messenger of Allah (ﷺ) and he said: 'Do not do so. For indeed one of you standing in the cause of Allah is more virtuous that his Salat in his house for seventy years. Do you not love that Allah forgive your sins and admit you* into Paradise? Then fight in the cause of Allah, for whoever fights in Allah's cause for the time it takes for two milkings of a camel, then Paradise is obligatory for him.'"

Source: Jami` at-Tirmidhi 1650 Grade: Hasan

**Mu'adh bin Jabal narrated that the Messenger of Allah (ﷺ) said:**

"Whoever fasts Ramadan, performs the Salat, performs Hajj to the House" - I do not know whether he mentioned Zakat or not - "except that it is binding on Allah that He forgive him, whether he emigrated in the cause of Allah, or remained in his land in which he was born." Mu'adh said: "Should I not inform the people of this?" The Messenger of Allah (ﷺ) said, "Leave the people to do deeds, for verily in Paradise there are a hundred levels, what is between every two levels is like what is between the heavens and the earth. Al-Firdaus is the highest of Paradise and its most expansive, and above that is the Throne of Ar-Rahman (the Most Merciful), and from it the rivers of Paradise are made to flow forth. So when you ask Allah, ask Him for Al-Firdaus."

Source: Jami` at-Tirmidhi 2530 Grade: Sahih

**Narrated Safwan bin Muhriz Al-Mazini:**

While I was walking with Ibn `Umar holding his hand, a man came in front of us and asked, "What have you heard from Allah's Messenger (ﷺ) about An-Najwa?"

*Ibn `Umar said, "I heard Allah's Messenger (ﷺ) saying, 'Allah will bring a believer near Him and shelter him with His Screen and ask him: Did you commit such-and-such sins? He will say: Yes, my Lord. Allah will keep on asking him till he will confess all his sins and will think that he is ruined. Allah will say: 'I did screen your sins in the world and I forgive them for you today', and then he will be given the book of his good deeds. Regarding infidels and hypocrites (their evil acts will be exposed publicly) and the witnesses will say: These are the people who lied against their Lord. Behold! The Curse of Allah is upon the wrongdoers." (11.18)*

Source: Sahih al-Bukhari 2441

**It is narrated on the authority of Ibn Shamasa Mahri that he said:**

*We went to Amr bin al-As and he was about to die. He wept for a long time and turned his face towards the wall. His son said: Did the Messenger of Allah not give you tidings of this? Did the Messenger of Allah (ﷺ) not give you tidings of this? He (the narrator) said: He turned his face (towards the audience) and said: The best thing which we can count upon is the testimony that there is no god but Allah and that Muhammad is the Messenger of Allah. Verily I have passed through three phases. (The first one) in which I found myself averse to none else more than I was averse to the Messenger of Allah (ﷺ) and there was no other desire stronger in me than the one that I should overpower him and kill him. Had I died in this state, I would have been definitely one of the denizens of Fire. When Allah instilled the love of Islam in my heart, I came to the Messenger (ﷺ) and said: Stretch out your right hand so that may pledge my allegiance to you. He stretched out his right hand, I withdrew my hand, He (the Prophet) said: What has happened to you, O 'Amr? replied: I intend to lay down some condition. He asked: What condition do you intend to put forward? I said: should be granted pardon. He (the Prophet) observed: Are you not aware of the fact that Islam wipes out all the previous (misdeeds)? Verily migration wipes out all the previous (misdeeds), and verily the pilgrimage wipes out all the (previous) misdeeds. And then no one as or dear to me than the Messenger of Allah and none was more sublime in my eyes than he, Never could I, pluck courage to catch a full glimpse of his face due to its splendour. So if I am asked to describe his features, I cannot do that for I have not eyed him fully. Had I died in this state had every reason to hope that I would have been among the dwellers of Paradise. Then we were responsible for certain things (in the light of which) I am unable to know what is in store for me. When I die, let neither female mourner nor fire accompany me. When you bury me, fill my grave well with earth, then stand around it for the time within which a camel is slaughtered and its meat is distributed so that I may enjoy your intimacy and (in your company) ascertain what answer I can give to the messengers (angels) of Allah.*

Source: Sahih Muslim 121

**Abu Huraira reported Allah's Messenger (ﷺ) as saying:**

Allah has mobile (squads) of angels, who have no other work (to attend to but) to follow the assemblies of Dhikr and when they find such assemblies in which there is Dhikr (of Allah) they sit in them and some of them surround the others with their wings till the space between them and the sky of the world is fully covered, and when they disperse (after the assembly of Dhikr is adjourned) they go upward to the heaven and Allah, the Exalted and Glorious, asks them although He is best informed about them:

Where have you come from? They say: We come from Thine servants upon the earth who had been glorifying Thee (reciting Subhan Allah), uttering Thine Greatness (saying Allah o-Akbar) and uttering Thine Oneness (La ilaha ill Allah) and praising Thee (uttering al-Hamdu Lillah) and begging of Thee. Be would say: What do they beg of Me? They would say: They beg of Thee the Paradise of Thine. He (God) would say: Have they seen My Paradise? They said: No, our Lord. He would say: (What it would be then) if they were to see Mine Paradise? They (the angels) said: They seek Thine protection. He (the Lord) would say: Against what do they seek protection of Mine? They (the angels) would say: Our Lord, from the Hell-Fire. He (the Lord) would say: Have they seen My Fire? They would say: No. He (the Lord) would say: What it would be if they were to see My Fire? They would say: They beg of Thee forgiveness. He would say: I grant pardon to them, and confer upon them what they ask for and grant them protection against which they seek protection. They (the angels) would again say: Our Lord, there is one amongst them such and such simple servant who happened to pass by (that assembly) and sat there along with them (who had been participating in that assembly). He (the Lord) would say: I also grant him pardon, for they are a people the seat-fellows of whom are in no way unfortunate.

Source: Sahih Muslim 2689

**Abu Musa Al-Ash'ari reported:**

The Prophet (ﷺ) said: "Allah, the Exalted, will continue to stretch out His Hand in the night so that the sinners of the day may repent, and continue to stretch His Hand in the daytime so that the sinners of the night may repent, until the sun rises from the west".

Source: Riyad as-Salihin 16 Grade: Sahih

**It was narrated from Abu Hurairah the Prophet (ﷺ) said:**

"If you were to commit sin until your sins reach the heaven, then you were to repent, your repentance would be accepted."

Source: Sunan Ibn Majah 4248 Grade: Hasan

**Narrated Ibn `Umar:**

Allah's Messenger (ﷺ) said, "Whoever drinks alcoholic drinks in the world and does not repent (before dying), will be deprived of it in the Hereafter."

Source: Sahih al-Bukhari 5575

**It was narrated from Anas that the Messenger of Allah (ﷺ) said:**

*"Every son of Adam commits sin, and the best of those who commit sin are those who repent.'"*

Source: Sunan Ibn Majah 4251 Grade: Hasan

**It was narrated from 'Abdullah bin 'Amr that the Messenger of Allah (ﷺ) said:**

*"Whoever drinks wine and gets drunk, his prayer will not be accepted for forty days, and if he dies he will enter Hell, but if he repents, Allah will accept his repentance. If he drinks wine again and gets drunk, his prayer will not be accepted for forty days, and if he dies he will enter Hell, but if he repents, Allah will accept his repentance. If he drinks wine again and gets drunk, his prayer will not be accepted for forty days, and if he dies he will enter Hell, but if he repents Allah will accept his repentance. But if he does it again, then Allah will most certainly make him drink of the mire of the puss or sweat on the Day of Resurrection." They said: "O Messenger of Allah, what is the mire of the pus or sweat? He said: "The drippings of the people of Hell."*

Source: Sunan Ibn Majah 3377 Grade: Sahih

**Narrated Abdullah Ibn Abbas:**

*The Messenger of Allah (ﷺ) said: Every intoxicant is khamr (wine) and every intoxicant is forbidden. If anyone drinks wine, Allah will not accept prayer from him for forty days, but if he repents, Allah will accept his repentance. If he repeats it a fourth time, it is binding on Allah that He will give him tinat al-khabal to drink.*

*He was asked: What is tinat al-khabal, Messenger of Allah? He replied: Discharge of wounds, flowing from the inhabitants of Hell. If anyone serves it to a minor who does not distinguish between the lawful and the unlawful, it is binding on Allah that He will give him to drink the discharge of wounds, flowing from the inhabitants of Hell.*

Source: Sunan Abi Dawud 3680 Grade: Sahih

**It was narrated from Ibn 'Abbas that the Messenger of Allah (ﷺ) said:**

*"Wailing over the dead is one of the affairs of the Days of Ignorance and if the woman who wails does not repent before she dies, she will be resurrected on the Day of Resurrection wearing a shirt of pitch (tar), over which she will wear a shirt of flaming fire."*

Source: Sunan Ibn Majah 1582 Grade: Hasan

**Narrated Sa`d bin Ubaid:**

*(the Maula of `Abdur-Rahman bin Azhar) Allah's Messenger (ﷺ) said, "None of you should long for death,*

for if he is a good man, he may increase his good deeds, and if he is an evil-doer, he may stop the evil deeds and repent."

Source: Sahih al-Bukhari 7235

**Narrated Abu Huraira:**

I heard Allah's Messenger (ﷺ) saying, "The good deeds of any person will not make him enter Paradise." (None can enter Paradise through his good deeds.) They (the Prophet's companions) said, 'Not even you, O Allah's Messenger (ﷺ)?' He said, "Not even myself, unless Allah bestows His favor and mercy on me." So be moderate in your religious deeds and do the deeds that are within your ability: and none of you should wish for death, for if he is a good doer, he may increase his good deeds, and if he is an evil doer, he may repent to Allah."

Source: Sahih al-Bukhari 5673

**Narrated Abu Hurairah:**

that the Messenger of Allah (ﷺ) said: "The adulterer is not a believer while he is committing adultery, and the thief is not a believer while he is stealing, but there is a chance for repentance; (if he repents, Allah will accept the repentance)."

Source: Jami` at-Tirmidhi 2625 Grade: Sahih

**It was narrated that Abu Sa'eed Al Khudri said:**

*"Shall I not tell you what I heard directly from the Messenger of Allah (ﷺ)? I heard it and memorized it: 'A man killed ninety-nine people, then the idea of repentance occurred to him. He asked who was the most knowledgeable of people on earth, and he was told of a man so he went to him and said: "I have killed ninety-nine people. Can I repent?" He said: "After ninety-nine people?!" He said: 'So he drew his sword and killed him, thus completing one hundred. Then the idea of repentance occurred to him (again), so he asked who was the most knowledgeable of people, and he was told of a man (so he went to him) and said: "I have killed one hundred people. Can I repent?" He said: "Woe to you, what is stopping you from repenting? Leave the evil town where you are living and go to a good town, such and such town and worship your Lord there." So he went out, heading for the good town, but death came to him on the road. The angels of mercy and angels of punishment argued over him. Iblis (Satan) said: "I have more right to him, for he never disobeyed me for a moment." But the angels of mercy said: "He went out repenting." (One of the narrators) Hammam said: "Humaid At-Tawil narrated to me from Bakr bin Abdullah that Abu Rafi said: 'So Allah sent an angel to whom they referred (the case). He said: "Look and see which of the two towns was he closer, and put him with its people." (One of the narrators) Qatadah said: "Hasan narrated to us: 'When death came to him he strove and drew closer to the good*

*town, and farther away from the evil town, so they put him with the people of the good town."*

Source: Sunan Ibn Majah 2622 Grade: Sahih

**Abu Hurairah narrated that:**

*The Messenger of Allah (ﷺ) said: "Whoever sits in a sitting and engages in much empty, meaningless speech and then says before getting from that sitting of his: 'Glory is to You, O Allah, and praise, I bear witness that there is none worthy of worship except You, I seek You forgiveness, and I repent to You, (Subḥānaka Allāhumma wa biḥamdika, ashhadu an lā ilāha illā anta, astaghfiruka wa atūbu ilaik)' whatever occurred in that sitting would be forgiven to him."*

Source: Jami` at-Tirmidhi 3433 Grade: Sahih

**Narrated Musa bin Talhah:**

*that Abu Al-Yasar said: "A woman came to me selling dates. I said to her: 'There are better dates than these in the house.' So she entered the house with me. I had an urge for her so I began kissing her. I went to Abu Bakr and mentioned that to him, so he said: 'Cover what you have done, repent, do not inform any one, and never do it again.' So I went to 'Umar and mentioned that to him. He said: 'Cover what you have done, repent, do not inform any one, and never do it again.' Then I went to the Prophet (ﷺ) and mentioned it to him." He said: 'Is this how you take care of the wife of someone who is away* fighting in Allah's cause?" Such that he had wished he had not accepted Islam until that very time, and he thought that he must be one of the people of the Fire." He said: "The Messenger of Allah (ﷺ) bowed his head for a long time, until Allah revealed to him: And perform the Salat, at the two ends of the day and in some hours of the night. Verily, the good deeds remove the evil deeds. That is a reminder for the mindful (11:114). Abu Al-Yasar said: "So I went to him and the Messenger of Allah (ﷺ) recited it for me. A companion of his said: "O Messenger of Allah! Is this specific, or is it for the people in general?" He said: "Rather it is for the people in general."

Source: Jami` at-Tirmidhi 3115 Grade: Hasan

**It was narrated that Jabir bin 'Abdullah said:**

"The Messenger of Allah (ﷺ) delivered a sermon to us and said: 'O people! Repent to Allah before you die. Hasten to do good deeds before you become preoccupied (because of sickness and old age). Uphold the relationship that exists between you and your Lord by remembering Him a great deal and by giving a great deal of charity in secret and openly. (Then) you will be granted provision and Divine support, and your condition will improve. Know that Allah has enjoined Friday upon you in this place of mine, on this day, in this month, in this year, until the Day of Resurrection. Whoever abandons it, whether during my lifetime or after I am gone, whether he has a just or an unjust ruler, whether he takes it *lightly or denies (that it is obligatory), may Allah cause him to lose all sense of tranquility and contentment, and may He not bless him in his affairs. Indeed, his prayer will not be valid, his Zakat will not be valid, his Hajj will not be valid, his fasting will not be valid, and his righteous deeds will not be accepted, until he repents. Whoever repents, Allah will accept his repentance. No woman should be appointed as Imam over a man, no Bedouin should be appointed as Imam over a Muhajir, no immoral person should be appointed as Imam over a (true) believer, unless that is forced upon him and he fears his sword or whip.'"*

Source: Sunan Ibn Majah 1081 Grade: Daif

**Umar bin Al-Khattab reported:**

*The Messenger of Allah (ﷺ) said, "Whoever of you performs Wudu' carefully and then affirms: 'Ash-hadu an la ilaha illallahu Wahdahu la sharika Lahu, wa ash-hadu anna Muhammadan 'abduhu wa Rasuluhu* **[I testify that there is no true god except Allah Alone, Who has no partners and that Muhammad ((ﷺ) is His slave and Messenger]***,' the eight gates of Paradise are opened for him. He may enter through whichever of these gates he desires (to enter)."*

Source: Riyad as-Salihin 1032 Grade: Sahih

**It was narrated that Ibn Ma'qil said:**

*"I entered with my father upon 'Abdullah, and I heard him say: 'The messenger of Allah (ﷺ) said: "Regret is repentance." My father said: 'Did you hear the Prophet (ﷺ) say: "Regret is repentance?" He said: 'Yes.'"*

Source: Sunan Ibn Majah 4252 Grade: Hasan

### Abu Hurairah narrated the Messenger of Allah (ﷺ) said:

*"Allah is more delighted with the repentance of one of you, than one of you is, when finding his lost animal."*

Source: Jami` at-Tirmidhi 3538 Grade: Sahih

### Aishah narrated:

*"There was no behavior more hated to the Messenger of Allah than lying. A man would lie in narrating something in the presence of the Prophet, and he would not be content until he knew that he had repented."*

Source: Jami` at-Tirmidhi 1973 Grade: Hasan

### Anas bin Malik reported Allah's Messenger (ﷺ) said:

*Allah is more pleased with the repentance of a servant as he turns towards Him for repentance than this that one amongst you is upon the camel in a waterless desert and there is upon (that camel) his provision of food and drink also and it is lost by him, and he having lost all hope (to get that) lies down in the shadow and is disappointed about his camel and there he finds that camel standing* before him. He takes hold of his nose-string and then out of boundless joy says: O Lord, Thou art my servant and I am Thine Lord. He commits this mistake out of extreme delight.

Source: Sahih Muslim 2747a

**Narrated 'Alqamah bin Wa'il Al-Kindi:**

*From his father: "A women went out during the time of the Prophet (ﷺ) to go to Prayer, but she was caught by a man and he had relations with her, so she screamed and he left. Then a man came across her and she said: 'That man has done this and that to me', then she came across a group of Emigrants (Muhajirin) and she said: 'That man did this and that to me.' They went to get the man she thought had relations with her, and they brought him to her. She said: 'Yes, that's him.' So they brought him to the Messenger of Allah (ﷺ), and when he ordered that he be stoned, the man who had relations with her, said: 'O Messenger of Allah, I am the one who had relations with her.' So he said to her: 'Go, for Allah has forgiven you.' Then he said some nice words to the man (who was brought). And he said to the man who had relations with her: 'Stone him.' Then he said: 'He has repented a repentance that, if the inhabitants of Al-Madinah had repented with, it would have been accepted from them.'"*

Source: Jami` at-Tirmidhi 1454 Grade: Hasan

**It was narrated from Abu Hurairah that the Messenger of Allah (ﷺ) said:**

"Allah laughs at two men, one of whom killed the other but they both entered Paradise. The first one fought in the cause of Allah and was killed, then Allah accepted the repentance of the one who killed him, and he fought and was martyred."

Source: Sunan an-Nasa'i 3166 Grade: Sahih

**Khalid bin Ma'dan narrated from Mu'adh bin Jabal that the Messenger of Allah said:**

*"Whoever shames his brother for a sin, he shall not die until he (himself) commits it." (One of the narrators) Ahmad said: They said: 'From a sin he has repented from."*

Source: Jami` at-Tirmidhi 2505 Grade: Daif

**Narrated Ubada bin As-Samit:**

*I gave the pledge of allegiance to the Prophet (ﷺ) with a group of people, and he said, "I take your pledge that you will not worship anything besides Allah, will not steal, will not commit infanticide, will not slander others by forging false statements and spreading it, and will not disobey me in anything good. And whoever among you fulfill all these (obligations of the pledge), his reward is with Allah. And whoever commits any of the above crimes and receives his legal punishment in this world, that will be his expiation and purification. But if Allah screens his sin, it will be up to Allah, Who will either punish or forgive him according to His wish." Abu `Abdullah said: "If a thief repents after his hand has been* *cut off, then his witness well be accepted. Similarly, if any person upon whom any legal punishment has been inflicted, repents, his witness will be accepted."*

Source: Sahih al-Bukhari 6801

**Narrated `Urwa bin Az-Zubair:**

*A woman committed theft in the Ghazwa of the Conquest (of Mecca) and she was taken to the Prophet who ordered her hand to be cut off. `Aisha said, "Her repentance was perfect and she was married (later) and used to come to me (after that) and I would present her needs to Allah's Messenger (ﷺ)."*

Source: Sahih al-Bukhari 2648

**It was narrated from Safwan bin 'Assal that the Messenger of Allah (ﷺ) said:**

*"Towards the west (i.e., the place of the setting of the sun) there is an open door, seventy years wide. That door will remain open for repentance until the sun rises from this direction. When it rises from this direction, faith will not benefit any soul that did not believe before or earn anything good through its faith."*

Source: Sunan Ibn Majah 4070 Grade: Sahih

**Abdullah bin Buraida reported on the authority of his father that Ma'iz bin Malik al-Aslami came to Allah's Messenger (ﷺ) and said:**

*Allah's Messenger, I have wronged myself; I have committed adultery and I earnestly desire that you should purify me. He turned him away. On the following day, he (Ma'iz) again came to him and said: Allah's Messenger, I have committed adultery. Allah's Messenger (ﷺ) turned him away for the second time, and sent him to his people saying: Do you know if there is anything wrong with his mind. They denied of any such thing in him and said: We do not know him but as a wise good man among us, so far as we can judge. He (Ma'iz) came for the third time, and he (the Prophet) sent him as he had done before. He asked about him and they informed him that there was nothing wrong with him or with his mind. When it was the fourth time, a ditch was dug for him and he (the Prophet) pronounced judgment about him and he wis stoned. He (the narrator) said: There came to him (the Prophet) a woman from Ghamid and said: Allah's Messenger, I have committed adultery, so purify me. He (the Prophet) turned her away. On the following day she said: Allah's Messenger, why do you turn me away? Perhaps, you turn me away as you turned away Ma'iz. By Allah, I have become pregnant. He said: Well, if you insist upon it, then go away until you give birth to (the child). When she was delivered she came with the child (wrapped) in a rag and said: Here is the child whom I have given birth to. He said: Go away and suckle him until you wean him. When she had weaned him, she came to him (the Prophet) with the child who was holding a piece of bread in his hand. She said:*

*Allah's Apostle, here is he as I have weaned him and he eats food. He (the Prophet) entrusted the child to one of the Muslims and then pronounced punishment. And she was put in a ditch up to her chest and he commanded people and they stoned her. Khalid bin Walid came forward with a stone which he flung at her head and there spurted blood on the face of Khalid and so he abused her. Allah's Apostle (ﷺ) heard his (Khalid's) curse that he had hurled upon her. Thereupon he (the Prophet) said: Khalid, be gentle. By Him in Whose Hand is my life, she has made such a repentance that even if a wrongful tax-collector were to repent, he would have been forgiven. Then giving command regarding her, he prayed over her and she was buried.*

Source: Sahih Muslim 1695b

### And the Messenger of Allah said:

*"Allah is more pleased with the repentance of one of you that a man in a desolate, barren, destructive wasteland, who has his mount carrying his provisions, his food, and his drink and what he needs with him. Then it wanders away. So he goes to find it until he is on the brink of death. He says: 'I will return to the place where I lost it, to die.' So he returns to his place and his eyes become heavy (falling asleep). Then he awakens to find his mount at his head carrying his food, drink and what he needs."*

Source: Jami` at-Tirmidhi 2498 Grade: Sahih

### Abu Hurairah reported:

Messenger of Allah (ﷺ) said, "Allah says: 'I am just as My slave thinks of Me when he remembers Me.' By Allah! Allah is more pleased with the repentance of His slave than one of you who unexpectedly finds in the desert his lost camel. 'He who comes closer to Me one span, I come closer to him a cubit; and he who comes closer to Me a cubit, I come closer to him a fathom; and if he comes to Me walking, I come to him running".

Source: Riyad as-Salihin 440 Grade: Sahih

**Narrated Al-Aswad:**

While we were sitting in a circle in `Abdullah's gathering, Hudhaifa came and stopped before us, and greeted us and then said, "People better than you became hypocrites." Al-Aswad said: I testify the uniqueness of Allah! Allah says: "Verily! The hypocrites will be in the lowest depths of the Fire." (4.145) On that `Abdullah smiled and Hudhaifa sat somewhere in the Mosque. `Abdullah then got up and his companions (sitting around him) dispersed. Hudhaifa then threw a pebble at me (to attract my attention). I went to him and he said, "I was surprised at `Abdullah's smile though he understood what I said. Verily, people better than you became hypocrite and then repented and Allah forgave them."

Source: Sahih al-Bukhari 4602

**It was narrated that Abu Hurairah said:**

"I went out to At-Tur and met Ka'b. He and I spent a day together, when I narrated things to him from the Messenger of Allah (ﷺ) and he narrated things to me from the Tawrah. I said to him: The Messenger of Allah (ﷺ) said: The best day on which the sun rises is Friday. On this day, Adam was created, on this day he was sent down, on it his repentance was accepted, on this day he died, and on this day the Hour will begin. There is no living creature on Earth that does not listen out from Friday morning until the sun rises, fearing the onset of the Hour, except the son of Adam. On (Friday) there is an hour in which, if a believer prays and asks Allah for something, He will give it to him. Ka'b said: Is that one day in every year? I said: No, it is every Friday.' Then Ka'b read in the Tawrah and said: The Messenger of Allah (ﷺ) spoke the truth; it is every Friday. Then I went out and met Basrah bin Abi Basrah Al-Ghifari. He said: From where have you come? I said: From At-Tur. He said: If I had met you before you went there, you would not have gone. I said to him: Why? He said: I heard the Messenger of Allah (ﷺ) say: Do not travel especially to visit any masjid except three: Al Masjid Al-Haram (in Makkah), my masjid (in Al-Madinah) and the Masjid of Bait Al-Maqdis (in Jerusalem). Then I met 'Abdullah bin Salam and said: 'If you had only seen me, I went to At-Tur and met Ka'b, and he and I spent the day together, when I narrated things to him from the Messenger of Allah (ﷺ) and he narrated things to me from the Tawrah. I said to him: The Messenger of Allah (ﷺ) said: The best day on which the sun rises is Friday. On this day, Adam was created, on this day he was sent down, on this day his repentance was accepted, on this day he died, and on this day the Hour will begin. There is no living creature on Earth that does not listen out from Friday morning until the sun rises, fearing the onset of the Hour, except the son of Adam. On (Friday) there is an hour in which, if a believer prays and asks Allah for something, He will give it to him. Ka'b said: That is one day in every year. 'Abdullah bin Salam said: Ka'b is not telling the truth. I said: Then Ka'b read (in the Tawrah) and said: The Messenger of Allah (ﷺ) spoke the truth; it is every Friday. 'Abdullah said: Ka'b spoke the truth; I know when that time is. I said: O my brother, tell me about it. He said: It is the last hour of Friday, before the sun sets. I said: Did you not hear the Messenger of Allah (ﷺ) say: If a believer prays, but that is not a time for prayer. He said: Did you not hear the Messenger of Allah (ﷺ) say: Whoever prays and sits waiting for the (next) prayer, is in a state of prayer until the next prayer comes? I said: Of course. He said: That is what it is."

Source: Sunan an-Nasa'i 1430 Grade: Sahih

### Abu Hurairah narrated that the Messenger of Allah (ﷺ) said:

"Allah created a hundred mercies, and He placed one mercy among his creation, they show mercy to one another by it, and there are ninety-nine mercies with Allah."

Source: Jami` at-Tirmidhi 3541 Grade: Sahih

**Abdullah bin 'Amr narrated that the Messenger of Allah said:**

*"The merciful are shown mercy by Ar-Rahman. Be merciful on the earth, and you will be shown mercy from Who is above the heavens. The womb is named after Ar-Rahman, so whoever connects it, Allah connects him, and whoever severs it, Allah severs him."*

Source: Jami` at-Tirmidhi 1924 Grade: Hasan

**Narrated Abdullah ibn Amr ibn al-'As:**

*The Prophet (ﷺ) said: The Compassionate One has mercy on those who are merciful. If you show mercy to those who are on the earth, He Who is in the heaven will show mercy to you.*

Source: Sunan Abi Dawud 4941 Grade: Sahih

**Abu Huraira said:**

*"A man came to the Prophet, with a child which he began to embrace. The Prophet said, 'Do you show mercy towards me?' 'Yes,' the man replied. He said, 'Allah is more merciful towards you than you are towards this child. He is the Most Merciful of the merciful."*

Source: Al-Adab Al-Mufrad 377 Grade: Sahih

**It was narrated from Abu Hurairah the Prophet (ﷺ) said:**

*"Allah has one hundred (degrees of) mercy, of which He has shared one between all of creation, by virtue of which you show mercy and compassion towards one another and the wild animals show compassion towards their young. And He has kept back ninety-nine (degrees of) mercy by virtue of which He will show mercy to His slaves on the Day of Resurrection."*

Source: Sunan Ibn Majah 4293 Grade: Sahih

**Narrated Abu Darda':**

*I heard the Messenger of Allah (ﷺ) say: If any of you is suffering from anything or his brother is suffering, he should say: Our Lord is Allah Who is in the heaven, holy is Thy name, Thy command reigns supreme in the heaven and the earth, as Thy mercy in the heaven, make Thy mercy in the earth; forgive us our sins, and our errors; Thou art the Lord of good men; send down mercy from Thy mercy, and remedy, and remedy from Thy remedy on this pain so that it is healed up.*

Source: Sunan Abi Dawud 3892 Grade: Daif

**Abu Umama that the Messenger of Allah said:**

*"Anyone who shows mercy, even to an animal meant for slaughtering, will be shown mercy by Allah on the Day of Rising."*

Source: Al-Adab Al-Mufrad 381 Grade: Hasan

**Narrated Usama bin Zaid:**

*We were with the Prophet (ﷺ) when suddenly there came to him a messenger from one of his daughters who was asking him to come and see her son who was dying. The Prophet (ﷺ) said (to the messenger), "Go back and tell her that whatever Allah takes is His, and whatever He gives is His, and everything with Him has a limited fixed term (in this world). So order her to be patient and hope for Allah's reward." But she sent the messenger to the Prophet (ﷺ) again, swearing that he should come to her. So the Prophet got up, and so did Sa`d bin 'Ubada and Mu`adh bin Jabal (and went to her). When the child was brought to the Prophet (ﷺ) his breath was disturbed in his chest as if it were in a water skin. On that the eyes of the Prophet (ﷺ) became flooded with tears, whereupon Sa`d said to him, "O Allah's Messenger (ﷺ)! What is this?" The Prophet (ﷺ) said, "This is mercy which Allah has put in the heart of His slaves, and Allah bestows His mercy only on those of His slaves who are merciful (to others)."*

Source: Sahih al-Bukhari 7377

**Ibn 'Umar reported:**

*The Messenger of Allah (ﷺ) visited Sa'd bin 'Ubadah during his illness. He was accompanied by 'Abdur-Rahman bin 'Auf, Sa'd bin Abu Waqqas and 'Abdullah bin Mas'ud. The Messenger of Allah (ﷺ) began to weep. When his Companions saw this, their tears also started flowing. He (ﷺ) said, "Do you not hear, Allah does not punish for the shedding of tears or the grief of the heart,* but punishes or bestows mercy for the utterances of this (and he pointed to his tongue)."

Source: Riyad as-Salihin 925 Grade: Sahih

**Abu Huraira said:**

"Two men sat in the presence of the Prophet and one of them was from a nobler family than the other. The nobler of the two sneezed and did not praise Allah, so the Prophet did not ask for mercy for him. Then the other man sneezed and praised Allah, so the Prophet, asked for mercy on him. The noble man said, 'I sneezed in your presence and you did not ask for mercy for me. This other than sneezed and you asked for mercy on him.' The Prophet said, 'This man mentioned Allah, so I mentioned him. You forgot Allah, so I forgot you.'"

Source: Al-Adab Al-Mufrad 932 Grade: Hasan

**Abu Huraira reported that the Prophet said:**

"There are three things which are all a duty for every Muslim:

to visit the sick, to attend funerals, and to say, 'may Allah have mercy on you' when someone sneezes if he praises Allah Almighty."

Source: Al-Adab Al-Mufrad 519 Grade: Sahih

**Narrated Abu Musa:**

The Jews used to sneeze in the presence of the Prophet (ﷺ) hoping that he would say: 'Yarhamukumullah (May

*Allah have mercy upon you).' So he said:
'Yahdikumullahu Wa Yuslihu Balakum (May Allah guide you and rectify your affairs).'"*

Source: Jami` at-Tirmidhi 2739 Grade: Sahih

**It was narrated that Abu Hurairah and Abu Sa'eed bore witness that the Prophet(ﷺ) said:**

*"No people sit in a gathering remembering Allah, But the angels surround them, mercy covers them, tranquility descends upon them and Allah remembers them before those who are with Him."*

Source: Sunan Ibn Majah 3791 Grade: Sahih

**It was narrated from Abu Huraira that:**

*A Bedouin entered the masjid and prayed two rak'ahs, then he said: "O Allah, have mercy on me and on Muhammad and do not have mercy on anyone else." The Messenger of Allah (ﷺ) said: "You have limited something vast."*

Source: Sunan an-Nasa'i 1217 Grade: Sahih

**Mu'awiya ibn Qurra reported that his father said:**

*"A man said, 'Messenger of Allah, I was going to slaughter a sheep and then I felt sorry for it (or 'sorry for the sheep I was going to slaughter').' He said twice, 'Since you showed mercy to the sheep, Allah will show mercy to you.'"*

Source: Al-Adab Al-Mufrad 373 Grade: Sahih

**Abdullah ibn al-'As reported that the Prophet said:**

*"Show mercy and you will be shown mercy. Forgive and Allah will forgive you. Woe to the vessels that catch words (i.e. the ears). Woe to those who persist and consciously continue in what they are doing."*

Source: Al-Adab Al-Mufrad 380 Grade: Sahih

**Narrated Abu Huraira:**

*I heard the Messenger of Allah (ﷺ) say: The wind comes from Allah's mercy.*

*Salamah's version has: It is Allah's mercy; it (sometimes) brings blessing and (sometimes) brings punishment. So when you see it, do not revile it, but ask Allah for some of its good, and seek refuge in Allah from its evil.*

Source: Sunan Abi Dawud 5097 Grade: Sahih

**Narrated Abu Huraira:**

*The Prophet (ﷺ) said: May Allah have mercy on a man who gets up at night and prays, and awakens his wife; if she refuses, he should sprinkle water on her face. May Allah have mercy on a woman who gets up at night and prays, and awakens her husband; if he refuses, she would sprinkle water on his face.*

Source: Sunan Abi Dawud 1308 Grade: Sahih

**Abu Hurairah narrated that the Messenger of Allah said:**

"Paradise and the Fire debated. Paradise said: 'The weak and the poor shall enter me,' and the Fire said: 'The tyrants and the proud shall enter me.' So He said to the Fire: 'You are My Punishment, I take vengeance through you from whom I will,' and He said to Paradise: 'You are My Mercy I show mercy through you to whom I will.'"

Source: Jami` at-Tirmidhi 2561 Grade: Hasan

**Narrated Abu Tamimah Al-Hujaimi:**

*from a man among his people, who said: "I went looking for the Prophet (ﷺ) but I was not able to find him. So I sat down, and then I saw a group of people, and he was among them, but I did not recognize him. He was settling some matter between them so when he was finished, some of them stood up with him and they were saying: 'O Messenger of Allah.' When I saw that, I said: "'Alaikas-Salam (upon you be peace) O Messenger of Allah! 'Alaikas-Salam (upon you be peace) O Messenger of Allah! 'Alaikas-Salam (upon you be peace) O Messenger of Allah!' He replied: 'Indeed "'Alaikas-Salam (upon you be peace)" is the greeting for the dead.' Then he came toward me and said: 'When a man meets his Muslim brother then he should say: "As-Salamu 'Alaikum Wa Rahmatullahi Wa Barakatuh (peace be upon you, and the mercy and blessings of Allah)." Then the Prophet (ﷺ) responded to my greeting, he said: 'And may Allah's mercy be upon you, and may Allah's mercy be upon you, and may Allah's mercy be upon you.'"*

Source: Jami` at-Tirmidhi 2721 Grade: Sahih

**It was narrated from Abdullah bin 'Amr that the Messenger of Allah(ﷺ) said:**

"Worship the Most Merciful and spread (the greeting of) peace.'"

Source: Sunan Ibn Majah 3694 Grade: Sahih

**Nawwas bin Sam'an Al-Kilabi said:**

"I heard the Messenger of Allah say: 'There is no heart that is not between two of the Fingers of the Most Merciful. If He wills, He guides it and if He wills, He sends it astray.' The Messenger of Allah used to say: 'O You Who makes hearts steadfast make our hearts steadfast in adhering to Your religion.' And he said: 'The Scale is in the Hand of the Most Merciful; He will cause some peoples to rise and others to fall until the day of Resurrection.'"

Source: Sunan Ibn Majah 199 Grade: Sahih

**Sa'eed bin Yasar narrated that:**

he heard Abu Hurairah say: "The Messenger of Allah said: 'No one gives charity from good sources – for Allah does not accept anything but that which is good – but the Most Merciful takes it in His right hand, even if it is a date, and it flourishes in the Hand of the Most Merciful until it becomes bigger than a mountain and he tends it as anyone of you would tend to his colt (i.e., young pony) or his young (weaned) camel.'"

Source: Sunan Ibn Majah 1842 Grade: Sahih

**It was narrated that Abu Hurairah said:**

*"The Messenger of Allah said: 'Those who walk to the mosque in the dark are those who are diving into the mercy of Allah.'"*

Source: Sunan Ibn Majah 779 Grade: Daif

**Abu Hurairah said:**

*"The Messenger of Allah said: 'When Ramadan comes, the gates of mercy are opened, the gates of Hell are closed, and the devils are chained up.'"*

Source: Sunan an-Nasa'i 2100 Grade: Sahih

**Narrated Abdullah ibn Umar:**

*The Prophet (ﷺ) said: May Allah show mercy to a man who prays four rak'ahs before the afternoon prayer.*

Source: Sunan Abi Dawud 1271 Grade: Hasan

**Abu Dharr narrated that:**

*the Prophet said: "When one of you stands for Salat then he should not smoothen the pebbles, for indeed it is mercy that he is facing."*

Source: Jami` at-Tirmidhi 379 Grade: Hasan

**Abu Huraira reported Allah's Messenger (ﷺ) as saying:**

Allah, the Exalted and Glorious, said: My mercy excels My wrath.

Source: Sahih Muslim 2751b

**Anas ibn Malik said:**

"A woman came to 'A'isha and 'A'isha gave her three dates. She gave each of her two children a date and kept one date for herself. The children ate the two dates and then looked at their mother. She took her date and split it into two and gave each child a half of it. The Prophet, came and 'A'isha told him about it. He said, 'Are you surprised at that? Allah will show her mercy because of her mercy towards her child.'"

Source: Al-Adab Al-Mufrad 89 Grade: Sahih

**Narrated Abu Huraira:**

I heard Allah's Messenger (ﷺ) saying, Verily Allah created Mercy. The day He created it, He made it into one hundred parts. He withheld with Him ninety-nine parts, and sent its one part to all His creatures. Had the non-believer known of all the Mercy which is in the Hands of Allah, he would not lose hope of entering Paradise, and had the believer known of all the punishment which is present with Allah, he would not consider himself safe from the Hell-Fire."

Source: Sahih al-Bukhari 6469

**Narrated Jabir bin `Abdullah:**

Allah's Messenger (ﷺ) said, "May Allah's mercy be on him who is lenient in his buying, selling, and in demanding back his money."

Source: Sahih al-Bukhari 2076

**It was narrated from 'Uqbah bin 'Amir Al-Juhani that the Messenger of Allah (ﷺ) said:**

*"May Allah have mercy on the one who keeps watch over the troops."*

Source: Sunan Ibn Majah 2769 Grade: Daif

**Narrated Abu Huraira:**

*Allah's Messenger (ﷺ) said, "When Allah created the creations, He wrote with Him on His Throne: 'My Mercy has preceded My Anger.'"*

Source: Sahih al-Bukhari 7453

**Abu Hurairah narrated the Messenger of Allah said:**

*"Indeed two men among those who entered the Fire will be screaming violently. So the Lord, Blessed and Exalted, will say: 'Take them out.' Then when they are taken out, He will say: 'What caused you to scream so violently?' They will say: 'We did that so You would have mercy on us.' He will say: 'My mercy for you is that you both go and throw yourselves where you were in the Fire.' So they will go. One of them will throw himself in, and He will make it cool and peaceful for him. And the other will*

stand there and not throw himself in, so the Lord, Mighty and Majestic, will say to him: 'What prevented you from throwing yourself in as your companion did?' He will say: 'O Lord! I hope that you will not return me to it after You have taken me out.' So the Lord, Blessed and Exalted, will say to him: 'For you is what you hoped for,' And so they will both enter Paradise together by the mercy of Allah."

Source: Jami` at-Tirmidhi 2599 Grade: Daif

**Narrated Anas:**

*The Prophet (ﷺ) said, "Some people will be scorched by Hell (Fire) as a punishment for sins they have committed, and then Allah will admit them into Paradise by the grant of His Mercy. These people will be called, 'Al-Jahannamiyyin' (the people of Hell).*

Source: Sahih al-Bukhari 7450

**Abu Huraira reported Allah's Messenger (ﷺ) as saying:**

*O Allah, I am a human being and for any person amongst Muslims upon whom I hurl malediction or invoke curse or give him whipping make it a source of purity and mercy.*

Source: Sahih Muslim 2601a

**Abu Huraira reported Allah's Messenger (ﷺ) as saying:**

*There is none whose deeds alone would entitle him to get into Paradise. It was said to him: And, Allah's Messenger, not even you? Thereupon he said: Not even I, but that my Lord wraps me in Mercy.*

Source: Sahih Muslim 2816c

**It was narrated from Anas bin Malik that the Messenger of Allah (ﷺ) said:**

*"This nation has been granted mercy (in the Hereafter) and its torment (in this world) is at the hands of one another. When the Day of Resurrection comes, each Muslim man will be given a man from among the idolaters and it will be said: 'This is your ransom from the Fire.'"*

Source: Sunan Ibn Majah 4292 Grade: Daif

**Narrated Abu Waqid Al-Laithi:**

*While Allah's Messenger (ﷺ) was sitting in the mosque with some people, three men came. Two of them came in front of Allah's Messenger (ﷺ) and the third one went away. The two persons kept on standing before Allah's Messenger (ﷺ) for a while and then one of them found a place in the circle and sat there while the other sat behind the gathering, and the third one went away. When Allah's Messenger (ﷺ) finished his preaching, he said, "Shall I tell you about these three persons? One of them betook himself to Allah, so Allah took him into His grace and mercy and accommodated him, the second felt shy* from Allah, so Allah sheltered Him in His mercy (and did not punish him), while the third turned his face from Allah and went away, so Allah turned His face from him likewise."

Source: Sahih al-Bukhari 66

**It was narrated from Abu Hurairah the Prophet said:**

"There are no two Muslims, three of whose children die before reaching puberty, but Allah will admit them to Paradise by virtue of His mercy toward them. It will be said to them: 'Enter Paradise.' They will say: 'Not until our parents enter.' So it will be said: 'Enter Paradise, you and your parents.'"

Source: Sunan an-Nasa'i 1876 Grade: Sahih

**It was narrated that Abu Hurairah said:**

"The Messenger of Allah said: 'Whoever relieves a Muslim of some worldly distress, Allah will relieve him of some of the distress of the Day of Resurrection, and whoever conceals (the faults of) a Muslim, Allah will conceal him (his faults) in this world and the Day of Resurrection. And whoever relives the burden from a destitute person, Allah will relieve him in this world and the next. Allah will help His slave so long as His slave helps his brother. Whoever follows a path in pursuit of knowledge, Allah will make easy for him a path to paradise. No people gather in one of the houses of Allah, reciting the Book of Allah and teaching it to one another, *but the angels will surround them, tranquility will descend upon them, mercy will envelop them and Allah will mention them to those who are with Him. And whoever is hindered because of his bad deeds, his lineage will be of no avail to him.'"*

Source: Sunan Ibn Majah 225 Grade: Sahih

**Ibn `Umar narrated the Messenger of Allah (ﷺ) said:**

*"Whomsoever of you the door of supplication is opened for, the doors of mercy have been opened for him. And Allah is not asked for anything – meaning – more beloved to Him, than being asked for Al-`Āfiyah." And the Messenger of Allah (ﷺ) said: "The supplication benefits against that which strikes and that which does not strike, so hold fast, O worshippers of Allah, to supplication."*

Source: Jami` at-Tirmidhi 3548 Grade: Daif

**It has been narrated on the authority of 'Abdullah bin 'Umar that the Messenger of Allah (ﷺ) said:**

*Behold! The Dispensers of justice will be seated on the pulpits of light beside God, on the right side of the Merciful, Exalted and Glorious. Either side of the Being is the right side both being equally meritorious. (The Dispensers of justice are) those who do justice in their rules, in matters relating to their families and in all that they undertake to do.*

Source: Sahih Muslim 1827

**Narrated `Aisha:**

*(the wife of the Prophet) I asked Allah's Messenger (ﷺ) about the plague. He told me that it was a Punishment sent by Allah on whom he wished, and Allah made it a source of mercy for the believers, for if one in the time of an epidemic plague stays in his country patiently hoping for Allah's Reward and believing that nothing will befall him except what Allah has written for him, he will get the reward of a martyr."*

Source: Sahih al-Bukhari 3474

**It was narrated that 'Ali said:**

*"I heard the Messenger of Allah (ﷺ) say: 'Whoever comes to his Muslim brother and visits him (when he is sick), he is walking among the harvest of Paradise until he sits down, and when he sits down he is covered with mercy. If it is morning, seventy thousand angels will send blessing upon him until evening, and if it is evening, seventy thousand angels will send blessing upon him until morning.'"*

Source: Sunan Ibn Majah 1442 Grade: Hasan

**Abu Bakr ibn Hazm and Muhammad ibn al-Munkadir were some people from the mosque who visited 'Umar ibn al-Hakam ibn Rafi' al-Ansari. They said, "Abu Hafs! Relate to us!" He said, "I heard 'Abdullah say that he heard the Prophet say:**

*"When someone visits a sick person, he dives into mercy to such an extent that when he sits with him, he settles in it."*

Source: Al-Adab Al-Mufrad 522 Grade: Sahih

**It was narrated that Ibn Dailami said:**

*"I was confused about this Divine Decree (Qadar), and I was afraid lest that adversely affect my religion and my affairs. So I went to Ubayy bin Ka'b and said: 'O Abu Mundhir! I am confused about the Divine Decree, and I fear for my religion and my affairs, so tell me something about that through which Allah may benefit me.' He said: 'If Allah were to punish the inhabitants of His heavens and of his earth, He would do so and He would not be unjust towards them. And if He were to have mercy on them, His mercy would be better for them than their own deeds. If you had the equivalent of Mount Uhud which you spent in the cause of Allah, that would not be accepted from you until you believed in the Divine Decree and you know that whatever has befallen you, could not have passed you by; and whatever has passed you by, could not have befallen you; and that if you were to die believing anything other than this, you would enter Hell. And it will not harm you to go to my brother, 'Abdullah bin Mas'ud, and ask him (about this).' So I went to 'Abdullah and asked him, and he said something similar to what Ubayy had said, and he told me: 'It will not harm you to go to Hudhaifah.' So I went to Hudhaifah and asked him, and he said something similar*

to what they had said. And he told me: 'Go to Zaid bin Thabit and ask him.' So I went to Zaid bun Thabit and asked him, and he said: 'I heard the Messenger of Allah (ﷺ) say: "If Allah were to punish the inhabitants of His heavens and of His earth, he would do so and He would not be unjust towards them. And if He were to have mercy on them, His mercy would be better for them than their own deeds. If you had the equivalent of Mount Uhud which you spent in the cause of Allah, that would not be accepted from you until you believed in the Divine Decree and you know that whatever has befallen you, could not have passed you by; and whatever has passed you by, could not have befallen you; and that if you were to die believing anything other than this, you would enter Hell"

Source: Sunan Ibn Majah 77 Grade: Sahih

**It was narrated from Ibn Umar that the Messenger of Allah (ﷺ) said:**

"(Allah says) O son of Adam! I have given you two things which you do not deserve (except by mercy of Allah): I allow you to dispose of a share of your wealth when you are on your deathbed, in order to cleanse and purify you, and my slaves pray for you after your life is over."

Source: Sunan Ibn Majah 2710 Grade: Daif

**'Abdullah reported that Allah's Messenger (ﷺ) got his head shaved (after slaughtering the sacrificial**

animal on the 10th of Dhu'l-Hijja), and so did a group of Companions, while some of them got their hair clipped. Abdullah said:

*Allah's Messenger observed once or twice:" May Allah have mercy upon those who get their heads shaved." And he also said:" Upon those too who got their hair clipped."*

Source: Sahih Muslim 1301a

**Narrated Zaid bin Khalid Al-Juhani:**

*The Prophet (ﷺ) led us in the Fajr prayer at Hudaibiya after a rainy night. On completion of the prayer, he faced the people and said, "Do you know what your Lord has said (revealed)?" The people replied, "Allah and His Apostle know better." He said, "Allah has said, 'In this morning some of my slaves remained as true believers and some became non-believers; whoever said that the rain was due to the Blessings and the Mercy of Allah had belief in Me and he disbelieves in the stars, and whoever said that it rained because of a particular star had no belief in Me but believes in that star.' "*

Source: Sahih al-Bukhari 846

**It was narrated from Yazid bin Thabit that:**

*they went out with the Messenger of Allah one day and he saw a new grave. He said: "What is this?" They said: "This is so-and-so, the freed slave woman of Banu so-and-so" - whom Messenger of Allah knew - "She died at midday and we did not like to wake you up when you were fasting and taking a nap." The Messenger of Allah stood (for prayer) and the people formed rows behind him. He said four Takbirs over her then he said: "If anyone among you dies while I am still among you, inform me, for my prayer for him is a mercy."*

Source: Sunan an-Nasa'i 2022 Grade: Sahih

**Narrated Abu Huraira:**

*I heard the Messenger of Allah (ﷺ) say: There were two men among Banu Isra'il, who were striving for the same goal. One of them would commit sin and the other would strive to do his best in the world. The man who exerted himself in worship continued to see the other in sin.*

*He would say: Refrain from it. One day he found him in sin and said to him: Refrain from it.*

*He said: Leave me alone with my Lord. Have you been sent as a watchman over me? He said: I swear by Allah, Allah will not forgive you, nor will he admit you to Paradise. Then their souls were taken back (by Allah), and they met together with the Lord of the worlds.*

*He (Allah) said to this man who had striven hard in worship; Had you knowledge about Me or had you power over that which I had in My hand? He said to the man who sinned: Go and enter Paradise by My mercy. He said about the other: Take him to Hell.*

*Abu Huraira said: By Him in Whose hand my soul is, he spoke a word by which this world and the next world of his were destroyed.*

Source: Sunan Abi Dawud 4901 Grade: Sahih

## It was narrated that Abu Hurairah said, 'I heard the Messenger of Allah(ﷺ) say':

"Allah said: 'I have divided the prayer between Myself and My slave into two halves, and My slave shall have what he has asked for.' When the slave says: 'Al-hamdulillahi rabbil Alameen (All the praise is to Allah, the Lord of all that exists),' Allah says: 'My slave has praised Me, and My slave shall have what he has asked for.' And when he says: 'Ar-Rahmanir-Rahim (The Mos Gracious, the Most Merciful),' Allah says: 'My slave has extolled Me, and My slave shall have what he has asked for.' And when he says: 'Maliki yawmiddin [The Only Owner (and he Ruling Judge] if the Day of Recompense],' Allahs says: 'My slave has Glorified Me. This is for Me, and this Verse is between me and My slave in two halves.' And when he says: ' Iyyaka na'budu wa iyyaka nastain [You (Alone) we worship, and You (Alone) we ask for help],' He says: 'This is between Me and My slave, and My slave shall have what he has asked for.' And the end of the Surah is for My slave.' And when he says: 'Ihdinas-siratal-mustaqeema, siratal-alldhina an'amta alayhim wa lad-dallin [Guide us to the Straight Way, the way of those on whom You have bestowed Your Grace, not(the way) of those who earned

*Your Anger, nor of those who went astray],'* He says: *'This is for My slave, and My slave shall have what he has asked for."*

Source: Sunan Ibn Majah 3784 Grade: Sahih

**Narrated Abu Huraira:**

*The people said, "O Allah's Messenger (ﷺ)! Shall we see our Lord on the Day of Resurrection?" He replied, "Do you have any doubt in seeing the full moon on a clear (not cloudy) night?" They replied, "No, O Allah's Messenger (ﷺ)!" He said, "Do you have any doubt in seeing the sun when there are no clouds?" They replied in the negative. He said, "You will see Allah (your Lord) in the same way. On the Day of Resurrection, people will be gathered and He will order the people to follow what they used to worship. So some of them will follow the sun, some will follow the moon, and some will follow other deities; and only this nation (Muslims) will be left with its hypocrites. Allah will come to them and say, 'I am Your Lord.' They will say, 'We shall stay in this place till our Lord comes to us and when our Lord will come, we will recognize Him. Then Allah will come to them again and say, 'I am your Lord.' They will say, 'You are our Lord.' Allah will call them, and As-Sirat (a bridge) will be laid across Hell and I (Muhammad) shall be the first amongst the Prophets to cross it with my followers. Nobody except the Prophets will then be able to speak and they will be saying then, 'O Allah! Save us. O Allah Save us.' There will be hooks like the thorns of*

*Sa'dan in Hell. Have you seen the thorns of Sa'dan?" The people said, "Yes." He said, "These hooks will be like the thorns of Sa'dan but nobody except Allah knows their greatness in size and these will entangle the people according to their deeds; some of them will fall and stay in Hell forever; others will receive punishment (torn into small pieces) and will get out of Hell, till when Allah intends mercy on whomever He likes amongst the people of Hell, He will order the angels to take out of Hell those who worshipped none but Him alone. The angels will take them out by recognizing them from the traces of prostrations, for Allah has forbidden the (Hell) fire to eat away those traces. So they will come out of the Fire, it will eat away from the whole of the human body except the marks of the prostrations. At that time they will come out of the Fire as mere skeletons. The Water of Life will be poured on them and as a result they will grow like the seeds growing on the bank of flowing water. Then when Allah had finished from the Judgments amongst his creations, one man will be left between Hell and Paradise and he will be the last man from the people of Hell to enter paradise. He will be facing Hell, and will say, 'O Allah! Turn my face from the fire as its wind has dried me and its steam has burnt me.' Allah will ask him, "Will you ask for anything more in case this favor is granted to you?' He will say, "No by Your (Honor) Power!" And he will give to his Lord (Allah) what he will of the pledges and the covenants. Allah will then turn his face from the Fire. When he will face Paradise* and will see its charm, he will remain quiet as long as Allah will. He then will say, 'O my Lord! Let me go to the gate of Paradise.' Allah will ask him, 'Didn't you give pledges and make covenants (to the effect) that you would not ask for anything more than what you requested at first?' He will say, 'O my Lord! Do not make me the most wretched, amongst Your creatures.' Allah will say, 'If this request is granted, will you then ask for anything else?' He will say, 'No! By Your Power! I shall not ask for anything else.' Then he will give to his Lord what He will of the pledges and the covenants. Allah will then let him go to the gate of Paradise. On reaching then and seeing its life, charm, and pleasure, he will remain quiet as long as Allah wills and then will say, 'O my Lord! Let me enter Paradise.' Allah will say, May Allah be merciful unto you, O son of Adam! How treacherous you are! Haven't you made covenants and given pledges that you will not ask for anything more than what you have been given?' He will say, 'O my Lord! Do not make me the most wretched amongst Your creatures.' So Allah will laugh and allow him to enter Paradise and will ask him to request as much as he likes. He will do so till all his desires have been fulfilled. Then Allah will say, 'Request more of such and such things.' Allah will remind him and when all his desires and wishes; have been fulfilled, Allah will say "All this is granted to you and a similar amount besides." Abu Sa`id Al-Khudri, said to Abu Huraira, 'Allah's Messenger (ﷺ) said, "Allah said, 'That is for you and ten times more like it.' "Abu Huraira said, "I do not remember from Allah's Messenger (ﷺ) except (his saying), 'All this is granted to you and a similar amount besides." Abu Sa`id said, "I heard him saying, 'That is for you and ten times more the like of it."

Source: Sahih al-Bukhari 806

## Abu Hurairah reported:

*When it was revealed to Messenger of Allah (ﷺ): "To Allah belongs all that is in the heavens and all that is on the earth, and whether you disclose what is in your own selves or conceal it, Allah will call you to account for it," the Companions of Messenger of Allah (ﷺ) felt it hard and severe and they came to Messenger of Allah (ﷺ) and sat down on their knees and said: "O Messenger of Allah, we were assigned some duties which were within our power to perform, such as Salat (prayer), Saum (fasting), Jihad (striving in the Cause of Allah), Sadaqah (charity). Then this (the above mentioned) Verse was revealed to you and it is beyond our power to live up to it." Messenger of Allah (ﷺ) said, "Do you want to say what the people of two Books (Jews and Christians) said before you: 'We hear and disobey?' You should rather say: 'We hear and we obey, we seek forgiveness, our Lord and unto You is the return."' And they said: "We hear and we obey, (we seek) Your forgiveness, our Lord! And unto You is the return." When the people recited it and it smoothly flowed on their tongues, then Allah revealed immediately afterwards: "The Messenger (Muhammad*

(ﷺ)) believes in what has been sent down to him from his Lord, and (so do) the believers. Each one believes in Allah, His Angels, His Books, and His Messengers. (They say), 'We make no distinction between one another of His Messengers' - and they say, 'We hear, and we obey. (We seek) Your forgiveness, our Lord, and to You is the return (of all)". When they did that, Allah abrogated this (Ayah) and Allah the Great revealed: "Allah burdens not a person beyond his scope. He gets reward for that (good) which he has earned, and he is punished for that (evil) which he has earned." (The Prophet (ﷺ) said): "Yes. 'Our Lord! Lay not on us a burden like that which You did lay on those before us (Jews and Christians)". (The Prophet (ﷺ) said): "Yes. 'Our Lord! Put not on us a burden greater than we have strength to bear". (The Prophet (ﷺ) said): "Yes. 'Pardon us and grant us forgiveness. Have mercy on us. You are our Maula (Patron, Supporter and Protector) and give us victory over the disbelieving people".

He (the Prophet (ﷺ)) said: "Yes".

Source: Riyad as-Salihin 168 Grade: Sahih

### Abu Hurairah narrated the Messenger of Allah said:

"Allah will gather mankind on the Day of Resurrection on a single plane, then the Lord of the Worlds will come to them and say: 'Let every person follow what they used to worship.' So to the worshipper of the cross, his cross *shall be symbolized to him, and to the worshipper of images his images, and to the worshipper of fire his fire. They will follow what they used to worship, and the Muslims will remain. Then the Lord of the Worlds will come to them and say: 'Do you not follow the people?' So they will say: 'We seek refuge in Allah from you, we seek refuge in Allah from you, Allah is our Lord, and we shall remain here until we see our Lord.' And He orders them and makes them firm.'"* They said: "And you will see Him, O Messenger of Allah?" He said: "Are you harmed in seeing the moon on the night of a full moon?" They said: "No, O Messenger of Allah." He said: "So you will not be harmed in seeing Him at that hour. Then He will conceal Himself, then He will come, and He will make them recognize Him, then He will say: "I am your Lord, so follow Me." So the Muslims will arise and the Sirat shall be placed, and they shall be placed, and they shall pass by it the like of excellent horses and camels and their statement upon it shall be, "Grant them safety, grant them safety." And the people of Fire shall remain, then a party of them shall be cast down into it, and it shall be said (to the Fire): 'Have you become full?' So it shall say: Is there more? Then a party of them shall be cast down into it, and it shall be said: 'Have you become full?' So it shall say: Is there more? Until when they are all included into it, Ar-Rahman (the Most-Merciful) shall place His foot in it and its sides shall be all brought together, then He will say: 'Enough.' It will say 'Enough, enough.' So when Allah, the Exalted, has admitted the people of

Paradise into Paradise and the people of Fire into Fire"- [He said:]- "Death shall be brought in by the collar and stood on the wall that is between the people of Paradise and the people of the Fire, then it will be said: 'O people of Paradise!' They will come near, afraid. Then it will be said: 'O people of the Fire!' They will come rejoicing, hoping for intercession. Then it will be said to the people of Paradise and the people of the Fire: 'Do you recognize this?' So they will-both of them-say: 'We recognize it. It is Death which was given charge of us,' so it will be laid down and slaughtered upon the wall [the one that is between Paradise and the Fire], then it will be said: 'O people of Paradise! Everlasting life without death!' And 'O people of the Fire! Everlasting life without death!'"

Source: Jami` at-Tirmidhi 2557 Grade: Sahih

**Narrated Abu Huraira:**

I heard Allah's Messenger (ﷺ) saying. "All the sins of my followers will be forgiven except those of the Mujahirin (those who commit a sin openly or disclose their sins to the people). An example of such disclosure is that a person commits a sin at night and though Allah screens it from the public, then he comes in the morning, and says, 'O so-and-so, I did such-and-such (evil) deed yesterday,' though he spent his night screened by his Lord (none knowing about his sin) and in the morning he removes Allah's screen from himself."

Source: Sahih al-Bukhari 6069

**It was narrated from 'Abdullah As-Sunabihi that the Messenger of Allah (ﷺ) said:**

"When the believing slave performs Wudu' and rinses his mouth, his sins come out from his mouth. When he sniffs water into his nose and blows it out, his sins come from his nose. When he washes his face, his sins come out from his face, even from beneath his eyelashes. When he washes his hands, his sins come out from his hands, even from beneath his fingernails. When he wipes his head, his sins come out from his head, even from his ears. When washes his feet, his sins come from his feet, even from beneath his toenails. Then his walking to the Masjid and his Salah will earn extra merit for him."

Source: Sunan an-Nasa'i 103 Grade: Hasan

**It was narrated from Abu Hurairah that the Messenger of Allah (ﷺ) said:**

"Whoever covers (the sin of) a Muslim, Allah will cover him (his sin) in this world and in the Hereafter."

Source: Sunan Ibn Majah 2544 Grade: Sahih

**Abu Dharr said:**

"Allah's Messenger said: "I surely know the first man who will enter the Garden of Paradise, and the last man who will emerge from the Fire of Hell. The man will be brought forth on the Day of Resurrection, and the command will be given: "Show him his minor sins, and let his major sins be hidden from him!" He will therefore be told: "On such-and-such a day, you committed such-and-such and such-and-such sins!" He will acknowledge [his sins] and not disavow them and he will be fearful of those sins that are major offenses, so the command will be given: "In place of every bad deed he committed, grant him a good deed!" He will therefore say: "I am guilty of sins that I do not see here!" Abu Dharr said: "I saw Allah's Messenger smile so broadly that his molar teeth showed!"

Source: Shama'il Al-Muhammadiyah 228 Grade: Sahih

**Narrated Safwan bin Muhriz:**

**A man asked Ibn `Umar, "What did you hear Allah's Messenger (ﷺ) saying regarding An-Najwa (secret talk between Allah and His believing worshipper on the Day of Judgment)?" He said:**

"(The Prophet (ﷺ) said), "One of you will come close to his Lord till He will shelter him in His screen and say: Did you commit such-and-such sin? He will say, 'Yes.' Then Allah will say: Did you commit such and such sin? He will say, 'Yes.' So Allah will make him confess (all his sins) and He will say, 'I screened them (your sins) for you in the world, and today I forgive them for you."'

Source: Sahih al-Bukhari 6070

**It was narrated from Abu Hurairah the Prophet (ﷺ) said:**

*"If you were to commit sin until your sins reach the heaven, then you were to repent, your repentance would be accepted."*

Source: Sunan Ibn Majah 4248 Grade: Hasan

**Abu Hurairah narrated that:**

*The Messenger of Allah said: "Whoever performs Hajj for Allah, and he does not have sexual relations nor commit any sin, then his previous sins will be forgiven."*

Source: Jami` at-Tirmidhi 811 Grade: Sahih

**Abu Huraira reported:**

*Verily the Messenger of Allah (ﷺ) said: The five (daily) prayers and from one Friday prayer to the (next) Friday prayer, and from Ramadhan to Ramadhan are expiations for the (sins) committed in between (their intervals) provided one shuns the major sins.*

Source: Sahih Muslim 233c

**It was narrated that Ibn 'Umar said:**

"*The Messenger of Allah said: 'Do not revert to disbelievers after I am gone, striking the necks of one another (killing one another). No man is to be punished for the sins of his father, or for the sins of his brother.'*"

Source: Sunan an-Nasa'i 4126 Grade: Sahih

**Narrated Abu Huraira:**

*The Prophet (ﷺ) said, "Whoever established prayers on the night of Qadr out of sincere faith and hoping for a reward from Allah, then all his previous sins will be forgiven; and whoever fasts in the month of Ramadan out of sincere faith, and hoping for a reward from Allah, then all his previous sins will be forgiven."*

Source: Sahih al-Bukhari 1901

**It was narrated that Abu Hurairah said:**

*"I heard the Messenger of Allah himself say: 'The Mu'adhdhin's sins will be forgiven as far as his voice reaches, and every wet and dry thing will pray for forgiveness for him. For the one who attends the prayer, twenty-five Hasanat (good deeds) will be recorded, and it is will be expiation (for sins committed) between them (the two prayers).'"*

Source: Sunan Ibn Majah 724 Grade: Hasan

**Ja'far bin Muhammad narrated from his father, from Jabir bin 'Abdullah who said:**

*"The Messenger of Allah said: 'My intercession is for the people who committed major sins in my Ummah.'" Muhammad bin 'Ali said: "Jabir said to me: 'O Muhammad! Whoever is not among the people of major sins, then there is no need in the intercession for him.'"*

Source: Jami` at-Tirmidhi 2436 Grade: Sahih

**Ibn 'abbas said:**

"The Messenger of Allah said: 'Perform Hajj and 'Umrah consecutively; for they remove poverty and sin as the bellows removes impurity from iron.'"

Source: Sunan an-Nasa'i 2630 Grade: Hasan

## Abu Hurairah narrated the Messenger of Allah (ﷺ) said:

"There is not a man who calls upon Allah with a supplication, except that he is answered. Either it shall be granted to him in the world, or reserved for him in the Hereafter, or, his sins shall be expiated for it according to the extent that he supplicated - as long as he does not supplicate for some sin, or for the severing of the ties of kinship, and he does not become hasty." They said: "O Messenger of Allah, and how would he be hasty?" He (ﷺ) said: "He says: 'I called upon my Lord, but He did not answer me.'"

Source: Jami` at-Tirmidhi 3604d Grade: Daif

## Abu Huraira reported Allah's Messenger (ﷺ) as saying:

The supplication of the servant is granted in case he does not supplicate for sin or for severing the ties of blood, or he does not become impatient. It was said: Allah's Messenger, what does:" If he does not grow impatient" imply? He said: That he should say like this: I supplicated and I supplicated but I did not find it being responded. and then he becomes frustrated and abandons supplication.

Source: Sahih Muslim 2735c

**Aisha reported:**

*Allah's Messenger (ﷺ) said: There is no trouble that comes to a believer except that it obliterates from his sins, even if it is the pricking of a thorn.*

Source: Sahih Muslim 2572e

**Aisha narrated that:**

*The Messenger of Allah said: "The believer is not afflicted by the prick of a thorn or what is worse (or greater) than that, except that by it Allah raises him in rank and removes sin from him."*

Source: Jami` at-Tirmidhi 965 Grade: Sahih

**Anas said that the Prophet said:**

*"Allah will say: 'Remove from the Fire whoever remembered Me one day, or feared Me while in a state of sinning."*

Source: Jami` at-Tirmidhi 2594 Grade: Hasan

**It was narrated from Abu Hurairah that:**

*The Prophet said: "Sins are expiated by well-performed ablution despite difficulties, increasing the number of steps one takes towards the mosque, (and waiting for the next prayer after prayer)."*

Source: Sunan Ibn Majah 428 Grade: Hasan

**Narrated Abu Huraira:**

*Allah's Messenger (ﷺ) said, "Whoever says, 'Subhan Allah wa bihamdihi,' one hundred times a day, will be forgiven all his sins even if they were as much as the foam of the sea.*

Source: Sahih al-Bukhari 6405

**Uqbah bin 'Amir narrated:**

*"I said: 'O Messenger of Allah! What is the means to salvation?' He said: 'That you control your tongue, suffice yourself your house, and cry over your sins.'"*

Source: Jami` at-Tirmidhi 2406 Grade: Daif

**It was narrated from Ibn 'Abbas that:**

*The Messenger of Allah (ﷺ) said concerning the person observing I'tikaf. "He is refraining from sin and he will be given a reward like that of one who does all kinds of good deeds."*

Source: Sunan Ibn Majah 1781 Grade: Daif

**Abu Sa'id and Abu Huraira reported that they heard Allah's Messenger (ﷺ) as saying:**

*Never a believer is stricken with discomfort, hardship or illness, grief or even with mental worry that his sins are not expiated for him.*

Source: Sahih Muslim 2573

**It was narrated that 'Abdullah said:**

*"The Messenger of Allah said: 'Perform Hajj and 'Umrah consecutively, for they remove poverty and sin as the bellows removes impurity from iron and gold and silver, and Hajj Al-Mabrur brings no less a reward than Paradise.'"*

Source: Sunan an-Nasa'i 2631 Grade: Hasan

**It was narrated that 'Uthman bin 'Affan said:**

*"I heard the Messenger of Allah (ﷺ) say: 'Whoever does wudu' properly, then walks to (attend) the prescribed prayer, and prays with the people or with the congregation or in the Masjid, Allah will forgive him his sins."*

Source: Sunan an-Nasa'i 856 Grade: Sahih

**Narrated Umm al-Ala:**

*The Messenger of Allah (ﷺ) visited me while I was sick. He said: Be glad, Umm al-Ala' for Allah removes the sins of a Muslim for his illness as fire removes the dross of gold and silver.*

Source: Sunan Abi Dawud 3092 Grade: Sahih

**Uthman bin 'Affan reported:**

*The Messenger of Allah said: He who performed ablution well, his sins would come out from his body, even coming out from under his nails.*

Source: Sahih Muslim 245

### Anas bin Malik said:

*"The Messenger of Allah (ﷺ) said: "Whoever sends salah upon me once, Allah will send salah upon him tenfold, and will erase ten sins from him, and will raise him ten degrees in status."*

Source: Sunan an-Nasa'i 1297 Grade: Sahih

### Ibn Ubaid bin Umair narrated from his father:

*"Ibn Umar was clinging on the two corners (in a manner that I had not seen any of the Companions of the Prophet doing) so I said: 'O Abu Abdur-Rahman! You are clinging on the two corners in a manner that I have not seen any of the Companions of the Prophet clinging.' So he said: 'I do it because I heard the Messenger of Allah saying: "Touching them atones for sins." And I heard him saying: "Whoever performs Tawaf around this House seven times and he keeps track of it, then it is as if he freed a slave." And I heard him saying: "One foot is not put down, nor another raised except that Allah removes a sin from him and records a good merit for him."*

Source: Jami` at-Tirmidhi 959 Grade: Hasan

### Thauban said:

*I heard Messenger of Allah (ﷺ) saying, "Perform Salah more often. For every prostration that you perform before Allah will raise your position one degree and will remit one of your sins".*

Source: Riyad as-Saliheen 107 Grade: Sahih

**It was narrated that Abu Rimthah said; "I came to the Prophet with my father and he said:**

'Who is this with you?' He said:' my son, I bear witness (that he is my son). He said: 'You cannot be affected by his sin or he by yours.

Source: Sunan an-Nasa'i 4832 Grade: Sahih

**A'isha reported:**

I said: Messenger of Allah, the son of Jud'an established ties of relationship, fed the poor. Would that be of any avail to him? He said: It would be of no avail to him as he did not ever say: O my Lord, pardon my sins on the Day of Resurrection.

Source: Sahih Muslim 214

**Abu Hurairah narrated that:**

Allah's Messenger said: "Shall I tell you that for which Allah will wipe out your sins, and raise your ranks?" They said, "Of course Allah's Messenger!" He said: "Performing Wudu well in difficulty, and taking many steps to the Masajid, and waiting for Salat after Salat, That is the Ribat."

Source: Jami` at-Tirmidhi 51 Grade: Sahih

**Narrated Um `Atiya:**

*We used to be ordered to come out on the Day of `Id and even bring out the virgin girls from their houses and menstruating women so that they might stand behind the men and say Takbir along with them and invoke Allah along with them and hope for the blessings of that day and for purification from sins.*

Source: Sahih al-Bukhari 971

**It was narrated from Tariq and Muharibi that a man said:**

*"O Messenger of Allah, these are Banu Tha'labah who killed so and so during the Jahiliyyah: avenge us! He raised his arms until the whiteness of his armpits could be seen and said:*

*"No mother's sin can affect her child," twice.*

Source: Sunan an-Nasa'i 4839 Grade: Sahih

**Abu Hurairah narrated that:**

*Allah's Messenger said: "When the Imam says: (Sami Allahu liman hamidah) 'Allah listens to those who praise Him. Then (all of you) say: (Rabbana wa lakal-hamd) 'O our Lord! And to You is the praise for whoever's saying concurs with the saying of the angels, then his past sins will be forgiven."*

Source: Jami` at-Tirmidhi 267 Grade: Sahih

**Narrated `Abdullah:**

*I visited the Prophet (ﷺ) during his ailments and he was suffering from a high fever. I said, "You have a high fever. Is it because you will have a double reward for it?" He said, "Yes, for no Muslim is afflicted with any harm but that Allah will remove his sins as the leaves of a tree fall down."*

Source: Sahih al-Bukhari 5647

**Ma'dan bin Talha Al-Ya'muri said:**

"I met Thawban, the freed slave of the Messenger of Allah (ﷺ) and said: "Tell me of an action that will benefit me or gain me admittance to Paradise.' He remained silent for a while, then he turned to me and said: 'You should prostrate, because I heard the Messenger of Allah (ﷺ) say: "There is no one who prostrated once to Allah, the Mighty and Sublime, except that Allah will raise him one degree in status thereby, and erase one sin thereby." Ma'dan said: "Then I met Abu Ad-Darda' and asked him the same question I had asked Thawban." He said to me: "You should prostrate, for I heard the Messenger of Allah (ﷺ) say: "There is no one who prostrates once to Allah, but Allah will raise him one degree thereby and erase one sin thereby."

Source: Sunan an-Nasa'i 1139 Grade: Sahih

**Abu Huraira reported Allah's Messenger (ﷺ) as saying:**

*He who performed ablution well, then came to Friday prayer, listened (to the sermon), kept silence, all (his sins) between that time and the next Friday would be forgiven with three days extra, and he who touched pebbles caused an interruption.*

Source: Sahih Muslim 857b

**Uthman said:**

*"I heard the Messenger of Allah (ﷺ) say: 'Do you think that if there was a river in the courtyard of anyone of you, and he bathed in it five times each day, would there be any dirt left on him?' They said: '(There would be) nothing.' He said: 'Prayer takes away sins like water takes away dirt.'"*

Source: Sunan Ibn Majah 1397 Grade: Sahih

**Abu Huraira reported that a person said to Allah's Messenger (ﷺ):**

*My father died and left behind property without making any will regarding it. Would he be relieved of the burden of his sins if I give sadaqa on his behalf? He (the Prophet) said: Yes.*

Source: Sahih Muslim 1630

**Amr bin Shu'aib, on his father's authority, told that his grandfather reported the Messenger of Allah (ﷺ) said:**

*Do not pluck out grey hair. If any believer grows a grey hair in Islam, he will have light on the Day of Resurrection. (This is Sufyan's version). Yahya's version says: Allah will record on his behalf a good deed for it, and will blot out a sin for it.*

Source: Sunan Abi Dawud 4202 Grade: Hasan Sahih

**Narrated Abu Huraira:**

*Allah's Messenger (ﷺ) said: "Whoever amongst you swears, (saying by error) in his oath 'By Al-Lat and Al-Uzza', then he should say, 'None has the right to be worshipped but Allah.' And whoever says to his companions, 'Come let me gamble' with you, then he must give something in charity (as an expiation for such a sin)."*

Source: Sahih al-Bukhari 6107

**Abu Huraira reported Allah's Messenger (ﷺ) as saying:**

*If anyone extols Allah after every prayer thirty-three times, and praises Allah thirty-three times, and declares His Greatness thirty-three times, ninety-nine times in all, and says to complete a hundred:" There is no god but Allah, having no partner with Him, to Him belongs sovereignty and to Him is praise due, and He is Potent over everything," his sins will be forgiven even if these are as abundant as the foam of the sea.*

Source: Sahih Muslim 597a

**Sa'd bin Abu Waqqas reported:**

*We were with the Messenger of Allah (ﷺ) when he asked, "Is anyone of you unable to earn a thousand good deeds?" One of those present asked: "How can one earn thousand good deeds in a day?" He (ﷺ) replied, "By saying: Subhan Allah a hundred times, then one thousand good deeds will be recorded for him or one thousand sins will be blotted out from his record."*

Source: Riyad as-Salihin 1431 Grade: Sahih

**Narrated Mihjan ibn al-Adra':**

*The Messenger of Allah (ﷺ) entered the mosque and saw a man who had finished his prayer, and was reciting the tashahhud saying: O Allah, I ask you, O Allah, the One, the eternally besought of all, He begetteth not, nor was He begotten, and there is none comparable unto Him, that you may forgive me my sins, you are Most Forgiving, Merciful.*

*He (the Prophet) said: He was forgiven (repeating three times.)*

Source: Sunan Abi Dawud 985 Grade: Sahih

**It was narrated from Anas that the Prophet (ﷺ) entered upon a young man who was dying and said:**

*"How do you feel?" He said: "I have hope in Allah, O Messenger of Allah, but I fear my sins." The Messenger of Allah (ﷺ) said: "These two things (hope and fear) do*

not coexist in the heart of a person in a situation like this, but Allah will give him that which he hopes for and keep him safe from that which he fears."

Source: Sunan Ibn Majah 4261 Grade: Hasan

**Narrated Al-Harith bin Suwaid:**

*`Abdullah bin Mas`ud related to us two narrations: One from the Prophet (ﷺ) and the other from himself, saying: A believer sees his sins as if he were sitting under a mountain which, he is afraid, may fall on him; whereas the wicked person considers his sins as flies passing over his nose and he just drives them away like this."*

*Abu Shihab (the sub-narrator) moved his hand over his nose in illustration. (Ibn Mas`ud added): Allah's Messenger (ﷺ) said:*

"Allah is more pleased with the repentance of His slave than a man who encamps at a place where his life is jeopardized, but he has his riding beast carrying his food and water. He then rests his head and sleeps for a short while and wakes to find his riding beast gone. (He starts looking for it) and suffers from severe heat and thirst or what Allah wished (him to suffer from). He then says, 'I will go back to my place.' He returns and sleeps again, and then (getting up), he raises his head to find his riding beast standing beside him."

Source: Sahih al-Bukhari 6308

**Narrated Abdullah ibn Mas'ud:**

*The Prophet (ﷺ) said: Our Lord Most High is pleased with a man who fights in the path of Allah, the Exalted; then his companions fled away (retreated). But he knew that it was a sin (to flee away from the battlefield), so he returned, and his blood was shed. Thereupon Allah, the Exalted, says to His angels: Look at My servant; he returned seeking what I have for him (i.e. the reward), and fearing (the punishment) I have, until his blood was shed.*

Source: Sunan Abi Dawud 2536 Grade: Hasan

**It was narrated from 'Abdullah bin 'Amr that the Prophet (ﷺ) said:**

*"When Sulaiman bin Dawud finished building Baitil-Maqdis, he asked Allah for three things: judgment that was in harmony with His judgment, a dominion that no one after him would have, and that no one should come to this mosque, intending only to pray there, but he would emerge free of sin as the day his mother bore him." The Prophet (ﷺ) said: "Two prayers were granted, and I hope that the third was also granted."*

Source: Sunan Ibn Majah 1408 Grade: Sahih

**Mus'ab bin Sa'd narrated from his father that a man said:**

*"O Messenger of Allah! Which of the people is tried most severely?" He said: "The Prophets, then those nearest to them, then those nearest to them. A man is tried according to his religion; if he is firm in his religion, then*

*his trials are more severe, and if he is frail in his religion, then he is tried according to the strength of his religion. The servant shall continue to be tried until he is left walking upon the earth without any sins."*

Source: Jami` at-Tirmidhi 2398 Grade: Hasan

**Aswad reported that some young men from the Quraish visited 'A'isha as she was in Mina and they were laughing. She said:**

*What makes you laugh? They said: Such and such person stumbled against the rope of the tent and he was about to break his neck or lose his eyes. She said: Don't laugh for I heard Allah's Messenger (ﷺ) as saying: If a Muslim runs a thorn or (gets into trouble) severe than this, there is assured for him (a higher) rank and his sins are obliterated.*

Source: Sahih Muslim 2572a

**Narrated Abdullah ibn Amr ibn al-'As:**

*The Prophet (ﷺ) said: Three types of people attend Friday prayer; One is present in a frivolous way and that is all he gets from it; another comes with a supplication, Allah may grant or refuse his request as He wishes; another is present silently and quietly with-out stepping over a Muslim or annoying anyone, and that is an atonement for his sins till the next Friday and three days more, the reason being that Allah, the Exalted, says: "He who does a good deed will have ten times as much" (vi.160).*

Source: Sunan Abi Dawud 1113 Grade: Hasan

**Narrated Abu Huraira:**

*Allah's Messenger (ﷺ) said," Whoever says: "La ilaha illal-lah wahdahu la sharika lahu, lahu-l-mulk wa lahul-hamd wa huwa 'ala kulli shai'in qadir," one hundred times will get the same reward as given for manumitting ten slaves; and one hundred good deeds will be written in his accounts, and one hundred sins will be deducted from his accounts, and it (his saying) will be a shield for him from Satan on that day till night, and nobody will be able to do a better deed except the one who does more than he."*

Source: Sahih al-Bukhari 6403

**Abu Sa`eed narrated that:**

*the Prophet (ﷺ) said: "Whoever says, when he goes to his bed: 'I seek forgiveness from Allah, [the Magnificent] the One whom there is none worthy of worship except for Him, the Living, the Sustainer, and I repent to Him (Astaghfirullāha [al-`Azim] alladhi lā ilāha illā huw, al-Ḥayyul-Qayyūm, wa atūbu ilaihi)' three times, Allah shall forgive him his sins if they were like the foam of the sea, even if they were the number of leaves of the trees, even if they were the number of sand particles of `Alij, even if they were the number of the days of the world."*

Source: Jami` at-Tirmidhi 3397 Grade: Daif

**It was narrated from Sa'd bin Abu Waqqas that:**

*The Messenger of Allah said: "Whoever says, when he hears the Mu'adh-dhin, 'Wa ana Ash-hadu an la ilaha illallah wahdahu la sharika lahu, wa ash-hadu anna Muhammadan 'abduhu wa rasuluhu, radaytu Billahi rabban wa bil-islami dinan wa bi muhammadin nabiyyan (And I bear witness that none has the right to be worshipped but Allah alone, with no partner, and I bear witness that Muhammad is His slave and Messenger, and I am content with Allah as my Lord, Islam as my religion and Muhammad as my Prophet),' his sins will be forgiven to him."*

Source: Sunan Ibn Majah 721 Grade: Sahih

### It was narrated from Abu Dharr that the Messenger of Allah (ﷺ) said:

*"What will you do, O Abu Dharr, when death overwhelms the people to such an extent that a grave will be equal in value to a slave?" I said: "Whatever Allah and His Messenger choose for me, or Allah and His Messenger know best." He said "Be patient." He said: 'What will you do when famine strikes the people so that you will go to the place where you pray and will not be able to return to your bed, or you will not be able to get up from your bed to go to the place where you pray?" He said: "I said: 'Allah and His Messenger know best, or whatever Allah and His Messenger choose for me." He said: "You must refrain from forbidden things." He said: "What will you do when killing befalls the people so that Hijaratuz-Zait is covered with blood?" I said: "Whatever*

Allah and His Messenger choose for me." He said: "Stay with those whom you belong to." He said: "I said: 'O Messenger of Allah, should I not take my sword and strike those who do that?'" He said: "Then you will be just like the people. Rather enter your house." I said: "O Messenger of Allah, what if they enter my house?" He said: "If you are afraid that the flashing of the sword will dazzle you, then put the edge of your garment over your face, and let him carry his own sin and your sin, and he will be one of the people of the Hellfire."

Source: Sunan Ibn Majah 3958 Grade: Sahih

**It was narrated that Humran bin Aban said:**

We were with `Uthman bin `Affan, he called for water and did wudoo'. When he had finished his wudoo`, he smiled and said: Do you know why I smiled? He said: The Messenger of Allah (ﷺ) did wudoo` as I just did wudoo`, then he smiled and said: "Do you know why I smiled?` we said: Allah and His Messenger know best. He said: "If a person does wudoo and completes his wudoo', then he starts to pray and completes his prayer, he will come out of his prayer free of sin as he came out of his mother's womb."

Source: Musnad Ahmad 430 Grade: Sahih

**Ka'b bin Ujrah narrated:**

"The Messenger of Allah said to me: 'I seek refuge in Allah for you O Ka'b bin Ujrah from leader that will be after me. Whoever comes to their doors to approve of their *lies and supports them in their oppression, then he is not of me and I am not of him, and he will not meet me at the Hawd. And whoever comes to their doors, or he does not come, and he does not approve of their lies and he does not support them in their oppression, then he is from me and I am from him, and he will meet me at the Hawd. Ka'ab bin Ujrah! Salat is clear proof, and Sawm (fasting) is an impregnable shield, and Sadaqah (charity) extinguishes sins just as water extinguishes fire. O Ka'b bin Ujrah! There is no flesh raised that sprouts from the unlawful except that the Fire is more appropriate for it.'"*

Source: Jami` at-Tirmidhi 614 Grade: Hasan

**Narrated Khalid bin Madan:**

*That 'Umair bin Al-Aswad Al-Anasi told him that he went to 'Ubada bin As-Samit while he was staying in his house at the sea-shore of Hims with (his wife) Um Haram. 'Umair said. Um Haram informed us that she heard the Prophet (ﷺ) saying, "Paradise is granted to the first batch of my followers who will undertake a naval expedition." Um Haram added, I said, 'O Allah's Messenger (ﷺ)! Will I be amongst them?' He replied, 'You are amongst them.' The Prophet (ﷺ) then said, 'The first army amongst' my followers who will invade Caesar's City will be forgiven their sins.' I asked, 'Will I be one of them, O Allah's Messenger (ﷺ)?' He replied in the negative."*

Source: Sahih al-Bukhari 2924

**Abu Dharr narrated that:**

*The Messenger of Allah (ﷺ) said: "Whoever says at the end of every Fajr prayer, while his feet are still folded, before speaking: 'None has the right to be worshipped but Allah, Alone without partner, to Him belongs all that exists, and to Him is the praise, He gives life and causes death, and He is powerful over all things, (Lā ilāha illallāh, waḥdahu lā sharīka lahu, lahul-mulku wa lahul-ḥamdu, yuḥyī wa yumītu, wa huwa `alā kulli shay'in qadīr)' ten times, then ten good deeds shall be written for him, ten evil deeds shall be wiped away from him, ten degrees shall be raised up for him, and he shall be in security all that day from every disliked thing, and he shall be in protection from Shaitan, and no sin will meet him or destroy him that day, except for associating partners with Allah."*

Source: Jami` at-Tirmidhi 3474 Grade: Hasan

**Sa'id bin Jubair said:**

*I asked Ibn 'Abbas (about the verse relating to intentional homicide in Surat An-Nisa') He said: When the verse "Those who invoke not with Allah any other god, nor slay such life as Allah had made sacred, except for just cause" was revealed, the polytheists of Mecca said: We have killed the soul prohibited by Allah, invoked another god along with Allah for worship, and committed shameful deeds. So Allah revealed the verse "unless he repents, believes, and works righteous deeds, for Allah* will change the evil of such persons into good." This is meant for them. As regards the verse "if a man kills a believer intentionally, his recompense is Hell" he said: If a man knows the command of Islam and intentionally kills a believer, his repentance will not be accepted. I then mentioned it to Mujahid. He said: "Except the one who is ashamed (of his sin)."

Source: Sunan Abi Dawud 4273 Grade: Sahih

**It was narrated that Mu'adh bin Jabal said:**

"I was with the Messenger of Allah (ﷺ) on a journey. One morning I drew close to him when we were on the move and said: 'O Messenger of Allah, tell me of an action that will gain me admittance to Paradise and keep me far away from Hell.' He said: 'You have asked for something great, but it is easy for the one for whom Allah makes it easy. Worship Allah and do not associate anything in worship with Him, establish prayer, pay charity, fast Ramadan, and perform Hajj to the House.' Then he said: 'Shall I not tell you of the means of goodness? Fasting is a shield, and charity extinguishes sin as water extinguishes fire, and a man's prayer in the middle of the night.' Then he recited: "Their sides forsake their beds" until he reached: "As a reward for what they used to do." [32:16-17] Then he said: 'Shall I not tell you of the head of the matter, and its pillar and pinnacle? (It is) Jihad.' Then he said: 'Shall I not tell you of the basis of all that?' I said: 'Yes.' He took hold of his tongue then said: 'Restrain this.' I said: 'O Prophet of Allah, will we be brought to account for what we say?' He said: 'May your mother not found you, O Mu'adh! Are people thrown onto their faces in Hell for anything other than the harvest of their tongues?'"

Source: Sunan Ibn Majah 3973 Grade: Hasan

**Narrated Abu Dharr:**

*I came to the Prophet (ﷺ) while he was wearing white clothes and sleeping. Then I went back to him again after he had got up from his sleep. He said, "Nobody says: 'None has the right to be worshipped but Allah' and then later on he dies while believing in that, except that he will enter Paradise." I said, "Even if he had committed illegal sexual intercourse and theft?" He said. 'Even if he had committed illegal sexual intercourse and theft." I said, "Even if he had committed illegal sexual intercourse and theft?" He said. 'Even if he had committed illegal sexual intercourse and theft." I said, 'Even if he had committed illegal sexual intercourse and theft?' He said, "Even if he had committed illegal sexual intercourse and theft, inspite of the Abu Dharr's dislike. Abu `Abdullah said, "This is at the time of death or before it if one repents and regrets and says "None has the right to be worshipped but Allah. He will be forgiven his sins."*

Source: Sahih al-Bukhari 5827

**Abu Hurairah reported:**

*Messenger of Allah (ﷺ) said, "While a man was walking on his way he became extremely thirsty. He found a well,* he went down into it to drink water. Upon leaving it, he saw a dog which was panting out of thirst. His tongue was lolling out and he was eating moist earth from extreme thirst. The man thought to himself: 'This dog is extremely thirsty as I was.' So he descended into the well, filled up his leather sock with water, and holding it in his teeth, climbed up and quenched the thirst of the dog. Allah appreciated his action and forgave his sins". The Companions asked: "Shall we be rewarded for showing kindness to the animals also?" He (ﷺ) said, "A reward is given in connection with every living creature".

Source: Riyad as-Salihin 126 Grade: Sahih

**Narrated Abu Hurairah:**

that the Messenger of Allah (ﷺ) said: "The adulterer is not a believer while he is committing adultery, and the thief is not a believer while he is stealing, but there is a chance for repentance; (if he repents, Allah will accept the repentance)."

Source: Jami` at-Tirmidhi 2625 Grade: Sahih

**It was narrated from Abu Dharr that the Messenger of Allah (ﷺ) said:**

"Allah the Blessed and Exalted says: 'O My slaves, all of you are sinners except those whom I have saved. So ask Me for forgiveness, I will forgive you. Whoever among you knows that I have the power to forgive and asks Me to forgive by My power, I will forgive him. All of you are astray except those whom I guide. Ask Me for guidance and I will guide you. All of you are poor except those whom I enrich (make independent of means). Ask of Me and I will grant you provision. Even if your living and your dead, your first and your last, your fresh and your dry, were all as pious as the most pious among My slaves, that would not increase my dominion as much as a gnat's wing, and if they were to be as evil as the most evil among My slaves, that would not detract from My dominion as much as a gnat's wing. Even if your living and your dead, your first and your last, your fresh and your dry, were to join together and each of them were to ask for all that he wishes for, that would only detract from My dominion as much as if one of you were to pass by the edge of the sea and dip a needle in it and withdraw it. That is because I am the Most Generous, Majestic. I give with a word; when I will something, all I do is say to it "Be!" – and it is.'"

Source: Sunan Ibn Majah 4257 Grade: Hasan

**Abu Ayyub Khalid bin Zaid reported:**

*Messenger of Allah (ﷺ) said, "Were you not to commit sins, Allah would create people who would commit sins and ask for forgiveness and He would forgive them".*

Source: Riyad as-Salihin 423 Grade: Sahih

**Narrated Abu Huraira:**

*Allah's Messenger (ﷺ) said, "The angels keep on asking for Allah's Blessing and Forgiveness for anyone of you as long as he is at his Musalla (praying place) and does not* do Hadath (passes wind). The angels say, 'O Allah! Forgive him and be Merciful to him.' Each one of you is in the prayer as long as he is waiting for the prayer and nothing but the prayer detains him from going to his family."

Source: Sahih al-Bukhari 659

**Narrated Abu Huraira:**

*The Prophet (ﷺ) said, "The prayer offered in congregation is twenty five times more superior (in reward) to the prayer offered alone in one's house or in a business center, because if one performs ablution and does it perfectly, and then proceeds to the mosque with the sole intention of praying, then for each step which he takes towards the mosque, Allah upgrades him a degree in reward and (forgives) crosses out one sin till he enters the mosque. When he enters the mosque, he is considered in prayer as long as he is waiting for the prayer and the angels keep on asking for Allah's forgiveness for him and they keep on saying: 'O Allah! Be Merciful to him, O Allah! Forgive him, as long as he keeps on sitting at his praying place and does not pass wind.*

Source: Sahih al-Bukhari 477

**Narrated Abu Sa'id Al Khudri:**

*Allah's Messenger (ﷺ) said, "If a person embraces Islam sincerely, then Allah shall forgive all his past sins, and after that starts the settlement of accounts, the reward of his good deeds will be ten times to seven hundred times* for each good deed and one evil deed will be recorded as it is unless Allah forgives it."

Source: Sahih al-Bukhari 41

**Tariq bin Ashyam reported:**

Whenever a man entered the fold of Islam, the Prophet (ﷺ) would show him how to perform Salat and then direct him to supplicate: "Allahumm-aghfir li, warhamni, wa-hdini, wa 'afini, warzuqni (O Allah! Forgive me, have mercy on me, guide me, guard me against harm and provide me with sustenance and salvation).'"

Source: Riyad as-Salihin 1469 Grade: Sahih

**Narrated Abu Hurairah:**

The Messenger of Allah (ﷺ) as saying: Our Lord who is blessed and exalted descends every night to the lowest heaven when the last one-third of the night remains, and says: Who supplicated Me so that I may answer him? Who asks of Me so that I may give to him? Who asks My forgiveness so that I may forgive him?

Source: Sunan Abi Dawud 1315 Grade: Sahih

**It was narrated that 'Uthman bin 'Affan said:**

"I heard the Messenger of Allah (ﷺ) say: 'Whoever does wudu' properly, then walks to (attend) the prescribed prayer, and prays with the people or with the *congregation or in the Masjid, Allah will forgive him his sins."*

Source: Sunan an-Nasa'i 856 Grade: Sahih

**It was narrated that 'Ata' bin as-Sa`ib said:**

*I entered upon Abu 'Abdur-Rahman as-Sulami who had prayed Fajr and was sitting in the mosque. I said: Why don`t you go to your bed, for it will be more comfortable for you? He said: I heard `Ali say: I heard the Messenger of Allah (ﷺ) say: "Whoever pray Fajr, then sits in the place where he has prayed, the angels will send blessings upon him and their blessings upon him will be: 'O Allah, forgive him. O Allah, have mercy on him.` And whoever waits for the prayer, the angels will send blessings upon him and their blessings upon him will be: `O Allah, forgive him, O Allah, have mercy on him."*

Source: Musnad Ahmad 1251 Grade: Hasan

**Abu Hurairah narrated that:**

*Allah's Messenger said: "Whoever continuously performs the two Rak'ah of Ad-Duha his sins will be forgiven, even if they be like the foam of the sea."*

Source: Jami` at-Tirmidhi 476 Grade: Daif

**Ali reported:**

*We were in a funeral in the graveyard of Gharqad when Allah's Messenger (ﷺ) came to us and we sat around him. He had a stick with him. He lowered his head and began to scratch the earth with his stick, and then said: There is not one amongst you whom a seat in Paradise or Hell has not been allotted and about whom it has not been written down whether he would be an evil person or a blessed person. A person said: Allah's Messenger, should we not then depend upon our destiny and abandon our deeds? Thereupon he said: Acts of everyone will be facilitated in that which has been created for him so that whoever belongs to the company of the blessed will have good works made easier for him and whoever belongs to the unfortunate ones will have evil acts made easier for him. He then recited this verse (from the Qur'an): "Then, who gives to the needy and guards against evil and accepts the excellent (the truth of Islam and the path of righteousness it prescribes), We shall make easy for him the easy end and who is miserly and considers himself above need, We shall make easy for him the difficult end" (xcii. 5-10).*

Source: Sahih Muslim 2647a

## Abdullah bin Mas'ud told how God's messenger drew a line for them and then said:

*"This is God's path." Thereafter he drew several lines on his right and left and said, "These are paths on each of which there is a devil who invites people to follow it."*

Source: Sharh At Tahawiya 525 Grade: Sahih

## Narrated Mu'awiyah:

*I heard the Messenger of Allah (ﷺ) say: Migration will not end until repentance ends, and repentance will not end until the sun rises in the west.*

Source: Sunan Abi Dawud 2479 Grade: Sahih

**Narrated Mu`adh bin Jabal:**

*The Prophet (ﷺ) said, "O Mu`adh! Do you know what Allah's Right upon His slaves is?" I said, "Allah and His Apostle know best." The Prophet (ﷺ) said, "To worship Him (Allah) Alone and to join none in worship with Him (Allah). Do you know what their right upon Him is?" I replied, "Allah and His Apostle know best." The Prophet (ﷺ) said, "Not to punish them (if they do so).*

Source: Sahih al-Bukhari 7373

**Hanzalah al-Kaatib, said:**

*I heard the Messenger of Allah say: "Whoever regularly offers the five daily prayers, with their bowing, prostration and wudoo', offering them on time, and realizes that they are truly prescribed by Allah, will enter Paradise."*

Source: Musnad Ahmed 18345 Grade: Sahih

**It was narrated that Ibn Abbas said:**

*Quraish said to the Prophet: "Pray to your Lord for us to turn (the mountain of) Safa into gold for us, and if it is turned into gold we will follow you and will acknowledge what you have said as you said it." He(the Prophet)* asked his Lord, and Jibreel came to him and said: If you wish, this Safa will be turned to gold for them, then whoever among them disbelieves after that, I will punish them with a punishment with which I have never punished anyone in the world before, or if you wish, we will open the gate of repentance to them. He (the Prophet) said: O Lord, no; rather open to them the gate of repentance.

Source: Musnad Ahmed 3223 Grade: Sahih

**Narrated 'Abdullah bin Sakhbarah:**

narrated that the Prophet (ﷺ) said: "Whoever seeks knowledge, he is atoning for what has passed (of sins while doing so)."

Source: Jami` at-Tirmidhi 2648 Grade: Daif

**Abu Bakr narrated:**

That the Messenger of Allah (ﷺ) said: "He who seeks forgiveness has not been persistent in sin, even if he does it seventy times in a day."

Source: Jami` at-Tirmidhi 3559 Grade: Hasan

**It was narrated from 'Abdullah bin 'Amr that the Prophet (ﷺ) said:**

"Allah accepts the repentance of His slave so long as the death rattle has not yet reached his throat."

Source: Sunan Ibn Majah 4253 Grade: Hasan

### Narrated Ibn `Abbas:

*The Prophet (ﷺ) narrating about his Lord and said, "Allah ordered (the appointed angels over you) that the good and the bad deeds be written, and He then showed (the way) how (to write). If somebody intends to do a good deed and he does not do it, then Allah will write for him a full good deed (in his account with Him); and if he intends to do a good deed and actually did it, then Allah will write for him (in his account) with Him (its reward equal) from ten to seven hundred times to many more times: and if somebody intended to do a bad deed and he does not do it, then Allah will write a full good deed (in his account) with Him, and if he intended to do it (a bad deed) and actually did it, then Allah will write one bad deed (in his account)."*

Source: Sahih al-Bukhari 6491

### Narrated Safwan bin Muhriz Al-Mazini:

*While I was walking with Ibn `Umar holding his hand, a man came in front of us and asked, "What have you heard from Allah's Messenger (ﷺ) about An-Najwa?" Ibn `Umar said, "I heard Allah's Messenger (ﷺ) saying, 'Allah will bring a believer near Him and shelter him with His Screen and ask him: Did you commit such-and-such sins? He will say: Yes, my Lord. Allah will keep on asking him till he will confess all his sins and will think that he is ruined. Allah will say: 'I did screen your sins in the world and I forgive them for you today', and then* he will be given the book of his good deeds. Regarding infidels and hypocrites (their evil acts will be exposed publicly) and the witnesses will say: These are the people who lied against their Lord. Behold! The Curse of Allah is upon the wrongdoers."

Source: Sahih al-Bukhari 2441

**Abud-Darda reported:**

*The Messenger of Allah (ﷺ) said, "He who follows a path in quest of knowledge, Allah will make the path of Jannah easy to him. The angels lower their wings over the seeker of knowledge, being pleased with what he does. The inhabitants of the heavens and the earth and even the fish in the depth of the oceans seek forgiveness for him. The superiority of the learned man over the devout worshipper is like that of the full moon to the rest of the stars (i.e., in brightness). The learned are the heirs of the Prophets who bequeath neither dinar nor dirham but only that of knowledge; and he who acquires it, has in fact acquired an abundant portion."*

Source: Riyad as-Salihin 1388 + Abu Dawud + Tirmidhi

**Narrated Abu Umamah Al-Bahili:**

*"Two men were mentioned before the Messenger of Allah (ﷺ). One of them a worshiper, and the other a scholar. So the Messenger of Allah (ﷺ) said: 'The superiority of the scholar over the worshiper is like my superiority over the*

least of you.' Then the Messenger of Allah (ﷺ) said: 'Indeed Allah, His Angels, the inhabitants of the heavens and the earths - even the ant in his hole, even the fish - say blessings upon the one who teaches the people to do good.'"

Source: Jami` at-Tirmidhi 2685 Grade: Hasan

**Abu Huraira reported:**

The Messenger of Allah said: "Is not the world cursed and everything in it? Except for the remembrance of Allah and what facilitates it, the scholar or the student."

Source: Sunan al-Tirmidhī 2322 Grade: Hasan

**It was narrated from Anas bin Malik that:**

The Messenger of Allah said: "Every caller who invites people to misguidance and is followed, will have a burden of sin equal to that of those who follow him, without that detracting from their burden in the slightest. And every caller who invites people to true guidance and is followed, will have a reward equal to that of those who follow him, without that detracting from their reward in the slightest.'"

Source: Sunan Ibn Majah 205 Grade: Hasan

**Narrated 'Ali bin Abi Talib that the Messenger of Allah (ﷺ) said:**

"Whoever recites the Qur'an and memorizes it, making lawful what it makes lawful, and unlawful what it makes unlawful, Allah will admit him to Paradise due to it, and grant him intercession for ten of his family members who were to be consigned to the Fire."

Source: Jami` at-Tirmidhi 2905 Grade: Daif

**Abu Sa'id al-Khudri reported that The Messenger of Allah said:**

*"It will be said to the companion of the Quran when he enters Paradise: Recite and ascend! Thus, he will recite and ascend one level for each verse until he recites the last one with him."*

Source: Sunan Ibn Majah 3780 Grade: Sahih

**Abu Al-Malih narrated from 'Awf bin Malik Al-Ashja'i who said:**

*"The Messenger of Allah said 'Someone came to me from my Lord to give me choice between the half of my Ummah being admitted into Paradise or intercession. So I chose the intercession, and it is for whoever dies and he did not associate anything with Allah."'*

Source: Jami` at-Tirmidhi 2441 Grade: Hasan

**Ja'far bin Muhammad narrated from his father, from Jabir bin 'Abdullah who said:**

*"The Messenger of Allah said: 'My intercession is for the people who committed major sins in my Ummah.'"* Muhammad bin 'Ali said: "Jabir said to me: 'O

Muhammad! Whoever is not among the people of major sins, then there is no need in the intercession for him.'"

Source: Jami` at-Tirmidhi 2436 Grade: Sahih

**Abu Hurairah reported that the Messenger of Allah said:**

"When a person dies, all action is cut off for him with the exception of three things:

Charity which continues, knowledge which benefits, or a righteous child who makes supplication for him."

Source: Al-Adab Al-Mufrad 38 Grade: Sahih

**Narrated Abu Sa`id Al-Khudri:**

Allah's Messenger (ﷺ) said, "Allah will say to the people of Paradise, 'O the people of Paradise!' They will say, 'Labbaik, O our Lord, and Sa`daik!' Allah will say, 'Are you pleased?" They will say, 'Why should we not be pleased since You have given us what You have not given to anyone of Your creation?' Allah will say, 'I will give you something better than that.' They will reply, 'O our Lord! And what is better than that?' Allah will say, 'I will bestow My pleasure and contentment upon you so that I will never be angry with you after forever.' "

Source: Sahih al-Bukhari 6549

www.ingramcontent.com/pod-product-compliance
Lightning Source LLC
Chambersburg PA
CBHW050253010526
44107CB00003B/309